Visions, Dreams & Rumours

Zoë Howe

A PORTRAIT OF

STEVIE NICKS

ZOË HOWE

OMNIBUS PRESS
London / New York / Paris / Sydney / Copenhagen / Berlin / Madrid / Tokyo

(A Division of Wise Music Limited)

Cover designed by Lora Findlay
Picture research by the author

ISBN: 978-1-9172-7407-4

A catalogue record for this book is available from the British Library.

Typeset in Garamond MT Std by Palimpsest Book Production Limited, Falkirk, Stirlingshire

Printed and bound in the Czech Republic

www.omnibuspress.com

Contents

Foreword by Vivien Goldman viii

Prologue 1
Part I – Daughter Of The Desert 7
Part II – On The Wings Of An Albatross 59
Part III – Bella Donna 159
Part IV – Never Break The Chain 281

Afterword 383
Pick 'n' Nicks - Stevie Nicks Fact File 389
Acknowledgements 397
Bibliography 399

Foreword

For much of her career, Stevie Nicks ducked being described as a witch, whether the people who tried to thus label her were pro or con that mystic wisdom. Yet she was an indisputable sorceress. Single-handed, she wove for us a new avatar of rock womanhood; as if casting forth one of her celebrated shawls like a net, she caught a global audience in its shimmering folds.

Weaving together a multiplicity of sources, original interviews with archive as Howe does here, is a classic biographers' approach. However it is Howe's own voice, empathetic and disarming, never brutal, ironic, that welds this book into a pleasure. Her asides feel like confidences exchanged between girlfriends in private. Unafraid to be critical, Howe's brisk, sometimes stern analysis is always tempered by a deep affection for the transformative power of this enchanting chanteuse.

Howe contextualises the evolution of Nicks' whirling, ethereal persona, grounding it in seminal books, notably Robert Graves' *The White Goddess* which illuminated Nicks as it did so many; and the ancient Welsh bards' epic *The Mabinogion*, which would inspire her for life.

Was Stevie Nicks the inventor of her celebrated Rihannon, or her channeller? Searching for female deities to align with, Nicks found that her initially imagined sorceress actually appeared in *The Mabinogion*. A spell was cast, entwining Nicks' art with ancient storytelling and the connection with this mythical past would forever shape Nicks' future.

The singer's own destiny was always apparent. When she was just a tiny tot, her hard-living, rambling musician grandfather paraded her to sing in bars. A prolific songwriter, her package of archetypal Botticelli beauty, vocal force and sense of performance made her a multi-level threat – particularly to some of those who claimed to love her most.

Others' insecurities would trigger her own and take a toll on her romantic life, as Howe sympathetically and sensibly chronicles. Due to aeons of conditioning, it takes a self-assured, not self-obsessed, evolved sort of feller to rise to the role of Great Woman's Mate and wholeheartedly revel in his partner's success. That classic friction often seems to have played a part in messing up Nicks' love affairs. Yet she is adept at channelling all that tortured passion into intimate musical confessions; communicating her emotional revelations with a poetic sensibility that touched multitudes.

The now mythic scandals and drazma (sic) of the band's interpersonal, near-incestuous relationships, chronicled in their mega-selling album *Rumours*, would not have penetrated as deeply without Nicks' naked evocations of emotion. Though as Howe emphasizes, underpinning those histrionic love affairs with alpha males was a profound kinship with some stalwart male buddies – and her girlfriends. Some were even exes of her exes, a rather particular bond. Those intense platonic female friendships, some becoming regular co-creators, seal Nicks' goddess aura and the divine feminine within the canon of rock.

Particularly tender is Howe's description of the connection between her female compatriot in "the Mac", as Howe breezily calls them – pioneering British blues singer, keyboardist and songwriter, the immaculate Christine McVie. This book helps us understand that if Nicks was a goddess, she revered McVie as a god.

Their connection played a profound part in Nicks' working process, which Howe lays bare for us here; her creation of a sacred creative space wherever she might find herself; her need to retreat and withdraw deep within in order to transmute trauma, whether internal or socio-political, into the gold dust she sang of so sweetly.

As Howe herself has spread ideas of the sacred feminine in previous work, it is no surprise that her approach to Stevie Nicks is so in tune with Nicks' artistry. She knows how to spin Nicks' incantations into desirable information for us readers, transporting us as we glean Nicks' journey from one who truly understands.

Vivien Goldman, May 2025

Prologue

Warner Brothers Studios, Burbank, California; 23 May 1997. A soundstage has been transformed into a mammoth concert venue; MTV's camera crew is ready to film the spectacle that is just moments away; backstage, one of the most important and intriguing bands in rock'n'roll history is preparing to play live together in front of thousands for the first time in 15 years. The MTV special will be titled *The Dance*. The band is Fleetwood Mac.

A petite woman with waist-length blonde hair, three days shy of her 49th birthday, glances nervously at the people around her; friends, ex-lovers, a quasi-family – albeit a seriously dysfunctional one. So many complications, so much love and so much acrimony have gone down between these five people, and yet here they are, ready to go on stage as a unit once more after all this time. Drummer and founding member Mick Fleetwood bends down to kiss Stevie Nicks, the perennially mystical 'Queen Bee' of the group, on the head. She tentatively clasps hands with the guitarist Lindsey Buckingham, their jagged chemistry undiminished and crackling between them, and not for the last time this evening. The lights dim, a hush falls over the restless crowd. It's time. Fleetwood pounds out quarter notes on his bass drum, percussion shimmering like shards of glass. Stevie raises her shawl and the riff to 'The Chain', a song that has never been more laden with significance to this band, begins, malevolent, mysterious. They are back.

Just two years previously, the idea of this seemed impossible to Stevie Nicks. Up until now, she had remained close to fellow singer-songwriter and keyboardist Christine McVie, but the third key writer in the group was not always 'friendly' towards Nicks. In fact, as Stevie saw it, Lindsey Buckingham "just plain doesn't like me". Stevie and Lindsey, as you almost definitely don't need telling, were teenage sweethearts, collaborators, star-crossed lovers, creative rivals, sworn enemies. The fly in each other's ointment.

Even now the pair are locked in an ongoing dialogue through their songs, searching for closure. Yes, there's a thin line between love and hate. There was also an awareness inherent in the group that the fractured romance between Nicks and Buckingham was one of the most compelling elements of their live show, let alone their songwriting. (Admittedly this was before the still very real volatility between Nicks and Buckingham became too much to bear, with Buckingham leaving Fleetwood Mac in 2018.*)

All the same, behind the onstage glowers and finger-pointing was a genuine, unbreakable attachment between two people who still seemed to yearn for something more, even if it was only during the time they were onstage together. What we saw when Fleetwood Mac reconvened on stage for *The Dance*, and in particular when Stevie and Lindsey locked eyes, was quite real; even in rehearsals, nothing like this had happened. There was something about singing those songs in front of an audience again that touched something deep within them both. The audience went wild, witnessing something so personal, a tender moment of not-quite closure for one of the most famous rock'n'roll love stories of all time. Fleetwood Mac obviously cottoned onto this, and they would certainly make the most of it onstage in the years ahead. But that's not to say there wasn't still something true at the core. They just blended reality with theatricality to spellbinding effect, and it worked.

After the final threads of the toxic Fleetwood Mac tapestry separated completely in 1995, no one within the circle imagined they'd be beating

* The band would continue with Heartbreakers guitarist Mike Campbell and Crowded House frontman Neil Finn, but after the death of Christine McVie in 2022, Stevie Nicks expressed to *Mojo*'s Bob Mehr in 2024 that there would be no more Mac without Christine.

a path to each other's door any time soon, although plenty were hoping for a miracle. On being asked (repeatedly) as to the possibility of a reunion, Stevie opined that Buckingham might do it if offered "an exorbitant amount of money", but if she wasn't getting a good vibe from him, something that was rarely there anyway, it just wasn't worth it. Money obviously wasn't an issue; no matter how much of it had been inhaled, smoked or imbibed during the boom years, there was still more than enough to ensure she didn't have to go back to the tension and upset of working with the Mac, or Lindsey, again.

Safer as this option was, it was sad and unsatisfying; loose ends remained untied, and there was still a sense of longing for what might have been, if only creatively – and not just for the people involved, by the way. Lindsey himself has admitted he is a "different man" now, and thousands of Fleetwood Mac fans remain obsessed with the idea of Lindsey and Stevie not just getting along, but getting back together. There are websites, blogs and YouTube channels* dedicated solely to poring over footage and imagery of the pair during happier times, cooing over each other, sharing meaningful glances, scars left by decades of hurt having been picked at repeatedly during a show consisting largely of songs that lament or berate each other.

The Fleetwood Mac story – a saga of incongruity even before Stevie and Lindsey joined – never really ended, even when each member of the band had supposedly closed the door on it. Stevie had always dreamed that, under different circumstances, they would reunite, and sure enough, those golden, binding threads that had become so frayed and ripped, slowly started to knot together.

Just weeks after the split of the 'final' Fleetwood Mac lineup in 1995 (bearing in mind that Stevie and Christine had left five years earlier, and Buckingham had quit in 1987) word was rife that Mick Fleetwood had started working with Buckingham on his solo album. Then Christine and

* You can buy mugs on Etsy that bear the words: 'Sorry, I can't talk, I'm busy thinking about the 1997 performance of Silver Springs where Stevie Nicks stares a hole through Lindsey Buckingham."

John McVie came on board. The following year, Stevie even recorded a duet with Lindsey for a movie (*Twisted*) and in May 1996, around the time of Stevie's birthday, the band reunited at a private Kentucky Derby gala at the home of Louisville actress/super-hostess Patricia Barnstable Brown. There they celebrated 20 years of *Rumours*, their seminal album post-Peter Green, and second album post-inclusion of Buckingham Nicks. The idea of a tour was floated and, assuming Lindsey would be the hardest to convince, Christine McVie organised a dinner at her house, which turned out to be "the most blatant form of what you might call an intervention," Lindsey remembered in an interview with *Rocky Mountain News*'s Mark Brown in 2004. "People got in a circle around me and said, 'You gotta do this thing'."

And so it began again, memories were dragged to the surface but conflict was at a minimum, love and caution prevailed, knowing which buttons not to press was key. Stevie and Lindsey were more stable in themselves than they had been for a long time; Stevie's addictions were in the past and Lindsey was now a family man, more settled and loving than his ex-partner had ever seen him. In each other's company, there was always the risk of falling into old patterns but, as Buckingham admitted, as long as they all kept an eye on themselves, the sweetness of the situation could shine through, fun could overtake friction, and a love that had never really disappeared would flourish, at least while the players were playing. "It's nostalgic," mused Buckingham. "You could cry over it if you let yourself. This was like the girl I used to live with again. No matter what, some kind of chemistry will always be there."

There is more to Stevie Nicks than Fleetwood Mac, and she's far from defined by a ruined rock'n'roll romance that will never go away, but that band, with its tragedies and mysteries and entanglements that would put Hollywood to shame, is what first brought her to the world's attention. All the same, her spellbinding presence, songwriting and unique voice – these are the elements that made sure she stayed in people's hearts for decades to come. As the pages turn and we journey through a fairytale life, with all the darkness and glamour that entails, we'll garner glimpses of inspiration, rock goddess lessons and nuggets of advice from one of popular culture's most enduring wise women, the symbolic white witch of rock 'n' roll who is always shapeshifting and evolving. After all, Stevie Nicks often refers to herself as someone who has taken the falls so 'the little rock stars who come after' don't have to. They probably will all the same, but it's the thought that counts.

So who is Stevie Nicks? Who is behind the mask, under the veils of chiffon and cashmere and gossamer dreams? Ask anyone and they'll have a different impression. Potent symbol of feminism as well as femininity. Mystical lady from the mountains. Soft-focus California dream girl. Hedonist. Witch. Strong and powerful. Frail and child-like. In need of solitude. In need of attention. Hard. Soft. Maybe she's all of these things. Maybe she's something else. One of the most enchanting things about Stevie Nicks is that she allows us to *be* enchanted; she never gives away too much, all the while making you think she's giving you everything. Her songs are emotional, but many of her lyrics are cryptic rather than confessional. Her doe eyes are wide open but there's an aura around her, like the vines protecting the sleeping beauty; they won't let just anybody through. She's like a silent movie queen, prizing the mystery, and her fans thrive on the enigma – it keeps them held as if under a spell. True, she allowed us into her home in her documentary *In Your Dreams*, but little is laid bare, and the home is a mask in itself: Nicks really lives in a flat nearby which remains private. We are allowed just so close, as is appropriate, and Stevie is very much at the controls, as she always has been. After an interview with *Vox* magazine in the nineties, unhappy with how the photographer had shot her abode, she organised a crew at her own expense to recreate her home at a Hollywood soundstage – all of her knick-knacks, her dolls, her trinkets were present, just lit more flatteringly for him to photograph again. Eccentric, yes . . . but who wants a rock star to be dull and predictable? We love them because they're more interesting than us, more free- thinking, independent and . . . yes, perhaps a bit strange.

Quixotic rock star moments aside, Stevie is a role model for many and it's easy to see why: she is uncompromising, she puts creativity first, she has cracked the code of being sexy but not over-sexualised and, after 50 years in the rock'n'roll business, she has been there, done that, shed the tears, done the drugs, got the platform boots and is still here to tell the tale. So for those who sometimes wonder, 'what would Stevie do?' – and let's face it, who doesn't? – it's time to wrap yourself in velvet, fling a shawl over your lamp, light the candles (maybe have a fire extinguisher handy) and pour some Courvoisier into your tea; you're about to find out, Stevie-style.

PART I

Daughter Of The Desert

Chapter One

Stevie Nicks might have lived a peripatetic life, but Phoenix, Arizona, with its sub-tropical desert climate and majestic mountain ranges, would always draw her back. Phoenix represented Stevie's roots, and in the rudderless life of a rock'n'roll star, having a sense of home and family is vital; Stevie still has a home in Phoenix to this day. The name of the place alone would provide an appropriate touchstone for Nicks as the years unfolded, that of a glorious bird, burning out only to rise back up from its own ashes, more spectacular than ever. Not a bad symbol for a rock star. While we're on the subject of symbolism, the zodiac indicates that Stevie was born under the sign of Gemini, a sign ruled by the element of air and the planet Mercury. The astrologically inclined may agree that these cosmic connections could explain her fascination with the heavens, mists and veils, her passion for diaphanous stage costumes and her life long love of ballet and the idea of the body in flight. Her signature song, 'Rhiannon', chronicles the tale of a white witch 'taken by the sky', after all, and what are dreams and visions but ethereal flashes of the unconscious?

Music was in Stevie's life from the beginning – in her blood, no less – thanks to her grandfather AJ, a musical free spirit who lived up in the mountains. AJ supported himself by playing pool, but his heart lay in country & western music, and he was a gifted multi-instrumentalist: harmonica, guitar, fiddle – you name it, he could play it. His dream to succeed as a performer saw him leaving his family behind to ride the freight trains and play in bars around the country. Little Stevie was inspired by her bohemian grandfather, and the day he visited with a trunk-full of 45s was the day her path was set and she found her voice. They sat together on the floor of her bedroom, listening to records back to back. AJ would sing to Stevie, and soon they were harmonising and trying out duets; "sing like you mean it, granddaughter", AJ would croon to the blonde-haired toddler by his side; "put your heart into it". Before long, they were inseparable, and AJ would take four-year-old Stevie with him to taverns across the mid-West where she would sing along with her grandfather and charm everyone, already quite the boxoffice draw. This was her first taste of success, of how she could affect an audience – not to mention make a little money: AJ would slip her 50 cents for her trouble. It would also prepare her for life as a touring musician; as Stevie would tell *Sounds* writer and musician Vivien Goldman in later years: "I learned how to make friends quickly, and quickly how to leave them. It toughened me and I'm very adaptable."*

The Nicks family moved to Los Angeles when Stevie was still very small, opening a Mexican-style bar where her mother would cook and the men of the family would hang out, but even after Stevie had started school the music flourished, and she was getting more and more confident, her talent radiating from her, very much in her element while singing to an audience. One of Stevie's favourite early memories was coming home from school and dropping in on the bar to find her father, her uncles and beloved grandfather in there, listening to music and singing together. "I can remember being there at about two in the afternoon," she recalled. "No one really in there . . . I remember singing with my granddad and feeling even at that young age that music was definitely going to be a part of my life."

AJ agreed. He knew he had a little star on his hands and decided he wanted to take his granddaughter on the road for a run of dates together. Jess and Barbara wanted to encourage Stevie too, but they weren't sure how wise it was to allow a five-year-old to go on tour and sing in bars. It was time to make a decision. Stevie's little brother Christopher had just been born and another move was on the cards – this time to Albuquerque, New

* 'Fleetwood Mac: John and Christine and Stevie and Lindsey and Mick . . .' Vivien Goldman, *Sounds,* 30 October 1976

Mexico – surely there was enough upheaval in their lives without their young daughter disappearing to perform like a miniature Vaudevillian for drunken strangers? The answer was 'no', an answer AJ did not wish to accept. After a huge row, he stormed out on the family, refusing to speak to them for two years. This sudden absence and bad blood broke Stevie's heart after having been so close to AJ; the first emotional storm of many to come.

Arguably, the arrival of Chris Nicks was a storm in itself, however. Stevie, the self-confessed 'little diva' was 'out of control', and her parents decided another child might bring a little balance to the family and show Stevie she wasn't the only person in the world. It did not go down well and it would take some years for the siblings to really get on. "I hated Chris," she would admit in an interview with *You Magazine*'s Maureen Paton in 2003."I would pull his hair and kick him . . . I'll be apologising to him for the rest of my life." As is often the way, her parents were typically far stricter with their first child than they were with their second, but as their only daughter she was still, as she once put it dreamily, "the star in my family's sky", and they encouraged her creativity and love of stories, fairytales, music and dance. Stevie collected shawls and swirled them around in her room, dancing and pretending to be Isadora Duncan, a ballet dancer whose free movement and emotional, joyous style would leave its stamp on Stevie's own way of moving. The idea of going to a strict ballet school where she couldn't express herself freely was anathema to her.

"I didn't want to study and kill myself; I knew I couldn't bluff my way through Russian ballet. So I had to figure out another way to do something wonderful without working at it."* Stevie combined her passion for dance and obsession with popular music, dancing like a rock'n'roll ballerina to the Beach Boys, the Ronettes, Mahalia Jackson, spinning in front of her mirror, working out routines and 'stage shows' with the help of her little brother, whom she would pay 50 cents to dance with her. All of the

* From the book *Everything You Want to Know About Stevie Nicks* by Ethlie Ann Vare and Ed Ochs (1984), via InHerOwnWords.com.

elements of everything Stevie loved and would love for the rest of her life – music, performance, escapism, dressing up (maybe not so much little brothers) – were aligning.

By the time the now music-obsessed Stevie was 15 years old, in 1963, yet another relocation was due for the Nicks clan – this time, they would be heading back to Los Angeles. If Stevie ever felt a tinge of nostalgia about her old bedroom as the removal van pulled up, her mother Barbara would urge her to look to the future, not the past. "There's always a better house," she would assure her misty-eyed daughter as she eyed the floor she'd danced on and the window she gazed out of for one last time.

Stevie's bedroom was so important to her simply because she spent so much time in it; it was a sanctuary where she could read, dance and, most importantly, dream. Barbara and Jess were protective of their daughter, and she was kept inside far more than the average kid in the sixties, but one advantage of this seclusion would be that the poetic, fantastical world she created became so powerfully formed that it would come to inform her whole persona, her outlook, and her future. It would bring her strength and comfort when life got tough, which it would. She believed absolutely in wishes and the power of the mind to make things happen, and would seek enchantment in the most mundane aspects of everyday life; even in the fact that she was extremely short-sighted. Without her glasses, the world was out of focus, turning a simple bare light bulb into a 'star' and treating her to 'amazing light shows' whenever she took off her spectacles. She later mused as to whether these early experiences of turning a disadvantage into something beautiful informed her mystical approach to everyday life. Trust Stevie Nicks to find magic in myopia.

School would take a little adapting to, largely because whenever Stevie started to get settled, the family had to move to another town. Being shy and having to meet new people so frequently wasn't the best combination, but Stevie had long since learned that if she wanted an easy life, she'd have to drop the anxiety – or at least hide it – and be flexible and friendly. She had to make friends quickly after all, or simply be on her own for the rest of the year until it was time to up sticks again, and these formative experiences served her well for the future. "I learned to get accepted quickly because I didn't have time to waste," she said. "To be snooty for six months until I decided to come down to earth and be a part of everything didn't work at all."

Arcadia High School, however, wasn't the easiest place to fit into; it was "hotsie-totsie, very cliquey, and lots of rich people went there". Stevie, on the other hand, was something of an oddball in comparison. Amid the trendy jocks and coiffed debutantes there was Stephanie Nicks. You couldn't miss her. "I dressed kinda crazy and I always had a big straw bag because I wanted to carry everything with me," she told singer, friend and collaborator Sheryl Crow for *Interview Magazine* in 2001. "If you talk to people that went to school with me, they would say, 'She was a little crazy, she loved her music and she was interesting'. I think I was very interesting to everybody."

Stevie might not have won over the popular kids in class to the extent that she was accepted into their gang, but she was confident enough in school to show off her talent for singing on a 'father-daughter' night. She and Jess, who also had a fine singing voice, chose to perform the Roger Miller song 'King Of The Road', a song that could almost have been written about AJ. They rehearsed for a week and certainly gave an unforgettable performance, not least because Stevie got the giggles within seconds of starting to sing. "I was singing away," recalled Jess, "and Stevie was singing away, and she gets to laughing, and I get to laughing and I'll be damned if she didn't wet her pants right there on the stage!"

"I got the giggles during the first line, 'Trailer for sale or rent' and I was just hysterical," said Stevie. "He [gave] me this look, like, 'How could you do this to me?'" Wetting yourself onstage in front of your classmates . . . this actually would have been a great time to change schools, but no, Stevie would remain at Arcadia for another academic year, and it would be a year in which several important things would happen to Stevie:

1) She would join her first band, The Changing Times – a vocal harmony group similar in style to the Mamas and the Papas, tuning in to the West Coast sound.
2) Shortly before her 16th birthday, a beehived Stevie was granted permission to take guitar lessons.
3) She would write her first song.

Barbara and Jess weren't sure whether their daughter's fervent wish for a guitar was just a whim, so they paid for six weeks of lessons with a Spanish classical guitarist who rented a guitar for her to learn on. Stevie took lessons twice a week and by the time the course was up, it was clear to Stevie's parents that this was no passing fad. Because her teacher had plans to go to Spain to study, he agreed to sell the small classical Goya guitar Stevie had been learning on to Barbara and Jess, and they planned to present it to her on her birthday. Stevie adored it (she still has it to this day) and immediately sat down and started to compose a song. It was already bursting out of her: a ballad about a teenage love that had gone unrequited. Perfect inspiration for a first song, and as she turned 16 years old, it was like a rite of passage. The song was, as Stevie admits, "pretty goofy, but it had a chorus and two verses and it had an end. From that second onwards, I knew I wanted to be a songwriter."

The song was titled 'I've Loved And I've Lost, And I'm Sad But Not Blue' – meaning she'd accepted that the boy she adored had decided to go out with her friend instead. History would sadly repeat itself 15 years later, and, again, the heartbreak would lead to a poem that would lead to a song. Painful as it could often be, these upsetting times were, in the words of the poet Robert Graves, "compost", and some beautiful blooms would burst forth as a result.

Stevie always wrote poetry; she was rarely seen without a pen in her hand, but this would be the first time she put her words to music. The boy she was writing about (who would no doubt be regretting his rejection of her a few years down the line) was "an incredible guy, and he ended up going out with my best friend. They both knew I was going to be crushed," she said.* The lyrics to Stevie's first song went thus: 'I've loved and I've lost, and I'm sad but not blue / I once loved a boy who was wonderful and true / But he loved another before he loved me / and I knew he still wanted her – 'twas easy to see.' "The words were incredibly trite," Stevie later said. "But I was so in love so it was totally stupid." By the time she had finished writing the song, Stevie was in floods of tears.

At least Stevie could admit that the tune was "pretty", and she was instantly sold on how cathartic the songwriting process was, and how you could end up with something so rewarding despite feeling so down. Emboldened by the encouragement of her best friend Robin Snyder who praised its potential, Stevie would even perform the song in high school assembly, and from this point forth she was never seen without her guitar. It was decided. Stevie Nicks was going to be a songwriter, and so began an obsession that has lasted for six decades and counting.

This early period gave her a "definite glimpse", as Stevie worded it, of things to come. She believed in her songwriting, which was crucial because she felt that not many other people did. But as long as she was happy, and Robin was by her side to spur her on, she knew she was developing a skill that would be hugely important to her. After all, she had no intention of working in an office, the idea of getting up at 8.30 a.m. to drive to a desk-bound job and a regular wage was repellent to her and she "knew instinctively" that "as a pretty little girl" with creative talent and obvious charisma, nine-to-five life was not going to work for her. Just a few years down the line she worked at a dental hygienist's clinic. She lasted three days and "wanted to die". 'I've Loved And I've Lost' was a glowing signpost to the future.

Barbara and Jess were sympathetic to their daughter's ambition and commitment to her art – they knew there were worse things for a teenage girl to get up to – and if they could hear chords being strummed and

* A boy by the name of Dave Young, a quarterback on the school football team, was apparently Stevie's first "proper" boyfriend, although pictures exist of him taking Stevie to senior prom, so no doubt this plaintive ballad is not about him.

the sound of that honeyed vibrato floating out of her bedroom, they never knocked on her door. They even let her miss dinner if she hadn't finished writing; they respected her dedication. "They could hear that I was working, at 16 years old, and would leave me alone," she told writer Jenny Boyd (sister of Patti Boyd, and Mick Fleetwood's then wife) for her book *Musicians In Tune*. But it wasn't just the writing that lit her up; Stevie was a natural performer and she wanted to share her songs with whoever would listen, which meant more performances at school assembly, appearances with folk groups, after-school clubs . . . any opportunity she could find to sing, she grabbed it. She'd found her vocation. "It's what I came here to do."

"There she goes," Barbara would note with concern as she contemplated her daughter's future. "Down the same path as her grandfather." But Stevie's fate and that of AJ Nicks would be dramatically different.

Chapter Two

Another move was on the horizon, one that would offer Stevie plenty of opportunity to sing and perform amid kindred spirits. Jess Nicks' work would soon take them to San Mateo, California, where Stevie would attend the Menlo-Atherton High School in 1966. She was, as Mick Fleetwood put it, 'an instant hit', being voted runner up for Homecoming Queen in her first year there. Songwriting and poetry had balanced her, giving her confidence, expressiveness and poise, which marked her out amidst many of her more awkward teenage contemporaries. Add to that her beauty, balletic physical grace, easy charm and an inner core of determination, and there was nothing she couldn't achieve. She was altering her look too; a move that would create a seismic shift in the way she saw herself. Gradually, Stevie Nicks was honing herself into a mini rock'n'roll star: "I had my hair streaked at the end of my tenth-grade year and got in a lot of trouble for it," she told *Allure* magazine in 1995. "They didn't just streak it blond . . . they streaked it silver. My hair was totally ivory. I was grounded for six weeks. But when my hair changed, everything changed. There was no way I was going back."

Apart from the shock hair-streaking incident, Stevie was generally still a "good girl" at this point. She rarely troubled her parents (occasional strops notwithstanding – her pouting was legendary), she took her ambition seriously and still rarely went out. However, there was one weekly event she would attend just to get out of the house: a 'Young Life' church meeting for students. "Nobody went for church," Stevie admits. It was just something to do, an outlet for kids who liked to sing and play music and meet up on an otherwise dead Wednesday night. It was at one of these low key parties that someone caught Stevie's eye; a "stunning" teenage boy with curly hair and intense blue eyes wandered in with his guitar, sat down and started to play the Mama and the Papa's hit 'California Dreamin''.

Stevie, immediately attracted to him, nonchalantly sidled over and joined in, singing the Michelle Phillips harmonies that she knew so well. "He was, I guess, ever so slightly impressed," recalled Stevie. The boy was playing it cool, but "he did sing another song with me." A connection had been made. The young guitarist was called Lindsey Buckingham, and Stevie had fallen just a little bit in love with him.

Lindsey Buckingham, a year below Stevie at school, was a born Californian, growing up in the moneyed Bay-area community of Atherton. The youngest of three sporty brothers, Lindsey found his heart lay in music as opposed to athletics early on in life, playing along to his brother Jeff's Chuck Berry, Elvis Presley and Everly Brothers records on a toy Mickey Mouse guitar. It wouldn't be long until Lindsey was given a proper guitar by his parents, who had noticed his early talent. He never took a lesson, however; the fiercely independent young Lindsey taught himself by feel and by ear. Lindsey loved folk music and the finger-picking style used on the banjo, aping the playing of The Kingston Trio, a folk group local to Palo Alto, near where he lived. By the time he'd reached his mid-teens, Lindsey Buckingham was ready to join a band.

His first group at school was the Fritz Rabyne Memorial Band, named after a pupil at Menlo-Atherton as a joke – whether the real Fritz Rabyne, a diffident German boy still very much alive at the time, took this as a compliment will remain a mystery, but his chronic shyness and the sudden popularity of his name was not a good combination. "He moved away and we never heard from him again," said Fritz founder Javier Pacheco.* "We hardly knew him to begin with!"

The band, eventually just known as Fritz, formed in the autumn of 1966 and started out with a lineup that included Jody Moreing on vocals,

* As told to FleetwoodMac.net, Q&A Sessions, July 5-24 1999.

her cousin Calvin Roper on guitar, Bob Aguirre on drums, Javier Pacheco on keys and Lindsey himself on bass, rather than guitar. He would later explain that this was because he simply didn't take to playing the then 'fashionable heavy rock style' on guitar. Pacheco took care of most of the songwriting duties and Fritz practiced regularly at Lindsey's house in Atherton.

The band had potential, and when Moreing, later a successful singer-songwriter, and Roper had to go to college, an opportunity arose to inject some new blood into the lineup. On guitar, Fritz recruited a musician called Brian Kane, and when it came to finding a replacement vocalist, the band tried out several new female singers, but nothing gelled. Lindsey, perhaps unsurprisingly, remembered the pretty girl who stepped up to sing with him over a year earlier and suggested they give her a call. Bob Aguirre found Stevie's number and invited her for a try-out. Although not everyone in the band was convinced according to Aguirre (presumably referring to Javier Pacheco), "I knew right away. It worked."

With Stevie, Fritz now not only had a new singer, but they had someone who could contribute new songs as well, hers having more of a country feel. Perhaps this is one of the reasons why there was some friction between Javier, who provided many of the songs, and Stevie. Even so, no one could deny that Stevie had something special about her that spelled success, and that was as threatening as it was promising. Stevie, on the other hand, would later admit that she "really had no idea what I was getting into when I said I would join Fritz." Still, it would provide the ideal training ground.

Fritz's first gig with Stevie was at the Quad at Stanford University. "A big deal," Aguirre told Fleetwood Mac fans in a Q&A in recent years. "Stevie did a version of Linda Ronstadt's 'Different Drum' that brought the house down . . . we had to do it again by popular demand. The writing was on the wall."

Some reports claim Stevie joined Fritz in 1968, but according to Javier Pacheco, the new members arrived in the late summer of 1967. And, as Stevie Nicks recalls, "within two or three months we were opening for

Hendrix, Janis Joplin, all the San Francisco bands." The chemistry was right, her voice and look was ideal and audiences loved her. Fritz was now no longer a school band, but one of the hottest groups in the Bay-area music scene and they had high hopes, rehearsing at least four times a week and putting huge energy into their shows. Stevie was already displaying a talent for theatricality, "acting" out her songs and mesmerising the audiences with her performances. This didn't always go down well with the rest of the band, however.

Pacheco recalled that Stevie's emotional interpretations were certainly memorable, but to him, it simply seemed like a "big put on", particularly when they performed the Buffy Sainte Marie song 'Codeine'. "Stevie doubled up and acted out withdrawal pains while she sang it," he remembers. "I used to complain about it . . . That was her showbiz side. But Stevie persisted and this always got noticed. People were moved by it. But she could also stir you with a simple country song as well."

Pacheco admits that, back when Stevie first joined the group and was finding her feet, he thought she was a shrinking violet who "couldn't cut it. As it became clear that she would be staying in the band, I became resigned to working around her vocal strengths and weaknesses," he later stated, with no small measure of snark. But as "resigned" as he was, he would also tease her mercilessly. "Stevie became the victim, and I was the big bad wolf," he recalled. "I was critical of Stevie, but her songs did move me, [and] her first Fritz songs have stayed with me."

While Stevie was doing her best to navigate the friction in Fritz, 5,437 miles away in London, the guitar prodigy Peter Green was forming the blues band Fleetwood Mac with drummer Mick Fleetwood and bass player John McVie, all three of them former members of John Mayall's acclaimed Bluesbreakers. Much was expected from this new lineup but only the boldest of clairvoyants could have predicted a future alliance between Fleetwood Mac and Fritz.

Sometimes, when being the only girl in a group of musos started to grate, Stevie would wonder why she stayed in Fritz. But in the years to come, she would look back and realise it was all unfolding exactly as it should have done. "It was preparation for Fleetwood Mac," she said. She also laid down her ground rules early: she was the singer. She was also a lady. There would be no heavy lifting, no helping out with carrying gear and no unloading the van. "I wanted to be a lead singer. I didn't want to carry a 21lb Les Paul," she said.

Stevie's parents were anxious that Stevie should back herself up with some employable skills – she was a smart young woman and could turn her hand to so many things – and while Barbara and Jess loved that Fritz was going well and were always supportive of Stevie's dreams, they wanted to see her get her education too. "My mom said, 'I totally believe you're going to be a singer and a famous songwriter. But just in case, I need you to take typing and I need you to take shorthand. And if you go to college, we'll pay for everything.' And I went. I think that you should get the best education you can, and then if you want to go off and be a total entrepreneur space cadet, that's fine. But if you are called upon to take care of somebody or keep something together, you gotta have studied something*." Stevie would also study Speech Communication at San Jose State University. Lindsey would join her the following year, majoring in art.

Unlike Jody Moreing, Stevie stayed with the band when college came calling; if she had to commute every week to gigs and rehearsals, so be it. Admittedly, she couldn't commit to as many practices as before, and this would irk some of her bandmates who practiced for hours every day, but had to put up with enquiries about the band "with the little brownish-blondish haired girl . . ."

"Those guys didn't take me seriously at all. I was just a girl singer and they hated the fact I got a lot of the credit," remembered Stevie in a 1977 interview for *Rolling Stone.* Actually, considering interviews given by her then bandmates in later years, it sounded like they were all rather attracted to her, but she was off limits or they behaved clumsily, and the

* As told to *Rolling Stone*, December 30, 1999, via InHerOwnWords.com.

'look but don't touch' vibe ramped up the tension. "I think there was always something between me and Lindsey," Stevie told *Rolling Stone*, "but nobody in that band wanted me as their girlfriend because I was too ambitious for them. But they didn't want anybody else to have me either. If anyone else in the band started spending time with me, the other three would literally pick that person apart."

Part of the problem, as far as Javier was concerned, was the obvious connection between Stevie and Lindsey. Nothing was technically "going on" between them at this point, but there was a serious frisson between them, and this split the band down the middle. Bob Aguirre took Stevie out on a few dates early on, and, for all of Pacheco's gruff dismissals of Ms Nicks, he admits they could have been "more than friends" if it wasn't for his "silly machismo and arrogance . . . [I] missed my chance to get closer," he told fans in his frank online Q&A with FleetwoodMac.net. "The main thing I regret is [that] Stevie and I did not become better friends, but just the opposite. She was 'on guard' with me." Boys, let this be a lesson to you – you may tease because you love, but pigtail-pulling rarely goes down well.

The repeated commute up and down the peninsula for shows might have been a little time consuming for the student Stevie, but it was worth it – speech communication was all very well, but Fritz's star was rising and they had become the go-to band for San Francisco support slots for all of the major names at all of the most prestigious venues. "We played the Fillmore, Winterland, the Avalon, simply everywhere," said Stevie.

Fritz had the chance to watch and learn from headline acts such as Santana, Jimi Hendrix, Janis Joplin, Creedence Clearwater Revival, Jefferson Airplane and many other enduring rock icons, working their magic on stage as Stevie and her bandmates stood, transfixed, in the wings. One of her most treasured memories is the time that, during a Hendrix show, the guitarist himself looked over and declared, "I'm dedicating a song to that girl over there." "That was a moment of greatness," Stevie remembers proudly.

Jefferson Airplane singer Grace Slick made an impression on Stevie too, not least her powerful voice and "slinkiness", which Stevie made a note of, learning from the best. This was the real education, never mind classes at San Jose State. And if this was the case, surely Stevie's greatest teacher at this point must have been Janis Joplin. When Fritz supported Big Brother & the Holding Company, Stevie was gripped by Joplin's performance, and how a 'plain', small and down to earth woman could suddenly go on stage and become a transcendent figure of such emotion and power.

"You couldn't have pried me away with a million dollar cheque," said Stevie. "I was glued to her. I said, 'If ever I am a performer of any value, I want to be able to create the same feeling that is going on between her and her audience'. Janis was tough but sang like a bird and could really hold that audience in her hand." This holy trinity of rock archangels – Grace, Janis and Jimi – taught Stevie the three qualities she would swiftly develop and prize within herself: sex appeal, attitude and humility.

Stevie might have adored Janis, but she didn't want to copy her completely, not least because Joplin's earthy character off stage was quite different to super-feminine Stevie's. Javier recalls Fritz sharing some of Joplin's Southern Comfort in the dressing room, and while they appreciated the headliner's gesture, they were somewhat shocked by Joplin's tough demeanour. "She could be very crude and unladylike, just like one of the guys," said Pacheco. "I don't think Stevie decided she wanted to be just like Janis after that initial meeting." Still, her cracked charisma and emotional performances made their mark and would be added to the mix of qualities Stevie was mentally collecting and absorbing in order to make herself even more of a potent onstage presence.

It wouldn't just be the stars themselves that Stevie was observing, but some of the more stylish members of the audience. One woman in the crowd caught Stevie's attention during Joplin's set. "I saw this girl in the audience wearing a mauvy pink chiffon skirt and very high cream suede boots," recalled Stevie. "Her hair was kind of Gibson Girl – she had some pink ribbons – and I thought that's it." The woman was swathed in layers, a combination of bouffant Victorian beauty, free- flowing gypsy chic and elegantly ragged street urchin style. Stevie didn't mind admitting that she "wanted to be her", and she would hold these images in her mind, looking out for items that fitted the image she wanted to create in markets and antique stores. One day she would have the opportunity to have exactly that look designed for her, but in the meantime, she would have to put up with off-the-peg threads. That didn't mean she couldn't look like a legend, however.

Stevie had done her homework; she knew that Janis and Grace bought their clothes at the hip Velvet Underground boutique in San Francisco and so, with her Goya guitar slung over one shoulder, Stevie would stride through the streets on a Saturday afternoon and kit herself out right there, just like her heroines. Bell bottoms, tunics, evening gowns, beautiful fabrics . . . the boutique was only small but it had everything Stevie needed to transform herself and, with money she'd saved from a job working part-time in a clothes store, she would "really splurge . . . I would carry my guitar in these clothes, and I would walk like a rock star – there was something about my posture and the ballet I had taken and I would be swathing through crowds of people thinking 'Do you know who I am?'" she laughs. "And I really believed it. It's like that thing, build it and they will come. I was thinking, 'I am going to be a big star. Soon.' I believed you could plant the seed in people's heads." Long gone were the days of ingénue Stevie. With hard work, the power of her focused intent and more than a little magical thinking, she was rebranding herself into a rock goddess; it was just a matter of time until the rest of the world caught up and commenced worship.

Thanks to the plum support slots Fritz were playing in San Francisco, it wasn't long until Fritz themselves were attracting attention from managers and agents who could see their considerable potential. It wasn't just Stevie and Lindsey who were ambitious; the whole group were keen to make it, and they were soon signed by a new manager, David Forest. Forest was as dogged as they were – he went from fronting his own business to working with Creative Management Associates in LA, and he worked hard to try to secure a record deal for the band. However, the road to rock'n'roll stardom rarely runs smoothly, and while Stevie and Lindsey understood Los Angeles was the place to be, the rest of the band didn't take to it, preferring "groovy San Francisco" to the "plastic" City of Angels. The strain was starting to show, and the different agendas within Fritz were becoming harder to reconcile. Lindsey no longer wanted to play bass, Brian would rather have been playing the blues and, as Javier later revealed, "We were being manipulated by outside forces." He felt Forest had 'dragged' the band to LA because he was working there "and wanted to continue to control and/or profit from the group. Dave hid from us the fact that Bill Graham had shown interest in managing the group, so Forest made us believe that LA was our only viable option."

But this was not the only thing that would precipitate the break-up of Fritz after five years of hard work and "musical apprenticeship", and draw two-fifths of the band to Los Angeles. The agent Todd Shipman was "trying to get traction for this band", remembers the producer Keith Olsen, then a starving engineer in Los Angeles. "[Shipman] started calling all the A-level producers asking if they'd be interested in going up and seeing them live in San Jose. When everyone turned him down, he went to the B-level producers – you see where this story is going – and nobody wanted to go. So he went to the C-level and, well, *they* didn't want to go. So he went to the D-list, which had my name on it. "I said, 'Sure, free trip to San Jose!' Little did I know they were going to pick me up in the band van which had no seats. I got to sit with the drums in the back, and I got to help set up . . . I was young, I didn't care. But I saw the band that night and I thought, 'There's something special here . . .' Lindsey and Stevie, when they sang together, they had this colour . . . Those voices were meant to sing together."

Keith felt instinctively that Stevie and Lindsey didn't need the rest of the band to succeed. However, he invited Fritz to come to Van Nuys in Los Angeles to cut a demo with him at the now legendary (but somewhat grubby) Sound City studio on Cabrito Road one quiet Sunday morning. It was a thrill to be asked, and, once they'd arrived at the innocuous-looking studio, the band's trepidation intensified thanks to a small hitch: the locks had been changed since Keith had last recorded there. All was not lost. Keith was nothing if not determined. "We broke into the studio by taking off the door. We came in, left the door on one side and recorded."

It was their first time in a proper studio and the resulting demo, naturally, was flawed but still strong. However, as Olsen listened to the track after the session, he realised that he loved it but . . . "something wasn't right. The band . . . there were too many weaknesses. I hate thinking about it or even talking about it now because they were such friends, but I said to Lindsey and Stevie, 'I'd love to continue to work with you but I think you would do better as a duo.' And, of course, that meant horrific consequences. These were the people they'd played with and I was suggesting that they break up the band; an awful thing to do, but that's reality sometimes. I was straightforward and honest and they said, 'Yeah, we'll think about it', and drove off."

Keith's conscience can rest easy – this wasn't the sole reason for the eventual split in 1971. The band was arguing more than ever and wanted to pursue different avenues, although this tempting glimpse of a possible future for Stevie and Lindsey would no doubt have been the tipping point. All you had to do was listen to the lyrics of Stevie's songs from just before that time to get a clear picture of how things were changing. Javier Pacheco remembers one of Stevie's songs was "right on the mark. The lyrics go: 'There's a deep sense of a funny kind of love . . .' Like a marriage after it has broken up. She was speaking of the coming downfall of Fritz. See, we were writing love and break-up songs to each other way back in 1970. This didn't just start with the Mac."

Chapter Three

Stevie and Lindsey might have told Keith they would discuss his controversial suggestion to leave Fritz behind, but there was little to think about; this was their dream becoming manifest, and Fritz was already starting to disintegrate. But Keith had not only set the Buckingham Nicks wheels in motion musically: it appears he inadvertently helped push their romance along as well. Stevie and Lindsey had retreated to the ramshackle but rock'n'roll Tropicana Motel on Sunset Strip after Fritz's session at Sound City to talk over the possibilities, but talking would soon develop into something else.

"Why it happened between me and Lindsey was because we were so sad that we had to tell the three guys in the band that nobody wanted them, only us," Stevie explained in an interview with *Rolling Stone*'s Fred Shruers. "It just happened."

Much to Stevie's parents' chagrin, she and her collaborator-turned-boyfriend were making plans to quit college and live together permanently in LA, with a view to pursuing what so many had pursued before them. The idea of Stevie leaving her precious education behind was bad enough as far as her parents were concerned, but her decision to move in with her musician boyfriend was almost too much for them to take.

The pair were almost ready to relocate when a bombshell hit. Lindsey's health had become poor, but he'd attempted to work through it. However, what first seemed like a dose of simple influenza turned out to be a bad case of mononucleosis (glandular fever), a painful and debilitating disease that leaves the sufferer no option but to lie flat and do nothing. Lindsey's main plan now was to recover in bed at his parents' house while trying not to die of boredom. This was a particular problem for Lindsey – he was fiercely creative but wouldn't have the energy to even lift his head for three long months. There were also just five TV stations to choose from.

Stevie, who often stayed over in the Buckinghams' living room, did her utmost to keep Lindsey entertained, bringing him food, playing records, telling him stories and trying to keep his spirits up. This experience of having to care for Lindsey as their relationship was still in its early stages bonded them even more. She "didn't mother him," recalls Keith Olsen, who remembers this frustrating period for Lindsey (and is especially sympathetic having suffered from mono himself). "She just poured her love out to him. It was such a love commitment." Music-wise, Lindsey insisted they should listen to the Everly Brothers, the Kingston Trio and the Beatles to study "form" – Stevie would rather have listened to Aretha Franklin, Diana Ross and Joni Mitchell instead (Mitchell's 1970 album *Ladies Of The Canyon* being a particular influence on Nicks) but she followed Lindsey's determined guidance, until she "burned out", at least. One day Lindsey, still horizontal, asked Stevie to pass him his guitar.

It was at this point that a change occurred that would inform how he played forever. "He didn't have enough strength to strum," explains Keith. "He only had enough strength to use his fingers. Now think about the way he plays guitar – it's all because of mono. He became this incredible super player who had a style all his own because of his illness. It was kind of a semi-flamenco finger-pick style but he's using the backs of his fingers really fast. He was able to figure out his soloing style because of that." Lindsey had always loved the finger-picking styles of bluegrass guitarists and banjo players in his youth, and this, combined with his often frenzied self-taught technique, helped him create a new sound altogether which would provide contrast to Stevie's mellifluous voice as she harmonised with his more urgent, plaintive tenor. Lindsey had never provided any songs for Fritz, but something had unlocked. To Stevie's great relief, Lindsey's health slowly started to improve, and her love and support would be rewarded with the creation of a new song titled 'Stephanie', a pretty, romantic instrumental. Another song he wrote during this enervating period was far darker in mood. 'I'm So Afraid', later a hit single for Fleetwood Mac, is not just an angry, hopeless depiction of how Lindsey must have been feeling physically, but is a stark window into his fearful, neurotic psyche. "I'll never change, I never will/ I'm so afraid of the way I feel . . ."

Lows were balanced by highs, and as Lindsey's strength picked up, so did their luck: Lindsey had recently been left a generous inheritance by an aunt he had never actually known, and as soon as he was able he used the money to buy an Ampex four-track tape recorder 'the size of a washing machine'. His father, Morris Buckingham, owned a coffee plant near the Cow Palace in Palo Alto, and he allowed Stevie and Lindsey to practice in the warehouse once the workers had gone home for the night.

The pair would write and work in that 'creepy' room from 9pm until dawn almost every night. "It was so scary that we locked ourselves in the room and didn't go out because it was a big warehouse," remembers Stevie. "If we heard things, we would just stay in there and keep the door locked."

Spookiness aside, the acoustics were good and it was here that Lindsey not only taught himself to use the four-track and get just the sound he wanted, but the duo would record their first demos as Buckingham Nicks, with a mind to return to LA and secure a record deal. 'Frozen Love' was one of the many songs written during this creative time and, as Mick Fleetwood later observed, it is thanks to this period of hothousing that Lindsey developed his meticulous producer's mindset that he would become noted for in later years. Soon, all of those nights working in Mo Buckingham's cavernous coffee plant would pay off. With a clutch of finished demos, Stevie and Lindsey slung the four- track in the back of their rickety car, headed back to LA and knocked on Keith Olsen's door.

"Lindsey set it up in my house and said, 'Listen to this.' I was so blown away. Oh my God. I took those demos and I started to go around to sell them," says Keith. Stevie and Lindsey's voices were perfect together, Olsen already knew that; but they also had the songs that would take them to the next level. Gold dust.

Lindsey and Stevie signed up with Keith's company Pogologo Productions and agreed to split everything down the middle. "It was the good old days," adds Keith. Buckingham Nicks obviously had an album's worth of beautiful, unusual songs in them, the only obstacle was lack of budget. This wouldn't be a problem for long. While shopping the tracks around, Keith had approached David Shackler, former head of A&R at major label Polydor. Shackler was instantly smitten by Stevie and Lindsey's demos. He would, in turn, sign Buckingham Nicks to Anthem Records, a subsidiary of Polydor. The mission was on.

Stevie and Lindsey moved in with Keith Olsen in his 'little house on the hill' in Van Nuys as a temporary measure while they found their feet in LA and looked for their own place. Olsen generously even allowed them to borrow his prized new Corvette when their own car conked out yet again. This was a decision he would regret, to say the least. He can laugh about it now but . . .

"I was going away to New York to mix a James Gang show in Central Park. I had this little Corvette, it had maybe 350 miles on it, it was a stick shift and I had to drive down to get the guitarist Domenic Troiano. We all met back in the Valley." Keith got out of his car to wait with the rest of the band for the limousine to take them to the airport, only to see Stevie emerging from the house "in her robe and furry slippers, hair in a towel." She evidently needed to use the car. Stevie had never driven a stick shift before, but that didn't stop her. Keith and the James Gang looked on with interest as she attempted to make her way down the drive.

"She finally gets it going but it's making all these noises," recalls Keith. "Roy [Kenner], the singer of the James Gang, looks at me and says, 'You'll never see that car again.' I said, 'Oh no, she'll get the hang of it, she'll make it.'" And she did. The car wouldn't, however. By the time Keith and the James Gang reached New York, disaster had struck. Entering his hotel room, Keith was alarmed to see a light flashing on his telephone, a message already waiting for him: "It's Lindsey. Call your house. It's kind of an emergency."

"I dial my house, and Lindsey picks up," continues Keith. "The first thing I say is 'Is everybody ok?' and he said, 'Yeah . . . But your car is in your neighbour's bedroom.' We're up quite a high hillside. Stevie had pulled the emergency brake and just left it in neutral, went click and got out of the car. It started to roll and about 40 minutes later there was a guy knocking on the door. 'Do you own a gold coloured car?' Stevie says, 'Well, sort of.' He said, 'It's in my bedroom.' It actually went off the cliff, rolled and went through his bedroom ceiling. It was the most unbelievable thing."

Olsen was clearly an understanding, supportive presence in their lives, but it was perhaps wise that Stevie and Lindsey were looking to move out, particularly as they would soon be in the studio together every day. Through Keith, the couple met Richard Dashut, a dark-haired, bearded maverick with a passion for British blues bands such as Fleetwood Mac, the Yardbirds and the Bluesbreakers, and a mischievous look in his eye. He'd started working at Sound City as a caretaker but within a week he was working with Olsen as an assistant engineer. Stevie and Lindsey got on well with him, and they were soon renting a place together in North Hollywood near Universal Studios. Through Dashut, Stevie would meet the musician Tom Moncrieff who would also stay with them from time to time, and remain a longtime collaborator of Stevie's for years to come.

And on the subject of Fleetwood Mac, after a promising start things had gone badly awry for Peter Green's already legendary blues band. Though fundamentally unstable, they'd hit big with the instrumental 'Albatross', a UK number one in 1968, and two number twos: 'Man Of The World' in 1969 and the riff-driven 'Oh Well' a year later. More to the point Green had emerged as a guitar great, his subtle textures and light touch contrasting sharply with the more exuberant styles of contemporaries like Clapton, Jeff Beck and Jimmy Page. Then, just as it seemed as if the Mac would join the superstar league, Green quit in circumstances that have never been fully explained, evidently disillusioned by success, struggling with mental health issues and seeking a higher purpose in life. A further blow occurred in 1971 when slide guitarist Jeremy Spencer abruptly upped sticks in LA during a US tour, electing to join a religious sect known as the Children of God, another eerie development that brought forth credible suggestions that the group might be cursed. Bassist John McVie recruited his musician wife Christine, née Perfect, formerly of the band Chicken Shack, to shore up the ranks. But by the early seventies the ship was listing badly, a succession of singers and guitarists failing to refloat the group that rhythm section Fleetwood and Mac struggled to keep on course – and worse was to come.

Despite sharing the apartment, money was tight and Stevie had to pick up waitressing work to cover the rent while Lindsey stayed at home, practicing guitar and writing. This might seem a little unfair, but Stevie has always insisted she was largely happy with the arrangement. She was "devoted to making it happen for him". Plus Stevie felt secure in her own ambition; she had her "$50,000" education, she knew she'd be all right, and she could see the bigger picture. It was going to take all of her strength and grit to get them where they needed to be but someone had to do it, and other than a spot of dodgy telesales, Lindsey wasn't up for casual work. He and Richard would bounce cheques at coffee shops and spend a lot of time smoking strong "opiated hash" with the singer-songwriter Warren Zevon, who often dropped by. Still, the energy Lindsey put into developing their songs made it worthwhile, and they were both utterly determined; it was, as Stevie put it, "our whole reason for getting out of bed." The scenes at home were tense, however, and it was no wonder so much dope was smoked – albeit not by Stevie at this point. She was more interested in preserving her voice.

"I believed Lindsey shouldn't have to work," Stevie insisted in an interview with *Spin* in 2007. "I believed he should just practice guitar and become more brilliant every day. And as I watched him become more brilliant every day, I felt very gratified. I never worried about not being successful; I wanted to make it possible for him to be successful. When you feel that way about somebody, it's easy to take your own personality and quiet it down. I knew my career was going to work out fine. I knew I wasn't going to lose myself." Occasionally Stevie would feel less generous on this subject, however, admitting to *Harpers Bazaar* with a twinkle in her eye that "Lindsey thought it would be selling out for him to work at a restaurant, so I did."

Stevie, writing in any scraps of spare time she could find, was working as a hostess at Bob's Big Boy burger bar – "I wasn't a waitress, I wasn't good enough!" – and using her charm to ease the way with difficult customers and earn good tips. The experience would stay with her and Stevie has subsequently always made an effort to be kind to waiting staff; she knows what they're going through, after all. "Whenever I'm helped in a restaurant these days I remember it," Stevie later said. "I'm glad, because I wouldn't like to have been in this roundabout if that made me forget the things that are truly of value."

Stevie also understood that she needed that time out at work every day to 'be independent' and maintain some kind of a routine. "When you're a tragic, starving artist, if you hang out at home you just get more tragic, so to go to that job for six hours a day was good. I said, 'You can sit around thinking about being famous, but somebody's gotta pay the rent, and it's obviously not gonna be you!'"

With hindsight, knowing that Lindsey would later complain about Stevie's relative lack of musicianship, and how much work he'd have to do to bring her songs to a standard he was happy with, it's hard not to consider how things would have turned out had Lindsey been the bread-winner while Stevie stayed at home and concentrated on developing her craft instead. Fellow singer-songwriter Patti Smith had a similar experience during her early "starving artist" years in New York City while living with the artist Robert Mapplethorpe. Patti worked tirelessly to keep a roof over their heads while Robert stayed in his cocoon and developed his art. What about her art? Either way, Lindsey and Stevie were a team in every sense and, as Lindsey later said, not a little dismissively, "Whatever her music was, I was always this soul mate who knew exactly what to do with it."

The relationship between Nicks and Buckingham consisted of equal parts fierce devotion and an even fiercer creative rivalry, qualities that would make their onstage presence completely compelling. Decades after they split, it seems the world is still rooting for Buckingham and Nicks, even though it's a love that can never be. It is surely rock's greatest and most difficult romance. At this point, however, Stevie and Lindsey couldn't have imagined that the world would be obsessed with their tumultuous relationship in years to come. They were just trying to get by, write enough material for the album and stay in love.

But the course was set, Sound City was happy to have them, and the record deal had been confirmed. An advance was paid by the label to cover studio time and living costs for everyone involved and finally they were having "a taste of the big time", as Stevie put it.

Richard Dashut wasn't the only friend of Keith Olsen's that would help Buckingham Nicks make their debut album something special; Tom Moncrieff would be very much on board, initially on guitar and later on bass, as would a guitarist called Waddy Wachtel, with whom Olsen had worked since the late sixties, and who subsequently secured a deal with Polydor subsidiary Anthem himself. Keith was keen to bring Waddy ("another of those super-players who is so creative", as Keith describes him) and Buckingham Nicks together, as he knew his playing would suit their songs. They hit it off immediately – Waddy bonded with Stevie over Dolly Parton, and Lindsey over smoking weed. With fellow Pogologo signing Jorge Calderon on percussion, the Buckingham Nicks family was complete and they were ready to record.

The recording of Buckingham Nicks in the grimily thrilling environs of Sound City made it all worth it; the musicians loved spending time together and they knew they were creating something beautiful. The opportunity for Stevie and Lindsey to play with musicians like Tom, Jorge and Waddy was also something they didn't take for granted. Plus they were making history – the legendary console at Sound City (now owned by Dave Grohl) was "the first big giant Neve console in America," says Keith. "I demanded that we buy this console, because I owned a piece of Sound City at that time. The first day we plugged it in and turned it on, I cut 'Crying In The Night' with Buckingham Nicks. Very first thing recorded on there."

The album was scheduled for release in September 1973, with the track 'Don't Let Me Down Again' confirmed as the first single. The album would be dedicated to Stevie's grandfather AJ, although the cover wouldn't exactly be grandpa-friendly.

Knowing that the photo-shoot was looming, Stevie splashed out her last $111 on a beautiful, "very sexy" white blouse to wear for the cover. It wouldn't be necessary, however. Waddy had suggested his brother Jimmy, now an art director, should be one of the photographers for the album artwork, and it was agreed Stevie could wear the blouse she was so proud of for some of the shots. Stevie felt she would "win", that they'd love the blouse and how stunning she looked in it; pure angelic hippy chic. However, halfway through the session, "one of the photographers came over and said, 'OK, it's time to take off the blouse.'"

The plan was that the cover should feature a bare-chested Buckingham and Nicks in moody black and white. Stevie hated the idea, and apparently wept while the shots were being taken. These nude pictures represented "the most terrifying moment of my entire life," she later said, and Lindsey was not interested in her trepidation, reprimanding her for being childish and unreasonable. But from this point, Stevie promised herself she would never let herself be compromised again. Instead, she would be sexy as hell 'under 18 pounds of chiffon and velvet' and always retain her mystique.

Stevie's family were mortified by the cover when they saw it. "It was a big shock, let me tell you," Stevie's mother Barbara told *The Arizona Republic*. "I just told her, 'We're going to have to think about this before we show it to Dad'. Stevie didn't want him to see it at all. But she was young then, and it's something she was talked into." AJ Nicks apparently wasn't too impressed with the album, according to Stevie, although, again, perhaps seeing his granddaughter ostensibly naked on the cover of a record might have been a little too much to take. Stevie, rather, believed there was more than an element of bitterness when it came to how AJ

Nicks felt about little Stevie's big moment, and a sense of what might have been had his own life as a musician taken a different turn.

To add insult to injury, the album was ultimately unsuccessful (except, curiously, in Birmingham, Alabama, where the disc apparently received a healthy amount of radio play). It failed to go gold, Polydor lost interest and Buckingham Nicks were swiftly dropped. Stevie and Lindsey were devastated.

"It was hard when you practice that hard and you sound that good and everybody tells you that you should be doing something else," Stevie told *Creem*. "You want to say, 'Obviously we're not from the same planet, because I didn't sit with this guy for five years and sing like this for you to tell me that nothing we do is commercial.' Lindsey and I just couldn't understand how we could sing a beautiful song and nobody liked it. It was like, 'We don't belong here, nobody understands us.'" However, it was time to shove despair aside and get back to work.

Writing and practising continued, Lindsey sparked up another doobie and Stevie found a new waitressing job, earning $1.50 per hour at Clementine's, an elegant LA restaurant with a 1920s theme. There was a lot of running around – Stevie was, she admits, probably in the best physical shape of her life – and the waitresses had to dress up as flappers, something the roguish Richard Dashut found quite hilarious. And when it was dinnertime back at home, Stevie would open the cupboards, rack her brain and "try to find ways of making Hamburger Helper different . . ." which wasn't quite so hilarious, especially when Stevie came home to find that a stoned Lindsey had put her electric skillet on the stove, "and cooked the Hamburger Helper in the electric skillet, which meant we had no more electric skillet, and no more Hamburger Helper . . ."

Sometimes Stevie would bring home a slice of pizza to share between herself and Lindsey, barely enough sustenance to fuel the night ahead. "I'd get home from my waitress job, then we'd have dinner, and then we'd start working at nine at night to two or three. Then go to bed, get back up, he'd work on the music and I'd go and be a waitress."

Chapter Four

After being dropped by Polydor, it was time to get motivated again – they needed to play more gigs and showcase their talent if they were going to bag another record deal. Buckingham Nicks were admittedly somewhat picky about where they played – shunning offers to form a Top 40 show band to "play the steak and lobster circuit on the West Coast", as Mick Fleetwood later described it; the money would have been more than welcome but the gigs were theirs "only if they'd play Top 40," explains Mick in his book *Fleetwood*, "because nobody, they said, would pay to hear Buckingham Nicks play their own songs."

They didn't want to compromise themselves or lose their focus, but shows were thin on the ground, and the ones they did play weren't always a success. *Billboard*'s Nat Freedland caught them at LA's Troubadour, dismissing them as a "lacklustre male-female duo who . . . showed a couple of songs with chart possibilities. Keyboard and drums would help focus their on-stage guitar sound." Their debut appearance on the East Coast the following spring at New York's Metro saw them display "both problems and promise". *Billboard* praised their "strong vocal punch" but felt their "twin strength was undermined" by the addition of other musicians, presumably Waddy, Tom and Jorge.

"Buckingham handles both vocal leads and lead guitar, a role that seems to be a bit taxing," wrote *Billboard*'s reviewer. "Ms Nicks also encounters problems, chiefly in her solo style, which points up the occasional roughness of her voice and the strident quality to her top end that makes duets bracing, but proves less than fruitful when she takes the stage alone."

Rock Magazine's Dan Hedges saw something special in Buckingham Nicks, describing their sound as "soaring" and berating Polydor's lack of support. "No, of course you've never heard of them," he wrote. "Thanks to their record company, few people have . . . Buckingham Nicks have created what may well be one of the finest American albums released over the last three or four years." Hedges went on to commend their haunting depth and inventiveness, a "welcome change of pace from [the] mindless bopping" that dominated the charts.

He was impressed by 'Crying In The Night' – "the obvious choice for that all-important hit single" – and noted 'Crystal' and 'Frozen Love' for their ominous beauty. "With a bit of luck," Hedges concludes, "a few influential radio stations will pick up on them and, maybe then (no thanks to Polydor), people will discover exactly who Buckingham Nicks are. After that, who knows? There might even be a second album." And the rest. Never mind "influential radio stations", Buckingham Nicks are living testament to how one random, indirect encounter with the right person can change everything. But let's not get ahead of ourselves.

Waddy Wachtel had become firm friends with Stevie and Lindsey thanks to their time together in the studio and on the road, and he would spend hours playing guitar with Lindsey and smoking dope at their house. Stevie would often come home from work to find Lindsey, Waddy and Richard sprawled on the floor and staring at the ceiling. Stevie would have to lift up their legs in her attempts to tidy the place up. "Oh yeah," Waddy laughed in an interview with *Black Cat.* "She had to step over us, for sure." Stevie rarely found it amusing at the time. "I was just living in a world with all of these guys and I wasn't relating to any of them," Stevie later recalled. "I was working and they were all practising guitar. I was a whole different kind of person, I was the mom, the camp director of the Cub Scouts . . ." Stoned Cub Scouts.

It wasn't easy to kick back and enjoy life when Stevie knew all too well that, despite her best efforts, poverty was creeping up on them again. In addition to the stress of trying to live two lives at once, she was often rewarded by "a cold shoulder" when she returned home from work.

"[Lindsey] wouldn't quite trust me about where I'd been or what I'd been doing. Rich and famous or starving and poor, we went through the same problems. He wanted me to himself but somebody had to earn some money."

When she wasn't working, the way Stevie wrote was completely different to Lindsey, and this also irritated him. Lindsey crafted a song from the foundations up, while Stevie went straight in with lyrics and melody, simple and quick, highly creative and unstoppably prolific. Put simply, she was a "radical" and he was a perfectionist. She would tell Australian TV show host Molly Meldrum in later years that "it needs to be perfect for Lindsey and so his perfection drives me crazy because I think he doesn't have any fun, and my radicalness drives him crazy because he thinks I'm not as good as I should be."

As a twosome, Lindsey and Stevie were, as Keith Olsen recalls, "always on the edge". The differences and the dramas . . . well, no one could do anything about that, but being poor just made them all the more tense. Olsen was keen to help, but the producer's well-meaning attempts to offer the couple money were rebuffed by Stevie – she would only accept it if she could earn it.

"So I said, 'Stevie, do you wanna clean my house?' and she said, 'Sure!' It was really funny. She'd show up in that old Toyota, it was barely worth driving, and I'd open the door and here's this woman, one of the prettiest, most elegant people in the world, looking like Carol Burnett when she dressed as a maid. That happened maybe four times, but that money was the difference between eating and not eating."

Never mind eating; it was also during this period that Stevie first tried cocaine. It may be an unlikely image, that of a cleaning lady having a quick toot but, for a joke, someone "had left a line of coke underneath something to see if I was a thorough house cleaner. And of course I was, and of course I found it."

Stevie and Lindsey might not have had the funds or the inclination at this stage to start hoovering up Columbia's finest on a regular basis, but they would soon be eating a little more frequently. Lindsey had just received the dream call, offering him the chance to tour for a month with Don Everly as the Everly Brothers, whom Lindsey had always revered. Evidently Don and Phil had fallen out to the extent that Phil was actually being "replaced". Stevie and Lindsey might have thought they had a complex relationship, but the Everlys were off the charts. Lindsey practised the songs obsessively in preparation and the proposed recording of Buckingham Nicks follow-up album would have to be postponed.

Stevie was more concerned that she was surplus to requirements. "Me and Lindsey were the original after-the-Everly-Brothers-Everly-Brothers!" – but she swallowed her pride, grabbed her beloved poodle Ginnie (a vital companion on this rather lonely trip), and drove Lindsey up to Aspen for two weeks of rehearsals before the reconstituted 'Everly Brothers' went out on tour.

While Lindsey was away, Stevie decided to make the most of being in Aspen and stayed there for weeks reflecting, linking up with a friend who lived locally and taking inspiration from the beautiful Colorado landscape. Stevie would read, write poetry, play with the dog . . . unfortunately this was before Stevie started to paint, but Aspen was a much-needed change of scene, and the snow-capped hills and fiery autumn colours would plant lasting images in her mind. Aspen seemed so tranquil and fresh in comparison to dirty, fast-moving Los Angeles. As Stevie gazed for hours at the mountains, fragments of song ideas came flickering through her mind. The sky and the snow were so clean and bright, almost mirror-like, but it was the reflective state this landscape would inspire in Stevie that would plunge her even further into contemplation.

Stevie's depression was coming to a head and she had plenty on her mind; money troubles aside, her beloved father Jess had been suffering from serious heart problems, forcing him to retire at just 49, and the weeks without Lindsey were lonely and paranoid. She also couldn't get over the fact that Lindsey was apparently living the high life with Don Everly, jamming with Merle Travis, Ike Everly, Roy Orbison, so many of their heroes – and she was in Aspen "with $40 and my dog and my Toyota that froze the day we got there," " she told *The Source* in 1981. "And we thought he was going to make lots of money. He didn't."

This was the first time Lindsey had been on tour without Stevie, and the anxiety this prompted would at least spark an idea for a song. 'Kind Of Woman', a suspicious paean to how 'darling' Lindsey Buckingham was, and expressed Stevie's fear that another woman was going to snap him up while he was on tour. "I was imagining groupies with the black feathers and the rhinestones and the boots and black stockings, and I was dying," she said. "So 'Kind Of Woman' was, you know, 'You didn't mean to meet her', you're going to call me and tell me that?" (For all of their difficulties, Lindsey has always insisted he was faithful to Stevie.)

To compound Stevie's misery, when Lindsey returned to Aspen he was in a black mood, "very angry with me . . . and he left me". Why he was so furious is a mystery; whether it was because he hadn't brought back as much money as he'd hoped for and was taking it out on her, whether Stevie roasted him with her suspicions of infidelity or whether it was simply because Stevie was having a much-needed break after such a punishing year and, as a result, was not earning their keep for once, we don't know. What we do know is a fuming Lindsey took the dog, got the car started and abandoned Stevie in Aspen, confused, cold and suffering from strep throat. Still, Stevie had reason to feel defiant. Temporarily.

"I had a bus pass because my dad was president of Greyhound," said Stevie. "So I said, 'Fine, take the car and the dog, I have a bus pass.'" Which would be all very well if it wasn't the day the Greyhound Buses went on strike. Stevie managed to find a phone, tearfully contacted her parents and "they unwillingly sent a plane ticket," she remembers, "because they didn't understand what I was doing up there in the first place." Stevie was wondering the same thing, and not for the first time. By the time she arrived back in LA, she was beside herself with distress and needed a friend; she certainly didn't want to go home to Lindsey. But again, from that pain, something beautiful and poetic would emerge. "Stevie and Lindsey's relationship, as you know, was always turbulent," remembers Keith Olsen. "They'd argue and things were said between the two of them that would hurt each other deeply. Stevie came over to where I lived in Van Nuys at about midnight and pounded on my door, crying like crazy."

"She sat on the couch, crying that she and Lindsey had had this fight, 'Oh God, I can't take it, I don't know what to do.' I had to do this commercial the next day at 9 a.m. . . ." continues Keith. "So, I just said, 'Stevie, if you feel this way, get it out.' I got my guitar out and handed it to her and said, 'Go in the bedroom and write about it.' And that's what she did. I fell asleep on the couch."

While Stevie was in Keith's bedroom, images of Aspen rushed back to her as she wept angry tears. She'd gazed at the 'snow-covered hills', in awe of their silent, detached beauty, aware that one sharp shout in their presence could be deadly, "the whole mountain could come down on you." She held the guitar and mused upon this again, likening the image to her situation with Lindsey, a love that was not without its sense of dread and tension. One false move and the entire delicate balance would be thrown, with catastrophic results.

"Everything could tumble," she said in a 1992 interview with radio personality Doug 'Redbeard' Hill. "When you're in Colorado and you're surrounded by these incredible mountains, you think 'avalanche'. It meant the whole world could tumble around us and the landslide would bring you down." Words she had jotted down as poetry in Aspen were summoned, and Stevie wrote the song "in about five minutes", murmuring the words and the melody in Keith's room while he slept next door, and picking out a simple, affecting tune on his guitar. This song has come to represent Stevie's loving relationship with her father, and the fear she felt for him when she thought he was dying, but at the time, it was very much about Lindsey, the man she had "built her life around". It was about "taking your ego down," Stevie has said. Considering it had just been crafted by a woman torn by despair, the result was tender, warm and mature. Like so many of Nicks's songs to come, this was a spell of healing and transformation.'

Keith Olsen: "She woke me up at 8 o'clock and said, 'I think I came up with something.' She played it to me, and it was 'Landslide'. Holy crap. The melody, the sentiment, the chorus . . . it was just perfect."

It is the beginning of 1974 and Fleetwood Mac seems to have reached the end of the road, so much so that manager Clifford Davis believes the group has imploded on him. While a state of confusion exists around the activities of the members of the real Fleetwood Mac, Davis, claiming he owns the rights to the group's name, recruits an entirely new band to become 'Fleetwood Mac' and embarks on a disastrous American tour. The original members of Mac sue Davis who countersues and the issue is eventually settled out of court. In the summer of 1974 the three remaining members of the group – Mick Fleetwood and John and Christine McVie – relocate to Los Angeles, determined to somehow restore their identity after the disquieting business of the bogus group. As if they hadn't had enough to worry about along the way . . . something or someone is needed to break this curse.

Once the storm had passed, Lindsey and Stevie prepared to hit the studio again and record album two. Sound City had generously suggested they could cut the record there for free, "without a record deal, and shop it around to labels afterward," engineer Richard Dashut would tell Mick Fleetwood for his book *Fleetwood*. "This was unheard of, but we had so much faith in what we were doing that some of it must have rubbed off."

Buckingham Nicks had plenty of material that they believed in and were keen to commit to vinyl; 'Monday Morning', 'So Afraid' and 'Landslide' were among the contenders, as was 'Long Distance Winner', one of many songs about "dealing with Lindsey", admitted Stevie to *Billboard*'s Timothy White in 1998. "How else can I say it? I bring the water down to you / But you're too hot to touch . . . [I'm] saying, 'I adore you . . . I'll stay with you, but you're still difficult.' It's just the age-old story: the inability to live with someone and the inability to live without them."

Stevie's parents were all too aware of how hard it could be for their little girl. They were always supportive: her father had always told her, "If you're going to do it, be the best, write the best, sing the best, and believe in it and yourself." But they were also increasingly shocked by how thin, sickly and unhappy their daughter had become. Was it worth it?

They knew Stevie was too determined for them to simply sweep her up and bring her home, but it was time to suggest an ultimatum: Stevie could continue trying to make it in LA for six more months, and should things not work out during that time, she would go back to college and be financially supported. Dejected and tired, Stevie agreed, but in the meantime, she and Lindsey really had to throw everything they had at this, their last ditch attempt at rock'n'roll success.

Business continued at Sound City. Buckingham Nicks, Waddy, Keith and Richard, the whole team were there, undeterred and eager to push forward and craft a new album that would grab the attention of the ideal label for them. But the winds of change were about to blow an unexpected situation their way. Buckingham Nicks might have been shopping for a label, but the tall, bearded man who'd just wandered into Sound City's reception was shopping for a studio.

"Mick Fleetwood came in to try and find a studio and a co-producer for his new album," remembers Keith. "The one right after *Bare Trees.* I played him some things that I'd done, and also I played him 'Frozen Love' by Buckingham Nicks." Lindsey Buckingham's ears pricked up when he heard their song being played loudly in the neighbouring studio, and he was surprised to see "this really tall guy stomping his feet to our song"

Fleetwood loved the song, loved the studio, and was impressed by the guitarist on the track, whose playing put him in mind of erstwhile Fleetwood Mac guitarist Danny Kirwan. Through the glass, Mick Fleetwood also spotted Stevie wafting around and, unwittingly, she made quite an impression on him*. Mick told Keith he liked the openness of the studio, and booked it for the next Fleetwood Mac album, with Keith Olsen co-producing. Not a bad afternoon, all told.

Recording sessions were booked in for February, March and the first

* Interestingly, when Mick Fleetwood described the first time he crossed paths with Buckingham Nicks in his book *Fleetwood*, the focus is actually very much on Stevie, not Buckingham. The chapter is titled 'Like a Charmed Hour and a Haunted Song', a lyric from Stevie's song 'Angel'. It opens with the Robert Graves quote from *The White Goddess:* 'Let the poet address her as Rhiannon, "Great Queen".'

two weeks of April 1975, and Keith Olsen finally breathed out for the first time in months. The idea of recording with Fleetwood Mac was a buzz, but so was the thought of being able to make rent . . . so when guitarist Bob Welch decided to quit Fleetwood Mac, it wasn't just a bombshell for the band.

After three years in one of the most tempestuous, twisted bands in rock, Welch broke the news that he could take no more on 31 December 1974. Happy New Year. Bassist and founding member John McVie tried to convince Welch to stay, reminding him solemnly that "it's rough out there" and that giving up Fleetwood Mac should not be done lightly. "It was a marriage," recalled Fleetwood. But Bob was determined and, as a result, the album would have to be shelved unless a solution could be found. Fleetwood Mac is nothing if not adaptable. Lineup changes were hardly unusual and Mick Fleetwood was in charge of keeping the wheels in motion.

"Mick calls me from the airport in LA," says Olsen. "He says, 'I have good news and bad news. Bob Welch has left the band and we won't be able to start the album in February.' I thought, 'Oh crap, I'm out of work, I'm going to have to go back on the hustle to find something for that time slot which I'm already too late for, I won't be able to pay my rent or my car payment . . .'

"I said, 'What's the good news?' He said, 'You know that guitar player? Would he want to join my band?' I said, 'You mean Lindsey? Lindsey and Stevie are kind of a set. You're going to have to take both.' Mick said, 'Well, do you think they would want to join my band?' And I said, 'I'll go and find out.'"

Whatever plans Keith and his date had for New Year's Eve were dropped. There would be no party, no dancing, no drunken kiss at midnight. Instead, they went straight to Lindsey and Stevie's house to put Fleetwood's proposal to them, and as hard as it might be to believe, they took some convincing. Stevie knew Fleetwood only really wanted Lindsey and, while it was encouraging that Fleetwood was potentially prepared to take them both, she was concerned about feeling like an also-ran. They were also reluctant to just drop their plans to try to make Buckingham Nicks a success after all of their hard work.

Keith Olsen continues: "For the next five hours, there's Lindsey, Stevie, myself and my date, who was sitting there thinking, 'God, this is really fun . . .' I sit there and try to convince them to join Fleetwood Mac. 'It's the best thing for your career . . .' and they're saying, 'But we're working on our new Buckingham Nicks album, it's going to be wonderful, we're going to pull in some of the players from the old Fritz band . . .' and here I am, second time around, trying to break up what they were doing."

While they mulled over the idea, the hours ticked by, 1975 arrived, bringing with it an incredible new era for Stevie and Lindsey if they could only see it. By 2 a.m. Olsen had managed to convince them to "try it for six or eight weeks". This would at least mean that a) they would be able to eat and b) so would Keith. The sessions could go ahead as planned and Fleetwood Mac would rise again. Keith's talented friends, in turn, would finally be in a band that had a chance of selling a decent amount of records.

"I thought, 'God, they could be on the road, they could make some money, they can expand their own personal art . . .' I just felt so good inside and they felt so tormented inside . . . That is exactly how it happened."

After Keith had left, Lindsey and Stevie were still wringing their hands over the situation. Lindsey was more reluctant than Stevie. He was convinced Buckingham Nicks was on the brink of real success with their follow-up album. "He was like, 'This record's happening'," remembers Stevie. "I said, 'Yes it is, but we are dirt poor and I don't want to be a waitress any more. If we don't do well in Fleetwood Mac then we'll quit, but let's save a bit of money, at least we'll be able to fix reverse in our car.' We always had to find a parking space where we could get out front-ways or we'd be stuck there all night . . ."

They needed another opinion from a trusted ally who knew their situation, musically as well as financially. Of course Keith wanted them to go for it, but Keith's financial situation was also riding on it as well.

Waddy Wachtel had just returned from a tour with Linda Rondstadt when his phone started to ring. "It was Lindsey," he recalled. "He goes, 'Man, I gotta run something by you. Mick Fleetwood wants us to join Fleetwood Mac. I don't know if we want to do it. You know, we got Buckingham Nicks . . .'

"I said, 'Lindsey, the only mistake you are making right now is you're on the wrong phone call. I want you to hang up and call Mick Fleetwood and tell him "Yes".' I knew that was an in for them. Buckingham Nicks was going to be an uphill fight, but Fleetwood Mac already had a name. Let them be your back up band, man. So that's what he did."

As soon as she could, Stevie went out to buy all of the Fleetwood Mac records she could get her hands on to case out what they were getting themselves into. As *Peter Green's Fleetwood Mac, Then Play On* (the only Mac record Lindsey was really familiar with), *Heroes Are Hard To Find* and everything in between blared from their speakers, Stevie realised that however much they wanted to move forward as a duo, they could learn so much from working with Fleetwood Mac, even if they just stayed for the recording.

She also loved the music and was pleasantly surprised to pick up on the mystical bent that informed their records, undoubtedly courtesy of Peter Green himself. This instantly chimed with Stevie's own spiritual sensibilities. But she also needed to feel that Buckingham Nicks could bring something to the table and actually enhance Fleetwood Mac as opposed to coasting along like passengers. She finally turned to Lindsey and said, "I think we can join this band, and not just be doing it for the money. We can add something."

It was time for Stevie to call her parents. Just half way through the six month limit they'd set, destiny had stepped in, a wish was granted, and Stevie and Lindsey's world would change completely.

Chapter Five

As Stevie and Lindsey listened to the back catalogue of Fleetwood Mac, Mick Fleetwood settled down in a rather more salubrious area of California to play the Buckingham Nicks album to fellow Mac bandmates John and Christine McVie. The pair were impressed even though, as Christine reiterated, it was "really only the guitar-player we were interested in". Stevie was an afterthought – they were simply prepared to do what they had to do to secure Lindsey, who wouldn't budge without his partner. But Mick didn't hesitate when he received Lindsey's terms, and there would be no audition.

Mick's only concern was that Christine wouldn't take kindly to another woman joining the band. "Mick and John said to me, 'If you don't like the girl then we can't have either of them, because they are a duo'," Christine said, admitting there was indeed some slight apprehension before meeting Stevie. She'd become so used to being the only woman in the band, but this was no alpha female neurosis – Christine was like one of the boys, and as it would turn out, it was a relief for Stevie to know there'd be another girl in the group. Stevie instantly saw Christine as a potential "pal", not a rival, and they were different enough for this never to be an issue – Christine was as earthy and cool as Stevie was ethereal and dreamy. "It was critical that I got on with her," McVie told *The Guardian*'s Tim Jonze in 2013, "because I'd never played with another girl. But I liked her instantly. She was funny and nice but also there was no competition. We were completely different on the stage to each other and we wrote differently too." It was decided, and Mick called the group's lawyer Mickey Shapiro to make it official.

Not everyone took the news well. When Stevie told the rest of the Buckingham Nicks band, it was, as Tom Moncrieff * recalled, devastating. "We were working on a killer second album, Richard Dashut was engineering, but we had no money or support, or any real way to get any further. The owner of Sound City, Joe Gottfried, had agreed to 'spec' us the time ('cuz I 'spec I won't get paid'). He was a great guy," Tom says. "We thought we should have had a future, but joining Fleetwood Mac was the only realistic thing Stevie and Lindsey could do."

The way in which the following Fleetwood Mac episode unfolded ties in with the sense of destiny and fortune that has always been intrinsic with the band. There would be no audition, although it wasn't as if Lindsey didn't offer. In fact, he was a little bemused by the Mac's open door policy.

"John and Mick have always been open to having a lot of different people in the band, which is odd," Lindsey told *Rolling Stone*. "I would never be able to do that. I would think it was real important to keep an identity. I remember being a kid, if a new member joined a group, I didn't like that at all. But that openness is what's kept them going for so long."

Mick Fleetwood has maintained that that combination of fluidity and fate, a "magic star" guiding them on, has been the driving force behind the band's extraordinary trajectory. There was always something of the esoteric about Fleetwood Mac, and there's no doubt that Stevie and Lindsey would bring so much more than anyone could have imagined – it was a serendipitous, if unlikely union. But this magic star of theirs was evidently intent on making things awkward for them as well. As magic stars go, this one had a warped sense of humour. It would rarely be easy, or comfortable, emotionally at least, in Fleetwood Mac. But magical, yes, in many ways it would be. For Stevie, Fleetwood Mac would be like a fairytale on acid; exaggerated, indulgent, colourful and Mick Fleetwood was the knight on a white charger, sweeping them up and away from

* From a 2000 Q&A with FleetwoodMac.net / The Ledge

destitution. Three months into her parents' kindly ultimatum, life had changed for the better. College was forgotten.

Arrangements were made for the band and their new members to meet up properly for the first time at El Carmen, a Mexican restaurant on West 3rd Street in Beverly Hills. Lindsey would meet Mick Fleetwood at his home in Fernwood, off Laurel Canyon, driving down together. John and Chris were heading down separately. Stevie, still in her flapper uniform after a day's waitressing, was already there when they arrived; "in two white Cadillacs, clunky, with big tail fins," remembers Stevie. "I was in awe."

Mick Fleetwood's grand entrance is something Stevie will never forget. She had always fantasised about English fairytale characters, lords and ladies, ancient royalty . . . and to Stevie, the eccentrically dressed Fleetwood, with his aristocratic manners and towering stature, was like "an English king," she told *Vox* magazine's Spencer Bright in 1992. "He was wearing a burgundy silk vest [waistcoat] with a watch-chain and a very long jacket that was nipped at the waist, and beautifully made pants. I was awestruck. I still am to this day of Mick's presence. The whole air around him is [of] power."

Christine and John swept in, Lindsey settled by Stevie's side and before long everyone was drunk on margaritas and having a ball. Fleetwood remembers "a lot of smiling". It felt right and Stevie, who had initially felt understandably intimidated by her new bandmates' sheer level of fame, soon fitted in. "I fell madly in love with all of them immediately. They made me feel wonderful." They also joked with Stevie that she should hang on to her day job at the fancy Clementine's, if only to keep them all going with doggy bags.*

"We all really got on well," confirmed Christine. "Stevie was a bright, very humorous, very direct, tough little thing. I liked her instantly and Lindsey too." Christine and Stevie were "complete opposites at either end of the personality spectrum", but crucially the one thing they did have in common was a wicked sense of humour. "We have a good laugh,"

* As told to Vivien Goldman, *Sounds*, 30 October 1976.

Christine told *Uncut Magazine* in 2003. "It is one of the primary reasons for anybody staying together, marriage, band, or whatever it is. The ability to laugh at things, and oneself, is really important."

Stevie was 27 but her childlike, exuberant demeanour and diminutive stature quickly marked her out as the "baby sister" of the band. Nobody else had nabbed that role – Christine was five years older for a start, and had been in the business far longer. Stevie recalls, "I thought it was very cool of a woman [not] to say, 'Oh, she's five years younger than me, I've worked for ten years on the road, killed myself, and here she is, our new front-woman!'"* Christine was never interested in grabbing the limelight anyway, unlike their new recruits. Both Christine and Stevie had grit and together they were "a force of nature", Stevie said, remembering what she'd told Christine when she first joined the band. "We're pretty tough by ourselves but together, we can't be beat."

There was, as there always seems to be with Fleetwood Mac, more than a little cosmic fortuity about the new development too – Christine's intuitive mother had cryptically left her daughter with the words "You will find it on Orange Grove . . ." before she passed away. Christine assumed she meant she was simply going to end up picking oranges in California, but when she met Stevie and Lindsey it all became clear: the couple lived on Orange Grove in Fairfax.

Fleetwood invited the newbies to have a jam the following day at 5 p.m. (i.e. once the hangovers had worn off) in a garage on Pico Boulevard, Santa Monica, but the first full-scale rehearsal took place in the basement of their booking agents ICM in Beverly Hills. Stevie and Lindsey might have been nervous but the energy together was perfect, and Christine, John and Mick were stunned by their vocal sound, which instantly infused their existing songs with a new power.

"I started playing 'Say You Love Me'," remembered Christine. "And when I reached the chorus they started singing with me and fell right into it. I heard this incredible sound – our three voices – and said to

* As told in 1981 to Sean Egan, *Fleetwood Mac on Fleetwood Mac: Interviews and Encounters.*

myself, 'Is this me singing?' I couldn't believe how great this three-voice harmony was." The sound of their voices together turned her skin "to gooseflesh". For Fleetwood, those early rehearsals with Stevie and Lindsey reminded him of the energy of the Peter Green/Jeremy Spencer days. "I also found Stevie to be the most endearing combination of beatnik poet and cowgirl."

The inclusion of Buckingham Nicks was, as Mick Fleetwood's then-wife Jenny Boyd put it, a "creative shot in the arm" – and Jenny had certainly seen Fleetwood's group undergo a few lineup changes in her time. Mick put the pair on a wage of $200 per week to start with. "We may have paid a little of their rent too," he recalled in his book *Fleetwood*, "but I can't remember. No one really had much money then, we were just surviving." It was all relative, of course – $200 a week was a lifeline to Stevie and Lindsey, who felt immediately rich. Just one week earlier they were eking out pizza slices. Fleetwood Mac may have been "just surviving" but they were surviving while driving Cadillacs and sinking margaritas. The fact remained, however, that, considering how successful they already were, they should have had more money at their disposal – but, as Fleetwood ruefully admitted, "everything was still in Bob Welch's name because we had no green cards that would let us earn money in the States. The $200,000 advance from Warner Bros to me, John and Chris went straight into Bob's bank account." Result? Welch was sent "one hell of a tax bill" for an album he wouldn't even be on.

Still, the money they apportioned for Stevie and Lindsey would make an instant difference to their lives. "I had hundred-dollar bills everywhere," Stevie told Sarah McLachlan for *Interview* in 1995, recalling pinning the notes up onto the walls of their apartment for fun. "Since we hadn't spent any money in five years, we didn't even know how to spend money. And I was putting hundred-dollar bills through the wash and finding them crumpled and detergented out, and hanging them on the line with the rest of our stuff." It wouldn't take long for Stevie to learn how to spend some serious cash, however: they left the apartment they'd been sharing with Richard for a new one on Hollywood Boulevard. She would soon get rid of the old Toyota and buy a 280 SL Mercedes convertible with a glamorous red interior. Then she really felt like a rock star. But something else that would quickly change was the fact that, while she had been 'the caretaker' of so many people since moving to LA, suddenly people were taking care of her.

Plans for the next album, the eponymous *Fleetwood Mac* (referred to by those in the inner circle at the time as 'The White Album'), were underway. Christine was writing songs at her home with John in Malibu, and Stevie and Lindsey, already armed with songs galore in demo form, headed over to run them past the rest of the band. After the assembled Macs had made themselves comfortable, Christine unveiled 'Sugar Daddy' and 'Warm Ways', to great approval. It was then time for Stevie and Lindsey to show off their wares. Neither party had any need for apprehension – the songs were, as far as the rest of the band were concerned, "tremendous" and fully formed. Lindsey had been "labouring over the harmonic guitars of 'I'm So Afraid' since at least 1971", according to Fleetwood, so it was no surprise that the demos were rather more than rough musical sketches.

'Monday Morning' and 'Landslide' were also on the tapes, and it was proposed that Fleetwood Mac should also record a new version of 'Crystal', which had featured on *Buckingham Nicks*. 'Crystal' was written by Stevie with her father and grandfather in mind, but she insisted Lindsey take the vocals as he interpreted it so beautifully. It was a strong song, and the lyrics were pure Stevie – "do you always trust your first initial feeling?"– and they were keen to hear how it would sound with more production. Another song Stevie presented to Fleetwood Mac was 'Rhiannon', a mysterious song that would soon come to define Nicks, not to mention light a fire under Fleetwood Mac's live shows, for more than 40 years to come. Stevie's demo was gentler and more sensitive than the song we know today, but that bright intensity and 'bird in flight' feeling, musically expressed by the lilting, rise and fall vocal melody in the chorus, was there at its core from the start.

The idea for 'Rhiannon' was sparked when Stevie was looking for reading matter to pass time in an airport three months earlier, possibly while waiting for her flight back to LA from Aspen around Halloween 1973. Stevie picked out the supernatural novel *Triad* by Mary Leader, and was very taken with two of the names in the story – that of Branwen, the female protagonist, (after whom Stevie would name an Afghan hound) and Rhiannon, Branwen's long-dead cousin who comes back to haunt her. Initially she "just thought it was a pretty name", but something about it inspired her on a deeper level. Within ten minutes, a song had formed. The lyrics, almost channelled, were about a compelling white witch, "taken by the sky", enchanting all who encountered her on a starless night; "who will be her lover?"

"It's just about a mystical woman [who] finds it hard to be tied down," she explained in 1976 in an interview with the broadcaster Jim Ladd. "What the band got really well was that uplifting of wings feel, you know . . . when you see a seagull and she's lifting up. Well, that's Rhiannon. She's moving up." And so was Stevie.

Later, however, Stevie would discover that the character she'd conjured, apparently from her imagination, actually existed in ancient Celtic mythology: Rhiannon was a Welsh "witch", a goddess who appears frequently in *The Mabinogion* – eleven prose stories collected from Welsh manuscripts that date back to the Middle Ages. "Rhiannon is the maker of birds and the goddess of steeds," Stevie explained of her findings. "She's the protector of horses. Her music is like a pain pill. When you wake up and hear her birds singing her little song, the danger will have passed. I realise that somehow I had managed to pen a song that went very much along with the mythical tale of Rhiannon."

"I just fell in love with the name, sat down, and wrote the song in about ten minutes," Stevie told Vivien Goldman for *Sounds* in 1976, "and found out later that the whole story is already written in Celtic mythology, Welsh mythology. It's very strange . . . and 'Rhiannon' onstage is very, very weird." Goldman suggested this was something to do with the collective unconscious, a "kind of a shared reference file of information referring back to pre-history and beyond . . . Walt Whitman puts it thus: 'I was the man, I suffered, I was there . . .' Stevie puts it like this: 'I'm sure that I was there at the time, and 'Rhiannon' somehow came through me.'"

"I started collecting butterflies in LA," Stevie continued, "after I'd joined the band, and 'Rhiannon' was recorded. Then, a year and a half later somebody gave me this book . . . This book was called *The Song Of Rhiannon*, and there's a picture of her at the beginning. She's sitting like this; she has really long flowing hair, and out of her mouth is flowing butterflies. I said, Lindsey, I've never read any of that stuff, but it's all there in the song. I figure I really didn't need to read it, I just think I was around at some point." And so, on her first album with Fleetwood Mac, Stevie's channelled 'Welsh witch' would find a home.

With the songs chosen and everyone "in love" with each other (this famously wouldn't last), Fleetwood Mac soon decamped to Sound City with Keith Olsen and Richard Dashut for the recording of *Fleetwood Mac*. "When we got into the studio, the magic started to happen, it really did," remembers Olsen. Lindsey fazed the band with his creativity (and occasionally irritated them with his strong ideas) and Stevie danced and whirled around the studio. "I had a feeling audiences were going to devour her," said Fleetwood, no doubt rather smitten.

The making of Fleetwood Mac that chilly February was largely smooth, by Fleetwood Mac standards at least. Everyone was excited by the sheer "newness" of it all . . . although that's not to say there wasn't tension. There would be some considerable clashing of egos between Lindsey and John, who didn't like taking orders from someone who had just joined the band. Lindsey was full of ideas, a natural producer, but perhaps he didn't have the best bedside manner when suggesting rhythms to Mick on the drums and basslines to McVie. John McVie was not only very protective and defensive of what he did, he was also "a consummate game-player" as Fleetwood puts it, and in addition was often rather drunk. McVie would often stop Lindsey in his tracks during moments of over-confidence and bossiness with the words: "Hang on, you're talking to McVie here." Maybe John's own ego needed checking, but either way it must have been inwardly not a little amusing to Stevie to see how others responded to Lindsey's forceful manner.

Still, Lindsey knew what he wanted and more often than not, he was right. The tracks were sounding phenomenal, although the music had changed: at one point John McVie looked at the two American flower children harmonising before him, turned to Olsen and said, "We used to be a blues band . . ." Keith looked back at him and retorted: "Yes, but now it's a much shorter trip to the bank."

Two vibrant new writers had joined the fray, and the resulting combination brought together gritty British rock and the sunshine of the West Coast with an added twang of country, courtesy of Stevie. They were becoming closer in sound and stature to the Eagles than the Bluesbreakers, and while Fleetwood Mac might never have had a US hit single up to this point, this would soon change thanks to their new magic ingredient – Buckingham Nicks.

Fleetwood Mac would pay tribute to the past, however, with the song 'World Turning', which had developed from the stem of an old Peter Green song; the band just jammed it and let it evolve in the studio. This track was only added because there weren't quite enough songs on the album, but its presence would provide a meaningful bridge between two very different Fleetwood Macs. Much of the development of this track would be down to Christine McVie and Lindsey, and Stevie was apparently more than a little rocked when she walked into the studio to see them singing it together. Stevie and Lindsey had never written together like that.

Stevie Nicks was three years away from her 30th birthday, but up to this point she barely drank or smoked, while Christine alone would be downing champagne within minutes of entering the studio, a cigarette ever-present in her free hand. There was also plenty of cocaine in the studio, indeed it was the first time really that any of them had gone for coke in a big way, but as Fleetwood puts it, "a toot now and then relieved the boredom of long hours in the studio." The proliferation of marching powder also suppressed their appetites, which was just as well – there was barely time to take a break to eat. They just worked and developed their studio tans.*

* A studio tan = not a tan. It was generally assumed that if a rock star looked tanned and healthy, their career was on the skids. They should be too busy working in a dark studio with no windows, or partying hard all night, to spend time lying about on the beach.

Long hours indeed would be spent recording 'Rhiannon'; the only really difficult track on the album to lay down. "The others were easy," Olsen said. "Like five takes, and the feel just kept getting better." But, as Stevie describes the character of her signature song, Rhiannon is "hard to tie down"; maybe that counts for capturing and pinning the song down on tape too.

"It was one of those songs that took over a day to get the basic track, and we're on analogue tape," explains Keith. "The first pass was kind of magical but had too many mistakes. The second pass was pretty good, but didn't have the magic and from there it went downhill. But I kept those two." By the end of the night, they still didn't have 'Rhiannon' the way they wanted it, and resolved to try again the following afternoon (never morning) when everyone was vaguely fresh. But Keith stayed back in the studio. He wanted to try something out.

"I started editing two-inch tape," he says. "And I just looped some sections – looping was done with a big physical loop of tape, and it would be transferred over to another machine. So if you listen to the end of 'Rhiannon', you will hear the mini scar in the cymbal crash that happens every time it loops around. There were, like, 14-15 cuts to put together that track. It was hard. Really hard." But it was worth it. By the time the band were back in the studio the following day, one of the strongest songs on the album – Stevie's song – had been transformed. The best of the previous day's parts had been blended to show off Stevie's luminous vocal, the haunting harmonies, the chiming keys and Lindsey's now-iconic guitar parts at their finest.

Part of the song's splendour would be sealed in the mixing stage. Engineers Richard Dashut and Ken Caillat would mix the radio edit of 'Rhiannon' and, after accidentally addressing Stevie as "Lindsey", Caillat was put under further pressure when Stevie took him aside and told him: "This has to be a great mix. This song is very special to me." She turned away, before turning back to add, "It's magic." She may well have been right; the song was so good, Ken admitted later in his 2012 book *Making Rumours*, that it "almost mixed itself". As they worked, Stevie whirled and pirouetted around the studio, her arms aloft, apparently in an altered state. "She believed she had magical powers," says Ken. "She probably thought she was chanting up a good mix from Richard and me." It must have worked: by the time their work was complete everyone was dancing, not just Stevie.

While the band worked, Mick Fleetwood, then acting as the band's manager, was having to field anxious calls from the label. Warner Brothers were sceptical about the band's tenth studio album after so many changes, so much trouble, so many cancelled shows and diminishing sales. But Fleetwood wasn't just delivering lip service in his attempts to reassure them – he genuinely believed the album was going to be their biggest yet. The joke within Warners was that Fleetwood Mac albums paid the lighting bills, generally 300,000 unit sales, nothing spectacular. The band knew *Fleetwood Mac* would be different, however, and Fleetwood was so adamant about it that he personally visited the office of then Warners boss Mo Ostin, accompanied by lawyer Mickey Shapiro, to demand either support or the freedom to find a more appropriate label. Fleetwood Mac had been on Warners' Reprise roster for years, but they needed their label to understand that what was coming would likely revolutionise how the band was regarded, not to mention their finances. Warners would be able to leave the lights on all night on what the Mac were about to pull in.

There was a nasty moment when the master tapes were briefly misplaced, but once they were found in a stack of tapes that were to be erased (best not to think about that too much), the individual members of the group were given copies of the record to take home and listen to in their own time. When Stevie took her copy back to the apartment and played it, curtains drawn, candles lit, she realised that she and Lindsey had accomplished what they set out to do when they first agreed to join Fleetwood Mac. "I said, 'This is a really nice album. There are some really pretty songs on it . . . And the voices sound beautiful, and . . . yes, we have added something. We have enhanced Fleetwood Mac.'"

PART II

On The Wings Of An Albatross

Chapter Six

As soon as the album was complete and the band members were happy with it, Fleetwood Mac went on an extensive tour; a venture that, again, Warners was not behind. The label didn't understand why the band would tour in May when the album was out in July – what was the point of going out on the road with no product to sell? Plus, this was a band not known for its stability. Warners shrugged their shoulders and refused to front the band any money for the tour, but Mick Fleetwood booked the dates anyway, all the while planning to dump Warners in favour of another major label, such as CBS or Arista.

The way they had been treated latterly was demoralising and, now Fleetwood Mac was practically a new band with exciting prospects the feeling was that, should the future be as bright as they anticipated, Warners didn't deserve a piece of that particular pie after having been so lackadaisical. "Our low status in those days was confirmed when our label took out an ad in *Billboard*," recalled Mick. "In the photograph Stevie was identified as Lindsey and vice versa. We were not amused."

Despite Warners' low expectations, the tour was a phenomenal success; the Mac initially played 3,000 capacity venues, opening for Loggins & Messina*, but by the end of 1975 they had played 90 punishing but triumphant headline shows in front of 20,000 people. The new mix of voices, personalities and songs would be a revelation for fans, and ultimately proved to the band – and the label – that they'd been right all along.

* Successful pop-rock duo Kenny Loggins and Jim Messina.

The tour certainly went well in terms of profile, but on a personal level a feeling of anxiety prevailed, and it radiated from everyone for different reasons. Christine and John's marriage would not last the course and Lindsey and Stevie, always a troubled couple, were constantly tugging at the seams of their relationship. Certain members of the crew were also feeling the strain: on Stevie and Lindsey's insistence, Richard Dashut had been appointed Fleetwood Mac's live sound engineer instead of then tour manager John Courage, who had been taking care of this duty quite happily for years.

Richard appreciated the gig and his friends' loyalty but he had never mixed live sound before and was extremely nervous. John Courage, meanwhile, was not impressed by the new development and encouraged the road crew to 'show him what the road's really like', leaving Richard to fend for himself in a Winnebago alongside some of the band's toughest roadies ("like cut-throat bikers on acid"). Before they embarked Courage rather cruelly instructed the other technicians to "keep him up all the way to El Paso", the first date of the tour on 15 May. He would be duly kept up for 48 hours, smoking dope and "consuming mounds of blow . . . I was a zombie when it was time to work". To compound matters, Richard, being such a close friend of Stevie and Lindsey's, would occasionally travel with the band in limousines. This didn't exactly engender a sense of crew solidarity.

There was more than a little casual sexism on the tour for Christine and Stevie to contend with too, and the sound of "get those broads off the stage" barked by Loggins & Messina's road manager Jim Recor (no doubt with a twinkle in the eye, but still . . .) was not unusual. Aside from wives or groupies, most of the crew were unused to having women on tour. While conflict was rife between the now disintegrating couples in the band, the general touring mood for Fleetwood Mac had nevertheless improved with Stevie and Lindsey, which is certainly saying something, as it was far from a relaxed expedition. But, as John Courage put it: "They were young, good-looking, friendly and fun to be with. Bob Welch was serious and moody and he went through depressing

A sun-lit Stevie Nicks in 1975, the year she and Lindsey Buckingham joined Fleetwood Mac. FIN COSTELLO/REDFERNS

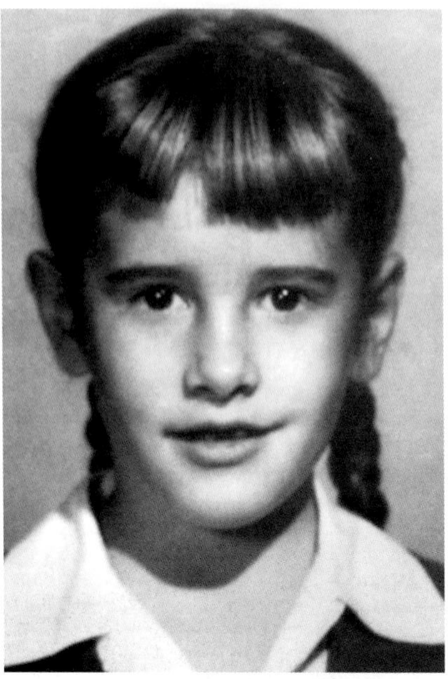

The young Stevie, who was already proving a talented singer and performer thanks to the encouragement of her grandfather, country and western singer AJ Nicks.

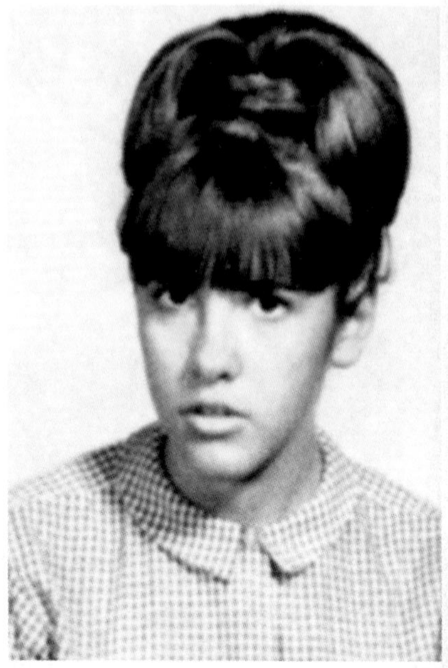

A beehived teenage Stevie working the sultry look in a high school photograph. Arcadia High School, 1965.

Stevie joined the Fritz Rabyne Memorial Band at the Menlo Atherton High School in California in 1967, and the band swiftly built up a following in San Francisco, supporting major acts including Janis Joplin, Jefferson Airplane and Jimi Hendrix. Here, Fritz band-mate Lindsey Buckingham poses by Stevie's side, and not for the last time.

Stevie attends the 20th Annual Grammy Awards ceremony with her devoted mother Barbara Nicks at the Shrine Auditorium in Los Angeles, California on February 23, 1978. Fleetwood Mac's *Rumours* would win the Album Of The Year category. RON GALELLA/WIREIMAGE

Fleetwood Mac in 1976. From left to right: Mick Fleetwood (drums), John McVie (bass), Christine McVie (keys, vox), Lindsey Buckingham (guitar, vox) and Stevie Nicks (vox). AP/PRESS ASSOCIATION IMAGES

Stevie recording a vocal take for the album *Fleetwood Mac* in 1975, Mick Fleetwood and Lindsey Buckingham in the background.
FIN COSTELLO/REDFERNS

Warner Brothers bosses Mo Ostin and Joe Smith join Fleetwood Mac (and Bugs Bunny) as they are presented with a gold disc for *Fleetwood Mac*, the first Mac album to feature Stevie and Lindsay Buckingham. JAMES FORTUNE/REX

Stevie with the man who briefly became her husband in January 1983: record executive Kim Anderson. Kim was the widower of Robin Snyder Anderson, Stevie's closest friend. RON GALELLA/WIREIMAGE

John McVie and Stevie display their contrasting sartorial styles onstage. MARVIN LICHTNER/TIME LIFE PICTURES/GETTY IMAGES

Producer Jimmy Iovine and Stevie attend the 10th Annual American Music Awards together. Iovine started working with Nicks on her first solo album *Bella Donna*, released in 1981. RON GALELLA/WIREIMAGE

A true 'girl's girl', Stevie always surrounded herself with female friends when on the road. RICHARD E. AARON/CAMERAPRESS

A wide-eyed Stevie charms the press on a cruise-boat in the harbour of Rotterdam, Holland, during the *Tusk* world tour, 1980.
BARRY SCHULTZ/SUNSHINE/RETNA/PHOTOSHOT.

times with us. But now I saw John and Chris and Mick enjoying themselves again."

Musically, the shows were strong and the tour proved an ideal testing ground for the new songs, a brave move in an era when unreleased material was rarely performed live. Still, old school fans were not disappointed and appreciated Lindsey's version of Peter Green's iconic 'Oh Well'. These were big shows for Stevie and Lindsey to play, but Loggins recalls watching from the wings and being struck by new girl Stevie's "innate awareness of how to work a large audience," he says. "Stevie has always impressed me as a unique artist and individual." Yes, Fleetwood Mac's new front woman was a natural, and this would be yet another reason for the growing agitation between herself and Lindsey. Buckingham was not happy that his girlfriend, whose simple but beautiful songs he had transformed into 'hits', had been "singled out as the star".

Stevie's charisma, voice and energy mesmerised the audience, particularly when the time came to unleash 'Rhiannon', which was "very, very weird" to sing live, according to Stevie. It would build to a raging, frenzied crescendo, quite different from the recorded version, and Stevie appeared to be transported to another plane as she performed it. "It's a real mind-tripper. Everybody, including me, is just blitzed by the end of it." Mick Fleetwood described Stevie's passionate performance of the song as "like an exorcism". Nearly 40 years on, the atmosphere 'Rhiannon' creates has hardly changed. It would always be, as Stevie says, a "heavy" part of the set. But no matter how much energy it takes out of her, she never tires of singing it.

Stevie always talked about Rhiannon as if she were a real person in her life, a kind of ever-present spirit guide whose intensity she has to keep at bay while performing the other songs in the set. "She just has to wait, that's all there is to it." Stevie was also protective of 'Rhiannon' to the point that she was against the idea of the song being released as a single. "I thought, 'What if my Rhiannon falls flat on her face.' It's not my choice to release her as a single, she is a mythological goddess [and] a brilliant, brilliant character . . ." said Stevie in a 1989 interview with

BBC One To One. "She simply is not for sale and has never been." This is all very well, but while 'she' might not have been for sale, the song definitely was, and it gave the band their first US hit.

The sheer scale of the shows was daunting and relationship difficulties were making Stevie feel increasingly alone, but she was going onstage armed with her precious songs and the spirit of Rhiannon urging her on. Cocaine also helped, something Courage ensured no member of the band was without. After their faithful tour manager had counted down the minutes until it was time for the band to face the crowd, they would line up and hold out their wrists, onto which Courage, or JC as he was known, distributed a toot's worth of the emboldening powder to see them onto the stage. As Stevie herself has noted, coke was viewed as a purely recreational drug at the time – she never imagined the damage it could inflict upon her, both mentally and physically. It was just as essential and routine a part of the backstage ritual as putting on her silent-movie star eye-makeup (and lots of it – what looked like too much close up was often just the right amount from the point of view of the audience), doing her ballet stretches and fixing her long, curly hair. For the 1975 tour, Stevie opted mostly for floaty, flowery printed chiffon tops and jeans. It would be a while until she took on her 'Rhiannon' look of black chiffon, handkerchief skirts, shawls and a top hat. However, the vision was already in her mind, and she pre-empted her own adoption of this look with the line "black robes trailing" in 'Sisters Of The Moon', a song she was working on during this tour. Before long, that image of a witchy rock 'n' roll high priestess would be a Fleetwood Mac mainstay.

By the time *Fleetwood Mac* was released on 11 July 1975, the band had flown to Detroit, taken in the Midwest and North-East of the US, and more dates were being added all the time. The album would set a record at the time for the most weeks on the chart before reaching the top, and by the following year, it would still be in the Top 10, selling over five million copies and winning the group five platinum discs and a gold one in the UK. The press praised it – although some journalists took time to get used to Stevie's 'harsh' voice in comparison to Christine's more silvery tones, a criticism that upset Stevie to the point she even considered quitting. The comments hadn't just pricked her ego; they reignited her paranoia that she was only there because of Lindsey and that she wasn't really wanted. However, Mick and Christine did their best to reassure her and her harmonies, particularly on Christine's song 'Over My Head', were duly praised, the single going straight into the Top Ten in November. Her own song 'Rhiannon' would surpass even this on release the following February.

Both fans and press were rightly excited for the future of Fleetwood Mac and, as far as the band was concerned, the new members were "blossoming" and this period on the road would seal them as a unit, musically at least. Away from the audience's adoring gaze, Stevie and Lindsey were fighting more than ever, and while Stevie often took refuge in Christine's company, Lindsey was largely out on his own socially, dedicating his time and considerable energy to composing instead. He would spend days on end with his tape recorders, working feverishly on songs. He was struggling with demons and neuroses, and it wasn't easy for him to be in a band that had existed successfully without him before he came along. He might have been the dominant partner in Buckingham Nicks, but this was Fleetwood Mac, and Lindsey didn't have the reins. At least if he kept writing and recording, he could pour his frustration into something productive.

Still, no one could deny the huge positive changes that had affected both Lindsey and Stevie: within just a few months of joining Fleetwood Mac, they had gone from destitution to fame – and not just in Birmingham, Alabama, where *Buckingham Nicks* had been such a cult hit*. It was confusing for them, an experience that, in a way, would strengthen their intense bond while onstage, but at the same time their partnership was

* In fact, just after joining the band, Buckingham Nicks were offered a headline show in Birmingham, which the Mac allowed them a night off to play. Stevie and Lindsey appeared in front of 6,000 fans and were treated like rock stars. After years of obscurity in LA this was something of a shock, but good practice for the levels of adulation to come, levels that would often reach 'scary' heights, as far as Stevie was concerned.

becoming more and more damaged. The whole tour was, to put it mildly, something of a culture shock.

The sudden level of attention frightened Stevie, and witnessing her new bandmates' raw, individual pain on a daily and nightly basis was jarring: John McVie's heavy drinking and despair over his failing marriage to Christine led to disturbing behaviour. Stevie recalled huddling with Christine in her hotel room as John paced the hotel corridors "just screaming her name," said Stevie. "It was horrible." Similarly there were times, certainly, that Stevie felt Christine was her "only friend" on the road, and vice versa. As soon as the press saw there were now two women in Fleetwood Mac, the questions started (and have never really stopped); they wanted a cat-fight, at least a little bitching. They wouldn't get it. Arguably Stevie and Christine's friendship ended up being the most successful out of the many relationships borne of Fleetwood Mac.

As Christine observed, humour was a vital part of what made it work from the start, and they weren't competitive, although Stevie later claimed she'd heard tales that Christine was indeed occasionally jealous of Stevie. All the same, "Christine never let me know, not one comment of: 'I could really have done without you.'" Stevie told *Mojo*'s Sylvie Simmons in 2007. "I'm sure there were times when I'm flying around the stage in my gossamer chiffon where she (thought) to herself, 'Wow, what's this? Fairy school?' Never once did she make me feel like that. She knew from the beginning I was real sensitive and that I love her so much that anything she'd say to me would cut like a knife."

The strain of heavy touring coupled with emotional conflict (and drugs) would have taken its toll on anybody. It soon led to Stevie becoming thin, tired and ill with frequent throat problems. Mick Fleetwood often saw her "melting into a corner wrapped in a shawl with a cup of tea, writing . . ." He was concerned to see her losing weight she didn't have to spare in the first place, but remembered her being "sweet and funny". She was putting a brave face on, as was Mick, whose marriage to Jenny Boyd also hung in the balance.

This gruelling tour – 90 dates in total – was the final straw for all of their respective relationships, and considering two of those relationships were within the band, Fleetwood Mac could have been forgiven for wanting to split up for the sake of their sanity, but there was no discussion of parting. Though Stevie herself seriously considered leaving from time to time during this tour, particularly after her parents came to the Phoenix show. They couldn't hide their horror at how drawn and skinny their usually bubbly, curvaceous daughter had become. She often had to be persuaded to eat and look after herself, and would tell Mick in later years: "When I joined I hadn't a clue it would be like this. I didn't know Chris and I would be sleeping on amps in the back of trucks. But I've decided I'm going to make it through and that no one's going to say, 'Oh, she can't cope.'" Again, she used the frequent periods of waiting around in venues to focus her feelings into songwriting, writing poems and songs such as 'Sisters Of The Moon' in her notebook backstage – acts of transmutation.

'Sisters Of The Moon' was inspired by the sometimes traumatic nature of being on tour, or more specifically, this first tour with Fleetwood Mac. It was hard, there were no limousines – not yet –and she just wasn't used to the lifestyle. She told radio interviewer Jim Ladd: "I walked out in front of a mirror and looked at myself and I was sick, I went, 'Oh, poor, sad little thing. She must be dying.'"

"I stood back and said, 'But you don't want to die and neither do I, so we must change this now. Soul, be my sister, I'm not going out on some cloud without you, and you look like you're on your way out. We'd better put this back together and realise that this is not such a frail creature.' So, [the lyric] 'intense silence as she walked in the room' was me looking at myself. And 'the people they love her . . .' that's after the gigs; there are a million people and you're being pulled every way . . . 'and they like to wrap her in velvet' like some sort of weird corpse? Not me. Do it to other rock'n'roll stars, baby, but I'm not doing that. I love life too much. But I was letting myself sink and sort of getting off on the fact I was so frail and blonde and pale."

She was starting to romanticise her own tragic potential, but it was when her parents stepped in and questioned what was happening that "it clicked." It's not hard to imagine the 'intense silence as she walked in the room . . .' however: the anxiety, paranoia and sense of isolation Stevie must have felt despite being suddenly surrounded by more people than ever. The people who 'loved her' were 'still the most cruel' – fans, the press, in some cases, the band. 'Some say illusions are her game . . .'

Female friendships were becoming ever more vital to Stevie on the road. 'She asked me: 'be my sister' . . .' (both 'she' and 'me' referring to Stevie herself) is just an open-hearted request not only to her own 'soul' or self, an appeal to take care of herself a little better, but also for a friend with no agenda. Not an easy thing to find at this level of fame and success. 'Friends' would be everywhere in the shape of hangers on and chancers, naturally. But as well as her strong kinship with Christine, the support Stevie gained from the presence of her old schoolfriend Robin Snyder, who joined her on the road as her vocal coach, was something that gave her strength. Robin, stable, beautiful and down to earth, didn't just help her friend to protect her voice from being worn ragged by relentless shows; she was also one of the only people who really knew Stevie.

Alongside Robin, other female friends were included in the sacred Stevie circle, most notably Mary Torrey and Christi Astbury, both of whom looked remarkably similar to Stevie, with angelic faces and long golden hair. Before long one of the most noticeable things about Stevie Nicks backstage at a Fleetwood Mac show would be her entourage of young women who were all curiously of a certain type – a Stevie type. They all looked as if Stevie had dressed them up like dolls from her own wardrobe. Perhaps it was a tactic to confuse the press. Either way, Kenny Loggins remembers noticing this shimmering little army "floating through the backstage area" with amazement.

"My first impression of touring with Fleetwood Mac was seeing Stevie and her acolytes . . . She seemed to collect talented, young, beautiful girls who would then dress like her and follow her around all the time. I'd never seen anything like it." It was as if having "mini-mes" around her gave her confidence; there was a protective, self-esteem-boosting perimeter wall around her at all times. It also helped having neutral parties around when Lindsey was in a bad mood – he was less likely to tear into Stevie if there was an audience of devotees witnessing the proceedings. Lindsey was, as Stevie herself put it, "scary" when he got angry.

Mick Fleetwood's own protectiveness and awareness of Stevie's vulnerability betrayed his affection for her at this early stage. He loved how 'silly' they could be together, and admits they're both 'old drama queens' (less of the 'old' please, Michael) but there was clearly more to it, and the super-sensitive Lindsey picked it up before even Mick did.

On one occasion, when Mick did get Lindsey out of the hotel to "have fun", he ended up being hit by a bombshell. The pair got stoned after a gig in Texas, and finally Lindsey had started to relax. But suddenly he turned to Mick and said, "It's you and Stevie, isn't it?" "I remember this hitting my psyche like a bolt of lightning," Mick mused in his book *Fleetwood*. "I really didn't understand. I could only stammer, 'Whaddaya mean?' But he didn't answer. The moment passed and it was never mentioned again."

But Mick even questions himself about his soft spot for Stevie at this stage – and he doesn't really have an answer: "Did I fall for her right away? I don't know, but she immediately felt like a soul mate." He was as transfixed as anyone when she worked her magic onstage. However, Mick kept his feelings to himself – and from himself, if his book is anything to go by – for as long as he could. Not only was his own marriage fractured, seemingly beyond repair, his mental health wasn't doing too well either. Keeping mind, body and spirit together in circumstances such as these was not easy.

Another complication, because there obviously weren't nearly enough on this tour, was that Loggins & Messina's tour manager Jim Recor had also become unsurprisingly attracted to Stevie. Presumably once he'd managed to get over the fact there were 'broads on the stage', he was struck by her presence, beauty and grace, which shone out in bold relief against the usual entourage of hairy roadies and sweaty male musicians

(Christine McVie being the other obvious exception here). Jim's own relationship with his wife Sara, a model (and later a close friend of Stevie's herself) was breaking down and confiding in someone as magnetic as Stevie, let alone travelling with her for the best part of a year, would not help matters.

The long-awaited final date of the tour was 22 December 1975, and in the spirit of rock'n'roll decadence, Richard Dashut and John Courage (now evidently reconciled) played Dodgems with their two rented station wagons in the icy Holiday Inn car park, smashing them into each other as the band looked on with jaded amusement. They had Christmas off, and they'd earned it. They already had a gold disc for the album and had proved themselves to Warners. Stevie and Lindsey were taken off their wage and made partners in the band. Fleetwood Mac was officially reborn. But as they steadily climbed the charts, behind the scenes there had never been so much turmoil. The McVies' marriage was over, with Christine now enjoying the attentions of the Mac's dangerously charming lighting director Curry Grant. Stevie and Lindsey, meanwhile, were barely surviving as a couple, although there was already the dreadful awareness that, if they did split up, they'd still have to see each other every day anyway. Neither of them would abandon Fleetwood Mac.

Meanwhile, Jenny Boyd had felt utterly abandoned in Topanga with the kids while Mick was working, and their failing marriage and his damaged lifestyle led to what Jenny herself describes as a "major-league breakdown . . . When I felt a little better, I told Mick that if we didn't separate I might do myself in. There was almost no reaction." Mick was obviously on the verge of a meltdown himself.

Whatever happened, come heartbreak, divorce, breakdowns, fights, illnesses, addictions and betrayals . . . for better or worse, Fleetwood Mac always had, and always would, come first. John McVie might have told Bob Welch it was 'a marriage', but it was obviously much more of a commitment than that. It was bigger than all of them, charging unstoppably like a wild-eyed giant, trampling innocents in its wake. The people within the band took their fun where they could, and extreme lows were matched by seemingly impossible highs, in every sense. If nothing else, they just had to keep moving forward. Soon after New Year 1976, one year after Stevie and Lindsey joined the band, Fleetwood Mac started work on their next album. None of them would survive unscathed.

Chapter Seven

Nineteen seventy-six would see a seismic shift in popular culture; it was the year that punk truly broke. It crackled outwards from New York and London via the Ramones, Television, the Sex Pistols, Adam Ant . . . but despite the rumblings of the more local, nascent punk movement in Los Angeles, Fleetwood Mac would be unperturbed by the growing craze that encouraged rock fans to hack off their hair and throw out all of their old records. The effects of punk are larger in memory than they were at the time and a majority of Mac fans would be hanging on to their treasured platters, waiting with bated breath for news that the band would be rolling into a town near them. No, the aggression and hardline purity of punk would not cause any difficulties for Fleetwood Mac. There was plenty of aggression – passive and otherwise – within the band itself. They had enough to worry about.

Cutting-edge groups such as The Clash and Talking Heads, however, made a certain Fleetwood Mac songwriter prick up his ears, inspiring an attempt to shrug off the full-fat West Coast AOR vibe of their music in favour of something harder and leaner. But at this point, Fleetwood Mac was lyrical soft rock to the hilt. The three writers – Christine, Stevie and Lindsey – had been busy working on new material matching that very description for the next album, the album that would later be titled *Rumours*.

Soon after New Year the band members, who had barely recovered from the Fleetwood Mac tour, reconvened to jam and rehearse ideas before heading to the studio. Mick had found a truly sinister place to practise: a dilapidated house in Florida with an unsettling atmosphere. Nature had already started to take over this empty place; there were frogs in the pool – "where we half expected to see William Holden floating face down", quipped Mick Fleetwood, in reference to the opening shots of *Sunset Boulevard.* Whether he had selected this location as a joke or not is unclear, but putting an already unhappy band in a deeply unhappy house would only engender further emotional bleakness. Lindsey would start to write the sour, feather-spitting 'Go Your Own Way' here with Stevie in mind.

Studio sessions were booked from 28 January, although they wouldn't be using Sound City this time. Mick Fleetwood felt it prudent to throw the group into a new situation, away from the stagnant and the familiar. It was healthy, perhaps, to change the scene during a "time of enforced creativity". So he booked a studio called the Record Plant in Sausalito, near San Francisco; a wooden, windowless place. Fleetwood had booked it out for nine weeks, which was somewhat optimistic. Making this album would actually take the band the best part of a year, not including overdubs, and recording took place in several different studios from North Hollywood to San Francisco to Miami, despite most of the band simply wanting to record at their homes. The whole process was, as Stevie describes it, 'horrifying'.

During the time Fleetwood Mac took to make this record, their second with Stevie and Lindsey, Keith Olsen had made albums with "[Arista Records boss] Clive Davis, The Grateful Dead, Santana, Foreigner, Pat Benatar, Rick Springfield, one after another, album after album while they were still working on *Rumours.* It's one of those things I'm happy I'm not involved with – when albums take over three months, you get lost . . ." Richard Dashut and LA-based engineer Ken Caillat were brought in, the house engineer being sacked for "being too into astrology". Interestingly Mick would give Dashut and Caillat a Chinese I Ching coin for luck, however. You evidently had to choose your oracle carefully around this lot.

Having Dashut on board was vital for both Stevie and Lindsey; he was an ally for them both and indeed close to the whole band, but while he was a sympathetic presence, he managed to remain largely neutral and good-humoured, which is more than can be said for the rest of the collective. As a result, Dashut became band confidante. By the end of the sessions, his ears would be thoroughly bent, as Ken Caillat remembered in his book *Making Rumours*. Now that Stevie had just left Lindsey, she was desperate for someone to confide in. The relationship wasn't technically "over" yet, but after the strain of the last tour, they'd had a huge fight at their flat and Stevie had had enough, grabbed her favourite things and left.

"I don't even remember what the issues were," Stevie told *Rolling Stone's Writers Notes* in later years. "I just got to the point where I wanted to be by myself. It wasn't good anymore, wasn't fun anymore, wasn't good for either of us. I'm just the one who stopped it." Before they'd joined Fleetwood Mac, Buckingham had always taken care of the music while Stevie worked to keep them alive, but now Stevie was considered a major songwriter in her own right – and she was grabbing a lot of the attention on stage. Stevie and Lindsey's romance was already rocky by the time they joined the group, and Stevie would sometimes wryly comment that the obsessive Lindsey loved his guitar more than he loved her. But she was now being celebrated as a star herself and she found that, in many ways, she just didn't need him as much as she did before. Neither of them had been "any comfort to each other" on the road, as Stevie put it, and the irritation was mutual. "I was frustrated. There was no love, everybody was too nervous."

The idea of being together every day in the studio after the most recent blow-up was not an appealing one, but they had no choice. It was devastating but, as Stevie noted, "devastation leads to writing really good things". At least Stevie and Christine could ensure there would be a few hours each day that would not be spent in the company of John and Lindsey. The studio had accommodation and while the boys of the company opted to stay there, the ladies chose to rent neighbouring condominiums by the harbour in Sausalito.

At her apartment, Stevie could attempt to relax, write to her parents, gossip with friends, stare out of the window at the water (the only panes of glass in the studio had engineers on the other side) and, very importantly, prepare her clothes for the day ahead. Let it be known that the chiffon-clad rock queen image was no stage act. This was now Stevie Nicks *all the time*, particularly in the studio, where she always looked stunning. The great care Stevie took over her outfits was at least partly because she was playing a part even offstage and the costume, or "uniform", as she refers to it, was her suit of armour. Unlike John McVie, who was perfectly happy in a pair of shorts, both Stevie and Lindsey, with his silk kimonos, velvet jackets and Byronic white shirts, knew the power of the right look and no mirror would go unchecked when Stevie or Lindsey were around.

They weren't the only ones in Fleetwood Mac to have a strong sense of the sartorial, of course: Christine wore fashionable bohemian threads, headscarves and boots, Mick preferred a more theatrical Victorian style with billowing sleeves, waistcoats, pocket watches and knickerbockers. Alongside Stevie and Lindsey they were like a rock'n'roll tapestry of archaic characters, knights, ladies, black-hearted princes . . . and then there was John, who just "looks like he's going to the beach" as Stevie once observed with affectionate amusement. Part of what was interesting about the band members' respective images was that they were so different. As Stevie herself attested, it wasn't enough to play music onstage, you had to give the audience something visual to enjoy as well. It went back to Vaudeville and Broadway; there was importance placed on entertaining all of the senses. Their audience would witness the show with their eyes as well as their ears, after all.

Mick never visited Stevie or Christine at their apartments, assuming it must have been "out of bounds to men". Not strictly true. Lindsey himself would occasionally swing by over the course of the next few months, "sleeping over", according to Stevie. These star-crossed lovers might have complained they could never have a clean break from each other, but they didn't help matters by hooking up out of sheer attachment, love and a bid to break the unbearable pressure. Richard Dashut recalled that almost everyone, "to relieve the tension, looked for sexual release, but even that didn't help. The only refuge was the music." What was about to transpire was "the craziest period of our lives". It would be a unique situation for an album to be recorded in, but one that ultimately made it even more compelling.

Always together, always upset, sarcastic barbs flying, substance abuse, not enough rest and increasing pressure from the label, anxious that the album should match up to if not better *Fleetwood Mac* . . . not only was it a huge achievement that such a stunning album would be produced under such stress, but it was also something of a miracle no one disappeared, had a coronary or committed a murder. *Rumours* was never just about showcasing beautiful songs. It was a narrative laid bare for all to read, a soap opera, a tangled movie plot that would ensnare anyone who listened. "It's simply a running document of what happened to us," Stevie would tell *Sounds* journalist Vivien Goldman in 1976. "It's a diary. It's a total lyrical story of what happened to us."

On the first morning of recording, Caillat recalls driving to the studio, his beagle Scooter by his side, and he observed ominous-looking storm clouds gathering as he approached Sausalito. Portentous indeed. Even Scooter would have to deal with some angst; he was about to meet Stevie's poodle Ginny and his high-octane friendliness would unfortunately be as unwelcome to Ginny as it was to Stevie.* Meanwhile, roadies bustled past, bringing in the daily haul of booze: Heineken, champagne, Courvoisier and honey for Stevie . . . Alcohol was generally eschewed by the technicians because it made it difficult to do their job and coffee was the order of the day, or at least it was at first. Cocaine would soon take its place. Stevie would drink and smoke pot. "She had the most time on her hands of anyone and was always looking for the right inspirational input," writes Caillat in *Making Rumours*.

* Ginny would, however, be very exuberant from time to time herself, if rumours of the dog's penchant for cocaine are to be believed. No wrap of the stuff could be left unattended when Ginny was around.

The Record Plant might as well have been chosen by Mick with one person alone in mind, subliminally at least. It had Stevie Nicks written all over it. A wooden building nestled at the bottom of a steep hill, it was hard to find, hidden by trees like "a secret haven" as Caillat observed. The only thing identifying it as the right place was the giant number – 2200 – painted on the wall by the front door, which also featured a carved 'band' of wooden animals playing instruments in a forest, like something out of a fantastical Kit Williams illustration. It was a rabbit warren to get lost in. Hobbit holes sprang to mind. The whole idea of the studio was to make it a 'getaway', far from the rest of the San Francisco music industry.

It would, however, become a prison in its own way. At the same time as the Mac's sessions there, the Eagles were recording in an adjacent studio – two bands with destinies very much entwined even if they didn't connect at this point. Some have opined that this claustrophobic period holed up and coked up, "trapped" in this dark, secret studio, was one of the key inspirations behind *Hotel California,* which was recorded there. The studio door opened out onto the street, glaring sunlight suddenly streaming in every time it was opened, a sudden, rude sense of the outside world rushing into this strange, stuffy twilight world of darkness and music and no small amount of mental torment.

Weeks would go by without sleep. From time to time, they thought they were all going insane. "They had brought amazing songs to the table," says Dashut. "But the sound needed to be coherent and arranged. One theory as to why [the album] took so long was that, because of the amount of cocaine being snorted, what felt like their 'best work' one day sounded dreadful the next, and everything would start again."

Something that would please Stevie would be the fact that the mics they were using had been used previously on Joni Mitchell's live album *Miles Of Aisles.* Joni was a heroine in Stevie's eyes. No one was allowed to approach her room when a Mitchell album had just been released. Stevie would be in there, lying on the floor, blasting the much anticipated record out of her trusty speakers, and was *not* to be disturbed. Any connection to Joni had to be a positive sign. Other than that, good omens were thin on the ground.

Thankfully, Stevie found somewhere to retreat. In the studio just next door, owned by Sly Stone, there was a dubious-looking "pit" which contained a black velvet bed, surrounded by drapes. The entrance was two giant red furry lips. It was often occupied by coke-chopping hangers-on whom nobody seemed to recognise, but Stevie often treated it as a little den, a secret place where she could think and write and get away from the others once the strangers and opportunists had left.

It would be in Sly's pit that "in about five minutes" Stevie conjured the song 'Dreams', although it was originally known as 'Spinners', simply because it reminded the band of a song by the band of the same name. She'd brought in her Fender Rhodes, set herself up in the darkness of the pit, and "it just flowed out". This slow, sad song detailed tenderly but honestly a kind of dialogue between herself and the subject of the song – clearly Lindsey. The lyrics instantly take us to the heart of the conflict: the desire for freedom and yet the crushing loneliness, "remembering what you had and what you lost . . ." This may not have only been a dig at Lindsey, however, but a confession of her own turmoil too. But there would be comfort and trust in a kind of spirituality, those intuitive "crystal visions" Stevie is so fond of (although "I keep my visions to myself" perhaps hints that Lindsey had heard one too many of these crystal visions for his liking), and some sense of anticipated healing, if not a resolution, by the end of the song. "When the rain washes you clean, you'll know . . ." is a reference to a Native American belief that the spirit is set free when the rain falls.

Having recorded her demo on cassette, Stevie was apprehensive about playing it to the rest of the band; she knew the themes within the song would resonate with them all. As it turned out, "everybody really liked it and we recorded it right away". Lindsey knew exactly what the song was about, of course, and even later would damn it with faint praise, describing it as "an interesting outcome for something that didn't have a lot of variety in terms of its chord structures, but tons of variety in terms of its melodic left and right turns . . ."

Stevie admits her songs always start as simple sketches; she'd present them to the band and then they would be arranged. This was rarely easy; handing over her songs meant handing over her control and apart from anything else, all of her songs were personal and precious to her. "I pretty much give it to them and say, 'Do with it what you may,'" she said. "I'm always there saying, 'Well, I'm not sure I like your way of doing it,' but on this particular album everything they did on my songs, I couldn't have done them better, even if I had the [musical] knowledge." It would normally be Lindsey doing the lion's share of the work on Stevie's songs; another thing that vexed him. It was bad enough seeing Stevie get so much credit, but the fact he was still expected to develop her tracks created even more resentment. "So you don't want to be my wife, my girlfriend," he said in an interview in later years, evidently still chagrined, "but you want me to do all that magic stuff on your songs. Is there anything else that you want, just like, in my spare time?"

From Lindsey's point of view, he had extra work to do because Stevie wasn't a musician; she supposedly just swanned in when she fancied with a song she wanted them all to hear, expecting a pat on the head. But arguably Stevie's technical musicianship didn't measure up to Lindsey's because during those formative years when he was practising guitar, she was keeping a roof over their heads. Nevertheless, the fact remained that, while Lindsey was so intrinsically tied to Stevie that he always knew how to work with her songs, sometimes he simply wouldn't do it. "He could take my songs and do what I would do if I had musical talent," Stevie said in an interview with USA Today. "When he wasn't angry with me, that is. That's why there's seven or eight great songs, and 50 more where he wasn't happy with me and didn't help me. Lindsey would say, 'I don't want this song on the record,' and I'd say, 'I hate you!' and I'd be out the door and at home making up speeches I wanted to deliver to him the next day . . ."

Part of Lindsey's irritation with Stevie was that her songwriting, despite her lack of technical musicianship, came so easily. As Ken Caillat noted, "She only knew about three chords, and she could make 30 songs out of them." It was difficult for Stevie to take criticism from Lindsey as a band member, as it was almost impossible to separate valid artistic appraisal from his anger concerning their situation. "It made for some hurtful times," he admitted, "and you had to push through anyway." But there were occasions when Stevie wanted to criticise his guitar parts when something wasn't working, or tear a strip off him for not getting it right, but in turn those would be the times that "he would really need comfort from me," Stevie said. "For me to say, 'It's all right. Who cares about them?' You know, be an old lady (wife) . . . [but] I was *also* pissed off because he hadn't gotten the guitar part on. So I'm trying to defend their point of view and at the same time trying to make him feel better. It doesn't work. I couldn't be all those things."

In the studio, Stevie invariably had to find something to do when the others were arranging their parts; she often sat behind Richard and Ken, smoking what was left of one of Lindsey's joints or sipping tea with a splash of Courvoisier (medicinal purposes, naturally). Stevie might have been the star on stage but she often felt in the way in the studio. Even as she danced and shook her tambourine with its trailing black ribbons, she knew that it would be Mick's tambourine parts that would be used, not hers. As Ken Caillat remembers it, she was mostly just trying to keep herself entertained, and her tambourine was always dampened with gaffer tape, as it would be on stage. It is the eternal problem for a singer – what do you do with your hands when you aren't actually singing? Stevie had found a solution, and it suited her whimsical image perfectly.

'Dreams' was, to say the least, a contrast to 'Go Your Own Way', which was an embittered 'kiss-off' aimed directly at Stevie in a major key but with a driving, almost brutal groove. The song that would end up on the album would be nowhere near as furious as the version that was first presented to the band. Caillat remembers in *Making Rumours* being "surprised at the intensity of his vocal, almost angry . . . [it] was pretty raucous."

Lindsey would claim that "loving you isn't the right thing to do . . .", hurting Stevie profoundly with the line "shacking up's all you wanna do . . ." insinuating a certain amount of promiscuity on Stevie's side which, she insists, "he knew wasn't true. It was just an angry thing he said". Saying it privately is one thing, proclaiming it on a record for the world to hear was another, and it would sting all the more that Stevie not only had to listen to it, she had to sing harmonies on the track, not to mention every night on tour when the time came.

But, snipes aside, Lindsey also exposed the fact he was still in love with her – "if I could, baby, I'd give you my world . . ." – and he was apparently confused as to why "everything turned around"'. But he was laying the blame at her feet and taking the high road, something that must have infuriated Stevie all the more. Stevie and Lindsey were communicating to each other through their songs, as they would continue to for decades to come, working out their pain and jabbing each other musically. They knew each other well enough to push the exact buttons required for maximum emotional damage. But in hindsight, Stevie also accepted that this was also just their way of processing their feelings, like keeping a journal or confiding in a soul mate. This was just that little bit more public . . .

"I write philosophically, he writes angry," she shrugged. "As a songwriter, I have to respect that he's gonna write about what's happening to him, and so am I." And so was Christine, although her songs were a little lighter* . . . she was in love with Curry Grant, which definitely took her mind off John, with whom she barely spoke unless she had to ask which key a song was in. 'Don't Stop (Yesterday's Gone)', the kindest, most positive, forward-looking song on the record, was written for him however, although 'You Make Loving Fun' was famously and rather brazenly written for Curry, making the situation all the more awkward. Still, John had put Christine through more than enough anguish with his drinking, which by

* Although, *Rumours* being a revealing emotional map of Fleetwood Mac's volatile year, it has been speculated that Christine's third contribution, 'Oh Daddy', was a contemplative ode to Curry, whose womanising was understandably wearing her down by this later stage. The final lines, 'And I can't walk away from you baby / If I tried' were provided by Stevie. Christine latterly claimed 'Oh Daddy' was written for Mick Fleetwood in the light of his struggling marriage to Jenny Boyd, however.

all accounts transformed his usually sweet 'crazy big brother' demeanour into something that was ultimately impossible to live with. It was frankly about time someone in Fleetwood Mac had some fun.

Chapter Eight

February 1976. The scene outside the studio was like a Christmas card and Stevie, wrapped up in layers, stayed in the warmth of the Record Plant, sipping her hot Courvoisier and honey, a Vicks inhaler never far from her grasp. (Rare was the day that Stevie wasn't complaining of a cold or a sore throat.) Lindsey had a new song to suggest, but he had to be careful to only play the chords when Stevie was around. The lyrics would only spark another argument, after all, but he couldn't hide them forever. The band sat around Lindsey while he strummed frenetically, a vigorous, chugging groove like an unstoppable train. He kept those lyrics a secret for as long as he could, unable to even reveal the name of the song, which just became known as 'Strummer' for want of something to call it. The song was 'Second Hand News', and no, the lyrics were not kind to Stevie: "I ain't gonna miss you when you go / Been down so long / I've been tossed around enough" and again, Stevie would eventually have to provide backing vocals, singing these very words and knowing exactly to what, and whom, they referred.

Stevie, understandably, was keen for the band to record another of her own songs now, and the following day would be the turn of the powerful, poignant 'Silver Springs'. This was a track written specifically for the album, as opposed to being an earlier Buckingham Nicks-era song, of which there were many. The evocative name was simply inspired by "a freeway sign that said Silver Spring, Maryland" which Stevie spotted when the band were on the road. A magpie for a pretty name with a touch of poetry to it, Stevie jotted it down in her notebook, even using the name Miss Silver Spring to check into hotels now and again. The real Silver Spring was named after a local river that was flecked with the mineral mica and sparkled in the sunlight. To Stevie, it was a fresh, flowing, celestial image to cleanse the soul of heartache, just like the rain in 'Dreams' and the beating wings of 'Rhiannon'.

'Silver Springs' was another musing upon the disintegration of Stevie's relationship with Lindsey. But while it was replete with sadness and even anger, there was no spite, as there was in 'Second Hand News'. As a song it was reflective rather than driving, like Lindsey's tracks. There is, however, an echoing of the sentiment of one of the more tender, frustrated lyrics in Lindsey's 'Go Your Own Way': "I know I could have loved you but you would not let me," is a direct emotional match for "If I could, baby I'd give you my world; how can I if you won't take it from me?" As Stevie said, "It wasn't quite over", because he was still visiting her from time to time, yet at the same time it really was. However, as long as they kept communicating to each other in song, never getting closure, on some level they would never break away from each other completely.

'Silver Springs' is, as Stevie rightly says, "a real heartbreaker", and builds in intensity, exposing her own volcanic emotions. Stevie told the *Arizona Republic* in 1997, explaining the sentiment behind the lines, "you'll never get away from the sound of the woman who loves you . . ." as "You will listen to me on the radio for the rest of your life, and it will bug you. I hope it bugs you . . . As far away as Lindsey goes from me, he'll never get away from my voice." Lindsey might have challenged her to beat it in 'Go Your Own Way' but these final lines of 'Silver Springs' keep him locked in, almost like a curse. It's symbolic that 'Silver Springs' would end up being the B-side to 'Go Your Own Way'; they were knitted tightly together even on vinyl, doomed to 'bug' each other for the rest of time.

The song was beautiful but the session started inauspiciously; Record Plant owner Chris Stone had wandered in with his friend Jimmy Robinson, who worked with him. A joint was passed around between the boys before work continued on 'Silver Springs', but before long everyone dispersed, everyone having had a toke from the joint feeling increasingly ill and discombobulated. The joint contained angel dust. "It ruined them for the rest of the day," said Caillat. Fortunately for Christine and Stevie, they hadn't smoked with Robinson, but there was nothing happening and no point in staying any longer at the studio that day. They would resume the following day – Friday, February 13.

The angel dust incident wasn't the only time the Mac would get inadvertently even more trashed than intended. Stevie's best friend Robin came by to visit the studio with some home-baked hash brownies, which were bound to go down well. Despite her repeated warnings regarding the considerable strength of these cakes, they were eaten with alarming gusto. The result was that, again, "not a note was played and the engineers went home," writes Caillat. "John and Stevie spent hours huddled in a corner, giggling like mad over a copy of *Playboy*."

'Silver Springs' would be further enhanced with experimental sounds courtesy of Ken Caillat, who added to the song's sparkle by using tape delay for 'an ethereal sound', and setting up a Lavalier mic to pick up the sound of Lindsey's pick on the metal strings of his Strat. The result was "a delicate, glasslike, musical box-type sound", very much evocative of "blue-green colours flashing", "shining autumns" and the mica shimmering away in that beautiful river in Maryland. Joint in hand, Stevie stepped up to the microphone which had been set up with a foam pop filter to get the ideal vocal sound. Ken instructed her to allow her lips to slightly touch the filter. The result was a "smooth, strong vocal," he explains. "We all knew this track was a winner."

The year was still young but the process of making the new album was already starting to pall; there were too many superfluous elements – entourages, drugs, expensive food that was never touched – which were holding things up and costing the band even more money, not that they noticed the latter at the time. It would have been all right if it was more of an enjoyable experience for everyone. Mick Fleetwood could see that a change of air and a bit of leg-stretching was required, and just as everyone was on the verge of losing their minds in the confines of the

Record Plant, he pulled together a ten-day European tour – Stevie and Lindsey's first time to Europe with the band. Stevie would stay close to her friends, giving Lindsey a wide berth. It was during this short stint, which took in a visit to Paris, that Stevie really saw the European drinking culture close at hand. It would have been rude not to join in. "Very easy to do over there, everybody there drinks like it's water," she said to Sarah McLachlan for *Interview*. "When I joined Fleetwood Mac, I was 27 years old and I never drank, and these people were used to getting on an airplane at nine in the morning and ordering a double Bloody Mary."

Other live shows would punctuate the year, chiselling the band out of the studio, but that isn't to say these sessions were all gloom, however; brief bursts of jollity did occasionally burn through the fog of ill-feeling. Mick would often try to lighten the mood with an impromptu skit, for better or worse . . . anything to raise a smile (although it was more likely to raise Lindsey's blood pressure, as he mostly just wanted to get on with it). The band members, on the rare occasions they wanted to be together outside of the studio, would also sometimes break for dinner at the Chinese restaurant Kowloon, six miles south-west of the studio on Pico Avenue. Kowloon was famous for its extremely strong cocktails, such as Mai Tais and Lindsey's favourite, Scorpions, which were sipped out of tureens with straws. The drunker they got, the more the tureens slipped, tipping into the menu and eventually soaking everyone's laps with alcohol. "We called this getting 'Kowlooned'," says Ken Caillat, who experienced many a dowsing there himself, and Lindsey himself was often inspired to kick off a food fight. Whenever Stevie went, she "wore a plastic cover-up which she would zip up, leaving only her face exposed." Wise indeed.

Another favourite restaurant to hang out in was Agatha's, where Lindsey would eventually succumb to the charms of a brunette waitress with hair as curly as his. Discovering this would leave Stevie bereft; she couldn't deal with him, but the thought of him finding pleasure in someone else's company was too much to bear and there would be frequent tearful rows in the studio. The incongruity of seeing Stevie and Lindsey blissfully singing the harmonies to 'You Make Loving Fun' side by side on tall stools before viciously turning on each other as soon as the take was complete was bizarre and the acrimony would take its toll on everyone. This was apparently the first real indication to Ken Caillat that they were having problems. He'd witnessed Lindsey flirting with other women at Agatha's in the evenings, but simply assumed they had an open relationship. Unfortunately the fighting infected the atmosphere to the extent that the usually civil McVies started arguing, too. Eventually both women walked out.

One of the many benefits of renting an apartment downtown was that Stevie and Christine were a little closer to civilisation, a little further from the madness and were able to frequent some glamorous shops. It was still relatively new for Stevie not to have to avoid going into stores at all, being so poor she couldn't bear to expose herself to temptation. Life had changed. She could now do – and buy – what she wanted. And by God, she did.

As well as fashionable clothes, shawls and make-up, Stevie and Christine would buy "little beautiful coke bottles that you wore around your neck," recalled Christine in a 2013 interview with *The Guardian*'s Tim Jonze. "Gold, turquoise, with diamonds . . . it was an aesthetic thing . . . The boys would be doing huge rails of coke while Stevie and I would [have] our little bottles with tiny coke-spoons that we'd wear on delicate chains." It was, "ladylike, more refined," concurs Stevie, admitting that it was actually acceptable at the time too. The payback would be "a complete bitch", however.

For Stevie, the ritualistic nature of drug paraphernalia tied in perfectly with "the candles, the incense, all that stuff". In her imagination, sparked by the romantic draw of cocaine and everything that surrounded it, a powerful character was coming to life like an exotic homunculus.

Drawing the shades in her apartment, lighting a candle and some sticks of Nag Champa incense, Stevie meditated on new ideas, humming quietly, words and couplets darting about in her head as the sweet smoke surrounded her like an aura. The following night in the studio, she would retreat to Sly Stone's overtly seductive hideout with her Fender Rhodes and a cassette-recorder, eventually emerging with a compelling demo. 'Gold Dust Woman' was ready to be unveiled for the first time. "Gold dust" naturally refers to that expensive powder that kept disappearing up rock stars' nostrils amongst other places (according to oft-dismissed rock'n'roll rumours), but Stevie herself has insisted the song wasn't "entirely" about cocaine – which, by the way, Stevie rarely bought; it was just "around". The lyrics also referred to her anger (dragons), fear (black widows) and an underlying anxiety of what effects sudden wealth, fame and power could have on a person. Stevie had had an insight of just how overwhelmingly "big" it could get; she just didn't assume it would grip her in the way that it would. The 'Gold Dust Woman' is the character and the story Stevie created to project those fears of the future onto, but it – she – was also a mirror that offered a grim flicker of the future. "Take your silver spoon", Stevie would sing, referring to the tiny cocaine spoon that dangled around her neck, "and dig your grave . . ." her lilting country twang providing an eerie contrast to the lyrics.

"I had a serious flash of what this stuff could be, of what it could do to you," Stevie told *Spin* in 1997. "And I really imagined that it could overtake everything, never thinking in a million years it would overtake me."

The line "rulers make bad lovers" refers to how powerful they had all become, how possible everything was, but also what that could potentially do to them in the long run. "I was definitely swept away about how big Fleetwood Mac was and how famous I suddenly was," she admitted. "I might be a ruler, but maybe I'd be a lousy lover," it being generally accepted that excessive cocaine use doesn't always make for the most fulfilling of sexual experiences either. Drugs weren't the whole story in 'Gold Dust Woman', however. The words also referred to 'groupie-type women', the femme fatales, manipulators and hangers-on who stared daggers at Stevie and Christine, but were all smiles whenever a male member of the Mac came into the room.

Stevie had taken a historical, fairy-tale image – a powerful, formidable "ancient queen" – and blended it with chemical abuse, broken love, shattered illusions and the wreckage of celebrity. This was your warning against too much of a good thing, although it's not as if it would curtail the band's frequent need for the white stuff. In fact, the evening was wearing on, and when Stevie entered the studio with her tape to play it to the rest of the band, they all broke for a 'bump' so they could feel perky enough to give it their attention and learn the parts despite the late hour. By the time the demo had been played, everyone "realised this was a very special song" said Ken Caillat. The demo was free from the ghostly wails and smashed glass percussion that augment the track we know and love, of course, but it was clear it could "take some very unusual sounds" to make it even more atmospheric and unnerving. Lindsey was already somewhat freaked out by it. "It's an evil song," he said. "Very dark, and I'm guessing that the acrimony was directed at me." Stevie has always publicly insisted she wasn't directly involved in witchcraft, but this song, coupled with her black clothes and love of the moon and Welsh witches, would be enough to convince the world she had considerable cosmic power and was not to be messed with.

After a 'transcension' into the small hours, they were getting somewhere and the song was already very different from the original demo, which was "harder and more rock'n'roll" as Ken remembers it. Lindsey played his Stratocaster through the Leslie, a sound Stevie loved, and she wanted to sing the work vocal in the studio with the band, so a directional mic and baffles were set up. After something to eat, a little cocaine, a joint and a splash of brandy, Stevie was ready to sing the first vocal take at around 3am. The studio was fully lit, which didn't suit the eerie mood of the song, and Stevie started to become more and more inhibited with every take. Eventually it was agreed that a change in atmosphere was required. The lights were dimmed and Stevie sat on a chair, wrapped herself in a cardigan and arranged her supplies around her – Vicks inhaler, tissues, a bottle of Calistoga mineral water and a carton of lozenges to ease her throat.

Jim Grissim from *Crawdaddy* was there, having just interviewed Stevie, and he watched the whole process unfold. "The song required a lot of power and an equal measure of feeling," he observed. "Stevie had achieved an astonishing command of the material and on the eighth take she sang the song straight through, nailing it perfectly." By the end of the take, as Ken Caillat remembers it, "Stevie was howling like a witch on fire." This would arguably be one of the most compelling tracks on the whole record. It would be matched in power by 'The Chain', the song that opened side two of the original vinyl album. "'The Chain' is really my song," Stevie would say. "We split [the royalties] five ways but the fact is I wrote most of those words and most of that melody."

The song had an awkward start in life; the rest of the band had been trying to work out why the groove they were working on wasn't happening, Stevie asked if she could help and while she was rebuffed, they soon realised the melody and chorus that she'd come up with on her own worked perfectly with the parts they were sketching into life. "If Stevie hadn't had that melody and those words, it would never have happened," insists Ken Caillat. "That's another example of how undervalued she was by the band at this point."

Richard Dashut has described *Rumours* as an 'aural collage' – there would be so many overdubs that the tapes actually started to wear out – but 'The Chain' is the ultimate composite track, and its title pays tribute to this. But it is also a clear nod to the symbolic emotional chains of Fleetwood Mac, unbreakable and strong, for better or worse. Stevie had come up with a melody on the piano, and, feeling there was something there and sharing it with the band, the other writers worked with her to develop it. She had also written another song with many of the words that would end up on 'The Chain'. And so these elements came together to provide the foundation of a shadowy song that, lyrically, would be almost frightening in its passion, again, like a curse – 'damn your love, damn your lies . . .'

Soon 'The Chain' would be more than just a great song; by the mere process of working it through as a band, it would be part of a healing process, uniting them and reminding them of what they had. Lindsey and Mick worked out the beginning, a simple bass-drum beat interlaced with the mysterious, Oriental sound of the Dobro guitar. They added the original chords from the chorus of a song called 'Keep Me There', Christine and Stevie thrashed ideas out on the piano, and John worked out a bass solo which "we all loved," Stevie remembers. "It's like, the monsters are coming!" It would be the first song written by the whole band and, while the sentiment was that of an intense, damaged love, it was a poignant conclusion of togetherness during the fractious year that would birth their album – originally titled *Yesterday's Gone* (a reference to 'Don't Stop.'

Whether flirtatious, confessional or downright confrontational, everyone's songs together simply sounded "like a bunch of rumours", as John McVie noted. It was the perfect title, and it also wryly referred to the flurry of sensationalist gossip about them in the music business and the press, members of which had gleefully cottoned on to their romantic complications and were now making all sorts of claims about who was now sleeping with whom.

"They said Stevie was sleeping with me . . ." Mick Fleetwood told Stephen Davis for the book *Fleetwood.* "Christine had run off with Lindsey, Stevie was seeing John and me on alternate Wednesdays, Stevie was leaving, Stevie had left months ago and this was why the album had been delayed, Stevie practised black magic and led a coven of witches in the Hollywood Hills . . ." Fleetwood Mac elected to use the British spelling of "rumours" when the time came, presumably in tribute to the Londoner who came up with it. It was scheduled for release in September 1976. That wasn't going to happen.

Albums weren't supposed to take this long. To put it into some kind of context, The Beatles recorded their first album in one day, all bar four tracks they'd already recorded, and Iggy Pop's *Lust For Life* took eight days to make, although, granted, there weren't quite as many people involved as there were in Fleetwood Mac. The Eagles, at least, would have been able to sympathise to a degree. Their own autobiographical album *Hotel California* took a painful nine months. The making of *Rumours* would leave even the generally cheerful Richard Dashut something of a broken man – and they weren't even half way through yet. He described the process as "boredom punctuated by sheer terror". There were occasional moments of joy, "but not many".

By March, Richard and Ken Caillat had "lost all ability to keep the band sane", as Caillat himself admitted. The drugs and associated paranoia were out of control and the daily start time was getting later and later. As soon as the group could take no more, Mick Fleetwood commanded them to "transcend", push through and keep playing into the night. These "transcensions" were frequent occurrences, but only tended to be participated in by the "coked up crazies", says Ken, meaning Stevie, Mick and Christine. John and Lindsey were rarely up for unnecessarily late nights – once the clock started to tick towards 3 a.m., Lindsey's tactic would be to say he was going to the bathroom . . . and just leave. But they didn't always have a choice and the intake of cocaine was largely motivated by the need to stay up and work.

Before long the band's body clocks incredibly confused. They were getting up at 8 p.m. to go to the studio and work through the night. A familiar scene would be Mick bending over the mirror for a toot of coke, huge eyes flashing and a wide grin appearing on his face. "The woods are lovely, dark and deep," he would recite. "But we have promises to keep, and miles to go before we sleep . . ." The verse he was paraphrasing, a favourite no doubt memorised during his public school days, belonged to the Robert Frost poem 'Stopping by Woods on a Snowy Night'. I think Frost was referring to a different kind of snow, but whatever works.

There would be a 'banquet' every night, like a Roman bacchanal, a drawn-out, drugged-up mess, according to studio owner Chris Stone. "The band would come in at night, party till one or two in the morning and then, when they were so whacked out they couldn't do anything, they'd start recording." In the meantime, hangers-on continued to party while the band tried to work. One favourite dealer of Mick's was going to be credited on the artwork for supplying them so freely, but he was executed before the album was released. That's right. Executed. Christine would later refer to the whole affair as a 'trauma'. And it wasn't nearly over yet.

The band would take a few well-earned weeks off, leaving the Record Plant several thousand bad vibes heavier, the walls still ringing with a confusion of vicious rows and potent music. Something else Stevie would leave behind was her romantic partnership with Lindsey, once and for all. "We were just finishing up the end of our songs in Sausalito and I said 'We're done, I think this is over,'" she said in an interview with Oprah Winfrey (*Oprah Winfrey's Masterclass*) in 2013. They were both devastated but they had to take time away from each other, because, as Stevie insisted, "No matter what it takes, our breaking up is not going break up this band. I'm not going to quit and neither are you . . ." And so another layer of bitterness started to harden – Lindsey Buckingham, according to Stevie, would never get over the fact that their relationship's demise was hastened by joining Fleetwood Mac.

"Lindsey always blamed Fleetwood Mac for the loss of me," she said. "Had we not joined we would have continued with our music but we probably would have gotten married, had a child . . . We were still young enough, destiny could have taken us another way. But destiny took us straight into Fleetwood Mac."

Chapter Nine

The year 1976 may have been one of disintegrating relationships for the Mac, but there were also new romances brewing. It would be the year Lindsey Buckingham met Carol Ann Harris who worked at the Producers Workshop, a studio in a seedy spot on Hollywood Boulevard between two adult cinemas. This was the studio where *Rumours* would be mixed.

Carol Ann Harris had long, blonde wavy hair and big searching eyes, not unlike Lindsey's last girlfriend, although she was something of a hard act to follow. Stevie wouldn't find it easy being around Carol for obvious reasons, and Carol herself would note the constant tension between Stevie and Lindsey, as if they weren't yet over each other. But Stevie herself had found new love: Don Henley, founding member, drummer and singer of the Eagles, a band Stevie had always loved. "He was cute, elegant, sexy. Such an interesting guy," she told *Spin*. She didn't have the best first impression of him, however.

During the hot, hazy summer of this fateful year, Fleetwood Mac would open for the Eagles on a smattering of US shows. The Mac and the Eagles had neighbouring dressing rooms on the first of these shows and, when Stevie entered to get ready for the show, she was confronted with a bouquet of roses and a card: "The best of my love . . . Tonight? Love Don", in a cheeky reference to the Eagles' 1974 hit 'The Best Of My Love'. Stevie hadn't even met Don yet and was apoplectic at the apparent proposition. She hadn't noticed John and Mick, who had bought the flowers and written the card, giggling like a pair of naughty schoolboys in the corner. Just as Stevie was on the point of rushing out to find Don and tell him exactly what she thought of his invitation, Christine quickly took her aside to explain that Henley wasn't to blame.

Quite unlike the false impression she'd had of him, Don was a Southern gentleman and his irresistible charm would impress Stevie when they did eventually meet. They had so much in common already and after crossing paths – as inevitably they would – on several occasions, it didn't take long for Don to pick up the phone and initiate something more. Lindsey, meanwhile, was observing everything as it happened. "I could see it coming," he said in an interview with Sean Egan (*Fleetwood Mac on Fleetwood Mac: Interviews and Encounters*). "It's strange, it's one thing to accept not being with someone, and it's another to see them with someone else, especially someone like Don, right? A big star in another group."

"It was 1976, right after [we] really made it, and the Eagles had been famous for a long time," remembers Stevie. "So he found a very different girl in me than in most of the women he was used to hanging out with, and we had a very special relationship because of that."

Don's star power and wealth was considerable. There would be Learjets sent to pick Stevie up and many other extravagances – all very nice, but subtlety and timing were not his strong points. The Eagles had started recording at Criteria Studios in Miami, and soon Fleetwood Mac would do the same. The Mac stayed at an idyllic house on the water. "It's romantic, it's pink, it's like Mar-a-Lago*," she said in a 1997 interview with Hole singer Courtney Love for *Spin*. "Anyway, he sends a limousine driver over with a box of presents for me and they're delivered right to the breakfast room where everyone's eating." And when she says 'presents', we're talking vast bouquets of flowers and fruits, an expensive stereo and a selection of "fabulous records . . ." all being loaded onto her breakfast table by the driver. "And I'm going, 'Oh no, please, this is not going to go down well.' Lindsey is not happy . . ."

Ostentatious displays of affection aside, the fact that Don was "a big star in another group" was a plus – there was an empathy, rather than

* A beautiful estate on Palm Beach, Florida, now owned by Donald Trump.

the imbalance there would have been between a rock star and a groupie, which is the sort of situation it's fair to assume Stevie is referring to with her earlier comment on "the women he hung out with". These two were on the same level.

Henley also taught her how to spend money like a star. "He didn't set out to do that, I just watched him," she continued. Henley thought nothing of buying a huge new house or a flashy car. One example of how well Stevie had learned from her paramour occurred in 1983 when, one night, "me and a bunch of my friends were up all night doing cocaine and watching that movie *Risky Business*. That's one of my favourites." She saw the 1979 Porsche 928 driven by Tom Cruise in the film, and decided she wanted it. "And I just made a call and that Porsche was delivered. I said, 'I want the same Porsche that's in *Risky Business*.' And I bought it that morning." In rose.

As Lindsey came to terms with seeing Stevie and Don together, he realised it didn't "bum him out" as much as he thought it might. At least, that's what he told the press, and possibly himself. In reality, it must have been difficult and confusing, but he relished the opportunity "to be Lindsey Buckingham" again, not just one half of a duo. Lindsey would even concede that "someone like Don is good for her . . . The whole breakup has forced me to redefine my whole individuality – musically as well." He also told *Rolling Stone* that once the loneliness lifted, he was "surprised we lasted as long as we did."

Seeing another successful musician outside of the band had its disadvantages too, however, especially in the sexist seventies music industry. Stevie remembered, in an interview with Liz Derringer for *High Times* in 1982: "I was up at Don's house having dinner with him and his manager, Irving Azoff (later Stevie's own manager). Glenn Frey of the Eagles walked in, looked at me and said, 'Spoiled yet?' Like, no mention of Fleetwood Mac. I was not even in the league of a singer. I was nothing more than a girl. My claws went out and I wanted to get out of there." Stevie, who would later reveal she found Frey rather "witchy" a compliment in Stevie-land – admitted she 'loved' him and that this was in the past, but this experience was one she wouldn't forget. "Going out with a very famous man, a rock'n'roll singer, and have people not relate to me like I even had a job . . ."

Stevie would also briefly date songwriter JD Souther, another man who was "very, very, very chauvinistic" and who in his time had cheated on girlfriend Linda Ronstadt with none other than Joni Mitchell. Stevie found JD "wonderful but very Texas". She realised that if she wanted any of these relationships with famous men to work, she had to refrain from ever talking about her own professional life to shield their fragile egos. "It didn't help my status with the man to bring up anything I did, so I didn't. And then you start saying, 'But I work too. I'm happening. I write songs, but you aren't giving me a break.'" It's not hard to see why Stevie has spent so many years of her life happily single.

September would see a return to LA smog, and to another studio where an artistic mutilation would take place. Yes, 'Silver Springs' might have been "a winner", but it was also too long – eight minutes in total, potentially taking up the space of two songs on the vinyl record. Ken Caillat recalled in his book *Making Rumours* having to sit with Stevie for hours trying to cut some of the many verses. "While we worked, tears ran down her face," recalled Ken, who describes Stevie's words as 'her obsession'. "[She sobbed] 'These lyrics mean so much to me, they're part of the story and we can't cut them . . .'" However, when it was explained that it was that or risk losing the song from the album, she agreed. Although, after several hours of hacking at her precious song, she was drained and emotional. The only other option would have been to lose one of her other songs, as it just wouldn't have been fair on the other writers to have such a long track on the album unless she was prepared to lose another of her own. Her eventual agreement was helped along by the understanding that she would receive fewer royalties should she opt for keeping 'Silver Springs' in its entirety and dropping another song.

"As soon as she realised this, it was as if a miracle had occurred," Ken Caillat writes. "The tears went away and she stopped resisting most of my edits. She was a business woman!" They successfully chopped 'Silver

Springs' down to 4.33 but, as it would later transpire, even this wouldn't be enough. They had just 22 minutes per side, and there was also concern regarding "how it would flow with the rest of the songs," said Ken. Fate stepped in when Stevie unfortunately elected not to come into the studio one day and while she was absent, someone voted 'Silver Springs' off the album altogether in favour of recording another of Stevie's songs to replace it. Lindsey suggested 'I Don't Want To Know', a song from the Buckingham Nicks days, a bright, up-tempo duet boasting tight, Everly Brothers-like harmonies. The band recorded the basic track without Stevie. All it needed was her vocal.

When Stevie swept in the following day, she was bemused that the band had recorded another of her songs without even consulting her – surely this meant she now had more songs on the LP than anyone else? Not quite. It was time to break the bad news. Lindsey had nominated Mick to tell her because his situation with her 'was already fragile'and Mick was the band leader. After a band meeting, he agreed, telling the others that he'd "let her know that we've all tried, but there's no other way to make this record perfect. She'll just have to trust us." Their attorney Mickey Shapiro had informed them sales for *Fleetwood Mac* were rocketing and the pressure increased to make *Rumours* the best it could be. They were already superstars, but two hit albums in a row would change their lives. The modus operandi was to make the record all-killer-no-filler, every song had to be a potential single and they had to be ruthless. But 'Silver Springs' was hardly filler, and Richard and Ken in particular were regretful about the decision.

Mick approached Stevie as if walking towards an incendiary device. He gently suggested they go out into the parking lot. "I knew it was serious," Stevie recalled in an interview with the BBC in 1991, "because Mick never asks you to go out into the parking lot for anything." He explained that the general consensus was that they wanted to use 'I Don't Want To Know' instead of 'Silver Springs', which was still too long and not upbeat enough to fit with the other songs. Stevie protested that she didn't want 'I Don't Want To Know' on the album, to which Mick reasoned, "Well, then don't sing it."

"I started to scream bloody murder," Stevie continued. "Probably said every horribly mean thing that you could possibly say to another human being." Stevie insisted she was one fifth of the band and she had a right to boycott 'I Don't Want To Know' – her own song, after all – but it was made clear that she could either get on with it and sing, put up with having just two songs on the album or leave. Angry and upset, Stevie eventually cooperated and sang it "with a gun to her head". But no one could deny that, as Richard Dashut said, "'Silver Springs' was the greatest song never to make it onto an album." The decision to put it on the B-side to 'Go Your Own Way' was further insult to injury.

Other songs of Stevie's that were recorded but not included on *Rumours* were 'Think About It' and 'Planets Of The Universe'. She was, as Ken recalls, "a little dismayed" they weren't selected but was building up a fine stash of work should she choose to release a solo album. It was restrictive for a writer as prolific as Stevie to provide just three songs per Fleetwood Mac album.

Warners were getting edgy: the album release had been postponed to February 1977 and they wanted reassurance. Mick Fleetwood organised a listening party, where only 'Dreams' and 'Go Your Own Way' would be revealed. By the end of 'Dreams', the studio executives were swaying to the music, and as 'Go Your Own Way' concluded they were even applauding. They asked for more, but Fleetwood told them they would just have to wait. He thought it best to quit while they were ahead. But the suits were already confident that, as they'd hoped, the next Fleetwood Mac album would match, even surpass Fleetwood Mac in sales and acclaim.

Mixing would continue at Studio B in the Producers Workshop, where Lindsey and studio manager Carol Ann Harris quickly became an item. Harris remembers the first time she met Stevie very well, describing her in her 2009 book *Storms* as: "a tiny hummingbird . . . brushing past in a blaze of colour on a cloud of patchouli and ylang ylang. I'd never seen anything so bright and dynamic before." Carol watched Lindsey's irritation around her, the chemistry still crackling between them. She also observed, with slight surprise, the reaction Mick Fleetwood always had around Stevie, straightening up in his seat, winking at her, flirting . . .

During this period, the shoot for the album artwork was arranged and the romantic, classical shot of Mick and Stevie on the cover would cause some controversy, if only within the Mac. The photographer Herbie Worthington, who had also shot the cover of *Fleetwood Mac*, ran the shoot and focused very much on Stevie and Mick to create a visual extension of the *Fleetwood Mac* cover image, which featured Mick towering over John McVie. Mick's pose would be similar on both covers, upright and aristocratic, and on the cover of *Rumours,* Stevie Nicks, bedecked in gossamer chiffon and wearing her black ballet slippers, entwined around him, arms apart like wings. Between Mick's legs were his trademark dangling wooden balls*, and in his hand was a crystal ball into which Stevie was gazing, 'crystal visions' indeed. Mick had wanted something 'special' and 'Shakespearean', an enigmatic work of art that would capture people's imaginations for years to come. However, the rest of the band were put out that Herbie was concentrating on just two members, rather than reflecting the group. The photographer wasn't trying to promote anyone over anybody else and there would be a group shot on the back, but Lindsey in particular was not pleased.

Contact sheets were sent to the band by December. Herbie had already chosen his favourite image from the session, and was pleased when the general consensus was to select the same one. Lindsey, however, "has never forgiven me for not being on the *Rumours* cover," he said in Ken Caillat's *Making Rumours*. "[He] came up and said, 'I wish I could have been on my own cover.' That's showbiz." Would it have been less of a problem if it had been Mick and Christine on the cover? Who can say?

After a brief but much-needed Christmas break in Phoenix, Stevie

* Fleetwood explained the balls in his *Daily Express* column in 2014: "At one gig in the early days, I came back from a toilet break with the lavatory chains, a ball attached at each end, wrapped around my waist. I did a solo, hitting the balls into the microphone, just to make the lads laugh. Talk about spontaneous expression! The funny part is, my balls never went away."

reunited with the band in Hollywood before New Year to add the finishing touches to *Rumours*. By 4 January 1977, everything was complete. Fleetwood Mac would celebrate finishing the making of *Rumours* at a French restaurant on Melrose, but Stevie would be conspicuously absent, as Lindsey was there with Carol Ann on his arm. They'd both had their romances since splitting up, but it was the first time he'd started seriously dating someone. Life after Stevie Nicks. Inconceivable. And, given the circumstances, impossible.*

Still, it was time to celebrate, and Stevie wasn't just walking away as soon as the work was done. She was planning a party of her own. Fleetwood Mac were exhausted but thrilled to have finally finished *Rumours* and yet they were still largely oblivious to just how strong this album was. Ken Caillat had given everyone a tape, and Stevie could think of no better way to hear the songs they'd all grown rather tired of than in the company of friends.

The party was arranged to take place at Stevie's brother Chris's house in Whitley Terrace, above the Hollywood Bowl. There they could also enjoy an impromptu screening of *Snow White And The Seven Dwarfs*, because Warners had given Stevie a copy of the Disney animation. Ever the child at heart. By 7 p.m., the drink was flowing and pot was being smoked. Ken Caillat, as instructed, had brought his Revox two-track machine, connected it to the stereo and rewound the tape while the assembled illuminati and members of the inner circle settled down with their drinks. It was a pleasant surprise for the band to hear the songs with fresh ears,

* Stevie and Lindsey were outwardly still seen as a team in many respects. Another album released in 1977 was Walter Egan's *Fundamental Roll*, a record that featured Buckingham Nicks on co-production duties and backing vocals (particularly, in Stevie's case,'Magnet And Steel' which would hit the Top Ten). Egan loved Buckingham's guitar work on *Fleetwood Mac* and, on Keith Olsen's urging, invited him and Stevie to work on his debut solo album. The three would become friends, but during the period *Fundamental Roll* was being made back at Sound City, the friction between Lindsey and Stevie became unbearable. Egan found himself refereeing their arguments (he also admits to "falling quite hard" for Stevie), and soon the pair were having to turn up separately in order for anything productive to happen at all.

not to mention a revelation to the other guests. Everyone applauded and whistled, and Fleetwood Mac lapped up the adulation. If this was a sign of things to come, they had nothing to worry about. Nearly a year in the studio for less than 40 minutes' worth of songs. But what songs they were.

They had gone beyond what they had set out to do – make an album that could outshine *Fleetwood Mac*, on which every track could be a hit. It was an instant classic; everybody in the room knew it. And yet they were, as Ken put it, "still so close to the album [they had] no idea what they had created."

Chapter 10

Some 800,000 copies of *Rumours* were shipped to dealers in February 1977, the biggest advance order in Warners' history. No doubt helping to boost sales was the compelling sense of intrigue swirling around the band, a complex psychodrama that gripped both the public and the press, who had just never seen anything quite like it. Journalists delighted in concentrating on the personal dramas within Fleetwood Mac and, outwardly, the band were generally good-humoured about it. In reality they were uncomfortable with the idea of presenting their raw emotional wounds to the rest of the world to pore over. But the soap opera was part of their image now, and always would be. It was also priceless PR and they were required to work it. *Rolling Stone* wanted to run a frank interview with the band to coincide with the release of the album. The piece, written by Cameron Crowe (the man behind films such as *Almost Famous*), would be titled 'True Life Confessions', and the band would be photographed for the cover by none other than Annie Leibovitz. Stevie was now receiving constant reminders that she'd made it, but this was a significant one. *Rolling Stone* was one thing. Being on the cover was another. But being shot by Leibovitz? Fleetwood Mac were entering a new stratosphere.

The shoot took place at a rented room in LA (although Carol Ann Harris has claimed it took place at Lindsey's house) and the group turned up, stepping over cables and manoeuvring around lights, needling each other and making straight for the champagne that Annie had wisely elected to provide. In Annie's memory, she'd brought "huge amounts of drugs" which they all consumed with enormous enthusiasm and before long everyone was "out to lunch". Stevie only recalls the champagne (although how anyone recalls anything from this day at all is amazing in itself). Either way, everyone caned it, and with good reason: Annie had just told the band members to get into bed with each other.

It was a courageous, funny idea. It was also raunchy, oozing with sex, partner-swapping and not to mention a sense of "hands up" humour in the face of pain and romantic complication. The rest of the world was amused by the stories about them, why shouldn't they show they could laugh at it all too? Arguably they weren't ready to, but still, Annie pushed them straight into the deep end without water wings, with interesting results. Stevie claims this shoot sparked the attraction between herself and Mick, although it would appear Mick at least had been smitten for some time.

"When Annie said she wanted us to lie down together on a big bed," said Stevie to *Rolling Stone* in later years, "it was like, 'Hmm, hope you have a backup idea.' I said, 'OK, but I can't be in bed next to Lindsey.' So I curl up next to Mick for the next three hours while Annie is suspended over us on a platform." Again, there are slightly different versions of the course of events, probably because most of the people involved were out of their minds on drugs and alcohol. Carol Ann Harris claimed the shoot took no more than an hour. Whatever, time is a liquid concept; liquid being the operative word in this case.

Stevie, looking like a little girl in a peach satin 1930s nightgown, dubiously wandered to the giant mattress that Annie had brought. The band members had been dawdling awkwardly, perhaps understandably, but as Harris recalls, the esteemed photographer would simply bark at them to come in once the set was ready. Time was money. "Come on, you guys," she shouted. "Quit fucking around in there, I need you in here now."

Christine was not keen to be next to John in the picture, their divorce was still fresh; so she was placed in the arms of a bare-chested Lindsey while a jean-sporting John was consigned to the other side of the mattress, alone and reading a copy of *Playboy*. In the middle was Fleetwood, covered partially by a thin white sheet, with a curled up Stevie smiling mischievously by his side. Lindsey admitted that "the idea for the photo wasn't all that funny", because the animosities in the band, particularly between himself and Stevie, were still very close to the surface. However, after "compartmentalising" their feelings (Fleetwood Mac are big on psychobabble) to get through the session, something happened. There are two versions of what that was, but the end result is the same – there was an intimate coming together of Stevie and Lindsey. The only matter of dispute is how long that intimacy lasted.

Here's Stevie's version, courtesy of *Rolling Stone*: "Lindsey and I got to talking about how amazing it was that not so long ago I was a waitress and he didn't have a job, and now we were on the cover of *Rolling Stone* with this huge record. And we lay there for two hours talking and making out. Finally, Annie had to tell us to leave, because she had rented the room for only so long. But in one afternoon she put Lindsey and me back together and also planted the seed for Mick and me . . . You want to know the power of Annie Leibovitz, there you go."

And Lindsey's: "We had this moment of not being able to avoid all that had been lost. We embraced for about 15 minutes, and Mick finally came over and said that people were starting to get uncomfortable."

Stevie is, as even the most devoted fan would surely agree, prone to the occasional exaggeration, but the important thing is that there was a moment of tenderness after all of the hurt. Carol Ann Harris was in the next room, by the way.

The band had been rehearsing for the *Rumours* tour since the beginning of February 1977 at Rat, a small studio in the San Fernando Valley. Soon they would transfer to the large sound stage (Soundstage B) at SIR studios on Sunset Boulevard, struggling to work every day for a month through howling wind and rain. It was a tough period for Stevie; Lindsey Buckingham was back to his usual, impatient self.

To cope with his moods, Stevie simply found herself getting smaller and smaller, "mouse-like, [I] would never dare offer a suggestion," she said. "It was like a living nightmare . . . everything about me seemed to bug him: my laughter, the way I could deal with a lot of difficult things, [it] all made him want to cringe. So I changed when I was around him." At least Stevie could retreat to her loyal coterie of whispering ladies in waiting, who offered comfort and company which, in turn, created an atmosphere that excluded everyone else. It was like a group of bridesmaids, or schoolgirls sharing secrets, talking behind their hands, sweeping hither and thither behind the Queen Bee.

The glamorous Carol Ann Harris had been invited to rehearsals by Lindsey which, as Lindsey no doubt predicted, would cause Stevie no small discomfort. John McVie's new girlfriend Julie Reubens tried to make Carol Ann feel welcome but, while she had the right look, there was no way she was going to be invited to join Stevie's loyal gang, who eyed her with suspicion.

Stevie would, according to Carol Ann, attempt to make sense of Lindsey's interest in her by assuming it was because of their similarity, which wasn't hard to see. Stevie also learned that they shared a birthday – May 26. Carol Ann wrote in her book *Storms* that Stevie took her aside during a break to tell her so, apparently adding, "You must be so much like me that it's almost mystical. No wonder Lindsey would go for you." Carol Ann "didn't know whether to laugh or scream", but sardonically offered that "John Wayne also was born on May 26 . . ." If this was Stevie's way to tentatively connect with Carol Ann, it had been rejected. If it was her way of trying to understand Lindsey's attraction by blatantly suggesting it was just because he was trying to find another Stevie, it had been flatly ridiculed. But for all Carol Ann's bemused wariness of Stevie, she concedes that her beauty was breathtaking and once she started to sing, even in rehearsals, the power was overwhelming. Stevie had become a fantasy figure for men and women alike, a combination of vulnerable child and powerful sex symbol, not that Stevie felt particularly comfortable with it herself.

"It annoys her," Christine said in a TV interview at the time. "People are happy to put her in the role of 'sex goddess, starter of trends . . .' [but] she's totally unaware. She goes on stage and does what she does . . .

as she says, she has nothing else to do with her hands. My hands and feet are occupied. She's free to do what she does and it contributes in a very positive way to the band."

The upcoming tour would see Stevie's onstage style come into its own, and it was an extension of her *Rumours* cover look. Gone altogether were the jeans and floral tops of the Fleetwood Mac tour. With the help of designer Margi Kent, who helped her design her 'uniform' for the *Rumours* artwork, she now had a capsule wardrobe that gave a nod to the character she had created in 'Rhiannon', and gave her greater stature. At just 5 ft 1, platforms – sometimes with heels as high as seven inches – were a must, usually in tan, cream or lilac, and were made by local Italian bootmaker di Fabrizio. Stevie's hallmark top hat (found in a thrift store in Buffalo on the Fleetwood Mac Tour) would also give much needed height. With these staple items, she never had to worry about not knowing what to wear.

Stevie's diaphanous skirts would move easily as she danced, and if there was air-conditioning or a breeze at one of their outdoor shows, they would flow hypnotically around her. And then there were the capes and piano shawls which, again, would give Stevie a bigger presence onstage as she raised her arms like wings. The effect was similar to that of the Victorian modern dance pioneer Loïe Fuller, who used voluminous fabrics in a similar way, swirling and moving like a butterfly, and, crucial in Stevie's case, visible from afar. One of Stevie's favourite capes, even today, is her fringed, sequinned 'Gold Dust Woman' cape, created by Kent in gold chiffon. It looked ethereal but had the strength to withstand show after show, and wearing a shawl that was specifically designed for that potent potion of a song only seemed appropriate – ceremonial, almost. It also helped to be able to put it aside afterwards, as if it could contain all of that dark energy that had been whipped up during the song, keeping it separate from the rest of the characters Stevie would inhabit during the course of a set. Before long, a Fleetwood Mac audience would be filled with Stevie-alikes, wafting about in drifty layers and top hats, going wild to 'Rhiannon'.

The Rumours Tour began on February 24 in Uniondale, New York. Fleetwood Mac would now be playing 10-15,000 capacity halls; the Jefferson Coliseum in Birmingham, Alabama, selling out within one hour because of the community's enduring love of Buckingham Nicks. The anticipation surrounding the tour was heightened by the fact that, by the end of February, *Rumours* had gone Platinum, one million copies sold within its first month of release.* To celebrate, the band partied for two days straight just before leaving for the tour, but in all the excitement, Stevie had forgotten she'd left her contact lenses in for the entire time, wearing off her cornea. Short-sighted at the best of times, Stevie now could barely see at all. For the first show, she had to be carried by piggy-back to the stage by John Courage. She desperately tried to avoid the spotlight hitting her eyes and was soon ordered by a doctor to have her eyes bandaged for several days. As Carol Ann remembers it, the opportunity to take advantage of Stevie's temporary lack of sight was too much to resist for some – even her adoring handmaidens.

"'They dressed her in outrageous outfits – 'You look really pretty today', we'd all grin – they put food and drink just out of her reach and set booby traps. Very childish, but we laughed like idiots." With friends like these . . . Still, it will have cheered Stevie to know that within days of setting off on tour her song 'Dreams' would be released, hitting the top of the charts by April; the only time Fleetwood Mac would go to number one in the US.

By the time the band played the Berkeley Community Theatre in San Francisco, Stevie's eyes had started to heal. It was a home crowd for Buckingham Nicks and both Stevie and Lindsey felt the pressure even more than usual. John Courage counted down the minutes from ten until the Mac had to be on stage while Stevie tipped her head upside down to brush her long home-permed locks, slicked on some extra lipstick, necked a vitamin pill and waited, giggling as Mick pranced towards her, his wooden balls clacking as he thrust his pelvis in front of her. Lindsey glowered

* At its peak, *Rumours* would earn Fleetwood Mac a gold disc twice a month, and platinum once a month. A year later it was still selling nearly 250,000 copies every week.

and Carol Ann watched them both, wondering if he still had feelings for Stevie.

The San Francisco show was mesmerising and the crowd loved it. Stevie, however, was bereft, throwing herself onto a couch backstage and sobbing. Robin Snyder, always at hand, rushed up to console her as she wailed that the show was a disaster, she'd missed a cue in 'Rhiannon' and Lindsey had to cover for her. Lindsey, meanwhile, was nursing his hands which were bleeding from his furious finger-picking, his face uncertain. Both Stevie and Lindsey were devoted to doing justice to their songs – 'Rhiannon' above all meant the world to Stevie – but it's fair to say that cocaine may also have been contributing to their constant uneasiness.

Every night, Courage would pour the usual amount of cocaine onto the back of every wrist before the show, the bottle-caps of coke lined up in the wings for whenever anyone needed a bump, and yet, as Nicks insisted to the *Guardian*'s Tim Jonze, "We really were tame back then. We had to behave. We'd play a gig, get on an aeroplane right after the show and leave for the next place. And we were watched like hawks. We had security outside each of our rooms so Chris and I were almost like travelling rock'n'roll nuns." Yes, it was difficult for men to get anywhere near Chris and Stevie which, from the way Stevie talks about it, was a reality that had its pros and cons. She spent a lot of time in her room just writing her journal, little notes in envelopes that she'd keep to look at in years to come. She had her friends, she had Christine – everybody else she'd give a wide berth. For the time being.

"We were cool onstage," she added. "But offstage everybody was pretty angry. Most nights Chris and I would just go for dinner on our own, downstairs in the hotel, with security at the door."

On 1 April, Fleetwood Mac flew to the UK to start the European leg of the Rumours Tour. Mick and John's concerns that they'd been 'forgotten' or abandoned by their die-hard blues fan base were quickly allayed – the band was greeted with enthusiasm, not to mention a raft of new fans won over by Stevie and Lindsey. This was a homecoming for Fleetwood Mac, and for those who had been sceptical about the dramatic change within the group? "We showed them our new tricks and changed their minds," said Mick.

The UK tour started right at the heart of England in Birmingham, near where Christine McVie was brought up. The flight was interminable, the food was dreadful and the weather was . . . well, English. To exacerbate the low mood, any warmth Stevie and Lindsey had shared during the *Rolling Stone* shoot had cooled considerably. "We hardly spoke," Stevie remembers. "We would get on and off the same plane without interacting at all."

The band became even sulkier when they reached the hotel, which wasn't as luxurious as they'd hoped. Yes, Fleetwood Mac might have essentially been a British band, but they'd been away for too long, they had a bigger following in the States now and while their fans were pleased to see them, their status in the UK just wasn't the same. *Rumours* entered the chart at number 34, eventually reaching the top by the following January. Stevie and Lindsey were a little shocked that the first date in the UK was at the Birmingham Odeon, which had a capacity of just over 2,000. They had been selling out 20,000 capacity venues back in the US.

To make matters worse, the Odeon itself had seen better days. Stevie kicked up a stink when she realised she had just one rack to hang her many wardrobe changes on backstage, Mick was whining for more cocaine and John McVie was just trying to get the radiator to work. The normally good-humoured tour manager John Courage was at the end of his tether, being the focus of all of the complaints, but somehow everyone got what they needed; the acoustics of the venue were perfect and the show was strong, perhaps the best on the UK leg of the tour.

Stevie might have been fearing a return to the bad old days of roughing it on her first tour with the Mac, but it wasn't all bad food and dirty hotel rooms – in fact, it would be on this leg of the tour that the band visited Eric Clapton's Italian-style villa near Ewhurst in rural Surrey, about 35 miles south west of London. The model and photographer Pattie Boyd, then Clapton's partner, was still technically Mick's sister-in-law (Mick's marriage to Jenny famously wavered between on and off), and the whole band decamped after a show to Clapton's sumptuous home. According to Harris, meeting Clapton was, for the American contingent, tantamount to meeting John Lennon, but as awe-struck as they were to meet the legendary guitarist, they soon settled in once the drugs and booze started to flow. The boys played darts while getting increasingly wasted (you can imagine how this ended) and Stevie hot-footed it up to Pattie's luxurious bedroom for some 'girl talk'. Eventually they came back down to find that Eric had brought down some more guitars and a jam session was about to kick off with another guest, none other than the Small Faces bassist and songwriter Ronnie Lane. As the snow fell outside and candles were lit, Stevie joined in with harmonies while the assembled rock royalty played the mournful 'While My Guitar Gently Weeps'. It was beautiful, if potentially slightly awkward considering the circumstances: 'While My Guitar Gently Weeps' was written by George Harrison, best friends with Clapton and Pattie's former husband – she had left him for Clapton in 1974. Next up was Clapton's yearningly romantic 'Layla', written for Pattie before their affair was out in the open. So, yes. Awkward. Still, it was the seventies and when it came to complicated domestic arrangements, the Mac were in extremely good company.

Eric Clapton wasn't the only blues guitar hero that Stevie and the group would encounter during their visit to London, as none other than Peter Green, Fleetwood Mac's long-lost founder, showed up at the hotel where they were staying. Looking wild and unkempt, he arrived with a ghetto blaster on his shoulder, blaring disco music, and knocked on their doors at night. On being granted entry, he sat on the end of their beds in silence. "Sadly he wasn't the Peter Green he must have been when writing 'The Green Manalishi'," said Stevie. 'The Green Manalishi', composed during Green's last months with the band, was inspired by a hallucination and evokes a sense of dread and mysticism. It's not hard to see why it's one of Stevie's favourite Green-era Mac songs.

"I always do those cries in the background when we do that song live. That makes me feel connected to him," she explained. "He was very far away when I saw him. I tried talking to him but he didn't want to talk, especially not about music and definitely not about Fleetwood Mac. He only wanted to watch."

Some of the cultural differences in Europe were hard to take for Stevie and Lindsey – in some parts of the UK they felt as if they were in the dark ages and the show they would play at the Pavillon de Paris, on the northern edge of the French capital, would literally make them sick. It was a huge space that had previously been used as a slaughterhouse, being as it was in the city's meatpacking district. There had been a bull-fight at the venue the night before Fleetwood Mac's show, the idea of which was bad enough but the stench of blood was still in the air, making everyone nauseous and turning Stevie "positively green". But, as always, the band rose to the audience's roar of approval as soon as they hit the stage. According to Mick Fleetwood, Stevie herself is an "audience addict" and as she worked her magic, teetering on her platform boots in front of the giant moon projection, her spell was cast on yet another converted audience. France has a deep love of the blues and rock'n'roll, but they took the new Fleetwood Mac very much to their hearts.

What was predictably hard for Stevie on this tour was that not only did she have to hear Lindsey sing 'Go Your Own Way', she had to sing the choruses with him. That "shacking up" line stood out in bold relief and, "every time those words would come out onstage, I wanted to kill him," she told *Rolling Stone* in 1997. "It was like, 'I'll make you suffer for leaving me.' And I did. It put me back in the place where Lindsey and I were when he wrote that song: back at our apartment [where he was] really angry with me. I had to revisit the world of the big fight every time he sang it."

One thing that would give her strength on stage in the light of all of this angst was a special gift from Don Henley, who had tapped into her love of English myths. It was a pendant that depicted Merlin the magician that she wore as a good luck charm. Considering her kinetic stage performance, whirling and spinning, it was amazing the charm didn't fly off. There was a show when it nearly went – she came offstage to find it hanging by the chain from her waist – but it didn't fall. "It didn't want to leave me," she said. Which is more than can be said for Henley when the time came to step up to the plate a little later down the line.

Stevie was treated like a queen by Don at first; after having endured years in the roles of "Mr and Mrs Intense" with Lindsey, when Don and Stevie did manage to score some time together, he showed her a very good time. But Henley was not keen on commitment and while Stevie had dreamed of family life as a young woman, she realised quickly that it would not be a possibility with him. This was no surprise to the Eagles crew, who watched him swing from "the ultimate Southern-charm gentleman" to "distant and unreachable". According to Marc Eliot's *Take It To The Limit*: "It was a pattern so familiar that it had become a running joke. Henley's favoured method of seduction became known as 'Love 'em and Lear 'em'," in reference to his penchant for picking up the object of his temporary desire in a Learjet. During Henley's "distant" patches, Stevie would direct her loneliness into writing and kept those she could rely on – her girlfriends – closer than ever on the road.

Chapter 11

The *Rumours* Tour was increasingly high octane and exhausting, so, to combat the fatigue and boredom, Fleetwood Mac ramped up the luxury: riders became more extravagant, travel was always first-class (no more sleeping on top of amps) and any sense of the whimsical or the eccentric was encouraged whole-heartedly to alleviate the dull downtime on the road. One example of this was the giant inflatable penguin that had recently joined the entourage, specifically to float above the band at outdoor gigs; though prone to erratic behaviour, at its best it rose to a full 70 feet tall. John McVie had always been fond of penguins, to the extent that they became the band's mascot. You'd find the tuxedoed little chaps lurking on the corner of album sleeves, printed on flight cases or emblazoned on Access All Areas passes. The inflatable was a bridge too far for some, however. When Mick Fleetwood's family attended a show, his father looked up at the bobbing inflatable and then looked back at his grinning son. "Penguins don't fly," were his simple but crushing words.

The major show for Fleetwood Mac during the summer of 1977 was undoubtedly Bill Graham's Day On The Green at the Oakland Coliseum, California, on May 7. They would play on the opening day of this outdoor festival, sharing the bill with the Doobie Brothers, Gary Wright and the Steve Gibbons Band. Every year the festival brought together the cream of the rock crop, but this year was particularly strong: on the days that followed Fleetwood Mac's show, the crowd would be treated to sets from the Eagles, the Steve Miller Band, Heart (with whom Stevie would later strike up a friendship), Peter Frampton, Boz Scaggs, The Beach Boys . . . it was a rock fan's dream.

Fleetwood Mac chartered a private Viscount 40 propjet from Van Nuys Airport to get to the show, and Stevie immediately commandeered a cosy area at the rear where she and her girlfriends snuggled up together and snoozed under a blanket. John, Mick and Lindsey sank beers with John Courage and Christine sat with the band's secretary Judy Wong*, drinking champagne and chain-smoking. Richard Dashut and Ken Caillat boarded the plane and as Ken wandered towards Stevie's den, Judy warned him off. "It's kind of Stevie's area," she explained carefully, no doubt having witnessed the cold front that could be expected by anyone venturing in uninvited. Ken later commented on "Stevie's fan club", as he referred to them, with some suspicion. "In the future, Stevie would have more and more 'friends' around her," he said. "They would take control of her appointments and we wouldn't be able to reach her when we needed to. Finally, we wouldn't be able to reach her at all."

The Day On The Green concert series was relatively new, only running since 1973, but it soon became an essential on the West Coast rock'n'roll calendar. On 7 May 1977, the great and the good of California cool were there to check out Fleetwood Mac. The crowd was 75,000-strong, the biggest audience Stevie and Lindsey had ever faced. Stevie: "I was standing in the middle of the stage thinking, 'This is the big time'." The show might have been in broad daylight – scuppering Curry Grant's atmospheric lighting – but the Mac created a potent atmosphere of neurotic energy, particularly during Buckingham's malevolent version of 'Oh Well', with Stevie hurtling across the stage with her tambourine, dancing wildly like a clockwork doll wound up just a few notches too tight. They quite simply

* Judy Wong was the subject of erstwhile Mac guitarist Danny Kirwan's song 'Jewel-Eyed Judy'. Kirwan has his own troubled story: loved by Peter Green for his passion and skill ("so into it that he cried as he played"), he ended up being fired after struggling increasingly with alcoholism and later lived rough on the streets. Just before being sacked, Kirwan had a fight with guitarist Bob Welch that turned ugly and precipitated his departure. Welch, a sufferer of depression himself, would commit suicide at the age of 66 in 2012. Kirwan died in 2018 at the age of 68 after contracting pneumonia.

weren't like anybody else on the bill, or any other bill for that matter. For Stevie, the show was one of the defining Mac concerts of the seventies and the seventies was a defining decade. There was something about it that had "a magic that really isn't there now", not just for Fleetwood Mac, but for all of the major rock bands who reigned during that era.

Stevie's designer Margi Kent joined the band on the road to develop further costume ideas. She worked alongside Curry Grant, "because if I did special costumes, we wanted to build according to the vibe of the lighting", she said. "Believe me, in those days every day was a story. They travelled around like a family, whether they were getting along or not, it's still a family." Margi would become a close confidante of Stevie's – to be in charge of her look was to be in an intimate position of trust, after all – and Stevie loved her, continuing to work with her to this day. She would even dedicate 'Landslide' to Margi during some of these early shows, an honour indeed.

During this tour, a witch's hat would be introduced into Stevie's ever-expanding wardrobe. It looked perfect silhouetted against the Halloween moon projected behind the drum riser, and, with her mystical demeanour and black robes, would add to the ever-rumbling speculation that Stevie really was a witch.

Critics were less concerned as to whether she was a practising occultist or not than they were by her vocal performance. There was always a seductive crack in Stevie's voice, but it was now becoming so hoarse it was affecting her range and tone. The ubiquitous cocaine and champagne backstage (and sometimes onstage) had their uses; they gave Stevie false courage to step out in front of thousands when she was at her most nervous and pepped her up, "like taking one of your mom's diet pills", giving her the energy to cope with her myriad professional and romantic pressures, fittings, interviews, shows . . . but soon she couldn't go forward without it. Those tempting bottle-caps filled with cocaine would be in the wings at every gig. Already high, "Stevie tripped off stage right during every single break to change shawl and snag a bottle cap of blow", according to Carol Ann Harris. At the end of the concert, everyone was presented with their own wrap of coke to take with them to the hotel to get them through the night. This may explain why Stevie's purse was always brimming with pills such as Quaaludes – she needed something to bring her down and allow her a few hours' sleep. The effect on Stevie's voice was becoming critical – the constant use (and chemical abuse) meant her voice was changing and getting lower. Robin, a voice therapist, was on hand to help her train and control her voice without strain, but it had little effect. Stevie's singing during this time would be described by *Rolling Stone*'s Peter Herbst as "growled incantations to rival Regan's (from *The Exorcist*), without Regan's exquisite control". He also commented on her 'sulkiness' between songs and physical instability; at one point 'frantic roadies' had to leap forward to prevent her from falling off the stage altogether.

Even so, fans were undeterred and 1977 was a huge year for Fleetwood Mac; a *Rolling Stone* poll awarded them the accolade Artist Of The Year, Rumours would be proclaimed Best Album, Stevie's song 'Dreams' would be voted Best Single and Nicks herself was nominated in the female vocalist category. *Rumours* also went to number one Stateside on 21 May, displacing *Hotel California* by the Eagles. It would stay at the top of the charts for eight months.

Such fame thrilled and frightened Stevie in equal measure. In September 1977, the band would be hailed once more at the prestigious Don Kirschner Rock Awards, scooping honours for Best Group and Best Album, partying briefly and then heading home. Even after all of the acclaim and applause, Stevie, driving home separately with her brother Chris, felt 'lonely' and 'scared'. No matter how many people Stevie surrounded herself with, she couldn't shake the feeling of isolation. Being with family helped, although she had little time to see her parents and many months often slipped by between visits. At least having her brother Chris nearby when she was in LA gave her something of an anchor.

The band could not have survived the tough, drug-addled *Rumours* tour without several much-needed breaks to punctuate the year. In some cases they were only a few days, in others Fleetwood Mac would be able to decompress for a month. During one break, Stevie decided to do a little mansion-shopping. The only problem was that Lindsey and Carol Ann had the same idea . . . and were interested in the same house in the Hollywood Hills. Rock star problems, eh? Stevie got there to view it first, to her ex-lover's fury. It was a beautiful day, "the scent of jasmine in the air . . ." as Carol Ann remembers it. "I gazed at the pink bougainvillea cascading down the walls and entry gates of old Spanish-style mansions . . ." Well, she was jolted out of her reverie when Lindsey parked the car outside the big white Spanish house they were due to see . . . and they heard Stevie's voice floating down from the balcony. She'd arrived an hour earlier with Robin in tow, and was tickled to see an unsmiling Lindsey below her, Carol Ann standing wanly by his side. After enquiring as to whether Stevie's realtor was "Satan", Lindsey discovered to his considerable chagrin that Stevie had been given the listing via his own realtor. Much teasing later, and insistence from Stevie that this was 'a girl's house' anyway, Lindsey relented. The triumph clearly warmed Stevie's cockles, because she invited them both – yes, Carol Ann was surprised too – back to her rental nearby. Stevie had to get ready for a photoshoot that was taking place in her house, but her brother Chris was there, as was an abundant stash of marijuana and coke. In a convoy of BMWs, off they went.

Stevie's home was not dissimilar to the house she'd just been viewing, built in the Spanish style, large and airy and protected by iron gates. The grounds were grazed by large statues of pink flamingoes and the outside walls were covered with trailing blossoms. Once inside, Carol Ann gazed in wonder at the tasteful opulence. There were lamps covered with silk scarves giving off a soft, coloured glow, Persian rugs strewn over polished wooden floors and, naturally, "candles everywhere, sitting on delicate tables next to photographs of Stevie and nearly everyone in the Fleetwood Mac family . . ."

Carol Ann Harris recalls in her book *Storms*: "The room was furnished with light wicker furniture that was almost buried under pillows covered in Laura Ashley fabric. Hanging from the ceiling was a wicker swing that moved gently in the warm breeze. In one corner stood a baby grand piano [with] a shawl thrown over it . . . and on a glass coffee table lay a large leather book titled *Magical Beings*. It was a room for Rhiannon and I loved it." Chris appeared, joints were rolled, Stevie brought out the marching powder and then scurried off to change for her shoot. For the first time, Stevie had shown some cordiality to Carol Ann, although she still rarely felt comfortable with her around. Even so, there would be moments of closeness in the coming years. Mostly it would be tricky as hell, of course, but one theory for Stevie's temporary friendliness was that she was in love. Yes, a curveball was heading Fleetwood Mac's way that would risk causing irreparable damage – and this was a group that had weathered more knocks than a front door.

Mick Fleetwood has said that his relationship with Stevie Nicks started in LA, just before they set off on the final leg of the *Rumours* tour that took in New Zealand, Australia and Japan in December 1977. And yes, Stevie was seeing Don Henley while Mick was still married to Jenny Boyd. Considering the already ridiculous levels of relationship tensions within the band, this was a disaster and Stevie herself was 'horrified'. Drugs and booze dissolved that extra level of propriety, however, and their feelings for each other temporarily overrode however devastated they were. Being together all of the time, taking comfort in each other . . . the boundaries had never been more confused.

During that rainy, muggy autumn, just before the final stint of the tour began, Mick would sneak away from home to be with Stevie and they would drive up and down Mulholland Drive together in his car. To make matters even more complex, Mick's parents were staying with him and this much-needed level of secrecy gave the situation an even more "supercharged aura of romance", as Mick put it. By the end of the first night of the tour in Auckland on 6 November, it had become a full-blown affair.

It was, according to Stevie, "the biggest surprise" and she still refers to him as one of her "great, great loves". But it would anger the band and once the news was out, hurt many people deeply, none more than

Jenny Boyd. "I loved these people," said Stevie, referring to the Fleetwoods. "I loved this family. It couldn't possibly have worked out, and it didn't." Mick and Stevie understood each other though. They laughed together, took solace in each other and were together almost all of the time. Both of them were fairly pickled too, and Mick in particular was in a state of some fragility. In addition to his out-of-control lifestyle and failing marriage, he was suffering from hypoglycaemia, and, while anaesthetising himself heavily, he was also trying to manage the band. Worse than all of this, however, was the fact that his father had just been diagnosed with cancer. Mick and Stevie were "in love"; this wasn't just lust or sadness or opportunism and their affection for each other lit up their otherwise rather traumatic days. But, with the clarity of hindsight, Stevie would later state in an interview with Oprah Winfrey that, "Mick and I would have never had an affair if we hadn't been . . . coked out. We were the last two people at a party and guess what? It's not hard to figure out what happened, and it wasn't a good thing, it was a doomed thing, caused pain for everybody, and led to nothing." Looking back at pictures of herself during that period, Stevie admitted that she thought she looked "beautiful" at the time, but now simply sees a woman who looks "unattractive and high".

We are granted a window into the band's mood at this time thanks to an hour of 'fly-on-the-wall' film shot during the Japanese dates on this tour. Fleetwood Mac are interviewed (often while drunk) as well as observed by a roaming camera. "What do you find interesting now?" asks the interviewer (also seemingly inebriated). Stevie Nicks smiles but clams up: "It's too personal . . ." When asked about Mick Fleetwood, she states wryly that he "loves attention. LOVES it." But Stevie is kind and light-hearted in the footage and doesn't object to a camera being in her face while she tries to put on her make-up before the show. She flirts outrageously with the crew, singing the vaudeville classic 'Shine On Harvest Moon' with them post-show, hugging and talking with one tech quite intimately and proclaiming a few moments later (when she spots the camera): "I'm having such fun with the crew . . . they're so much more fun than the band!"

We see a little girl from the audience approach after the rest of the crowd has gone, the young fan having found Stevie's ring which had flown off during the show. Stevie is thrilled and the child is rewarded with a hug, a kiss and Stevie's own black poncho. Robin is by Stevie's side at all times, providing support and humour right up to the moment Stevie steps out in front of the crowd. "Every night she's at the side of the stage," says Stevie. "And I say, 'Oh, I'm so tired,' and she says, 'Oh, it's OK, I can probably do it,' and she probably could!"

Lindsey Buckingham is given less screen time in this documentary, but what we do see is him storming into the dressing room exclaiming: "I'm sick of playing! Hate it! We need a vacation." Yes, they did. They had never worked so hard. But by the time 1978 dawned, they would all be multi-millionaires. Stevie as a principal songwriter was earning big money, her lifestyle utterly different to how it was three years previously. Everyone would celebrate the end of their tour in December with a mammoth pre-Christmas shopping spree and Stevie gave a gala New Year's Eve party at her house to honour their incredible year, and the year to come. AOR was healthier than ever – *Never Mind The Bollocks* by the Sex Pistols might have been welcomed by rock critics as it grabbed headlines through shock value and stripped back three-chord immediacy, but punk had little chance of stealing Fleetwood Mac's commercial thunder. Nevertheless, its angry, wipe-the-slate-clean influence would creep into their next album via the restless energy of new wave disciple Lindsey Buckingham.

Chapter 12

Stevie, Christine and Lindsey had all been working on new songs for the next album; expectations were high and Warners wanted another *Rumours* – which had scooped a Grammy in February 1978 and was still at number one in the US charts. Stevie wrote compulsively, not just because she was expected to, but for herself.

Christine referred to Stevie affectionately as "the mad songwriter" and Stevie was inclined to agree. "I thought, 'They're right. I am mad. There's no place for another song.'" But she had amassed so much material, there was only one thing for it; it was time to consider the option of a solo career, an option that had been suggested to her by more than one record executive, keenly aware of her appeal and potential as an artist in her own right. Stevie didn't want to leave the band but she did want to express her creativity and use her songs, many of which she would present to Fleetwood Mac only to have them rebuffed anyway. The wheels were already quietly in motion for a side project, which would soon exist, not always harmoniously, alongside the Mac.

Meanwhile, Lindsey had been fired up by punk, having caught live shows by bands such as The Clash while in London. Witnessing the spirit, attitude and simplicity of the new movement, Lindsey looked back at his own band with more objective eyes and he saw that Fleetwood Mac were just one of the many groups seen as pompous, indulgent dinosaurs by the punks. Lindsey didn't want to be any of those things, and saw an urgent need to push the Mac up and out of the rock'n'roll rut, even if he had to force them. There were three writers in the band, but Lindsey wanted to use punk as an influence on their follow-up to *Rumours* and, as we can now hear from listening to *Tusk*, if Stevie and Christine didn't follow suit . . . well, that was just too bad, and as a result, the writing styles on this record had never been so diverse.

Lindsey knew *Rumours* would be hard to follow, so, with his own songs at least, he would go in a totally different direction. By the middle of the *Rumours* tour, Lindsey had already written a fierce clutch of songs, including 'That's All For Everyone', 'Not That Funny' and 'What Makes You Think You're The One?' He was also tired of using his 'best ideas' to improve Stevie's and Christine's songs. Instead, he would concentrate on "broadening the [band's] palette," and if it took aggression on his part to chisel the rest of the band out of 'complacency', so be it – he wasn't exactly known for his soft-soaping bedside manner anyway. The way he used punk as an inspiration was more in terms of attitude than as a direct musical influence however; the grooves he was coming up with were less 'punk' and, at times, more of an angry, stabbing bluegrass-meets-ELO vibe. He was experimenting, and in the true nature of the new wave, he was free to make mistakes and think laterally, rather than stick to an old formula. If it ain't broke . . . then break it anyway.

Sessions for the next album were arranged to take place at the Village Recorder studio in Santa Monica, a former Masonic temple previously used by sometime Beatles guru the Maharishi Mahesh Yogi as a centre for transcendental meditation. Any lingering vibes of serenity were soon to be well and truly dissipated now the Mac were booked in. But before recording got underway, there was time to grab a few weeks' holiday before the band had to reconvene. Stevie was desperate to get away and rest while she could, so, with Christi, Robin and new best friend Sara Recor by her side, she flew to Maui in Hawaii, where she planned to do little more than simply lie in a hammock and stare at the sea and the sky, studded with more stars than she had ever seen – more stars than you could see in smoggy LA anyway.

Sara and Stevie had become friends against all odds; Sara was married to Jim Recor, with whom Fleetwood Mac had worked while touring with Loggins and Messina. Stevie and Jim had, as we know, struck up an affectionate friendship, but apparently no more. After meeting Stevie for the first time on Jim's urging, Sara coolly enquired as to whether Stevie was "Jim's little road friend?" Despite this somewhat excruciating introduction, Stevie would later become firm friends with Sara. "After a while I didn't care about what might have happened between my husband and Stevie," Sara had told Carol Ann Harris. "It was pretty much over between Jim and I. At the very least Jim had a crush on her, but who wouldn't?"

Together, they rented a house in Maui, a favourite destination for the members of Fleetwood Mac. It was tranquil, peaceful and separate from their chaotic lives in California or on the road, so it wasn't surprising that Stevie would 'bump into' Mick Fleetwood. Mick had escaped there too, ostensibly to spend some time alone to sort his head out, but the fact Stevie was there too may well have been a clincher. Mick was having a meltdown due to pressure and fear – fear of the future and of what was going to happen to his beloved, cancer-stricken father. Both of Mick's parents were in LA staying with Jenny at Mick's family home, seeking holistic alternatives to aggressive chemotherapy. Mick would soon return home to give his family the support they so desperately needed from him, but he was in need of help himself. In the meantime, Jenny had to take on much of the emotional heavy lifting.

While in Maui, Stevie would meet a young woman with whom she would build a lifelong bond. During an evening at the Blue Max club, Stevie's attention was caught by a striking brunette singer called Sharon Celani. Sharon had stepped onto the stage to sing 'Poor, Poor Pitiful Me', a song written by Stevie and Lindsey's old friend Warren Zevon and made famous by Linda Ronstadt. Sharon's voice impressed Stevie, who was already considering who she would want around her when – not if – she launched her own career and formed her own band outside of Fleetwood Mac. Stevie recalled to the DJ Jim Ladd in 1983: "I walked up to Sharon and said, 'My name is Stevie Nicks. I know you love being in Hawaii but

. . . if I ever have a band, if I ever do a record, will you consider coming and singing with me?' And I didn't know this girl, this could have been an unpleasant person that I'd just nailed myself into a relationship with. I didn't know. I took it solely on the way that she sang 'Poor, Poor Pitiful Me'."

But Stevie, who then joined Sharon onstage for a number herself, would find that her instinct was correct about Sharon – who naturally said "yes" in response to casually being offered the chance of a lifetime. From Stevie's point of view, she just loved the idea of having two backing singers to work with, not just on one record, but for all of her future work. The other singer to join the fray would be Lori Perry, whom Stevie and Lindsey had met through her husband, producer Gordon Perry, and Keith Olsen – the man all roads seem to lead to – in the early 1970s. A dream team was being formed. Having two girls to sing with, as well as gossip and spend time with, was ideal for Stevie. The musicians she wanted to pull around her for her own music were all male and Stevie was a true "girl's girl", after all.

Once the various Mac members were back in LA, Lindsey and Carol Ann decided to have a barbecue at their home in June Street, a "death row inmate's last meal", according to Carol Ann – they both knew the rest of the band would be shocked by the songs Lindsey had been working on in the home studio he'd constructed, and no small amount of hostility was anticipated. His new, short haircut alone had not gone down well on the whole – the detachment from the rest of the band that it represented went far beyond the visual. With the new coiffure, a rejection of his usual satin kimono tops for well-cut suits and dark make-up now lining his electric blue eyes, Lindsey had transformed himself, with Carol Ann's help, from poetic romantic lead to abrasive, sexy rock'n'roll Mephistopheles. He was shrugging off the tired hippie culture and impatiently waiting for the rest of the band to follow suit.

Everyone came to the party except Stevie, but Carol was wrong to assume it was down to the fact she was avoiding her. If she was avoiding anyone, it was Jenny. It all became clear when Carol Ann spotted a tearful Mrs Fleetwood lingering on her own at the party and took her aside. Jenny knew Mick's infidelities were nothing new – anyone who has read the memoir *Fleetwood* will know he was utterly at the mercy of the demands of what he referred to as 'the old veal viper' – but groupies were one thing. An affair with Stevie, a veritable member of the family, was another.

The situation within and around the band generally had also reached such a stage that Jenny was now more worried about her daughters than anything else, and the amount of hedonism to which they were potentially exposed. She wanted to take her girls back to the UK and away from Mick and the damaging Fleetwood Mac scene. Jenny also told Carol Ann that "Mick was terrified that Lindsey would go ballistic when he found out he and Stevie were sleeping together." Lindsey's anger was widely feared . . . but when Mick finally sat Lindsey down and told him, the reaction was a simple "Oh. OK."

"I didn't feel betrayed by Mick," Lindsey insisted to *The Independent*'s Lucy O' Brien in 1998. "Quite honestly I'd have been surprised if it hadn't happened. Stevie and I had long since parted company and she'd had several boyfriends in between." All sounds so reasonable and easy going, doesn't it? But the inevitable hurt would bubble volcanically beneath a sardonic exterior. Jenny herself was angrier with Mick than she was Stevie, but seeing "the other woman" at John McVie's wedding to Julie Reubens that April would be the moment that pushed her over the edge. The feeling at the wedding was one of magnanimity – it even took place at Christine McVie's Hollywood home, suggesting a certain level of *noblesse oblige*. But then Stevie arrived, and committed the ultimate wedding faux pas: she was wearing white.

One might think that the mere presence of Stevie Nicks at one's nuptials alone would guarantee an unfortunate upstaging of the bride, but for some reason, she went that step further. *Rolling Stone* reported that she was a "vision in white" – again, that's Stevie, not the bride – and she graciously accepted the many compliments flooding her way with quips and humble brags: "Thank you . . . it should be nice for what I paid for it." This was apparently too much for Jenny Fleetwood. The pair were later heard by Carol Ann having it out in Christine's walk-in wardrobe, Jenny pleading with Stevie to think of the children, Stevie trying to defend herself. Robin Snyder, alerted by the sudden conspicuity of Stevie's absence, found them and swooped in, calming Stevie down and gently extricating her.

Work began on the album that would be *Tusk* in May 1978, the beautiful early summer weather seeming like an auspicious sign, not that the band and crew were going to see much of the outside world for a while. The band was called for 3 p.m. (early for Fleetwood Mac) at Studio D, the Village Recorder, where they would record on a state of the art console, designed specifically to suit their needs. The idea for this album was that they would have their own studio built with a view to save money. Fleetwood Mac were gifted at many things, but economising was not one of them.

Their studio, which lay behind an unmarked iron door, was private, luxurious and comfortable. They knew if they were staying for any length of time, their second home would have to be exactly as they wanted it. Champagne was flowing from day one – not something that suggests a particular desire to stick to a tight budget. The decor in the studio was opulent; there were little stars on the domed ceiling in the listening room, plump sofas, remote-controlled baffles and beer on tap. There were also the usual tables covered in the most expensive gourmet salads, sandwiches and cheese boards, none of which would be necessary because all the band wanted was cocaine. There was plenty of that too. Hangers-on would come and go, perhaps to a lesser extent than on *Rumours*, but one new member of the inner circle would be a Beach Boy, hard partier and all-round big kid Dennis Wilson, now seeing Christine McVie. He was pretty expensive too.* Despite the call time of 3 p.m., Stevie turned up

* Dennis Wilson once expressed his love for Christine by booking gardeners to transform her back garden into a heart-shaped paradise for Valentine's Day. She was thrilled by the gesture. She was less thrilled when he then handed her the bill for it.

around 5 p.m., much to Buckingham's chagrin. He was already tense because the songs he had written and intended to use for this album were a departure from their previous work together and he knew his ideas would meet resistance. He also had no intention of compromising. Warners might have wanted *Rumours* Part Deux, but in Lindsey's opinion, *Rumours* had been a step into fresh, uncharted territory, therefore Tusk would have to be just as brave and innovative, if not more so, and the plan was to make it a double album. He decided to let Christine and Stevie play their demos first to ease everyone in before delivering the punch with angry songs such as 'Not That Funny' and 'What Makes You Think You're The One?' with its punchy ELO-inspired piano chords – brilliant but bitter, radiating strangulated fury and barely repressed contempt (towards Stevie, no doubt) with blatant lyrics such as "What makes you think I'm the one / who will love you forever?"

When Stevie finally did turn up, Ginny the poodle scampering along at her feet and a gaggle of 'girl fans' helping her with her many bags, Carol Ann Harris remembered her grand arrival was one befitting the "queen of rock she most definitely was . . . in a flowing dress made of antique scarves, with jade and gold bracelets jangling against her thin wrists . . . It was an entrance that would have made Elizabeth Taylor proud . . ." she wrote in her book *Storms*. Booze and chatter soon flowed as the ice broke and the vibe softened a little – until Mick discovered someone had crashed into his prized new (uninsured) sports car while he was inside. There would be plenty to distract him, however. Stevie's studio outfits, each more ravishing than the last, were, by all accounts, for Mick's benefit. Stevie's songwriting on this album reflects their affair, which changes as the time spent making *Tusk* passes. The relief and fun of 'Angel' would morph into sadness, almost grief, in 'Storms'.

With plans to make the album something of an epic affair, the writers in the band had an opportunity to include more of their work – a great relief to Stevie. But despite this extra scope, the process of making the record was agonising from the start. There was less sense of cohesion than ever between the band members, not just artistically but physically:

Stevie would ensure she was only there if she was needed, learning from the experience of having sat around killing time during the last two albums, and even John McVie would end up recording his parts separately so he could go sailing, the one way he could get far away from the band and not be on call.

At one point even Lindsey announced he wanted to record some tracks at home. Being in the studio wasn't exactly an attractive proposition for anyone: Lindsey, essentially at the helm of the project, was more divisive and controlling than ever, and no amount of gourmet sandwiches or champagne could soften the effects of that. His manner towards Stevie was, as she had predicted it would be, often harsh, sarcastic and cold; Lindsey might have found new love in the arms of Carol Ann, but that wouldn't make it easier between the two former lovers, and Stevie's writing would often bear the brunt of Lindsey's jabs. He was pulling away from her stylistically, apart from anything else – but just because his writing was changing didn't mean hers would be, nor would Christine's.

"*Tusk* was mainly Lindsey's conception, dream, everything he ever wanted to do," Stevie told *The Record*'s Michael Goldberg in 1982. "Everybody just figured that for whatever his reasons were, it was important that he do that and we just sort of sat back and let him do it. I don't mean to sound blasé or anything. I was there. I just didn't have very much to do with it. Because if I had had much to do with it, it wouldn't have been a double album and it wouldn't have been crazy." Fortunately for Stevie, she found she could escape from the studio a little more frequently than the others, which gave her time to record a duet with Kenny Loggins, with whom Fleetwood Mac had recently toured. Nicks loved duets, and she loved Loggins' music. She didn't need her arm twisting, although if she had known what a disciplinarian he was going to be, she might have thought twice.

"I call him 'Slave Driver Loggins'," she quipped to *High Times* in 1982. "He cracked the whip on me for two days to get that particular performance. And I was downright angry at points where I was going, 'I'm not going to do this,' and he said, 'Yes you are.' He's a real good producer, he got exactly what he wanted." The outcome was the soft-rock ballad 'Whenever I Call You "Friend"', which would be included on Loggins' album *Nightwatch*.

"I think I pushed her harder than she was used to in the studio," admits Kenny. "I just wanted to make a difficult song seem easy and fun, and she certainly delivered that." To be fair, Kenny was "always impressed with how dedicated she was, how savvy she was to her marketplace and her audience, and what a hard worker she was at all times. The girl really knew what she wanted and was not afraid to go after it." There were no two ways about it, Stevie was a star – and she knew how to work it in every way. Not only was she always flanked by her entourage, "it seems she had a full-time on-staff photographer," recalls Loggins, "just to catch her when she was in the mood to pose . . ."

Chapter 13

Stevie's songs on *Tusk* – 'Sara', 'Sisters Of The Moon', 'Angel', 'Beautiful Child' – all had hit potential and would arguably turn out to be the strongest on the record, although Lindsey would have contested that *he* was generally responsible for bringing both her and Christine's songs up to 'hit' standard. As usual, Stevie had to work up her courage when presenting her work to Lindsey. No one had the balls to criticise Lindsey's songs, however. He radiated an intimidating aura that warned off anyone who might question his musical decisions. As Stevie said, it was just easier to sit back and let him take the reins.

Stevie already had 'Sisters Of The Moon' to bring to the table, the song she had started writing on her first major tour with Fleetwood Mac. The upbeat 'Angel' was initially Stevie's attempt to "write a rock'n'roll song," she admitted in the 1980 *Tusk* documentary, but it soon took on a life of its own. "It started out being much sillier [but] it didn't end up being silly at all. When I started it I thought, 'This is good for me, since I write so many intense, serious, dark songs . . .' I wanted to write something that was up. It starts out that way but there is a definite eeriness . . ." In the studio, she stamps her peep-toe platform-clad feet to the music and sings her vocal, swishing her skirts by her sides, the energy building as the song progresses.

The band sipped on margaritas as they worked, but no cocktails could dull Stevie's edginess around fractious Lindsey, especially when she had to work with him on the harmonies of 'Angel' – yet another song at least partly inspired by him – at the grand piano. The song features typical Stevie themes – dreams, the wind, charmed hours, haunted songs, angels, yet more dreams, but there are also direct references to feelings tied to a past relationship: "When you were good, you were very, very good . . . I still look up when you walk in the room . . . and we both pretend . . ." The lines will have come from her notepads of poetry, thoughts and moments jotted down, and so there may be flashes of Mick, of Don, even (a cad, yes, but when he was good . . .). But at its core the song really is about Lindsey, whom, despite everything, she still has to stop herself from automatically "reaching out" to. It's about the love that might have been, and a new understanding that was proving hard to achieve.

The 'pretending' in 'Angel' may also refer to the affair with Mick and the need for discretion despite the fact everyone now knew what was going on. Overseeing this *ménage-à-quatre* would be the spirit of Rhiannon, as well as an indirect nod to family shining through in the line 'So I close my eyes softly / Till I become that part of the wind . . .' "There's a man in the story of Rhiannon and his name is Arawn, the great lord of darkness, the man who possesses the power to take or give life, but he only takes life . . . because of pain," Stevie explained in an interview with broadcaster Jim Ladd in 1979. "Aaron is my father's name, and also my brother's [middle] name, and my grandfather's name. So Arawn is many things to me." Of the lyric, Stevie expands with a reference to the ancient story: "And so Arawn touched the twins with his hand so that they would sleep. And in that sleep there will be no pain. And in that nonexistence of pain there will be happiness, because it was only given with great love. And this was in a haunted song, and a charmed hour, and this was the angel . . . of my dreams."

Stevie's transcendent song 'Sara', meanwhile, would braid her feelings for Mick, her protective "great dark wing", and her then best friend Sara Recor. One night in July, as the scent of jasmine floated through the window, blossoms warmed by another balmy day of California heat, Stevie refreshed her make-up, lit the candles and sat at the piano, sketching out a song from some simple chords, singing softly over the top, her notepads of self-penned poetry lying open nearby. When it came to writing or drawing, Stevie always ensured the atmosphere was just right when she "felt the power"; candles and incense are always present, but she often does her hair and make-up to make for a sense of ceremony, maybe even changing her outfit, so that "when I do sit down to create, all the channels are open." The channels were certainly open tonight. By the time the song was finished, it encompassed "a vast bunch of people" in her life, and she "fell in love" with the track she'd created, and everything, everyone, it represented.

The demo Stevie would record of 'Sara', with Tom Moncrieff on bass and singer Annie McLoone on strong, echoing harmonies, was over seven minutes long. In fact, the original version was over a quarter of an hour long and consisted of 16 verses. Stevie had a lot to say, and 'Sara' was veering more towards an epic saga than a pop song as a result. The process of chopping it down to size would be as hard as ever – "It got edited down to 14 minutes, down to 11 minutes, down to nine minutes, down to seven minutes, down to four minutes and 40 seconds," she told broadcaster Tommy Vance in 1994. "I was at the point where I went, 'Is the word Sara even going to be left in the song?'" – but a longer demo, with Stevie on piano and vocals, would be revealed in later years on the enhanced *Tusk* release. On listening to that magical early recording, one hears Stevie uttering the words "I wanna be a star! I don't want to be a cleaning lady . . ." before she launches in. One thing you can say for Stevie Nicks: no matter how wealthy she became, she never forgot those lean years.

'Sara' was, as Stevie states, her "most personal song" – personal not only to herself but to Fleetwood Mac and what they were all going through – but while writing always had a strong therapeutic benefit, Stevie actually found she had more fun writing this than almost all of her other songs to date. "I knew 'Sara' would be popular because I loved writing [it]," she said. It was hypnotic, soft and veiled in a mist of melancholy, but part of Stevie's enjoyment in writing 'Sara' was thanks to the simple healing process of wallowing, a feeling encapsulated in the evocative line: 'Drowning in the sea of love, where everyone would love to drown . . .'

"[It's] self-indulgence," Stevie admitted in later years, explaining the lyric with a chuckle. "Don't we all love to lay face down on our bed and go, 'I'm so miserable, don't bug me, I want to hurt! Don't even bring me tea . . .!'? I love to walk around in the throes of passionate miserability. I made that word up years ago. I don't like to suffer and I hate pain but I want to suffer to the point that I go to the typewriter and write down all of my marvellous philosophy as to why I'm suffering – I love that part of it."

As Stevie worked on the song at her home, with Sara herself by her side, Mick would turn up in his bright red Ferrari to develop the brush work Stevie wanted to accompany what had already been recorded for the demo. It took him three days to get it right but, as Fleetwood himself put it, "The result was, in many ways, the ultimate Fleetwood Mac song of that era, the late seventies, breathless, ethereal, almost ecclesiastical and somehow reverent, as Stevie pays tribute to her muse."

Despite the title, the muse was not just Sara. "[Sara] likes to think it's completely about her, but it's really not. It's about me, about her, about Mick, about Fleetwood Mac . . ." There is also what sounds like a knowing reference towards Stevie's first meeting with Lindsey – "I think I had met my match . . . he was singing . . .". Everyone who meant something profoundly to Stevie seems to be featured in this song. It's no wonder it was so long at first.

'Sara' also reached out to Don Henley; the line 'When you build your house, call me home . . .' referred to the charming Eagle himself, as the building of a fabulous home for Henley was indeed underway. And, as Stevie recalls, "I was in it before it was finished." But it would not be 'home' to her.

'Sara' was a special name for Stevie and was always "the poet in my heart, for sure." It was a name she loved to sing, and 'Sara' would almost become another musical spirit, just like 'Rhiannon', to accompany her invisibly onstage. There was a spiritual connection, almost commitment, to this name, and the uncharacteristically ambiguous nature of the lyrics led to some speculation on the song's release the following December, not least when Stevie explained that, if she ever had a little girl, she would name her 'Sara'.

But when questioned about the song himself in later years, Don Henley would later cause ructions by blurting out a shockingly personal piece of information in an interview with *GQ*. "I believe to the best of my knowledge [Stevie] became pregnant by me," he said. "And she named the [unborn] kid Sara, and she had an abortion and then wrote the song of the same name to the spirit of the aborted baby." Whether true or not, this blunt, all too public treatment of such a delicate subject was staggering. Stevie herself refused to comment beyond revealing that Henley "had to make many an apologetic phone-call" before they could be friends again.

Indiscreet as his statement was, one can see from the lyrics how Don got there – "Now it's gone, it doesn't matter what for . . . there's a heartbeat and it never really died" – and a devastating decision such as this would explain the 'passionate miserability' that gently washes over the whole song. Stevie herself has indicated there was indeed more than one 'lost child' in her life.

Summer had morphed muggily into autumn, and Halloween, normally Stevie's favourite time of year, was just around the corner. Stevie adored dressing up, in case you hadn't noticed, as did the whole of Fleetwood Mac, who had something of a gothic, twisted fairy tale about themselves. But Halloween 1978 would mark a change in Stevie's life. Yes, there would be dressing up, there would be a party at Lindsey's, there would be booze and blow and roller-skating and loud music . . . but there would also be a moment at which someone's feelings were transferred irrevocably from one beautiful woman to another. Stevie needed her great dark wing more than ever, but he was already preparing to build a nest elsewhere.

As the witching hour struck, Sara Recor arrived at the party, looking as glamorous as ever. She caught Mick Fleetwood's eye as she went to find Stevie. There was no more than a perceptible flicker between the two individuals, but something was already brewing.

It was around this time that Sara could almost always be found at

Stevie's house. Her marriage to Jim had passed the point of no return, and Stevie's glorious home was the ideal sanctuary. The two women adored each other despite the fact Jim had, as we know, been a little in love with Stevie himself in the past. Sara and Stevie played music together, sang and larked about, referring to themselves as 'The Twang Sisters' as they sang country songs to entertain people and make each other laugh.

Another who was frequently at Stevie's house during this time was Mick. Sara was secretly attracted to him from the moment she first met him and the feeling was evidently mutual, the chemistry between them growing every time Mick came round to visit Stevie. When, one day, they found themselves alone in Stevie's house, Mick invited Sara to go for a drive, taking her to the little house he had bought for Jenny – now vacant – on Little Ramirez Canyon. No one said this was going to be classy. He'd told Sara he and Stevie were over (although apparently Stevie herself hadn't yet been informed of this development) and this was the prompt Sara needed to allow her bottled up feelings for Mick to pour out, and vice versa. Everyone in the Mac camp was insecure and in need of approval, love and comfort; they would hold onto each other as the emotional sea around them became choppier, often with scant regard for boundaries.

The thrill of new love aside, this new situation was messy to say the least. Both Mick and Sara loved Stevie, both felt bad about Jenny, and then there was Jim, with whom Mick was still friends. Jim would be remarkably civilised about it, giving Mick his blessing. Stevie's position was obviously a little different. She might have been seeing Henley, but what she saw as the simultaneous loss of Mick and her closest friend Sara would break her heart. As always, out of the pain would come some of Stevie's most heartrending songwriting, her private emotions exposed through her lyrics. One of the songs that lays bare Stevie's reaction to this break-up would be 'Storms'.

When Stevie brought in a demo of this sensitive song, ringing with tenderly expressed heartache, she broke down when Lindsey elected to attack it almost immediately. All of Stevie's songs are personal, but to pour acid on 'Storms' was tantamount to harpooning a dove. Carol Ann was in the room and watched him "going over her new song bit by bit, pointing out how this part was crap, the next part needed to be raised or lowered by two octaves and this section desperately needed a new melody line – he tore it apart. By the time he finished . . . he smiled and said, 'I like it, Stevie, it just needs some work, that's all.'" Stevie bit back, and, as Carol Ann remembers, "The end result was always the same: a vicious battle over her music . . . without fail the parts that Lindsey didn't like were the parts that Stevie loved." Stevie already felt betrayed and hurt by her lover and her friend – and again, she would have to see that ex-lover in the studio every day, just as she had when she broke up with Lindsey during *Rumours* – but to have her work berated, work that so honestly conveyed her hurt, was just too much.

Lyrically, perhaps Lindsey took it personally; there are references to wondering how much she really cared about the subject of the song, inferences to a love gradually fading out of her life, but he may also have been subliminally punishing Stevie for having loved someone else so much that she could write a song like this – a raw composition clearly musing over Mick, a fact that will no doubt have been painful for Lindsey to accept. 'Every night you do not come / Your softness fades away . . .' creates an image of an extra-marital relationship: her lover isn't always able to be there with her. 'She said, "Every night he will break your heart . . ."' is possibly a reference to a warning from Jenny Boyd, delivered during their argument in Christine McVie's closet on John and Julie's wedding day. Tellingly, Stevie's lyrics in this song also allude for the first time to a kind of acceptance that her life as a touring musician simply cannot include a relationship without there being some measure of angst. She has loved before, but in the past she "did not deal with the road".

'Storms' is one of the songs Stevie is most proud of, referring to it as a "beautiful poem" full of wisdom and understanding, not just of Mick's motives but her own feelings. It was about coming through the other side. "It was probably one of the most terrible times of my life getting over the idea that Mick and I weren't going to be together," she has said. The storms in the title, of course, refer to Stevie's own tempestuousness. She wants to 'give something warm' to her friend as they part, but she had never been a blue, calm sea. Nevertheless, as Stevie maintains, her relationship with Mick could never have worked, too much pain had already been caused by it and, while Fleetwood Mac seemed to be the incredible unbreakable band, this might just have been the catastrophe to shatter it once and for all. 'Beautiful Child', Stevie's fifth song on *Tusk*, also detailed the love affair with Fleetwood, their age difference, the confusion and the awareness of how wrong it all was, mingled with an inability to let go. 'I'm tall enough to reach for the stars / I'm old enough to love you from afar . . .' lyrics evidently speaking as Mick, and written, presumably, before his feelings for Sara became known, when the only major problem between Mick and Stevie was that theirs was ultimately a forbidden love.

In the studio post-split, Stevie and Mick were largely silent with each other*– yet another Fleetwood Mac cold war – and while obviously extremely upset, Stevie refused to speak about what had happened with anyone, feeling understandably betrayed and less able to trust than perhaps she'd ever felt before. The band worked on. It didn't help that the decision to name the album Tusk was inspired by one of the many pet names Mick Fleetwood used in reference to his own penis. It was one thing having Mick posing around with unambiguous wooden balls dangling between his legs, but to basically name an album after his own genitals, particularly after having just proved that they were often in charge when it came to decision-making, was the height of poor taste in Stevie's eyes. She even threatened to quit the group over it, but of course, she didn't, and of course, the name Tusk stayed. In the meantime, the general vibe in the studio wasn't helped by Lindsey's "décor". "Lindsey had tusks on

* However, Mick would still gallantly leap to Stevie's defence whenever her honour was at stake, most notably when, in August 1979, LA punk band The Rotters released a single called 'Sit On My Face, Stevie Nicks', which was played frequently on the rock radio station KROQ until Fleetwood himself "demanded that they stop playing it," *Creem* reported in their story about the debacle (cheekily titled 'The Best Seat In Town').

the wall and all these weird Polaroids. I thought this must be what hell is like. With speakers," said Stevie in a 2011 Q&A at the Grammy Museum.

The title track itself, with its distinctive staccato riff, was born of a simple groove Lindsey Buckingham used to play during sound-checks while Richard Dashut got the mix they wanted. It was Mick Fleetwood's suggestion that they develop the riff into a song – the song that would be the album's first single – and this may explain why 'Tusk' is heavy on the drums, with Lindsey Buckingham's double-tracked octave-apart vocal soft and viper-like over the top during the verses before bursting into the chorus, all feral shouts and primal screams. It sounded fierce, but it needed something extra, something that the Mac had never done before.

While brainstorming in the studio, something reminded Mick of a holiday he had spent in Barfleur, France. One Sunday morning he awoke (rather earlier than he'd have liked to, the fact it was morning at all should tell you that) to the strident sound of a brass band marching around the town square below. Once he'd accepted that they weren't going to go away, Mick watched from his window and was inspired by the festive atmosphere the brass band had created, and how their presence was bringing everyone together – people were appearing in their droves to hear and see them. Remembering that feeling, Mick put it to the rest of the band that it would be fun to recreate that marching band sound and atmosphere . . . only in a much, much bigger way. With the help of the University of Southern California's Trojan Marching Band, Fleetwood Mac would take over the Dodger Stadium in LA to record the single and, famously, the video for 'Tusk'. Fleetwood didn't just want the band to play, he wanted them to have the space to march as well, and there would be plenty of room for that.

John McVie was the only Mac-member absent – he preferred to be in Tahiti instead – so he was represented by a cardboard cut-out. It was a relief for the band to be out of the studio, and recording in the open air and the sunshine was a unique situation. Stevie, in her summer dress, did a spot of baton twirling as the band played, and she and Robin roller-skated around the vast space during down time. The video concludes with the band playing as they march around the track; their only audience – Fleetwood Mac themselves – watch from the stalls and cheer them on, Stevie waving her straw hat in the air with excitement. There was, as Stevie has observed, something tribal about the song, and indeed the album. Tapping into that tribal quality led to the band themselves becoming like 'warriors' in their mind-set, which Stevie believes is the reason that the almost interminable process of making the album didn't see them all off completely. "*Tusk*, was very native, very African," Stevie told ABC Australia's Molly Meldrum. "Mick thinks he is a Watusi warrior and . . . he is! I would sit and write for days, it was like: these are the sacred steps back up to the top of the sacred mountain of this jungle . . . That's what *Tusk* was. Everything on *Tusk* was very warrior-esque, which is probably one of the reasons why 13 months didn't kill us all; we went to another kind of world for *Tusk*."

It would be experiences such as the recording of the 'Tusk' single and video that would make the process a little more fun and diverse, although while Stevie admits she enjoyed making *Tusk* more than *Rumours,* there were elements that also drove her crazy – having to be there at 2pm every day, for example: crack of dawn in Rock Star Land. What made this call-time even harder to face was the fact that, once in the studio, much time would be wasted, from her point of view, on 'blues jams' that went on for hours, work-outs that didn't involve her anyway. The prospect of this was rarely conducive to dragging herself out of her perfumed bed chamber.

"We had a digital person that I never understood the whole [time] why he was there," she continued. "I called him 'Mr Didge'. For 13 months we went to the studio every single day at two o'clock . . . and you are not late for a Fleetwood Mac session – they come and get you and kill you. So [you're there] from two o'clock in the afternoon – which is a horrifying time of day to even be up – until eight or nine the next morning, and then it's like, 'Let's jam! Let's play the blues! Da da da da- da!!' And you can't leave [the room] because you're part of this band . . ." Quibbles aside, the work was strong, not to mention abundant, but Mick was concerned a split was on the cards, not least because of the starkly different styles of songwriting that were now etched in very bold relief.

Stevie and Christine's songs were especially radio-friendly, but Fleetwood was still uneasy – Warners had told him they'd have to sell 500,000 copies just to break even, the way they were spending – and Lindsey, meanwhile, felt betrayed by the general lack of enthusiasm. Every writer in the band was respectively honing their own voice, so was this going to lead to disinterest in the band and a flurry of solo projects that would take over and tear them asunder? Whatever was on the cards, *Tusk*, for all its compelling qualities, would lack a unified voice and this was an indication of things to come. Meanwhile, the expenses had rocketed and *Tusk* would go down in history as the most expensive album produced up to that point, reportedly costing over $1 million (although this claim was a myth, according to Mick Fleetwood, who insists the Eagles broke that record. Those Lear jets won't pay for themselves). Still, figures were neither here nor there – the fact was that Fleetwood Mac had gone way over the top.

"When we moved out of the studio it looked like [a] house that we'd lived in," Stevie giggled. "There had to be 350,000 Polaroids plus stuffed animals hanging upside down, you know, rabbits* . . . Everything that we all owned, yarn and crocheting stuff, and paints. We had all our art supplies . . ." It was chaos, but after over a year in a confined space, they had to create their own corners inside of that, a corner that felt like home, otherwise they'd lose their minds. There was also so much equipment in the studio that, by the end of the 13 months it had taken to make *Tusk*, it would take an entire week and a large truck to shift it all back out again. The bills were mounting, and the intention to make it a double album would mean it was also expensive for fans. Warners were not convinced by the idea at all. The record industry was in the midst of a slump and Mo Ostin feared *Tusk* lacked commercial appeal, but Lindsey was determined, no matter whether anyone else in the band agreed. Christine McVie

* Essential studio staple, rabbits.

and Stevie had wrinkled their noses in bemused disdain as Lindsey whacked a Kleenex box in the toilet (not a euphemism) to get just the percussion sound he needed – and Lindsey's experiments were not all that welcome on their watch at the time either, even if Stevie has said that, with hindsight, she can appreciate *Tusk* much more than she did while they were making it. It was ahead of its time, but listening to the same songs for over a year was "a drain", she admits, and would make it hard for anyone to view the music objectively.

Lindsey had been trying to push Fleetwood Mac forward, to "shake people's preconceptions of pop" – a noble quest, but this, and his statement that selling copies was not his priority, didn't instil the label with confidence. Stevie shared Warners' view that it would be expecting too much of fans to part with $16 in one fell swoop, and the label considered releasing the album as separate discs "to soften the blow" of the cost. Price wouldn't be a problem at all, however, when the Westwood One rock radio station elected to play the entire album on air, allowing people to tape it. Fleetwood was furious, but Stevie Nicks was, according to Ken Caillat, more concerned with the cover of the album and the 'Tusk' single, which came out on September 19, 1979 (and went straight into the top ten in both the UK and US), just under a month before the album's release. The dilemma of who would end up being showcased on the cover, a la *Fleetwood Mac* and *Rumours,* was avoided altogether on both lead single and album because the image used would be that of Caillat's dog Scooter, biting the leg of his master's jeans. Stevie wasn't a fan of Scooter at the best of times, but this was a bridge too far.

"[Stevie] wasn't happy about that at all," wrote Ken in *Making Rumours,* even suggesting that when the decision regarding the cover art was made, Stevie "put a hex on Scooter. Then when he died four years later in 1983, Stevie said, 'I'm glad, Ken. Your dog had that album cover that should have been mine.'"

Chapter 14

Work on *Tusk* had been hard, and the upcoming tour would be even harder, but just before *Tusk* was released and dung the intense period of tour rehearsals, there would be a brief moment during which the band emerged into the light to be given the mother of all pats on the back: on October 10, 1979, Fleetwood Mac would be honoured with the 156th star on the Hollywood Walk Of Fame.

It was a surreal situation. The band first had to congregate inside the famously tacky Frederick's of Hollywood lingerie store on Hollywood Boulevard while hundreds of fans waited outside. At least this would give the frazzled band something to laugh about. Frederick's staff even presented them with commemorative underwear – well, it would be rude not to – while *Rumours* blasted through the speakers outside. Finally the big moment arrived, heralded by 100 USC Trojans charging through the shop playing 'Tusk'.

When the Mac finally sloped out into the street, looking every inch the cool, consummate rock stars, drinks in hand, they were invited to the podium to address the excited devotees before them. Mo Ostin thanked Fleetwood Mac for basically making them a ton of cash; John McVie, looking insouciant in sunglasses, deadpanned: "Thank you all for being . . . er . . . Americans . . ." and Stevie couldn't resist blessing the crowd for "believing in the crystal vision. Crystal visions do come true," she said dreamily. It was a little closer to what fans probably wanted to hear, but Stevie's little speech made Carol Ann and Lindsey snigger like naughty school-children. "We knew she was saying it from the heart," said Carol

Ann in her book *Storms*. "But quoting it against a backdrop of push-up bras and fuck-me heels . . ." That evening, a star-studded gala party was held in Beverly Hills to celebrate the Mac's achievement. It was a classic rock star shindig and everyone who was anyone was there (even the often reclusive Beach Boy Brian Wilson turned up).

Once the hangovers had worn off, Fleetwood Mac would resume rehearsals for the *Tusk* tour at the Sunset Gower studio complex. Mick Fleetwood remembers the soundstage, previously used by Busby Berkeley and Fred Astaire back in the golden era of Hollywood, as "immense, old, damp" – the walls rang with history, and it was twice the size of the studio used for the *Rumours* tour rehearsals. The constant chilliness did nothing for Stevie's respiratory health – fragile at the best of times – and even her dog Ginny developed a wheezy cough. Colds would abound, and self-medicating was in full flow.

The members of the Mac were frequently bored or simply exhausted, but *ennui* was, as always, balanced up by the kind of luxuries that would make Henry VIII feel quite at home. "Everything was being done on a scale that made the *Rumours* tour look like a poor man's road trip," wrote Carol Ann, who would visit Lindsey during the rehearsals and look on in wonder at the extravagance required to make day-to-day living bearable for the band. There was a Japanese masseuse; a daily banquet that was largely ignored, as always (Stevie had recently had root canal treatment anyway); the crew expanded, equipment was updated and two black tents were added to the stage plot. Every night, one would be erected on either side of the stage. One contained Stevie's many wardrobe changes, while both would contain plenty of blow for the band to enjoy without even having to leave the stage during the concert. The rehearsal site itself was so large, Christine could easily cycle around the room on her bike, her dog chasing after her, without even coming close to crashing into anything.

Meanwhile, Lindsey noodled on his guitar, and Stevie rushed around in high heels and leg warmers, returning to the safety of her ubiquitous gaggle of girlfriends whenever she had the chance, even during songs. That support network was more vital than ever as rehearsals were tough, most of the Mac were reluctant to be there at all, and there was now a new level of competition for Stevie to cope with. Her powerful, 'white witch' stage persona that reliably grabbed the spotlight on stage now had a rival in the shape of a dark prince: the new-look Lindsey Buckingham, who, with the help of his eyeliner, darkened, angry brows and sharpened cheekbones (thanks to a little contouring make-up) now looked "completely Satanic", according to Carol Ann Harris. He was giving Stevie a run for her money, and he'd certainly get plenty of attention during the *Tusk* tour, often for all the wrong reasons. That "Satanic" look was, by accident or design, reflecting his inner demons, and those demons were planning to accompany him live on stage, with some disastrous results.

It was no secret to the world that Fleetwood Mac had had their problems, but Stevie now insisted in interviews that their troubles were in the past, assuring journalists with a smile that "Fleetwood Mac is the rock in my life. We realised we could come through anything. The band is strong." And they were, but that didn't mean that, away from the public gaze, the Fleetwood Mac family was even close to functioning healthily. At least people were now talking less about the band's personal relationships and more about the music. For now.

The time spent making *Tusk* marked the longest the band had ever been in the studio, and similarly the *Tusk* tour would be an epic odyssey, a year on the road taking in 113 shows between October 26, 1979 (at the Pocatello Mini Dome, Idaho) and September 1, 1980 at the magnificent Hollywood Bowl, taking in the rest of the States, Japan, Oceania and Europe along the way. The *Tusk* tour saw Fleetwood Mac at the peak of their excess, setting a new level of rock star extravagance. There were limos for everyone – stage crew included – and commercial flights were abandoned altogether in favour of well-stocked private airliners. This wasn't unusual rock'n'roll behaviour once an act reached a certain level. Led Zeppelin had hired the flying "shag-carpeted gin palace" that was known as the Starship, after all. It was simply practical, there was less waiting around and any chances of offending anyone or getting arrested were minimised. One of the planes chartered by Fleetwood Mac was

Caesar's Palace's 'Chariot', a private Boeing 707 which was previously a passenger jet, and had also last been used by the Zep themselves a year earlier, as the Starship had been permanently grounded due to engine trouble. Caesar's Chariot was fitted with comfortable, overstuffed seating, there was a bar (obviously) and private rooms. There was also, famously, a Hammond organ. All the essentials, basically. It would cost $2,500 per day to hire the plane.

Mick Fleetwood has always maintained that this was the tour that nearly "killed the band" – and it would notably be the final tour with the profligate Fleetwood himself as manager – but they were going out in style if that was the case. Every whim was met, the masseuse was always on hand, the champagne and cocaine were already staples – it's almost pointless even mentioning them now. No one was going to be suffering from substance withdrawal and, thanks no doubt to the excess of many lovely things, the dressing rooms post-show were always crammed with people and record executives (mostly people too), including Danny Goldberg and Paul Fishkin, co-owners of new label Modern Records. Modern had recently signed Stevie exclusively as a solo artist. Stevie and Paul had also spent some time together romantically (in fact Goldberg has asserted that Stevie had dumped Fishkin for Fleetwood). He was "sweet and wonderful and understands [the lifestyle] as well as anyone," Stevie mused in an interview with *People*, although she would add, perhaps by way of warning, "I'm not interested in playing around but I do get terribly lonely on the road . . ."

Fishkin first met Stevie Nicks at a Warners Bros convention in 1976 where, on the first night of the event, she was going to play the *Rumours* album to the company for the first time. "She was sitting with George Harrison and I was introduced to her," remembered Fishkin. "I hardly knew who she was, she wasn't a 'star' yet." Paul would make a lasting impression on Stevie by being in the right place at the right time that night, rescuing her from a potential dousing from over-excited Warners executives. Her new hero.

"The guys were about to throw her in the pool," Fishkin told Robert

Llewellyn in his 'Carpool' series of interviews. "They were having a big party for the opening night of the convention, and she turned to me and said, 'I'm terrified of water'. So I was the big protector, I saved her." As a reward, Stevie invited Fishkin up to her suite with a handful of other executives – this isn't going where you think it is – and played them the album. "We were the first ones to hear it, it was before she'd played it at the convention. I remember dancing around, over the beds, it was crazy, an incredible moment." The pair would remain friends after this memorable first meeting, and Modern Records was formed in 1978 essentially *for* Stevie's solo career, the distribution deal being firmed up with Atlantic in June 1979. While much of the real work would go on hold as Stevie "completed her recording and touring obligations to Fleetwood Mac", by the time she was ready, everything would be in place. This was a development that Stevie would be keeping from Mick Fleetwood for the time being, believing that the news might not be well-received. Fleetwood Mac required commitment, and Mick was already panicking that the band members were pulling away from each other. His concerns were hardly allayed when, at the LA press conference for the tour, the majority of journalists wanted to know whether Stevie was leaving, or whether the band were likely to break up. Was this their final hoorah? This may have been one of the reasons Mick was throwing money at everyone and everything to make sure they had the best time they could possibly have.

One story from this tour that would go down in history, much to Stevie's considerable irritation, was the tale that Stevie and Christine demanded their hotel rooms be painted in their favourite pastel colours in advance of their arrival – pink, in Stevie's case. This has been heartily refuted by Ms Nicks. "I never had to have a pink room! I'm not even a pink person," she retorted. Not denying any other pastel colours there, one notes.

Still, even if it was true, it's almost possible to see some kind of rock star logic in having a thread of continuity when travelling from city to city, hotel room to hotel room, for an entire year. (Yes vocalist Jon Anderson, for example, required his own teepee to be erected in every dressing room for this same reason.) But Stevie insisted to *The Guardian*'s Tim Jonze that "all I wanted, and this is what I got, was the presidential suite at hotels. We were elegant people and we wanted a place to sleep after the show that was beautiful . . . From the first day I joined Fleetwood Mac, we got a first class ticket and a limousine picked us up. So it's their fault that I'm like this!" If there was just one presidential suite available, Stevie and Christine would flip a coin. The boys in the band didn't get a look in, although it's fair to say they probably weren't roughing it either. That said, what with Stevie knowing she would be away for so long, there was a little tightening of the purse strings (whether that was the intention or not) when she sold her fabulous Hollywood home – dubbed 'Fantasyland' by frequent visitors – in favour of a smaller beachfront condo.

That aside, everything else was getting bigger and bigger on Planet Mac and, with Mick Fleetwood acting as bursar, any hopes of breaking even had gone straight out of the window. But while the tour would not be a financial success, the *Tusk* shows were staggering to witness, so huge and impressive that, once the band had hit the stage, they were rendered as small as "toys, puppets," observed *NME*'s Richard Gabel. This wouldn't mean they or their performances were in any way lost; there was something about Fleetwood Mac that meant they were perfectly at home in vast venues. "The space gives them grandeur, since they command it with amplification and volume. They must be Gods," Gabel breathlessly concludes. But the difference between the sometimes playful backstage Stevie, dancing about with a plastic brush sticking out of her hair, and the poised rock queen on stage, was stark. The audience was rapt as Stevie told her stories through song, the energy building until it appeared almost as if she was speaking in tongues, particularly in 'Sisters Of The Moon', her mysterious chanting and gibberish were "like soothsayer's words", as the always entranced Mick Fleetwood remembers it.

'Rhiannon' was as dramatic and spell-binding as ever, even casting a spell over its own creator, it would seem. On this tour, Stevie seemed transfigured by the energy she'd conjure up in the form of Rhiannon, a form so strong and powerful it would apparently be champing at the bit to take her over all through the show, to "carry me off". Stevie would show *Rolling Stone's* Daisann McLane photographic evidence of her temporary transfigurations. "This is Rhiannon, without a doubt," she said, handing over a photograph of herself performing the song – a picture that apparently looked nothing like her. "You see, it turns." She then pulled out another photograph, this time one of herself with Lindsey onstage. "This is the killer. The pale shadow of Dragon Boy, always behind me, always behind me." McLane observed that she was speaking "almost to herself, in a hoarse whisper" at this point. "Carried off" indeed. So Lindsey was now Dragon Boy. The 'dragon' in 'Gold Dust Woman' represented anger, so that would certainly make sense.

Lindsey Buckingham's fearsome new look was pulling focus, but so was the way he was performing his songs, screaming with fury, sending the crowd wild. Stevie had her own characters onstage, but Lindsey's stronger persona seemed to have an emboldening effect – he would charge towards the front of the stage, his solos infused with new energy and his behaviour becoming . . . well, a little insane. There was now a war onstage between the white witch and the prince of darkness. His high levels of tension reflected the fact that he was being held responsible for the band's new direction on *Tusk,* and the mixed reaction it garnered. The passing of Lindsey's father, Morris Buckingham, only added to Lindsey's disordered state.

The final shows of the decade took place on home turf at San Francisco's Cow Palace, close to Morris Buckingham's old coffee plant where, back in the day, Buckingham senior had allowed Stevie and Lindsey to work on their songs through the night. Stevie would dedicate the final show to Morris. Just over a week earlier, on December 5, 1979, Stevie's treasured 'Sara', the album's second single, was released, peaking at number seven in the US charts. Given the circumstances and the changes the band members had undergone, even since the conception of the song, it was often difficult and emotional for Stevie to sing it live. It was as if she was re-opening those wounds again and again, and soon she would have to take a hiatus from singing 'Sara' onstage until a little more time had passed.*

The band spent Christmas with their loved ones (i.e. not each other), reconvening in February 1980 for their first shows of the new decade that took place in Japan before they moved on to Australia. While the band were technically "off" during January 1980, work was already underway for *Bella Donna,* Stevie's debut solo album, and it was time to let Mick Fleetwood know about it. According to Fleetwood, the letter he received from Stevie was "full of portents, news and admonitions." She wasn't just telling him she had her own career to think about now, she was taking the opportunity to deliver some home truths and go into a bit of a paranoid stream of consciousness to boot, noting that "it is a fearful time. Things are becoming less exciting and more real." Stevie also expressed her fears regarding what was happening politically; the diplomatic crisis between the US and Iran was at its height, with 52 American hostages held at the US Embassy in Tehran; the Soviet army was moving into Afghanistan . . . and, Mick recalls, Stevie informed him "that I was a cheap bastard, so she was sending the girls in our office an extra $250". The letter was signed 'Katherine DeLongpré'†, one of her many pseudonyms and characters ('Lily' being another). These names were masks to

* 'Sara' would be at the centre of further consternation, albeit for different reasons, the following year. A certain Carol Hinton of Rockford, Michigan, attempted to sue Nicks for plagiarism, claiming she had sent a song called 'Sara' to Warner Bros in the latter part of 1978.The lyrics bore some similarities – both apparently sharing the line "drowning in the sea of love" – but Stevie proved she had recorded her demo in July 1978, some months earlier than Hinton's supposed submission. Eventually Hinton dropped the suit, accepting Nicks had not plagiarised her work. Regarding the ordeal, Stevie told *Rolling Stone* in 1981: "I never said she didn't write the words she wrote. Just don't tell me I didn't write the words I wrote. Most people think the other party will settle out of court, but she picked the wrong songwriter. To call me a thief about my first love, my songs, that's going too far." It was "just a farce", Mick Fleetwood observed.

† Katherine de Longpré was a 17th-century saint known for her largesse; her disposition is likely to have resonated with Stevie, who is known to be generous. It's worth noting that Orange Grove, where Stevie and Lindsey once lived, joined Delongpre Avenue in Hollywood; this may have been when the name first caught her attention.

hide behind, useful when putting your feelings in writing, should the letter ever fall into the wrong hands.

*

"One more time, on the plane. Lindsey is his usual asshole self. I am coming to the conclusion that Lindsey and I are at an end. So sad to see good love go bad . . . Seattle. Worried about Christine. Wishing some spiritual guidance would come from somewhere. Where are the crystal visions when I need them?" An extract of Stevie's journal from the time of the Tusk *tour.*

"Tragedy and music make for great writing," Stevie would say, in reference to her letter-writing and feverish journal-keeping. She will have had plenty to get out of her system once the tour had resumed, because, by March 1980, Lindsey's rage was spilling over like molten lava. After touring the US and Japan, Fleetwood Mac hit Australia. They greedily fell upon every substance they could possibly inhale, having just arrived from Japan where recreational resources were somewhat limited. This post-withdrawal binge, plus the simple reality of having to spend every day with each other, was a combination that would affect both Lindsey and Stevie in different ways, neither of them positive. The situation was a ticking time-bomb, and by the time they were to play Melbourne's Festival Hall on 11 March, Lindsey was ready to explode. The way his behaviour was turning was almost as if he was possessed by something mischievous and malevolent and, unsurprisingly, he was targeting Stevie. It was hard enough having to be in the same room or on the same flight as "someone who hates you" but Lindsey's fury was now starting to bleed into the show.

The band, coked up and looking elegantly wasted, hit the stage, greeted by the usual roars. While it was not unusual to see Lindsey glaring at Stevie during her songs, Lindsey, who had apparently been drinking heavily, stepped up his hostility, determined to upstage her. At one point he lay down on his back and continued to play, writhing about and grinning up at an enraged Stevie as she screeched at him for ruining 'Rhiannon'. Despite Stevie standing over him yelling, Lindsey remained exactly where he was for three songs. But this wouldn't be the worst of his actions that night. As Stevie delicately placed her glittering shawl over her head and the opening beats to 'Sisters Of The Moon' kicked in, with an evil glint in his eye, Lindsey grabbed one of Stevie's spare shawls from the wings and whirled around, lampooning her performance.

"Stevie made it through the song and abruptly walked off stage and didn't return," wrote Carol Ann. "The show was over. Not one band member talked to Lindsey backstage, but he didn't seem to care." On top of the prodigious amount of drinking Lindsey had been doing, he had also been suffering from fits and had been prescribed Dilantin, an anti-epileptic drug which controlled his seizures. Taking both in combination was not recommended. Aware that not just Stevie, but the entire band and crew were unhappy with him, Lindsey attempted to control his runaway behaviour for the next few shows. Stevie must have been dreading what he was going to do next, but he played well and kept himself to himself.

But just as Fleetwood Mac were allowing themselves to relax a little, confident that the latest storm had passed, on 20 March – the 59th show on the tour at the Athletic Park in Wellington, New Zealand – Lindsey went completely out of control. Pulling his jacket over his head and twirling around in a repetition of his cruel send-up of Stevie's dancing, this time, during 'Rhiannon', Lindsey proceeded to ruin the night and put his own position in jeopardy by resorting to behaviour that would put his previous sarcastic imitations in the shade.

"I thought, 'Well, that's not working for me,' but I didn't do anything," Stevie would add in a 2013 interview with the *Daily Mail*'s Adrian Deevoy. "This must have infuriated him, because he came over and kicked me. I'd never had anyone be physical with me in my life. Then he picked up a black Les Paul guitar and he just frisbee'd it at me. He missed, I ducked – but he could have killed me." The kicking continued as Stevie desperately soldiered on. And all in front of 60,000 traumatised fans.

Carol Ann Harris was watching, horrified, from the wings. "The kick[s] seemed to stun her. Stevie frantically tried to stay away from his steel-toed cowboy boots and the whole show fell apart." Lindsey's own memory of this night is hazy, but for everyone else, it was hard to forget. "I'm not sure that happened," Buckingham told *The Guardian*'s Tim Jonze in later years. "Oh, it happened, all right," confirmed Christine McVie.

Everyone was "freaked out", as Fleetwood recalls and there would be no encore. The crowd yelled for more but their heroes would not return, all of them now running "at breakneck speed back to the dressing room to see who could kill [Lindsey] first", remembers Stevie. Bodyguards waded in to attempt to prevent the inevitable. Stevie was flying towards Lindsey, who was "slumped miserably on a bench", as Fleetwood puts it, but Christine was faster. Stevie has often credited the tough, practical Christine for absorbing much of the ugly side of being on the road with the Mac, and she would certainly be doing that tonight. Lindsey rose as an irate, tight-lipped McVie charged towards him, and before he could say anything she had struck him hard across the face. Then she threw her drink at him just to underscore the point. "Don't you ever do this to the band again," she hissed before storming out to cool off.

"I think he's the only person I ever, ever slapped," Christine told *Rolling Stone* in later years. "I just didn't think it was the way to treat a paying audience, aside from making a mockery of Stevie like that. Yes, she cried. She cried a lot." The tour would continue but there was serious discussion behind the scenes of sacking Buckingham and replacing him with their old friend Eric Clapton, a fellow survivor of the British blues wars of the sixties.

Lindsey himself looks back on those shows philosophically, admitting that the band's temptation to let him go was "well-founded", and that he had behaved unprofessionally. "Stevie and I could never quite find each other after *Tusk*," said Lindsey in later years, a note of therapy-speak creeping through. (Although who wouldn't need therapy after years in Fleetwood Mac?) Their broken relationship had been like a marriage in Lindsey's eyes, and one within which he had the upper hand. Lindsey didn't react well to not getting his own way, although his attitude would change once he had a family in later years. But at this point in the story, the torture of having lost Stevie but never being able to really move on was working its way out in all sorts of ways that were rarely constructive.

"You have to understand that this was someone I met when I was 16," explained in an interview with *Mojo Magazine*'s Phil Sutcliffe in 2003. "I was completely devastated when she took off. And yet, trying to rise above that professionally, I produced hits for her, I had to do a lot of things for her that I really didn't want to do. If I kicked her onstage, that was . . . something coming through the veneer. There has been a lot of darkness." The word "darkness" has come up more than once in connection to the ongoing saga of Stevie and Lindsey. On being asked if she would ever get back together with Lindsey, Stevie once dismissed the idea, insisting she would never want to go back to "that darkness".

This extensive tour kept barrelling along, no matter how hurt, tired or trapped the members of the group felt, and the amount of drugs needed to dull the pain would cause problems in all sorts of ways, not least because, thanks to their growing and not unfounded reputation as one of the world's most hedonistic bands, once they'd hit Europe in May, they were stopped by customs officers. After Stevie and Christine were subjected to humiliating body-searches, tour manager John Courage put his foot down and changed their transport plans. For the European leg of the *Tusk* tour, they would be travelling by private train through Germany and into France and Holland. This was all very well, and the train itself was luxurious and comfortable, but the Mac rather went off it when they realised that the lounge car of their train, with its gold light fittings, wooden interiors and velvet drapes, had once belonged to Adolf Hitler, and it came complete with an elderly attendant who had served the Führer himself. They all stayed in their own sleeping quarters after discovering that sinister little piece of living history.

A stop-off in Switzerland was eventful, according to the memory of the late Montreux Jazz Festival boss Claude Nobs. The week Fleetwood Mac descended on the lake-side town, the weather was gloriously warm, so it was with some concern that hotel staff were informed of smoke rising from the chimney of, no doubt, the presidential suite after the band had checked in to their glamorous new digs. It may have been Switzerland, but it was hardly the right weather for getting a blazing fire going in the hearth. It wasn't difficult to tell whose room it was coming from, for those on the inside track. Stevie Nicks loved a good fire (a safe one, anyway), and it was quite normal for her to have fires burning in every room in the house, no matter what the weather was like outside. She'd crank up the air conditioning if she had to, but the dancing flames inspired her and created the right atmosphere for songwriting. (Her mother would despair of her fuel bills, but Stevie didn't care.)

Meanwhile, a member of the hotel staff was sent up to the room to ensure all was well, but after knocking on the locked door, there was no response. There was simply an eccentric fire-loving superstar inside who was spending some quality time with her stash of coke, and did not wish to be disturbed, but the porter didn't realise that. As black smoke continued to billow from the chimney, the fire brigade was soon called and, legend has it, as the door of the room was broken down, Stevie immediately threw the mountain of coke straight onto the fire in a panic, the powder igniting in a bright blue flash.

Drugs were one thing on the road, but sex was another. Stevie has, to Christine McVie's own slight bewilderment, claimed that both women in the band were like "rock'n'roll nuns". This might sound unlikely, but the point she so often makes on this subject is that the double standards in the music industry were off the charts – and it was all the more noticeable when you were in a mixed-gender band. The clichéd image of a rock star was generally that of a promiscuous, hedonistic male. That was "the romantic idea", Stevie grumbled to *The Guardian*'s Tim Jonze. But what about female rock stars? Why was the same behaviour seen in such a completely different way? Even now, female artists who live in exactly the same way as male rock stars are regarded with disapproval, while the men are revered all the more. But the other reason it was difficult for Christine and Stevie to have male companions with them on tour was because the situation was far from straight-forward; you had two estranged couples in one band – three if you count Stevie and Mick. "[Boyfriends] would just get stomped on," says Stevie. "For me to have a guy out on the road with us, and have Lindsey glaring at him the whole time? Or for Christine to have a guy and John flip him off?"

The European shows were as huge as the American extravaganzas. On the first day of June, the Mac played an outdoor show at Munich's Olympic Horse Riding Stadium, supported by Bob Marley & the Wailers in front of a wildly excited crowd. But the warmth and affection the band had had for fans during the *Rumours* tour had transformed, in many cases, into impatience and fatigue, sentiments neatly encapsulated by the badges Ken Caillat had made for everyone for the *Tusk* tour. The buttons proclaimed the words: Tell Your Story Walkin', as if to say "move along, I've no time for you, whatever you have to say, say it on your way out". It was a weary example of the dark, cynical humour needed to get everyone through each day. Richard Dashut, so frequently the glue in the Fleetwood Mac family, had decided to leave and it felt as if things were falling apart for good.

The *Tusk* tour concluded at the Hollywood Bowl on 1 September 1980. Despite being so close to their respective homes, John Courage insisted the band stayed at L'Ermitage hotel in Beverly Hills, banning them all from going to their own homes. He needed them on the spot, and gathering them together for the show once they'd dispersed would be like herding cats. The concert was, naturally, a huge success; all of their Hollywood friends turned out for them, and the after-tour party was as Saturnalian as ever. However, the fact remained that the tour had barely broken even despite the hard graft and massive, sold-out shows. Mick Fleetwood had just been trying to keep everybody happy, but his thriftless attitude meant that no one had actually made any money. Three weeks after the end of the *Tusk* tour, a meeting would be held at Mick's home to discuss it. But this was far from just a band meeting. The respective Macs were accompanied by their lawyers. Mick tried to defend himself – and his 10 per cent – but Stevie had a new manager of her own, the super-sharp Irving Azoff (who also managed the Eagles) and he was, "ruthless as he took charge of the inquisition", Carol Ann Harris remembers in *Storms*. "He told Mick there would be no in-house managing of his new client, Ms Nicks [and] he made it clear that Mick had done a horrific job of looking out for the band's best interests over the past two years."

The band, not surprisingly, "felt we deserved a break," Christine said. "And we took that break. We took a *long* break." A break from each other, yes, but side projects beckoned. Everyone was desperately in need of a fresh creative outlet, and Stevie for one would be working harder than ever. The seed of her solo career had been tended in the dark for long enough. It was time for it to bud.

PART III

Bella Donna

Chapter 15

By the end of the *Tusk* tour, Stevie Nicks was, by her own admission, in terrible shape."I was so tired and sung out. I was so 'Landslide-ed' out and so 'Rhiannon-ed' out that I thought if I had to do that set one more time I was going to go nuts," she told Vicky Greenleaf and Stan Hyman for *Rock* in 1983. Paul Fishkin and Stevie had already started Modern, a record company that would be "special", with "high principles", as she put it. Stevie's romance with the dark-haired, rakish Fishkin – "the one man in my life who was truly good" – had foundered but their friendship and professional collaboration would continue and, with the utmost belief in Stevie and her work, he and co-conspirator Danny Goldberg "set the Ferris wheel in motion".

While Stevie knew Fleetwood Mac wouldn't feel comfortable with the development, she – and her Modern Records cohorts – felt strongly that it was the right thing to do, and at the perfect time. One of the reasons Mick Fleetwood insisted *Tusk* should be a double album was so the writers of the band had room to stretch; Mick was anxious they would be tempted to move on if they weren't given a little more space. Now he felt his fears had become a self-fulfilling prophecy. Everyone in the band was worried, 'angry', even, when Stevie told them her news. They believed it would harm Fleetwood Mac whether Nicks was successful in her venture or not.

Naturally Stevie herself was terrified of tanking, but if she wasn't allowed to express her creativity more fully, she risked sinking into a serious depression. Stevie had always felt like "the baby sister, the one that is left out. That's what I used to get upset about. They were not even close to using my full potential." Her bandmates questioned her decision, but she simply explained she was looking for "an outlet for my songs," and reassured them that she did not want to leave.

Nicks was exhilarated by the prospect of finally being able to expand her ideas rather than having to limit them, shelve them or watch them being taken apart and rearranged for Fleetwood Mac; she'd be the focus in the studio and she'd also be free to explore the influences that were close to her heart and in her bones, like country music. But a solo career would also relaunch Stevie as a different kind of "brand". Up until now she had been seen as just another dimension of Fleetwood Mac, and a rather floaty, flaky one at that.

Paul Fishkin and Danny Goldberg (also "besotted" with Stevie, albeit silently so) saw her in a different context, and were amazed that she had such little clout in the Fleetwood Mac infrastructure. Fishkin believed her to be one of the "hottest female artists" around and knew she could easily be taken seriously as a solid rock singer if she was given the opportunity. "She was a rocker, her whole thing was Janis Joplin," Fishkin reminds us. This was one of the most exciting moments in Stevie's life so far – being able to step away from the Mac and think, "What do I want to do next?" She might have felt like the White Queen on the chess board, being moved around by the hands of fate before, but Stevie was finally in charge. The next step was finding the right people to have around her in order to make her new project the best it could be.

Stevie had been writing and working on demos throughout the *Tusk* tour, and had a sketch in her head of what she wanted for her new album. What Stevie really wanted was for *Bella Donna* to be just like a Tom Petty record. Stevie had been a fan of Tom Petty & the Heartbreakers ever since she'd heard their eponymous debut album. It was in November 1976, while Fleetwood Mac were still working on *Rumours*, and Tom's "Florida swamp-dog voice", Mike Campbell's guitar and Benmont Tench's keyboards had Stevie smitten. "Tom had the same influences we had – the Byrds, Neil Young, Crosby, Stills and Nash – but he dropped in lots of serious old blues," Stevie told *Rolling Stone* in 2010. "And Tom is such a great singer and so charismatic onstage. I became such a fan that if I hadn't been in a band myself, I would have joined that one."

Stevie desperately wanted Tom Petty to produce *Bella Donna,* or at the very least write her some material, and as she was surreptitiously working on her game-plan during the *Tusk* tour, she approached him with the idea. Stevie and Tom had plenty in common, but at first Petty could only see the differences – and he was somewhat dazzled by this "larger than life" star, a "Cecil B. DeMille movie" personified. "She was this absolutely stoned-gone huge fan," Petty recalled in an interview with Paul Zollo for the book *Conversations With Tom Petty*. "And it was her mission in life that I should write her a song. We [the Heartbreakers] didn't quite know whether to like Stevie or not, because we saw this big corporate rock band, Fleetwood Mac – which was wrong, they were actually artistic people – but in those days, nobody trusted that sort of thing and we kept thinking, 'What does she want from us?'" Benmont Tench was also ambivalent at first:

"I had seen Fleetwood Mac play, and with Stevie I just didn't get it," he told *Classic Rock*'s Bill deMain. "She could sing, oh hell yes. But I didn't know what was going on with the top hat and the twirling and the witchy stuff. But then I bought the single to 'Go Your Own Way' and flipped it over, and there's 'Silver Springs'. Good Lord, what a song. The second I heard that, I went: 'Now I get it. That's Stevie. She's not faking. She's for real. She's not a poser in the least. She's a creative perpetual-motion machine. This is somebody I'd really love to play music with.'"

Tom Petty would also be turned around: he already loved Stevie's singing voice, and eventually agreed to produce a song for her. Stevie was impressed by him from the off. "He was pretty much what I expected. There's not a fake bone in his body," she said. But Tom wasn't used to working with "girls", not least one with a Hollywood entourage – and he'd definitely never worked with anyone like Stevie Nicks. "It was a completely different world from anything I had seen. She was very sweet and we liked her," Petty told *American Songwriter*. "But she had a whole different work ethic than we had, and there were a lot of hangers-on."

After working on one track, Tom gently informed Stevie that he would be too busy to help her out with the production of the album. What he could do, on the other hand, was put Stevie in touch with Jimmy Iovine, who had produced Petty – as well as Patti Smith, John Lennon and Bruce Springsteen – and would be a good foil for Stevie in the studio. Tom and Stevie would soon become close themselves, of course. "She would come to my house and just hang out and play records. We'd sit around and play the guitar and sing . . ." This would be the beginning of a lasting and creative friendship. And yes, Stevie would eventually get that song from Petty. She would also nab the Heartbreakers, who would play on the album themselves, amongst a roll-call of top LA session musicians and, of course, "the girls" – Sharon Celani and Lori Perry – Stevie's backing singers. This would be their debut recording together, and Stevie had been sending them demo tapes so they could practice the songs wherever they happened to be. They were all dedicated to making the new sound that Stevie craved for her album, that of a female "Commodores", as Stevie put it. She had brought Sharon with her on the *Tusk* tour as her dresser to get her accustomed to life on the road and they had all remained in close contact with each other as the plans for *Bella Donna* unfolded. Everything had long been in preparation and nothing was happening by accident. But Stevie was also nervous about going into the studio alone – Sharon and Lori gave her confidence and created a buffer, which was all the more necessary when Stevie discovered that the tough, serious-minded Jimmy Iovine would not tolerate the usual Fleetwood Mac 'party' atmosphere during sessions, and friends were largely banned from the studio.

Stevie would have to alter her whole way of life if she was going to work with Iovine, and the process would see her evolving emotionally, a metamorphosis Stevie herself would welcome. She was already 33, but after having been cosseted and indulged for so long, she realised there was so much more to life when you make your own decisions and fend for yourself. Stevie was fed up of being treated like a child, but if she wanted that to change, then *she'd* have to change first. No one had expected it of her before. She was often vulnerable, childlike, a princess, a star whose every whim was met, a romantic who played with make-up and dressing up boxes, was fascinated by children's stories and had, as every rock star did, everything done for her. Stevie had also shied away from being a "women's libertarian", she found it easier to deal with men in the music business with wide-eyed softness and a girlish smile.* But now someone demanded maturity from her, and Stevie rose to it, realising that being older was actually "wonderful", she told music writer Liz Derringer. "You see things clearer. You don't have to get so crazy. You're a woman, not a child. You're the only one who's here and no one is going to save you. My mom has been telling me that for years. And I call her sometimes and she'll say, 'I wish you'd let somebody take some of this pressure off your little bitty shoulders for a moment, Stevie.' And that's what I did. I gave it to Jimmy. I said, 'Here it is, here's the pressure, here's my weird life, here's how crazy it is. Now figure out how to make this album.'"

Stevie and Jimmy arranged to work together after being introduced by Tom Petty towards the end of the *Tusk* tour, but Jimmy Iovine would need some convincing. Stevie was excited to meet him, but he made it clear that she would have to knuckle down and "be a soldier". If she wasn't prepared to do that, they simply would not be working with each other. Iovine believed Stevie had probably been spoiled in Fleetwood Mac, protected like a "baby egg". He warned her that, if they were to assemble a crack team of session musicians around her, Stevie would have to rise to it and then some. "It's not a part-time job," he insisted. "You can't trick the band, they have to believe it. If they feel like this is a hobby of yours, they're going to treat it like a hobby. If that's what you want to do, I'm not interested." She had much to prove – not just to her audience, but to him. Jimmy required commitment from her, and the excesses she was used to in the studio would not be tolerated. The languor of Los Angeles, reflected in the months, years even, one could spend in a California studio while the weed was passed along the line and also-rans

* Stevie has since confirmed that she is and always has been a feminist.

lurked, waiting for crumbs, was nowhere to be seen. Stevie had a fast-talking young New York producer on her hands with no patience for pampered rock princes and princesses. There was work to be done.

"He said, 'I know you're used to being the midnight cat queen that comes in whenever you feel like it and completely wreck the studio . . . this is not how you are going to do this album," Nicks told ABC in 1981. "'For a start, you only have three months, and in the second place, I don't want to waste my time with a cartoon.' I just thought, 'Wow, I guess he doesn't think I'm that big of a deal, he's threatening to leave and we haven't even started the album yet!'"

This was the first time anyone had spoken to Stevie Nicks quite so directly, and it shocked her into getting focused. After taking a deep breath, she quietly assured Jimmy that this was all she had wanted to do since she'd started writing songs. She was looking forward to recording in a different, more immediate way anyway, and was aiming for more of a live feel after the painstaking production of *Tusk*. That said, she was also "scared to death, because I didn't know whether I was able to conform to this new disciplinary way of life . . ." But Jimmy Iovine would be the perfect person to guide her through and get the album cut in time, because, by the time they started work, she really did only have three months – not a long time in Fleetwood Mac's world. Admittedly, Stevie had plenty of work prepared in demo form, but Iovine had to finish work on Tom Petty's latest album *Hard Promises* before he could start working with Stevie, while Fleetwood Mac had recording sessions booked for their next album, *Mirage,* in Spring 1981 – and, as Stevie herself has said, when Fleetwood Mac tell you they need you to be somewhere, you go. Not that that's a situation many of us will have been in.

Stevie would hardly be languishing as she waited the long six months until her sessions could get underway, however. While waiting for Iovine, inspired by his hardline work ethic, she rented a house for her and the girls to move into and practise together every night. The Heartbreakers' Benmont Tench, who would be credited as the album's musical director, would visit and play the grand piano as they worked through the songs,

Lindsey Buckingham and Stevie performing onstage during the often nightmarish *Tusk* tour in 1979. Stevie and Lindsey's personal war raged both on and off stage. RICHARD E. AARON/REDFERNS

Stevie raises her wings and prepares to take flight with Fleetwood Mac. She quickly found having winged, diaphanous costumes gave her small frame greater physical presence onstage. RICHARD E. AARON/REDFERNS

Stevie and Mick Fleetwood (not pictured) join former Fleetwood Mac guitarist Bob Welch for the star-studded California Jam 2 at Ontario, California, March 18, 1978 NEAL PRESTON/CORBIS

Fleetwood Mac pose for photographers backstage at the 5th American Music Awards held at the Santa Monica Civic Auditorium on January 16, 1978 in Santa Monica, California, where they were honoured for their album *Rumours*. MICHAEL OCHS ARCHIVES/GETTY IMAGES

Fleetwood Mac and their road manager John Courage pose with promoter Bill Graham before hitting the stage for the *Day On The Green* concert in Oakland, California, hosted by Graham himself, April 26, 1976. NEAL PRESTON/CORBIS

Stevie in hypnotic mode during a backstage shoot, 1985, Los Angeles, California. Some say her intense gaze was largely down to being extremely short-sighted. Either way, the camera loves it. DONALDSON COLLECTION/MICHAEL OCHS ARCHIVES/GETTY IMAGES

Stevie and best friend Robin Snyder Anderson.

Fleetwood Mac at the unveiling of their star on Hollywood's Walk of Fame, Hollywood Boulevard, 1980. Somewhat comically, they'd had to wait inside the notoriously trashy lingerie store Frederick's of Hollywood before greeting the public. NEAL PRESTON/CORBIS

Stevie in contemplative mood on a carousel horse. Perhaps she'd have preferred the ghost train. NEAL PRESTON/CORBIS

Stevie and her beloved backing singers Sharon Celani and Lori Perry perform together onstage, during the *Bella Donna* tour, 1981. Sharon and Lori continue to sing with Stevie to this day NEAL PRESTON/CORBIS

Tom Petty and Stevie belt out 'Stop Dragging My Heart Around', their hit duet from *Bella Donna*. LYNN GOLDSMITH/CORBIS

Stevie would often use choreographers to create high concept pop videos that tapped into her love of ballet. NEAL PRESTON/CORBIS

Stevie was always deluged with bouquets of flowers from adoring fans at both Mac gigs and her solo shows. Here she is at the Rock N' Run benefit at UCLA, California. RICHARD E. AARON/REDFERNS

Stevie, Mick Fleetwood and Billy Burnette of Fleetwood Mac perform on stage, Ahoy, Rotterdam, June 14, 1988. PAUL BERGEN/REDFERNS

Stevie high-kicking in time like a rock'n'roll gypsy ballerina, and by the time October swung around and Stevie could finally sweep through the doors of LA's Studio 55 with Jimmy, "we were so ready to make that record. It just goes to show you what you can do if you want to." Still, while Jimmy was working with Tom and the weeks passed by, Stevie was starting to feel "very edgy . . . No one really knew where I was. I was also starting to feel very unimportant and very sorry for myself. I was ready to begin *Bella Donna* and it seemed like it would just never happen." But it would – as would an almost inevitable romance between herself and Iovine.

Some of the songs Stevie had already written specifically for the album included 'How Still My Love', 'After The Glitter Fades' and the country-inflected 'Think About It', which Stevie had saved after it had been rejected from *Rumours*. "Stevie knew," wrote Ken Caillat, "that regardless of whether she was performing her songs with Fleetwood Mac or on her own, she would certainly be expanding herself as a solo artist. 'Fine with me if the band doesn't want my songs, I'll just do them by myself!'" And for those songs, their time had come. As Stevie herself had observed, too often she would present the band with a clutch of songs and they'd choose the ones she liked the least anyway.

Stevie would make copies of her demo cassettes for "everybody in my life, there must be thousands of them out [there]", so almost all of the songs she had earmarked for *Bella Donna* and beyond had been run past Fleetwood Mac first. There were just two exceptions. "They were welcome to anything I wrote," Stevie said in later years. "Except, I would say, 'Bella Donna' and 'Edge Of Seventeen'. 'Bella Donna' was written to be the meaningful word of this album, and I couldn't give them that." The title track, in some ways, would echo some of Stevie's sentiments as explored in 'Sisters Of The Moon' – a beautiful, exhausted woman who is on the verge of fading away, her "face becoming thin" as her life in the fast lane took its toll. This comes over in the various meanings of the song and album title itself: "bella donna" can be simply the Italian for "a beautiful woman", it's a term of endearment Stevie liked to use, but belladonna is also a baneful herb, known as deadly nightshade, a herb that can bring rest, sedation, and death. To be approached and handled with care.

"The woman was so tired, that the woman could have disappeared," said Stevie, referring to the lyrics in 'Bella Donna', although "the woman" – i.e. her – had made some progress over the past few years. This version of her own self was, at least, not dying as she'd feared during the *Fleetwood Mac* tour. Her armour was tougher now, but the fatigue and pressure was still great. "It was just too difficult for me. I never thought my face would become thin, I have a lot of trouble losing weight as it is, and I became thin and unhappy. All the wonderful things that money could buy could not change the way you feel inside when you're by yourself in a hotel room at night." But in 'Bella Donna', Stevie's words soothe her own psyche. "Ooh, my Bella Donna . . . Come in out of the darkness." "The title *[Bella Donna]* is about making a change based on the turmoil in my soul," she explained to *Rolling Stone*. "You get to a certain age where you want to slow down. The title song was a warning to myself and a question to others." She had answered her own prayer in 'Sisters Of The Moon' – her soul had become her own sister.

Once Stevie entered the studio during the warm, foggy October of 1980, part of what would make *Bella Donna* a success was the "family" of hand-picked musicians Stevie gathered around her. One was her old friend Waddy Wachtel. "She and I hadn't seen each other in years, but she wanted me there," he said in an interview with *Black Cat*. "I was thrilled. That's where I met Jimmy Iovine and [engineer] Shelly Yakus, a well as the basis of her first touring band, Benmont Tench and Roy Bittan." The multi-instrumentalist Bittan, also known as The Professor, was another redoubtable talent, a key member of Bruce Springsteen's E Street Band since 1974. All in all, over 20 musicians would play on Bella Donna. Their presence motivated Stevie to work even harder. It was all about "the right people in the right room together," she would tell *Bam Magazine*'s Blair Jackson shortly after the album's release. "You have to look good with Russ Kunkel, Waddy [Wachtel], Roy [Bittan] and Mike

[Campbell] of the Heartbreakers. With Tom Petty and Don Felder out there you're certainly not going to stand up there and be terrible. You're going to do the very best you can from the first time you sing. You don't want to look like a jerk in front of all these guys!"

Heartbreaker Benmont Tench would be the musical director on the album, and Tench recalled initially wondering what this solo project would mean for Fleetwood Mac: "It's a big deal the first time you do a solo record," Tench told *Classic Rock*'s Bill deMain in 2003. "And remember, back then, if somebody in a huge band made a solo record, your first thought was: 'Wow, is the band breaking up?' It was really unusual and risky to step away. But Stevie may have just gone: 'Look, I've got these songs, let's do a record without the family baggage there was around Fleetwood Mac." And it would be, as he put it, "song after song after great song," with the combination of Stevie's voice and those of her backing singers Lori and Sharon giving him goosebumps on the regular.

A feature of the album would be a duet with Don Henley on the ballad 'Leather And Lace', which the pair had recorded in demo form back when they were dating. A tender expression of foreplay – "give to me your leather, take from me my lace", 'Leather And Lace' seemingly reflects an erotic moment of courtly love. Written originally by Nicks for Waylon Jennings and Jessi Colter's duet album of the same name but never used, Stevie took it back for herself. This was a good decision – it would be the second single from *Bella Donna*, and a top ten hit in the *Billboard* Hot 100 on its release in October 1981. The star power of Don Henley didn't hurt, but as Henley himself was initially sceptical as to whether Stevie had the discipline to pull off her own solo album, or the strength to break away from Fleetwood Mac, so this duet – and its subsequent success – was satisfying to Stevie in more ways than one. With Jimmy's help, Stevie would soon be showing all of her doubters what she was capable of away from the Mac. "I have my own life," as she sings in 'Leather And Lace', "and I am stronger than you know."

To have Don on her album was "the greatest compliment anybody could give me", Stevie told *Rolling Stone*. "I have striven to live up to the songwriting of Don Henley and Glenn Frey, Jackson Browne and Joni Mitchell. I learned a long time ago that I'd have to work very hard to get even a blink from any of them, not as a woman or a performer, but as a writer." Stevie's male contemporaries were "pretty chauvinistic" and she would often struggle to be taken seriously. "They resent my success," she once said. "I see it in their eyes, 'How did this dingbat manage to get everything she wants?'" She just had to shrug it off and keep going, building up the bubble in which she lived to shield her from outside forces that threatened to distract her or upset her balance. There would be no drifting off or indulgence on these sessions. Stevie had to match Jimmy Iovine's rod of iron with the best performances she had in her. In fact, the intense, determined Iovine would get "the most incredible performances" out of everyone, even if he had to drive the musicians up the wall to get results.

"By doing that he made you feel like, 'OK, I'll show you,'" Stevie continued. "Once he was in the middle of the room while we were recording. He had his headphones on and all of a sudden he turned the beat of the song around. He [looked] at [drummer] Russ Kunkel and motioned him to change the tempo. And I'm watching Russ start to play what Jimmy's saying and I'm blown away. My eyes can't believe that they're seeing this guy [Iovine] bouncing around the room looking like some kind of little elf, telling all these famous guys what to do. And they're following his every move."

Iovine had the energy, the ideas and the power to get what he needed musically out of anyone, and for all of his hard-line tactics, Stevie had fun in the studio. It was a completely different way of working for her, and she was loving the space – physically and mentally – Jimmy had created for her album to take shape. They spent hours in the studio together, danced around to her songs, Stevie would tease him and Jimmy would allow his softer side to come through, encouraging her as he brought up the vocal on 'After The Glitter Fades'. "Does it sound good enough?" Stevie asked him after a take. "Sounds beautiful," he assured her. (That gentle side was relatively rare, however. Stevie would have to draw the line when it came to protecting her backing singers from his domineering manner. However her efforts would be swiftly curtailed with the bark: "Shut up and let me work with them.")

'After The Glitter Fades', from the Buckingham Nicks-era, is a poignant, observant ballad exploring the theme of the music industry and Hollywood as one who was once an outsider ('Well, I never thought I'd make it here in Hollywood . . .') and is now a "rock'n'roll woman" going through all of the extreme peaks and troughs that such a life entails. And is the heartache worth it? Always. "Even though the living is sometimes laced with lies, it's all right . . ."

Written before joining Fleetwood Mac, Stevie had predicted her own future – not just the success, but the listlessness – with this song. Just a few years after writing 'After The Glitter Fades', everything Stevie touched would indeed appear to turn to gold, and while sometimes dazed by drugs and exhaustion, "the dream keeps coming even when you forget to feel". But sometimes the dream would become a nightmare, and soon a tragedy would strike, leaving the music world, and beyond, stupefied, grief-stricken and paranoid. December 1980 would be a frightening time to be a rock star.

Chapter 16

BBC news report, December 8th 1980: Former Beatle John Lennon has been shot dead by an unknown gunman who opened fire outside the musician's New York apartment. The 40-year-old was shot several times as he entered the Dakota, his luxury apartment building on Manhattan's Upper West Side, opposite Central Park, at 2300 local time. He was rushed in a police car to St Luke's Roosevelt Hospital Center, where he died. His wife, Yoko Ono, who is understood to have witnessed the attack, was with him.

The death of John Lennon, assassinated by Mark Chapman on that cold December night, sent shockwaves throughout the entire world, but for those who had been close to him, the devastation was unimaginable. Lennon had been a close friend of Jimmy Iovine's and they worked together on the former Beatle's album *Menlove Avenue* (released posthumously in 1986). In the liner notes to her 1991 release *Timespace,* Stevie recalls Jimmy talking about Lennon "many times; about [their] incredible friendship, how John had taken Jimmy in and taught him to record. He was his teacher . . . and I was entranced because I could not imagine these two together." Jimmy adored John Lennon – to work with the man who had kick-started his love of music was a huge thrill, but getting to know him was, as Stevie described it, a "real-life fairytale" – although what they really had in common was a little more earthy.

The pair had been talking casually together during a flight when Lennon asked Iovine: "Why'd you get into music?" Iovine told *Esquire*'s Cal Fussman the story in 2013. "So I thought about it – okay, okay, I got to fucking answer this question right! – and said, 'John, I saw you guys on Ed Sullivan and it was incredible. My friends, everybody felt the same. And then I saw the Rolling Stones a little later and I thought, I want to be part of this . . .' He goes, 'That's cool.' And I said, 'John, why did you do it?' And he says, 'To get laid.' And I felt completely ridiculous, because that's why I did it!"

On the dark day that Stevie and Jimmy received the news of Lennon's murder, "a terrible sadness set in over the house." Jimmy was torn up with anger, misery and confusion, to the point that nothing Stevie could say would help. Stevie also had her own anxieties – as someone very much in the public eye, there was suddenly the feeling that it could have happened to her, or any of her famous friends. After realising Jimmy wanted to be alone with his grief, Stevie left for Phoenix, still her home and the home of her extended family. There her ailing uncle, also called John, was on his deathbed and she would sit by his bedside holding his frail hand. His son – another John – sitting on the floor nearby. As always, through heartache came inspiration; her uncle's failing health, and the loss of John Lennon, would jointly spark what would become Stevie Nicks' signature song – 'Edge Of Seventeen', opening with the memorable words: 'Just like the white-winged dove . . .'.

"The line: 'And the days go by like a strand in the wind . . .' that's how fast those days were going by during my uncle's illness, and it was so upsetting to me." She would visit frequently until, one day, "sometime right about sunset, he turned his head slightly to John, and then to me, and his hand slowly let go of mine. I did run out into the hallway, but no one was there . . . and the white-winged dove took flight . . ."* The white-winged dove, naturally, would represent a spirit set free, inner peace finally taking over . . . but Stevie would later realise the white-winged dove was originally indigenous to the Arizona desert, a pigeon-like bird often seen perching on cacti – so there was another resonant connection to home in this song.

* *Timespace* liner notes, 1991.

The title, 'Edge Of Seventeen', would come from Stevie's patchwork songwriting style and magpie-like ability to pluck jewels from the most everyday of sources. The name of this song was given to Stevie accidentally by Tom's first wife, Jane. Making conversation, Stevie asked Jane how old she was when she first met her husband. "She said, in her very Florida swamp accent, 'I met him at about the age of 17.' I thought she said, 'At the *edge* of 17.' I just went . . . 'Oh, Jane. This is fantastic.' And I just wrote it right down. I said, 'I'm going to use that in a song.' I was really good friends with her, so she dug it."

Stevie sat at the piano and poured her emotions into writing the song; she knew her uncle would have wanted her to use her mourning constructively and write, rather than sit around and cry. But despite its motivation, the song Stevie wrote would be musically far from melancholy. 'Edge Of Seventeen' was, as Waddy Wachtel observed, "magic, explosive". It had an electrifying sense of tension and strength. There was nothing wallowing about it, although there is a yearning quality in Stevie's vocal.

"I cried in the middle of the bridge," she told *Vox*'s Spencer Bright in 1992. "About 'the sea never expects it when it rains but the sea changes colour, but the sea does not change' . . . And so with the slow graceful flow of age, I went forth with an age-old desire to please. It was like, 'well we have to keep going now'. And I wanted that song to have all that energy of us going on." And that energy was written into the track, to the extent that every time Stevie sings it, she "goes back to that week. In my mind, my little time-space, I'm back in the house finding out that news . . . That's why I can sing 'Edge of Seventeen' just like I wrote it yesterday."

Recording 'Edge Of Seventeen' with her band made Stevie feel supported and she was humbled by the effort they poured into it, their "heart and soul". "It was like they held my elbows so I could stand really tall and sing that song for my uncle and for John Lennon . . . And understand that we were doing what both of them would have wanted us to do."

It would take two nights to get the track recorded and the plan for the arrangement was to muster a similar feel to The Police's 'Bring On The Night' – something they certainly achieved. The groove was suggested by drummer Russ Kunkel and it would be Waddy who played that now famous one-note riff; it was tough on the wrist but he refused to use an echo effect, playing every stroke himself. He had to admit that, when it came to this track, he "didn't know what the hell we were doing", although he "dug it", which is, of course, the main thing. Waddy hadn't heard 'Bring On The Night', but understood what was required musically and duly delivered. So it was with some horror when he later realised just how similar the intros to the two songs actually were. "I had the radio on, and on comes what sounds like 'Edge of Seventeen' – and all of a sudden, there's Sting's voice! I thought, 'We ripped them off completely!' I called Stevie that night and said, 'Listen to me, don't ever do that again!'"

'Edge Of Seventeen' was a showcase for Lori and Sharon's voices, lighter and airier than Stevie's rich, rasping contralto, like silver to gold, and, having practised so diligently with Stevie around the piano, they now instinctively came to know what harmonies were required and when. They also knew when Nicks was feeling insecure or lonely, and they would back her up when she wanted to stay late at the studio even if the rest of the band were desperate to sleep. Nicks is a workaholic and Sharon and Lori knew how much she needed them to stay on the same track as her, even when no one else would or could. Stevie needed constant reassurance, but that in turn would be rewarded with loyalty and generosity, to put it mildly. She required "praise" from those around her, as Danny Goldberg recalled, "but she put considerable energy into making [them] feel important" and on an equal footing. Stevie went to some effort – albeit in vain – to try to get her designer Margi Kent an in with *Vogue* magazine. In fact, she was so devoted to her friends that she had a clutch of 24-carat gold crescent moon pendants made, so she could distribute them among those she loved. Jimmy Iovine refused to wear one. According to Danny Goldberg, the highest compliment Stevie could pay would be to say you were "very Rhiannon" and the macho Jimmy wasn't too keen on that either. "I am not 'very Rhiannon' . . ." he protested. But back to

Sharon and Lori. Stevie explains: "They make my life easier. If I get tired and drop out, they pick it up for me. If I don't want to sing alone when I'm recording, then one of them just quietly sings along, smiles and acts happy. I have to have people around me that love to sing and work, otherwise I feel like Alice in Wonderland because I don't relate to anybody, and nobody relates to me.

"The girls stay [late at the studio], even though they also want to sleep, because they'll know that maybe I'll write that special song, or that special emotional thing we wanted to get on tape will be gotten for the rest of our lives – we all feel it's a 'rest of our lives' proposition that we're talking about here." And it would be.

Stevie would work as long as she had to, zoning out at the piano, almost channelling in order to produce the kind of songs that could match up to 'Rhiannon'. Helping her along were, Stevie believed, "spirits from the air", guiding presences that she would tune into instinctively, drawing strength and inspiration. Another more earthly form of assistance was on hand, thanks to the odd slug of brandy – something Jimmy Iovine wasn't especially approving of – and voice coach / right-hand woman Robin was generally nearby to administer a much needed toot of cocaine when Stevie needed to keep up the momentum, as we hear on a leaked recording (audible on YouTube) of Stevie working on a demo of the song 'Julia' with Shelly Yakus. It is the dead of night; Shelly is clearly exhausted but Stevie is determined to write on, huskily murmuring her lyrics – all "riding through the snow" and "horses that run like the wind" she plays the song on the piano, eventually puncturing the magical mood by announcing, "I want a toot! This is important!" to Robin. The song was driving her crazy, but she couldn't go to bed until she'd conquered it.

There is just one note causing her a problem, "it fucking haunts me!" she yells, before surmising that there is "somebody up there who wants me to do something with this fucking note . . . Stupid thing. I'm sorry, Shelly," she adds with a smile in her voice. "You have to understand that I'm neurotic. I'm not only neurotic but I'm schizophrenic too . . ." "Good combination . . ." replies Shelly, wryly. Her frustration is tangible; she'd written the song just the night before and played it for Robin "perfectly". This is just a window into how much every single song Stevie writes means to her.

Tom Petty might not have been producing but Jimmy Iovine "desperately"wanted him to write a single for the album – he wasn't confident that there was one as yet, and to include a duet with a star like Petty would work on every level. Having spent time together, drinking wine and singing at his home, Tom knew he and Stevie could "make a pretty good sound" together, so, after a little urging from Jimmy, Tom sat down at home with his guitar and Stevie's voice in his head, and wrote the poignant 'Insider'. It took him a day to complete and the result was, as Petty observed, "one of my best songs [up] to that point. I loved it." He loved it a little too much to give it away, however. Petty duly took it to Jimmy Iovine, who "flipped. He thought it was incredible . . . he said, 'God, when I asked for a song, I didn't expect this!'"

Stevie was conflicted about the idea of using a song that wasn't hers on her debut solo album, but she loved Tom, and she would love 'Insider', which was replete with Nicks-esque lyrics involving "dangerous backgrounds" and "dark angels". For a Tom Petty super-fan like Stevie, having a duet with the man himself on her record was always going to be special. However, after the pair recorded their vocals, and the hallmark sound of the Heartbreakers was added, Petty was getting "a little depressed about giving away this song. It *hurt* me when I did the track and the vocals." Eventually Tom had to tell Stevie he just was too attached to it to give it to her. He wanted his song – their duet – on *Hard Promises*. "She said, 'Well, I can relate to that. I completely understand. I'll take something else.'"

That "something else" would be the song 'Stop Draggin' My Heart Around', written by Petty and Mike Campbell. Stevie fell in love with it when she heard it – although it wasn't actually written with her in mind. The track was already in existence, and, as Petty remembers, "all they did was take [it] and overdub Stevie onto it." Tom sang the chorus and bridge with Stevie and it took just a few hours to lay down the vocals, Stevie working out the lyrical expression and dynamics by writing down dashes and exclamation points on her lyrics pad. (When she asked Tom if he does the same thing, he simply replied: "I barely got through school.")

With those two distinctive voices over the inimitable sound of the Heartbreakers, no one was surprised when 'Stop Draggin' My Heart Around', released in July 1981, soared into the top ten on the *Billboard* Hot 100, while *Bella Donna* itself would rocket straight to number one the same month. "[The song] was a huge hit," admitted Petty. "But we [the Heartbreakers] were on a Stevie Nicks album . . ."

The main problem would be that Petty's own single 'A Woman In Love (It's Not Me)' missed out on being the hit it could have been, as it was scheduled for release just weeks before 'Stop Draggin' My Heart Around'. "It was an awkward position for us," Petty remembered in Paul Zollo's 2005 book *Conversations with Tom Petty,* "because ['Stop Draggin' My Heart Around'] was billed as Stevie Nicks with Tom Petty & The Heartbreakers. Radio programmers didn't want to have two Tom Petty & the Heartbreakers songs around the same period, especially while one was getting this extreme amount of airplay."

On the upside, working together on the song would firm up Tom and Stevie's friendship, and it would only build over the years to come. The paparazzi and tabloid press weren't generally interested in rock stars but Stevie was a little different – she was sexy, adventurous, beautiful and mysterious – and column inches were often filled with speculation about her love life, linking her with almost every man she was seen within six feet of. Stevie was irritated by the insinuations and insisted she was a "very quiet lady" who liked to be at home. All the same, the press intrusion and rumour mill would mean Stevie and Tom would have to give each other a wide berth for a while, which upset her enormously.

Something that had everybody talking was the rapport between Petty and Nicks, a rapport that was somewhat different to the connection between Nicks and Lindsey Buckingham. The reason for this was largely because they weren't and had never been involved in the biblical sense, according to Stevie. "I think we'll write together eventually," she told *Bam Magazine*. "You see, Tom and I aren't in love with each other, or haven't been in love and out of love. We're just good friends so we probably could write together. Lindsey and I have so much behind us that it would be difficult to sit down and get into lyrics. As it is he asks me, 'Who's that one about? What are you talking about in that line? What does that mean?'" And who could blame him?

"Even when we were lovers, we were never really best friends," Lindsey said. "We've always competed, ever since we started going out together back in 1971." And that competition continued apace outside of Fleetwood Mac too; while Stevie had been working on *Bella Donna*, Lindsey had been furiously completing his own debut album *Law And Order*. Stevie wished him well – apart from anything else, she knew that if her album was a bigger hit than his, there would be hell to pay.

"I love Lindsey," she insisted to *The Record* in 1982. "And I wanted Lindsey to make it. If his album is more successful than my album, I would be so glad . . . I was saying, 'let it go straight to the top', because it only makes my life easier when Lindsey is happy." *Law And Order* would be released on 3 October 1981, Lindsey's 32nd birthday, hitting number nine in the US charts. Four days later, *Bella Donna* would go platinum. Happy birthday . . . The rivalry was as dogged as ever and, if this was a race, Stevie was in the lead in terms of star power, and she always would be – no matter how hard Lindsey worked.

It wasn't just about her songwriting, it was about her look – she was the perfect pastel-shade, strong-yet-soft-focus icon for the new decade. Her vibrant imagination and visual appeal also meant Stevie was attracting attention from other areas of show business, and there had already been plans to make a Rhiannon movie, for example. While mission Rhiannon was afoot, Danny Goldberg was sent to meet Evangeline Walton, the fantasy author who had written novels including 'The Song Of Rhiannon', part of the series based on the ancient Welsh *Mabinogion* manuscripts that Stevie had been inspired by. Walton, based in Tucson, Arizona, was in her seventies at the time and Danny was taken aback to note that her skin was bright purple – as a child she had been prescribed silver tincture to ease a bronchial disorder. Being very pale-skinned, she had absorbed the tincture which turned her skin grey, darkening to a vibrant plum colour as she aged. But she was bright and happy, and listened to Danny with great interest, graciously agreeing that Stevie could use her stories, expecting nothing unless the film actually went ahead. Danny carefully explained that Stevie's plans were "a little tenuous". "Don't worry dear," responded Walton with a twinkle in her eye. "All true artists are a little neurotic."

A meeting with Columbia bore little fruit when it was discovered they wanted to dump the Welsh mythology and just use Stevie's songs for a remake of the witchy Kim Novak classic *Bell, Book And Candle* instead but the treatment, thanks to Danny Goldberg's dogged efforts, was eventually bought by United Artists. Paul Mayersberg, who wrote the screenplay for the David Bowie movie *The Man Who Fell To Earth*, was brought on board and, while Rhiannon was ultimately never made, Stevie was just happy to be receiving professional attention (and payment) away from the Mac. Danny would be receiving his own "Stevie moon" necklace for his efforts.

Another Stevie moon pendant would, of course, be given to Margi Kent, whose intuitive designs for Stevie's costumes both on tour and for album artwork provided another way for Stevie to express herself and strengthen her image. For the *Bella Donna* cover shoot, with her favourite photographer Herbie Worthington once again at the helm, the outfit Stevie wears is "the same as the one I wore on *Rumours*, except it's opposite, it's white," she explained to *High Times*. "It's a strange turnaround that I've come from black to white . . ." Coming in out of the darkness, a la 'Bella Donna', no doubt.

The change is also likely to have been connected to the fact that the "Stevie is a witch" gossip had now gone haywire and, as a result, she was attracting some unsavoury attention. Stevie loved wearing black but she eventually had to ask Margi to design a wardrobe-full of new stage clothes in cheery colours, her "Easter egg outfits" as she called them, so that the rumours could die down. As to whether she would cast black spells on people, Stevie assured *High Times'* Liz Derringer: "I don't do that. That's stupid, and anyone that [thinks that] that is making up their own character [that] has nothing to do with me. I love good witches. I like the good witch of the north, Glinda. My love of that fantasy fairy-tale thing is the good part."

It was also Margi Kent's job to ensure that Stevie's stage look for Fleetwood Mac did not threaten to upstage the rest of the band – particularly with Lindsey being so sensitive about who was getting the most attention at that time. "We would specifically tone it down because Stevie was getting way too much air time," Margi laughed in an interview with *District MTV*. "We had to keep it politically correct, it's hard for her not to stand out because she's a very dramatic performer, but we had to scale back. She had to be respectful of everybody's position in the band, she is a band member and she feels that way." But, when Stevie would finally tour to promote the record in the autumn of 1981, "we went crazy," remembers Kent. "Everything was colours, textures and feathers."

The outfit on the front of *Bella Donna* was longer than that of Stevie's *Rumours* costume, and instead of ballet slippers, Stevie would be wearing her now trademark suede platform boots, made by "my little cobbler who's seventy years old. A five-foot one-inch-tall person needs six inches. I get far on these boots. They are very out of style and I don't care. I love them." Stevie also hunted down the perfect platforms whenever she was on tour, scouring flea markets and boutiques, finding them in rose-pink, lilac, grey . . . pretty, soft colours. "We searched London," she recalled, "and I found one pair that was like a size five, and I wear a five and a half or six, but I bought them anyway. I stuffed my little feet into them." Before long Stevie had amassed 25 pairs, and one show would see her change platforms three or four times.

The *Bella Donna* costume represents Stevie's enduring desire to "give a fairytale" to people, and the white bird she is holding (Max, a pet belonging to her brother Chris) also connects with that. Fairytales, myths, dolls, puppets . . . even the Muppets – Stevie loved them all and they all resonated with her mission to encourage more escapism in a dark and difficult world. "If that's the only thing I can do, well, that's fine."

The German artist Sulamith Wülfing was also a great influence on Stevie's style. Stevie had collected her books, filled with luminous pictures of fairies, angels and trolls, since the early seventies. Flicking through the pages, "on the road, late after concerts . . ." gazing at the fantastical images gave Stevie great comfort, and eventually she taught herself to draw just by looking at Wülfing's illustrations. "I think she's probably a lot like me," said Nicks of Wülfing. "The world kind of scares her and freaks her out and she just wants to do this one thing, and she did it."

Prior to the release of *Bella Donna* in the summer of 1981, Fleetwood Mac would be getting together to record *Mirage*. Everyone had interrupted their own projects to fly to France for the sessions, and rather grudgingly so at that. Meanwhile, Stevie had promised herself she would keep her lip buttoned regarding her solo work – she knew if she allowed her excitement to spill over it would not go down well.

After the intensity of working on *Bella Donna* and an extra two months working on demos for the next Fleetwood Mac album, spending springtime in the French countryside might have sounded idyllic, but the reasons for recording at the Château d'Herouville were not. Mick had declared himself a resident of Monaco for tax reasons, and the Château was the only viable option financially. And so, with debts up to their ears, rumours of a split swirling around them and trepidation prickling through their veins, the five members of Fleetwood Mac made the long journey to Herouville, 60 miles outside of Paris. Mick Fleetwood, finishing his own solo album *The Visitor*, would meet them there.

The dilapidated eighteenth-century house had been converted into a studio and had seen the likes of David Bowie, Pink Floyd and Iggy Pop pass through its mouldering doors, not to mention Elton John, who had named his 1972 album *Honky Château* after it. The album included the single 'Rocket Man' and was hugely successful, so maybe the Château had enough enchantment to help the Mac create their best album to date.

That was the idea, anyway. It was time to return to the *Rumours* formula after Lindsey had been allowed off the leash for *Tusk*.

Carol Ann Harris' appraisal of the Château was that it was "icky. Damp, spider-and-ant infested, almost no modern amenities . . ." They were all used to being spoiled, and admittedly the luxuries had become essentials – they made the tensions between each other easier to bear. But the food provided was good and the Château also had, according to Carol Ann, "an ominous, supernatural feel." Which surely made it perfect for Fleetwood Mac. The press were convinced the next Fleetwood Mac album would never come out, so a bit of supernatural assistance would not have gone amiss, ominous or not.

Mick Fleetwood arrived "as the sun was rising on the day we were to begin recording," he remembered in the book *Fleetwood*. "We drove down the long tree-lined lane and saw Stevie peering out of the leaded-glass window, looking like Queen Guinevere in the misty early light. It was as if she were waiting for us, being the dawn-type lady that she is." The missing piece of the Mac jigsaw had arrived, the spirit of *Rumours* was being drawn upon and the adventure of the Fleetwood Mac album no one believed would ever appear had begun.

Chapter 17

Fleetwood Mac's modus operandi for *Mirage* was to make an "updated version" of the sound of *Rumours*, the album that had served them all so well. Admittedly, they were older now and had different preoccupations and the rich seam of fury that ran through *Rumours* belonged to *Rumours* alone, but to go into the studio with the atmosphere of that album in mind was certainly the idea. Meanwhile, the charts were dominated by the likes of Blondie, the Pretenders, Michael Jackson and Diana Ross, artists with a serious core of rock or soul but a strong pop sensibility. Fleetwood Mac were unsure whether they could move on from simply being seen as the kings and queens of 1970s rock – as Lindsey had been trying to encourage for some time – but they would. The dream team of Richard Dashut and Ken Caillat would be working with them again, money would be treated with a little more respect and the whole album would take a relatively short time to record. One of the reasons for this, perhaps, was the fact that everyone was just itching to get back to their own projects and their own lives, none more so than Stevie, who would be joined for a while at the Château by Jimmy Iovine.

As well as having to witness the pair's canoodling, Lindsey was irritated to see Jimmy advising her all the while. It was hard enough for Stevie and Lindsey to see each other with new partners, but the fact Iovine was a prestigious producer who was driving Stevie in a different direction would grate on a professional level as well as a personal one. Stevie had hoped that the fact everyone was now developing their own careers away from the Mac would bring greater balance, make everyone happier and also potentially take the heat off her a little – "If we're both doing a solo project, then you're not going to be angry with me . . ." she said at the time. But Lindsey, for one, felt frustrated that every time he was about to start work on new solo material, the band would steam in and so he would have to use the ideas he had for his own projects for the Mac recordings instead. And yes, he would still be angry with Stevie, not least because, as always, less was expected of her in the studio than of him – and thus she wouldn't have to give as much to the Mac as he would, as producer, arranger and writer.

Stevie's focus was split, the press and the public's hopes were highest for her solo career even though Lindsey, Mick and Christine were working on side projects themselves and, as Lindsey saw it, this caused Stevie to change, and her commitment to waver. She was, apparently, "flexing some emotional muscles that she feels she can flex now that she's in a more powerful position," Lindsey said to *The Record*'s David Gans. "There's a certain amount of leeway in how you can interpret Stevie's behaviour, but there's no denying that her success is making her feel she can pull things she wouldn't have felt comfortable pulling before. Most of them aren't particularly worthwhile but she's venting something, loneliness, unhappiness or something." Her "baby sister" vibe no longer seemed to wash with some – what had once been seen as charming vulnerability was now regarded by critics such as Gans himself as "childish" and "awkward", but Stevie remained resolutely herself despite the criticism: "I can't do what I do if I don't retain some innocence and spirituality," she told *Playboy Magazine*. "You'd see a definite change in my lyrics if I became hardened. I'm not interested in existing on that critical level most people live on."

Buckingham simply opined that she felt "out of her depth", being the only one who wasn't technically a musician. Stevie herself would insist that her loyalty to the Mac never faltered at all, however, insisting that the "special knowledge" as referred to in her pre-Mac song 'Crystal' now came to represent to her the unspoken awareness within the band that they would never leave each other. Even so, while she might not have been 'leaving', she was elsewhere in spirit.

A polite silence was maintained regarding Stevie's own solo work, in her presence at least. "They knew if they ripped [it] apart, I wouldn't give them any more songs," Stevie said. "Remember, 'Dreams' – which is just me – is the only gold single that Fleetwood Mac ever had." Behind her back, it was a little different. Lindsey felt Stevie's writing was supposedly "flaky", and sniggeringly referred to 'Stop Draggin' My Heart Around' as 'Stop Draggin' My Career Around',* later publicly dismissing Stevie's work as "a little hard to take seriously". In the meantime, however, they had a job to do, and they had to do it together. At least the strange charms of the Château would distract them from each other for a while.

The Château had an interesting history; once used as a courier relay station between Versailles and Beauvais, it would be painted by Van Gogh, who was buried nearby, and it was once a residence of the Romantic-era composer Frédéric François Chopin. Music was already in its bricks, but the house's rock'n'roll heritage was even more fascinating. Converted into a residential recording studio by Gigot composer Michel Magne in 1962, ten years later it would be the site of the oddest Grateful Dead gig the band had ever played. The Dead were booked to play a free outdoor festival nearby, but the heavens opened and the event was rained off. The band, staying at the Château, decided to play at the house itself, and anyone who happened by was welcome to come and join the party. "We didn't even play to hippies," remembered frontman Jerry Garcia in Blair Jackson's *Garcia: An American Life*. "We played to a handful of townspeople in Auvers. The chief of police, the fire department . . . Everybody had a hell of a time – got drunk, fell in the pool . . ."

David Bowie later arrived to work on *Pin Ups* and *Low* with Tony Visconti and Brian Eno, all of them convinced the place was haunted by the ghosts of Chopin and his mistress George Sand, to the extent that the Thin White Duke himself refused to sleep in the master bedroom. Fortunately, there were 29 other rooms to choose from.

"There was some strange energy in that Château," Tony Visconti

* 'Weird Al' Yankovic would parody the song himself in 1983 with the track 'Stop Draggin' My Car Around'.

confirmed in a 1999 interview with *Uncut*. "The master bedroom had a very dark corner, right next to the window ironically, that seemed to just suck light into it. It was colder in that corner too. I took the bedroom because I wanted to test my meditation abilities. It felt like it was haunted as all fuck, but what could Frédéric Chopin or George Sand really do to me, scare me in French? Eno claims he was awakened early every morning with someone shaking his shoulder. When he opened his eyes no one was there." This might have been handy as an alternative to an alarm clock, but knowing that most rock stars don't like to commence work until the more civilised time of two or three in the afternoon, one can see how this early wake-up call might not have been appreciated.

Bedrooms aside, there were other areas of the house that could tell some intriguing stories if only the walls could speak, not least around the main staircase. The Bee Gees recorded the soundtrack to *Saturday Night Fever* there, thanks to its natural reverb, but they were not the first artistes to utilise that part of the house. "So many pornographic films [were] made at the Château," said Robin Gibb. "The staircase, where we wrote 'How Deep Is Your Love?', 'Stayin' Alive', all those songs, was the same staircase where there've been six classic lesbian porno scenes filmed. I was watching a movie one day called *Kinky Women Of Bourbon Street**, and all of a sudden there's this château, and I said, 'It's the Château!' These girls, these dodgy birds, are having a scene on the staircase that leads from the front door up to the studio. There were dildos hanging off the stairs and everything. I thought, 'Gawd, we wrote 'Night Fever' there!'"

The Mac put their own stamp on the place by having the rooms they were using redecorated and it was a romantic, atmospheric place to record; no doubt the esoteric side of the house's background appealing to Stevie's love of the unknown. The band weren't especially worried about hostility from the "other side", even if soft rock, the musical direction in which Fleetwood Mac were increasingly heading, wasn't Chopin's thing. No, there was enough earthly aggravation to keep them occupied, and Carol

* The film was actually called *The Kinky Ladies Of Bourbon Street*, but to be fair to Robin, the title was probably the least memorable thing about the movie.

Ann Harris recalls being quite disturbed by the raging arguments that would occur "every night" in the studio. Meals on the other hand, were eaten together (albeit in silence) and whenever there was an opportunity to go for a walk in the vast, wild grounds around the house, they would take it – and walk as far away from each other as possible. On one occasion, as Mick Fleetwood prepared to go for a ride on the stunning mare that lived in the stable, Stevie swept out of the house and mounted it before he could hop on himself, cantering off into the distance, "her long cape billowing behind her".

Ken Caillat's dog Scooter might have gone to the great dog basket in the sky, but the engineer had brought his new puppy 'Pal' with him, and the grounds of the Château were perfect for a pooch to play in. During down time, it made a change to be able to leave the studio and be refreshed by cool French air rather than choked by LA smog, so as often as they could, Ken and Richard Dashut headed out to play with the model helicopters they'd just bought. One day, as Richard and Ken went outside to do a spot of flying, Richard commented that he hadn't seen Pal for a while. The dog had been locked into Lindsey's rented Peugeot the night before, and by the time Ken found him and flung open the car door, he saw that the puppy had basically chewed through the interior of the car. "All the headliner had been torn into shreds and was hanging down like a kelp forest with the light from the dome light streaming through," Ken remembered in his book *Making Rumours*. "Dashut hit the ground rolling with laughter . . ." No doubt this didn't exactly help to lift Buckingham's mood.

The songs Stevie brought to the table for *Mirage* included 'Straight Back', written just after the *Bella Donna* sessions and detailing the wrench of leaving LA and Jimmy to go back to Fleetwood Mac: a sanguine comparison between her solo career and the band. An earlier Nicks composition that also made the cut was 'That's Alright', a sweet, uplifting country ballad with a lachrymose twist. Stevie had attempted to get 'That's Alright' on a Mac album ever since she joined the band, but it was never deemed to have the right feel. The song, originally titled 'Designs Of Love', was written before Stevie and Lindsey moved to Los Angeles for the first time, and is a departure from the other tracks on *Mirage*, of which many by Lindsey harked back to a fifties, Bobby Vee feel (notably 'Oh Diane' and, in parts, the emotive 'Book Of Love'), while Christine's inclusions tapped straight into the early eighties soft-rock vibe, with super-smooth, prismatic songs like 'Hold Me' and the inoffensive 'Love In Store'. Buckingham and Nicks' songs always had an edge that Christine's didn't, to these ears certainly, but McVie certainly knew how to write a radio-friendly hit.

Another song Stevie presented to the collective was 'If You Were My Love', written just after she had concluded her sessions with Tom Petty & the Heartbreakers for *Bella Donna*. "I had so much fun that I was really bummed out when it was over," Stevie lamented. "That's when I wrote that song." Interestingly, the song is written to a potential lover, as the title indicates, and the line, 'Well, they say everyone must remain faithful . . .' betrays a possible crush. Whatever, the song would be rejected from *Mirage*, as would the unusually defiant 'Smile At You'. This song was written at Stevie's home 'El Contento', a pink Spanish-Moorish property in the Hollywood Hills that in the 1920s had been the residence of silent movie beauty Vilma Banky. Stevie loved it, not least because she was fascinated by the shadowy history of Banky, but Stevie also found it conducive to write and reflect there because Tom Moncrieff had built her a studio to focus and work on demos. Her time at El Contento was, appropriately, a happy one. If she wasn't in the studio, according to Danny Goldberg, she would be in the kitchen "making tacos" or in the living room, hunched over her precious Bösendorfer piano, one of her first major purchases when the royalties rolled in.

Some have hinted that 'Smile At You' was refused by Lindsey when he discovered she had written it with Tom Moncrieff's assistance, although Moncrieff himself maintains he has no memory of working on the song at all, and Stevie would simply explain that it was a "bitter" song, and they weren't really in that place when they were making *Mirage*. Either way, Moncrieff, who was staying at El Contento at the time, had often helped Stevie develop her work when Lindsey just couldn't face it. Lyrically,

'Smile At You' gives a rare glimpse of Stevie's own "flaming" fury for once; most of her dedications to Lindsey were kind and philosophical rather than barbed; that was more his style. Whatever the motive for shelving the song, it wouldn't turn up on a Fleetwood Mac record until 'Say You Will' in 2003, which is a shame: the inclusion of this song might have given *Mirage* the grit so many Mac fans felt this album lacked.

As always, there would be no shortage of material from Nicks, and, just as reliably, Stevie would have to stifle her hurt whenever one was passed over. "Stevie writes constantly," observed Christine McVie. "And all her songs are like babies to her even though some of them are rubbish." Christine was becoming impatient that Stevie didn't sit down and finish one song rather than "cranking them out all the time".

Still, for every few songs that were "rubbish" there would be a 'Gypsy' – Nicks' defining moment on *Mirage*, and possibly of the decade. 'Gypsy', written in 1979 and saved from the *Bella Donna* sessions, was a song that, once recorded, would be described by Mick Fleetwood as one of Fleetwood Mac's "greatest works of art. It crystallises that period of the early 1980s when we were looking back on our youth." Even Buckingham considers 'Gypsy' their "best collaboration" musically.

'Gypsy' takes us wistfully into Stevie Nicks' past, lifting the veil on her broke but happy years in San Francisco; queuing up for rock shows outside the Fillmore Auditorium, rifling through the racks of beautiful clothes at the Velvet Underground boutique and dreaming of stardom. This song was a tribute to those psychedelic days, and how little Stevie had really changed. "Every place I live still looks pretty much like my apartment in San Francisco," Stevie said in an interview with *The Record*. "The clothes I wear . . . that doesn't change. I love long dresses, I love velvet, I love high boots. I love the same eye makeup. I still have everything I had then."

A sensitive soul, Stevie once decided to cheer herself up by moving into one of the smaller rooms in her 'English' house in Doheny, recreating her old room in San Francisco: pulling her mattress onto the floor, moving her speakers, plants and "junk" into a room "about as big as [a] sofa . . .

I just lived in there for about three months," she told the broadcaster Jim Ladd in 1982. "It was really like living back in my apartment before I joined Fleetwood Mac. I'm very comfortable living in one little room with my bed on the floor and lace tacked up at the windows." There was a comfort in tapping into the "gypsy that remains" as Stevie put it, and cocooning herself in nostalgia; those formative years in San Francisco would always have a special place in Stevie's heart. There are references to Robin Snyder's "bright eyes", and the line "lightning strikes, maybe once, maybe twice" refers to the treasured friendship Stevie had found with Robin. "One time in your life you find a very good friend," explained Stevie. "And maybe if you're incredibly lucky, you might find a second. [The lyric] 'It all comes down to you' means you have to look very hard." As much as it is inspired by Robin, this song must also be connected to Lindsey too, Stevie's soul mate, both of them navigating life together at that time, both of them "facing freedom with a little fear", side by side. The line: "she is dancing away from you now . . ." must have cut Lindsey deep. But this lyric would also take on a devastating new resonance in the near future.

Once the album was complete, a *Mirage* listening party was held at the Château, to which the band invited a select group of lucky listeners including tennis stars John McEnroe and Vitas Gerulaitis, who were competing at Wimbledon that year. The band played ping pong with them and stayed up all night playing the record over and over again. After weeks of tension, it felt good to play the tapes to new ears; the songs were light-hearted, soft and . . . well, rather anodyne. They tried to cast the *Rumours* spell once again, but there was one thing missing. "Passion," Christine admitted in later years. That hot-blooded anger that had spiked *Rumours* with a ferocious, sharp-toothed *je ne sais quoi* had transmuted into frosty detachment.

*

Nineteen eighty-one was the year of the music video – the medium had found its home in the groundbreaking new music video channel MTV, and artists were able to express themselves and reach out to fans more widely. The posters pinned to the walls of a thousand bedrooms were coming to life. Australian director Russell Mulcahy was considered a leading proponent of the music video during the eighties; he was the man behind Buggles' 'Video Killed The Radio Star' promo, meaningfully the first pop video broadcast on MTV, and, naturally, when Fleetwood Mac started to talk about having their own videos made for the *Mirage* singles – due for release in 1982 – he was top of the list, as was Steve Barron, who had already directed videos for Adam & the Ants ('Antmusic'), the Human League ('Don't You Want Me?','Love Action') and Simple Minds ('Promised You A Miracle'). These artists, all pop titans of the new era, were considerably younger than Fleetwood Mac. Maybe Mulcahy and Barron could sprinkle a little visual stardust on them and ensure they could stride confidently into this glitzy new decade, taking their place alongside the younger stars with ease and shaking off any "seventies rock dinosaur" once and for all.

For the 'Hold Me' video shoot, Barron and his crew took the band to the Mojave desert where a series of surrealist Magritte-inspired tableaux were set up. The set included jagged spikes of broken mirror sticking out of the sand (surely an inauspicious sign in itself), mountains of discarded guitar parts and John McVie and Mick Fleetwood gooning about as archaeologists. Christine, meanwhile, searches for Lindsey in the desert and sings plaintively to camera while the "mirage" itself – Stevie, clad in trailing red silk – preens on a *chaise longue* and is painted by Lindsey, before struggling doggedly across the sand in her platform boots with the canvas under her arm, which she was not particularly happy to do. In fact, it sounds as if none of the band were particularly happy to do anything. They were hot, they were exposed and they couldn't stand each other. Producer Simon Fields remembers the shoot being "a fucking nightmare".

"It was 115 degrees on this sand dune," Stevie told ABC's Molly Meldrum in 1986. "No one in Fleetwood Mac even saw the other scenes that anybody did, because if you walked out of your trailer for five minutes, you died of asphyxiation because it was so hot . . ." Stevie's friends would tease her for getting the easy job, but she insists it was far from luxurious. "I'm lying on that *chaise longue,* and it's 115 degrees, and they're saying, 'We need you to look dreamy,' you know . . . I'm going to look dreamy and then I'm going to die!"

It was not just the heat that was causing tempers to prickle. "[They] were, um, not easy to work with," Barron said carefully.* "Four of them – I can't recall which four – couldn't be together in the same room for very long. They didn't want to be there. Christine McVie was about ten hours out of the makeup trailer. By which time it was getting dark." Fields also was not having a good time. Despite the cute and cuddly comedy archaeologist look, John McVie was steaming drunk and "tried to punch me," recalls Fields. "Stevie Nicks didn't want to walk on the sand with her platforms. Christine McVie was fed up with all of them. Mick thought she was being a bitch, he wouldn't talk to her." Another day in Paradise.

Hanging around for hours and being bossed about was not Fleetwood Mac's favourite way of spending three days – Stevie alone had plenty of that to contend with as it was – but the video shoot for 'Gypsy' would also be painful as it interrupted Stevie's first serious attempt at kicking cocaine, no doubt on the urging of strait-laced Jimmy Iovine. A stint at a rehab centre would have to be abandoned as Russell Mulcahy's shoot had been scheduled and could not be changed.

Again, the band were not comfortable in each other's company, but Mulcahy seemed to know how to deal with them. "It was like the best mom in the world," Stevie enthused later. "I wish we could find a producer like Russell for Fleetwood Mac . . ." (Take that, Lindsey.) However, Mulcahy had to be strong with the group, warning them not to "mess with me", according to Nicks. He also impressed Stevie because of his commitment to reflecting 'Gypsy' visually, which he went to great lengths to do. The result would be completely over the top, featuring Stevie as a pouting, bubble-haired ballerina, Stevie as a nymph, skipping theatrically through an enchanted forest, glitter raining down upon her, Stevie as a

* From Craig Marks and Rob Tannenbaum's 2011 book *I Want My MTV: The Uncensored Story of the Music Video Revolution.*

1930s ingenue navigating her way through the grime and glamour of Hollywood . . .

The 'Gypsy' video would be long – over five minutes long, in fact. It would also be the most expensive music video ever produced at the time and required several locations, many dancers and myriad costume changes, which will have appealed to Stevie. Mulcahy, having heard the song and its story, spent several hours Chez Nicks where he "looked at my closet and he looked at my crystal balls and all my stuff that I have," remembers Stevie. Knick-knacks, dolls, dresses and trinkets would all find their way into the video, which sees Stevie in her cluttered, comforting little bedroom practising her ballet; a dream-like, Vaseline-smeared image that soon becomes a black and white 1930s Hollywood movie, with the members of the band as the stars. The result would be the first ever "World Premiere Video" to be screened on MTV come the single's release in 1982, but, again, this would be a difficult shoot thanks to the interpersonal difficulties within Fleetwood Mac. Stevie was exhausted and desperate for cocaine, a bottle of which had been brought to her in secret before being discovered and confiscated before she could even have a toot. She also wasn't thrilled to have to dance with – and be kissed and caressed by – Lindsey during one of the scenes. The sight of her former love with another woman at breakfast might have made her "absolutely ill", but similarly she "didn't want to be anywhere near him".

"I certainly didn't want to be in his arms," she said. "If you watch the video, you'll see I wasn't happy. And he wasn't a very good dancer." The following scene in which Stevie rushes out into the rain-swept street after their awkward dance nearly saw her "decapitated" as one of the rain machines swooped a little too low. This would have been history repeating itself, in Stevie's opinion. She is convinced that, in a past life, she had been "put to death, like Marie Antoinette", she told *Bam Magazine,* because she has great trouble putting her head back, even in "the beauty parlour, I can't put my head back in the sink for a shampoo."

As for the cover of *Mirage* itself, featuring Christine, Lindsey and Stevie in Lindsey's arms, Stevie's head was thrown back dramatically: "I hated posing for that more than life," Stevie insisted. In the near future, when she was required to throw her head back again during the video for her single 'If Anyone Falls', the director "had to call in a back-up singer to do it. I called her my stunt neck."

*

Bella Donna was released in July 1981 – an instant hit, and a record that would rise swiftly up the charts. But Lindsey Buckingham believed that the immediate triumph of her debut solo album would not assuage the emptiness she continued to try to fill with drugs, romance and escapism. "Stevie has never been very happy," he said to *The Record*'s David Gans in 1982. "And I don't think the success of her album has made her any happier. In fact it may have made her less happy."

Stevie on the other hand believed he was simply jealous, and his resentment would lead to the usual hurtful, insulting behaviour. "He wasn't ever able to revel in any kind of joy for my success for *Bella Donna*," recalls Nicks in an interview with *The Times*' Chrissy Iley. "He would always start an argument – 'We're really not here to discuss your solo records, Stevie.' I gave him a signed copy of *Bella Donna.* He left it leaning against the recording studio wall for a month. I took it back, crossed his name out, and gave it to somebody else." It obviously still meant so much to Stevie that Lindsey approved of her work, and a snub like this mortified her, particularly seeing as so many lines on the album were about him.

Critically acclaimed, publicly lauded, *Bella Donna* was a tour de force. *Rolling Stone* magazine proclaimed Stevie the 'Queen of Rock'n'Roll' and by September 1981, the album had reached the top of the *Billboard* chart. But on the very day *Bella Donna* was proclaimed number one, Stevie received a distressing phone call about her closest friend. Robin Snyder had been diagnosed with leukaemia. She was the only one who could calm Stevie down in any circumstances, the one who had listened to every song Stevie had written since the age of 16, the one who knew how to protect Stevie's greatest asset – her voice – and now, at the age of just 33, she was dying. Stevie "just went crazy", and a black cloud of grief and fear now overshadowed what would otherwise have been a time of celebration. There was an upsetting irony in the fact that, when explaining the concept of 'Bella Donna' to Waddy and the band in the studio the year before, Stevie took great pains to clarify that the song was serious, it was not just about an attractive girl *per se*, but a beautiful woman who was becoming worn ragged by the rigours of rock'n'roll. It detailed Stevie's own fears for the future if she didn't slow down. The bella donna character was suffering. Now Robin, who had been by Stevie's side on the road and in the studio since day one, was suffering too.

"[This] should have been the time when I was the most happy and self-confident," Stevie would tell *Bam Magazine*. "But I felt the most helpless, because all the money in the world couldn't save this woman's life."

Chapter 18

Stevie's promotional dates for *Bella Donna,* titled the White-Winged Dove tour, would begin on 27 November in Houston, Texas, continuing until mid-December. Under the unbearable pall of Robin's illness, and reminded of her own warnings to herself in her album's title track, Stevie would take a different tack to touring this time. She was in charge now, after all. Stevie told press before embarking on the dates that the White-Winged Dove tour would be nowhere near as extensive as the average Fleetwood Mac odyssey. Nobody would "die from touring", she promised.

Stevie's own health problems had forced her to slow down, having been diagnosed with bronchial spasmodic asthma. "Everything that I do is wrapped up in my lungs," she admitted, so it made sense to take a little more care. "I need rest real bad," she told *Playboy*. "I also need some exercise. I don't want to be this romantically fragile character everyone thinks I am. The image is fine, but not if you have to go to hospital for it. For my asthma, I have to take these miserable pills that make you feel like someone put something weird in your Perrier." She was getting older, a process she intended to respect. Or that was the intention, at least.

Stevie and her band would take in Houston, Dallas, Oakland, Tempe and would conclude with five nights at the Fox Wilshire Theatre in Los Angeles on 13 December, with the show being recorded for an HBO special. The set featured Stevie's best-known Fleetwood Mac songs, including 'Gold Dust Woman', 'Sara', 'Angel', 'Dreams' and show-closer 'Rhiannon', a glittering haul of *Bella Donna* songs, of course, and 'Gold

& Braid', which she had developed with Tom Moncrieff, and one that remains a fan favourite to this day.

The entire process would be an utterly different experience for Stevie – she was on her own, at least in the sense that she was now the main focus on stage, the sole reason fans had bought their tickets. The responsibility was great, and Stevie was extremely nervous. But with Lori and Sharon by her side, bolstering her while she sang, Margi's new designs draping her form and some of her favourite musicians behind her, Stevie was free to fly with confidence. Wild-haired guitarist Waddy Wachtel, who had been in Stevie's life since she had first moved to LA, was bursting with pride as he witnessed his friend truly transform into a rock star in her own right. "It was extraordinary to see Stevie become this rock'n'roller," he told *Black Cat*. "Because when I met her she was this little folk girl. One night I said to her, after we did the first show of her tour, 'Stevie, you really impressed me. Standing on stage with you, you are a rock'n'roller, my girl.' She thought I was kidding. 'Get outta here!' she said. But I was totally serious. She's incredible."

Waddy's defining moment with Stevie would arguably be that iconic, scratchy riff on 'Edge Of Seventeen'. He had valiantly refused the use of an echo effect when it came to playing it in the studio, but onstage he realised that this song could be rather more labour intensive, not least because Stevie often used the opportunity, while he played the introduction, to have a quick breather. "I'd be standing there, playing that riff for around three minutes, before she'd even start singing," he laughed. "By the end of the tour I was able to break walnuts with my right hand."

A particularly special moment would be Stevie's show at the Oakland Coliseum, a favourite venue of hers and a place she had long fantasised about playing as a solo artist. As the lights went down and more than 10,000 lace-clad fans anticipated the entrance of their heroine, a mature gentleman in a dapper grey suit approached the microphone. "Ladies and gentlemen," he began. "Please welcome my daughter, Stevie Nicks."

It was, as *The Record* reported, "an emotional moment" for both father and daughter, and indeed everyone present, and once Stevie had hit the stage, she told the audience – "This is the big one for me." Stevie later admitted that the first time she asked her father Jess Nicks to introduce her onstage he "almost had a heart attack". But Jess, now a concert promoter himself, stepped up for his daughter. There was already show-business in his genes, as we know . . . "He went on the road with us for a month, [but] he thought my organisation could have been run a little better, so he went home," Stevie laughed. "Bye, Dad!"

Margi Kent had designed an entire new wardrobe for Stevie for the tour – feathers, lace, chiffon, colourful saris, everything Stevie loved ramped up to the highest degree; finally there was no one she had to worry about upstaging. While the black clothes of yore had been jettisoned (for now), fans were pleased to see that Stevie's swirling shawls were still an important part of her stage-wear. "Over the years they've become really superstitious things for me," Stevie later said. "They're like special good luck charms."

"The princess on-stage is my combination of [Russian prima ballerina] Natalia Markarova and Greta Garbo and the elegant rock'n'roll that I love . . . it's hard to be a fairy princess 50 per cent of the time and just be a nice lady the other half. But I like my real self better," she would tell *Rolling Stone*, although the "real self" and the "fairy princess" would often merge, and the sense of the spiritual and the mystical was always important for Stevie, giving her strength and, ultimately, defining her. Her intense gaze was also commented on as if Stevie was a seer who could gaze into the very depths of one's soul. As psychically attuned as Stevie no doubt was (and is), the reality was more likely to be that her eyesight was very poor, and she was probably just trying to focus.

Even though the "witchy" threads had been put into mothballs, Stevie's mysterious "wise woman" quality would mean that some fans were worshipful to the extreme. One night, Stevie emerged from the stage door after another triumphant show to find a weeping girl waiting for her. "I can never walk away from someone in tears," Stevie told *Playboy*. "She said, 'Will you sign my arm?'" Innocently, Stevie agreed; if it was going to cheer a wailing fan up, where was the harm? But to Stevie's horror, the girl returned the following night and proudly displayed her arm, which was now tattooed with Stevie's name, just as Stevie herself had signed it.

"I grabbed her and told her, 'Don't ever have someone cut into your arm with my name. It's stupid and I'm not happy about it.' Her reaction was more tears. Another night, one of her friends asked me to sign her arm. I told her, 'I'm not touching your arm. And if I ever find out that you got my name tattooed on you anyway, I'll sue. Don't put that on me. I'm not here to bring pain. I'm here to bring you out of pain.' It bummed me out. I felt like I'd come out the wrong door."

Another difficulty for Stevie was that, now she was a bona fide star, ordinary things such as going out for dinner with her girlfriends were almost impossible without being approached, or worse. It was symptomatic of the gulf between how men and women were, and in many cases still are, perceived.

"It's fine for the guys," Stevie complained, "but if we [girls] go down to Le Dome for a drink or to the Rainbow for spaghetti, we're classified as loose, roaming women. Me and some of the other female singing stars, like Ann and Nancy Wilson (Heart) and Pat Benatar can't just go out boogying with our girlfriends."

Stevie was now too recognisable to go out without being mobbed, but she had also been "securitied up to my neck" for seven years, so the idea of going out alone was actually frightening. She wasn't used to it anymore and, ultimately, came to accept her fate, holding wild parties in her home instead.

"People say [the security] is for my safety," Stevie told *Playboy*'s David Rensin in 1982, before giving a rather disconcerting conclusion: "Women are getting raped all the time. And I don't need to get raped, because I'd never get over it. That's when my songs would stop. That's when my belief in the world would die. I know it happens, but it happening to me is another story. It tends to take away one's spontaneity."

That the Stevie of 1982 could imagine the trauma of rape would necessarily be any more shattering for her than it would be for anyone else is hard to reconcile, but one can only assume the narcissistic world of a then coke-addled rock'n'roll star is a place where not everything makes sense, and the feelings of whoever is at the centre of it are simply deemed more important, more sensitive and more worthy of protection than anyone else's. It's not something anyone could imagine her saying or thinking now, but it's important to note that Stevie, at that time, was also "edging towards an emotional crisis", as she put it, becoming more and more dependent on cocaine in a bid to cope with her increasing work-load and the misery of Robin's sickness. Her life was in a state of confusion.

At least there were some "truly spectacular moments" the White-Winged Dove tour. At the end of the final show in Los Angeles, an emotional Stevie was practically bent double trying to carry the hundreds of bouquets flung at her during the show. As Stevie herself observed, the mere fact that no one had been heard to shout "Where's Don? Where's Tom Petty? Where's Lindsey?" was a success in itself. By the end of 1981, Stevie had never felt more like a star. She had also never felt more in need of care. She had her friends, her dogs and cats and her dazzling two-fold career, but she still occasionally hankered for family life, wishing she had "a little girl, even a little boy". Even so, Stevie also knew her relative sense of freedom was something she couldn't give up easily, and that included serious relationships too. Perhaps this was also her way of protecting herself after having been hurt.

Stevie had written that "the sea of love" was where everyone aspired to drown themselves, and her life had been bursting with romance, but now "I need to get to know Stevie again," she said. "I need to be able to paint all night without making someone feel horrible because he's waiting for me to come to bed." Stevie was conscious of the fact that her chosen path would often leave a partner hanging as she skipped around the world, or turned up late at night too tired to pay him any attention. On the other hand, the men who did understand her career were also those who invariably wouldn't commit, or who would break her heart. The sea of love could be turbulent and cruel. Whether or not her motive for shying away from domesticity in its traditional sense was due to an underlying fear of loss, Stevie felt it best to steer clear of the water altogether and use her head, not her heart, for the time being. Besides, her love and warmth was needed elsewhere.

Nineteen eighty-two crawled to its feet under a cloud of foreboding and sickness – Stevie's priority was cheering Robin up but she was feeling justifiably bereft herself. There was no escaping the inevitable: Robin had months to live. Despite the terminal diagnosis, Robin and her partner Kim Anderson did their best to live their lives, deciding to marry soon after the shattering results came through. Robin would even become pregnant – a legacy for Kim, the Warner Bros rep she had met while touring with Fleetwood Mac. Robin was given the option of terminating the pregnancy and prolonging her own life, but she refused.

During the spring, Stevie whisked Robin to the tranquil sands of Hawaii to give her a break and create some lighter memories during this, the final year of her life. Once back in California, Robin would be cared for at the City Of Hope Cancer Center. The treatment was aggressive and before long, she had lost so much weight she was unrecognisable. Seeing her friend like this was unimaginably hard for Stevie and, at first, Stevie would visit the centre "high on coke" and having drunk "half a bottle of brandy on the way there, because I couldn't stand it. She said to me, 'Don't come back until you're not high'." Stevie told *The Guardian*'s Craig McLean in 2011.

Robin's courage and fortitude inspired Stevie, who found herself wanting to paint and draw more in a bid to channel her grief more prolifically. Jimmy Iovine rushed out and found whatever he could to sate Stevie's artistic urges – namely some "stupid little kindergarten paints and some paper" – and, with a glass of water by her side for her brushes (and a glass of wine for herself) Stevie started to render the image of a mystical pyramid, her first painting. Not only was art a way of escaping the pain and entering a meditative state, but it gave her a chance to create pictures for Robin to have on the walls of her hospital room, to lift her spirits and assure her she was always with her in her heart, even if she couldn't be there in person.

"When you paint or draw something, you carry it around for days or months or years," Stevie explained. "If you have a dog or a cat, they'll seek out that painting to sleep on because it has your essence in it. So I started to draw so I could pin something up on her wall and be with her, knowing this wasn't a letter I'd just jotted out, or a song, but an image that would constantly occur when she looked at that, that would say, 'She's here'." Stevie's sensitive, intuitive artwork would be heavily influenced by the fantasy illustrations of German artist Sulamith Wülfing as we know, and the bright, celestial images will have no doubt brought great comfort to Robin. Knowing there was at least something she could do for her ailing friend will have consoled Stevie alike, who otherwise was at a loss to know what she could do to help.

On June 18, the radio-friendly Fleetwood Mac album *Mirage* was released, spending 18 weeks in the US Top Ten, and for the first time since *Rumours* returning the band to number one, where it would remain for five lucrative weeks, having knocked British rock band Asia's eponymous album from pole position. However, the circumstances around the Mac – and the album – were such that no one in the inner circle felt especially excited by it; Lindsey had lost his mojo after being reined in post-*Tusk* and simply shrugged his shoulders on *Mirage*, taking a wilfully "passive role", as he put it. For all of its strengths, that lack of Buckingham electricity showed. Many critics and fans felt the album was a little too soft and pedestrian for their liking. It is the oddball tracks, such as Lindsey's 'Empire State', an ambiguous, whispered love song to New York from a true blue West Coast boy, and, of course, 'Gypsy', that really carry the record aloft. Nevertheless, the album would go double-platinum, the first single 'Hold Me' peaked at number four in the US, becoming one of the band's biggest hits in America, and Stevie's 'Gypsy', released in August, would reach the respectable position of number 12.

The launch party for *Mirage* was held a month after the release of the record itself, which came out a whole year after Fleetwood Mac left the Château, due to overdubs and remixes at the hands of Lindsey Buckingham and Richard Dashut. One wouldn't want to suggest that everything about

Mirage reflected the dearth of energy in the studio, but the reality was that everyone's priorities were elsewhere. A party is a party, however, and a typically decadent jamboree would occur at the SIR soundstage in Hollywood as a gale howled outside. More than 200 people turned up at the cavernous site to drink champagne under the flashing disco lights, and the various members of Fleetwood Mac regarded each other civilly, with Lindsey even inviting the band and their partners back to his place in Bel Air.

Stevie insisted on riding back with Carol Ann (which surprised her, let alone everyone else) while suggesting Jimmy and Lindsey should drive back together too – no doubt her intention was to spend a little quality time with the devil's dandruff*, which Jimmy didn't approve of her using. This was her first hit of the night, and she must really have wanted it to have chosen to ride with the girlfriend of her ex.

But, according to Carol Ann's book *Storms*, as the radio blared and their blonde locks flew about in the wind, Stevie opened up to her, shedding a tear over how brave Robin was in the face of cancer, and complaining affectionately about Jimmy Iovine telling her what to do all the time. She "wanted to please him . . . he's a lot like Lindsey". Carol Ann laughed and agreed that being with Lindsey was no walk in the park. "I've learned that everything I do is watched – and if he's in a mood to disapprove of something then I find out quickly . . . Sometimes I feel as though I need to ask permission for every move I make," Carol Ann confided. Stevie sympathised, adding warmly (according to Carol Ann) that "all of my girlfriends and I are sisters of the moon. I've given every woman I love a little half-moon necklace to wear. I'd give you one too, but it would drive Lindsey crazy . . ."

Parties aside, the sense of lethargy around *Mirage* would spill over into the promotional tour, which ran from the beginning of September to the end of October 1982. At just two months long, it didn't last anywhere near as long as the average epic Mac tour and would take in only key

* I've mentioned cocaine so many times in this book so far I'm running out of alternative names for it.

American cities. "I'm not that excited about touring myself," Buckingham told *The Record*'s David Gans bluntly. Warners executives no doubt read this interview with their heads in their hands.

Everyone knew Lindsey preferred tinkering in the studio at the best of times, but now there was an added pressure. "People have been waiting for us to break up for years, and the subject's coming up again," he continued. "The most likely one to disappear is Stevie, but there's no way of telling whether she wants to go off and not be a part of the band . . . at other times it's the opposite." "Would Fleetwood Mac survive her departure?" asked Gans. "Why not?" retorted Mick Fleetwood. After all, there had been plenty of lineup changes within the band, gifted musicians and compelling personalities moving in and out of the ranks like pawns on a chess-board. Was 'White Queen' Stevie really any different?

Stevie had always flatly denied any suggestions she might be planning to leave Fleetwood Mac, but Paul Fishkin, protective of Stevie as an artist and as a friend (and an asset), publicly asserted that, ultimately, "If it came down to her making a decision in terms of her career or their career, I know which direction I would push her in." Having essentially two lives was time-consuming, energy-draining and complex, not to mention something of a conflict of interests. Also, as far as those in the Nicks camp could see, the Mac were not making Stevie especially happy, while at the same time her presence in the band was only enhancing their work and their stage show.

Money certainly wouldn't be a problem on the *Mirage* tour. The band would be paid $800,000 to play a single set on September 5 at the inaugural US Festival in California on a bill that included Jackson Browne and Jimmy Buffett, but the vast pay-checks did little to boost morale. Nor did the great quantities of drugs and alcohol that were available to them at all times. From the moment Fleetwood Mac arrived at the amphitheatre in Houston, Texas, for the first show of the tour, it was, as Carol Ann Harris remembers, "immediately apparent that this tour was nothing like the *Rumours* or *Tusk* tours."

Footage of the *Mirage* tour displays a band that is almost out of control.

Lindsey and Stevie scream their harmonies at each other in 'The Chain', eyeing each other with what can only be described as mutual loathing.

During his solo on 'Sisters Of The Moon', Lindsey appears to barge Stevie with his guitar, prompting Stevie to take comfort from her fans who reach out with flowers and hungry hands, as if she were a religious icon weeping miracle tears before them. On one clip she is indeed weeping, tears streaming down her face. Carol Ann recalls that many of the shows were not up to their usual standard, but unlike the early days, when the slightest mistake would have had Stevie on the verge of a panic attack, or Lindsey flying into a rage, the band "had little to say about it. Everyone headed for the drinks table, picked up powder-filled bottle caps and changed into their street clothes to head back to the hotel." They were numb, preoccupied and frankly, with the exception of Mick and John, nobody wanted to be there. The news that was just around the corner was the tipping point that ensured this tour would be swiftly curtailed.

On 5 October, the tragedy Stevie had been dreading came to pass. Just days after giving birth three months prematurely to a baby boy, Robin Snyder Anderson died. Stevie went into a tailspin, tearfully calling Lindsey's hotel suite on the day she received the news – he had known Robin nearly as long as Stevie, after all.

There was no time to reflect or grieve and almost everything would prove a trigger for Stevie to burst into tears. A song on the radio, a picture, a scent . . . but most evocative for Stevie would be the material she had written herself – 'Gypsy' in particular would be a song Stevie would have to have a break from for a while. There was so much of Robin woven into that song as it was, and now this brave "breathtaking" woman was dancing away from her, leaving her memory with those who loved her, just as the lyrics stated. It was too close to the bone.

"[Robin] walked me through life, taught me how to sing, how to use my voice. She made sure before she left this planet that I was all right. As I questioned [whether there] would be life after Fleetwood Mac, I certainly questioned would there be life after Robin," Stevie said. She would find that, of course, there was, "except that it's not the same, not near as special."

Understandably, discussions were soon underway within the band to abandon any further plans to tour *Mirage,* and by the end of October, Stevie, Lindsey and Christine informed Mick and John that they would not continue after the scheduled US tour dates concluded in November. "There would be no European or Far East tour," confirmed Carol Ann Harris. "With *Mirage* at number one for two straight months, the band was over it. They wanted a long break from Fleetwood Mac, and they couldn't give a damn about record sales . . ."

The tour was too short, in Mick Fleetwood's opinion, and failed to do the album justice. "As soon as we left the road, *Mirage* died after five weeks at number one," he noted, John Cougar's *American Fool* steaming in to take its place. However, some things are more important than promoting a record. Mental health, for example. Stevie, for one, was self-medicating furiously, plans were already in motion for her next solo album, and she also desperately needed time to get over the anguish of losing her closest friend. But she also needed to figure out what the future would hold for Robin's baby Matthew. Stevie was his godmother, after all.

The caption to Stevie Nicks' 'Rhiannon' painting, dedicated to Robin Snyder Anderson:

'Rhiannon' was started at the onset of Robin's Leukaemia – last August – she died last Tuesday – She was originally finished for Patrick at the City of Hope – she died while she was still in her grey stage – I finished her in brilliance upon Robin's death – because Robin was brilliant – May she be a patron of driving this disease away – it cannot live this cancer – amongst Rhiannons [sic] bright colors – she was a bright light girl – and we will fight on white light – S. Nicks, 1982

Chapter 19

"When Stevie passed 30 and had not gotten married, I honestly did not think she ever would," Jess Nicks told local glossy *Arizona Living*. "When a woman goes that long being single, and particularly when she's hugely successful, usually her career is so important that she won't get married. So at 34, when she did get married, it was quite a shock to her mother and me." As it was to the rest of Fleetwood Mac and, indeed, Stevie's fans.

Stevie's fairytale wedding on 29 January, 1983 would not cause ructions because of jealousy, nor because she had inevitably spliced herself with a charismatic fellow rock star who was destined to let her down. It was because the man she married was Kim Anderson, husband of her best friend Robin who had died just three months earlier. The intentions behind the bizarre nuptials were honourable if misguided – Stevie, as godmother, felt responsible for frail, premature baby Matthew and was anxious to support Kim during his darkest hour. She also needed help herself; Stevie was often hysterical, lying on the floor in the night, screaming and crying, beating her fists. Robin's death was, she has said, "the worst thing that ever happened to me. The only person that could comfort me was him, and the only person that could comfort him was me."

"I was determined to take care of that baby, so I said to Kim, 'I don't know, I guess we should just get married.' It was a terrible, terrible mistake. We didn't get married because we were in love, we got married because we were grieving and it was the only way that we could feel like we were doing anything." The decision was 'split-second', informed not just by the need to take positive action and care for the child, but also by the fact that, rather more unsettlingly, Stevie was so present in Kim's life, and so similar to Robin in many respects, "a little part of him thought that I was her reincarnate," she said in an emotional 1990 interview with *US Magazine*.

There would even be moments during the months ahead when, Stevie admits, "He thought I *was* her. When the light was down, he wasn't sure whether it was Stevie or Robin. I would say something and turn away and he would think she had come back." Both of these mourning souls were evidently suffering from their own personal breakdowns while trying to be strong and find a way through it for the sake of the child.

But Stevie was also "falling in love with this little baby that basically Robin had died for. We decided to get married, and nobody understood. Nobody. My parents thought it was the most crazy thing, and they thought I was nuts anyway . . ."

Stevie's family felt that, while Kim was "pleasant", the marriage was a bad idea. It was also too soon after Robin had died. While the belief that she had to marry Kim was simply borne of bewildered despair and wanting to do the right thing, it was regarded by some as being in rather poor taste. And apart from anything else, it was upsetting to the Nicks family that Stevie's wedding should not be an event celebrating the fact she had ostensibly found "the one", but a bittersweet, confused declaration of friendship and support. As her father said, "When she makes up her mind to do something, nobody can change it," and, as Stevie saw it, she was stepping up for Robin's sake.

When Stevie called her friends with the news, nobody knew how to react, but everybody was united in their discomfort. "I remember calling Don Henley and saying, 'Don, I'm getting married to Kim. Will you come to the wedding?' He said, 'No,' and hung up. Then he called back a couple of days later and said, 'All right, I'll come,' and that is the same reaction I got from every person I called."

The bride wore symbolic black lace over white and a dazed smile, the ceremony took place on the beach at sundown outside Stevie's new home in the Pacific Palisades, and the couple were married by Philip Wagner, the same minister who had given comfort to Robin as she was dying. Robin had been a member of the Hiding Place Church, a community of born-again Christians who "emphasise the supernatural in its worship". Wagner had been "trepidatious" about marrying Kim and Stevie – "I had to know where Stevie was at with the Lord," he told *Rolling Stone* – but a simple ceremony went ahead despite the circumstances. There were no "thees and thous", according to Wagner, just "a little five-minute thing about their relationship to the Lord and little miracles happening. Then we did some quick vows, they exchanged rings, and we had a little communion."

Paul Fishkin was in attendance, loyal as ever, the only person who "understood the emotional trauma" of the entire fifteen months, according to Stevie. She felt questioned and judged by everyone else. Christine McVie and Mick Fleetwood ventured to the ceremony. Lindsey gave it a wide berth.

The development sent the whole band reeling, and Lindsey in particular was horrified. While unhinged behaviour was, as Carol Ann had observed, "the rule instead of the exception" in the world of the Mac, this was "beyond the pale", she wrote in *Storms*. "But when I thought of the grief Stevie had shared with me on the night of the *Mirage* party, I could only speculate that it was this grief that was responsible for a type of temporary insanity . . ."

Once the rice had been thrown and the unhappy couple returned home, attempting to process what was happening, Stevie threw herself immediately into work. And "immediately" is no exaggeration: she wrote the dynamic 'Stand Back' on her wedding night, having been inspired by hearing Prince's new song 'Little Red Corvette' on the radio as they drove to Santa Barbara for their "honeymoon". A demo was recorded at the hotel that evening, and a collaboration was just a phone call away . . .

As always, writing songs and honing existing work for the new album was ongoing in the run-up to the sessions, as was the recording of demos.

Sharon Celani, who had moved into Stevie's house (the library, to be precise) had to be on hand at all times should inspiration strike.

"Sharon's always been a real big help to me for songwriting," Stevie said in a radio interview at the time. "Sometimes I can write the song but I can't get it together to run up and down stairs and plug the tape recorder in, find a tape that doesn't have anything on it, figure out why the tape recorder doesn't work . . . why there's no batteries in the house, it's the middle of the night and I'm having a nervous breakdown because this is an important epic song I'm trying to write here and nothing works . . ."

Recording for Stevie's second solo album *The Wild Heart* would take place variously at A&R in New York, the Goodnight studio in Dallas, Sunset Sound in Los Angeles and the familiar turf of The Record Plant and Studio 55, with the stoic Jimmy Iovine once more at the helm. The process was economical time-wise, but Stevie would have little opportunity to be at home with Kim and Matthew. This might not have been such a bad thing – as we know, it was confusing for Kim to have Stevie around and more often than not he "would not let me take care of Matthew" anyway, which rather defeated the object of having got married in the first place.

When asked about how motherhood was working out for one so frequently away, Stevie glossed over the subject, saying that Matthew has "his own little path" and that he was going to be all right. He had a nanny, Bridget, who looked after him, which was just as well, because "I wasn't allowed to even go into the nursery unless [Kim] OK'd it," Stevie later revealed and, unsurprisingly, this strange version of domestic life was only going to get more peculiar. "He changed the phone numbers, nobody was allowed to come over unless he [approved] it," Stevie told BBC Radio 1's Nicky Horne. "He became so possessive of me that he wouldn't let me out of the house." Sessions for *The Wild Heart* couldn't come too soon.

The album, dedicated to Robin, would be a therapeutic process for Stevie and once again, she gathered her favourite musician friends around her, including Tom Petty, Benmont Tench, Roy Bittan, Waddy, Don Felder, Michael Campbell, Lori and Sharon. Mick Fleetwood would be present, adding drums to the track 'Sable On Blond' and collaborating with Stevie on synths, and co-writing several songs would be the Texan singer-songwriter Sandy Stewart, "an incredible writer and incredibly funny, nice person."

Sandy came to Stevie's attention when someone handed a tape of Sandy's melodies to Stevie one day. Nicks was "so inspired, I wrote the lyrics to ['If Anyone Falls'] and 'Nothing Ever Changes' that night. From that day onward, Sandy and I considered ourselves kind of the Rodgers & Hammerstein of rock. If someone can write a track that I really love, I'll be glad to write a song to it, because I've got about 800,000 pages of words . . ."

Stevie was impressed by Sandy's sound, and had been keen to tap into the dominant trend of synth-pop sweeping the charts. Culture Club, Prince, Kim Carnes, Ultravox . . . all were utilising synthesisers but in a style less stark than the electronic music of the previous decade. To hear Stevie's spiked-honey voice against a wall of velvety synths would be a jolt for those who simply had her pegged as a 1970s relic, clinging to what had worked in the past. Stevie embraced modernity and innovation, she just wanted to merge it with her own unique style rather than completely reinvent herself.

Both the evocatively titled 'Sable On Blond' and 'Wild Heart' had been written the previous year, just after Stevie moved into her "horrifyingly bad, awful, terrible house in the Pacific Palisades". The Palisades is a glamorous, affluent beachside area north of Los Angeles and, as we know, Stevie was a stone's throw from the ocean, but there was something about the place she couldn't love, not least the fact that she came back from her *Bella Donna* tour, spent and desperate for the respite of home, to find there was no heating. "And I was all alone with no phones, like a mountain woman."

What would Stevie Nicks do in a situation like this? "I freaked out . . ." Yes, and? "And I wrote 'Sable On Blond' and the verses to 'Wild

Heart'. Me and my piano." That's more like it. 'Sable On Blond' was a "serious statement", according to Stevie. The song threw a spotlight on her feelings about maturing, learning to be alone, "to be one colour" after surrounding herself with people and noise and work, blocking out her emotions with drugs. She needed a place where she could just live with herself and train herself to be stronger. It wasn't easy, but drawing on the legend of Excalibur, Stevie explained to *Rock Magazine*: "The sword is there for protection, but you don't call upon it unless it's absolutely necessary. During that period in my life, I was learning how not to call on the sword." The sword could well represent cocaine. However, it may also represent the wrong type of man. She was still surrounded by dashing rock'n'roll "highwaymen" who were all too easy to fall in love with.

And so this brings us to the song 'Wild Heart'. Its fierce warmth is mingled with sadness, a characteristic of many of Stevie's songs. But this one represents the anxieties and fears Stevie was battling with all the more clearly, "all the darkest places of your mind", as Stevie put it, rather tellingly. "It definitely takes you through your nervous breakdown, and through your recovery and through your survival."

Stevie would record a demo with Sandy Stewart, Sharon and Lori, and the result was, in Stevie's words, "a killer". It had to be if it was going to lend its name to the album itself. If the song wasn't strong enough, Stevie would have simply had to change the album title, but "I played it for Tom Petty and he said, 'This is an epic.'" Now that Stevie had proved herself with *Bella Donna*, she insisted on more of a "party" atmosphere in the studio, and the presence of friends was more welcome than it had been during the previous album process. Iovine no doubt loosened his grip a little, particularly as he could see how important it was for Stevie to have the people she loved around her at this point in her life.

"*Bella Donna* was really intense," Stevie told Mary Turner for *Off The Record*, "because it was an unproven white-winged dove who could have crashed into the side of the mountain; everybody was hesitant about it, so I was really dedicated." That isn't to say Nicks wasn't just as committed to *The Wild Heart*, but the pressure was also lifted considerably thanks to the storming success of its predecessor. The turnaround would be relatively swift, however; the release date for the album would be 10 June 1983, which certainly focused the mind.

When it came to the mood of the album, Stevie visualised a direct thread between the characters of this and her previous release: 'Bella Donna' was coming of age and venturing out with more courage – which Stevie herself was doing musically as a solo artist. "It's like Bella Donna's heart is wild all of a sudden," Stevie told *Rock Magazine*. "She's surer of herself now, so she's taking more chances." Where *Bella Donna* was reflective and poetic, *The Wild Heart* would be, as its name suggests, "strong and emotional, no holds barred".

The themes of pain, death and rebirth would loom large, for obvious reasons. Mortality and change were on Stevie's mind. "This album is more rock'n'roll," Stevie would later state. "Which is good for me – it certainly keeps you young. If you can't rock and roll, you're old." No one could have predicted Robin would have been taken at such an early age, and the ordeal had opened Nicks' eyes and shown her she needed to make the most of her life, to "rock a little", as she often said, as opposed to too much, or not at all.

One song destined for *The Wild Heart*, stashed away from previous years, would be 'Beauty And The Beast', written on the road with Fleetwood Mac during the *Tusk* tour. It was inspired both by Mick Fleetwood around the time of their affair, and Jean Cocteau's dream- like 1946 movie *Beauty And The Beast*, a favourite film of Stevie's. The story itself resonated strongly. "Beauty And The Beast surrounds me," Stevie explained. "Everybody I know is either being the Beauty or the Beast." At the heart of the fairy story was a sense of "desperation", Stevie observed. At the time of writing the song, she was witnessing Mick Fleetwood's sadness as his father was dying of cancer. After the tour visited Dallas, Mick flew straight to his father's bedside after the show, arriving 45 minutes before he died.

Stevie's friend and sometime producer Gordon Perry had a studio in Dallas, and the day after the show, Stevie went there and recorded a demo of 'Beauty And The Beast' on the piano. The studio was "magical" and church-like, and the experience of recording the song there for the first time is a moment that Stevie has always held close to her heart. There was a reverence that suited the sentiment of the song. "Everybody has to remember how special everybody is . . . this is the story of Beauty and the Beast: how special we are to each other."

'Beauty And The Beast' would be at the centre of one of Stevie's most lavish sessions yet. "I'm someone who's oblivious to being able to do anything in the studio in a mere three hours," Stevie quipped, although she treated the session with the gravitas she felt it deserved, walking in in a long black gown, a glass of champagne in her hand as she greeted the musicians and approached the microphone.

"I wanted them to feel like they were the most special orchestra that ever existed," Stevie told the audience at the Wild Heart concert in Dallas in 1983. "They don't even have any idea what they gave me, how precious it is."

The pensive 'Nightbird' is Stevie's direct dedication to Robin's memory, and lyrically it has a connection to 'Edge Of Seventeen' (which refers to the "call of the nightbird" Stevie heard after her uncle John passed away). In the song, Stevie speaks of not having been 'ready for the winter', for the sadness that was to come, and plaintively addresses the spirit of her departed friend, asking her, "When I call, will you walk gently through my shadow?"

The song was written with Sandy Stewart in Stevie's living room, taking just two hours to complete, "with her synthesiser and me pacing". All of Stevie's songs are special to her, and all of them would go on to have a life of their own once she had presented them to the world. But 'Nightbird' had a particularly serious purpose; Stevie hoped that, through this song, she would play her part in helping to beat cancer.

"Maybe 'Nightbird' will inspire somebody to do some research," Stevie said. "Maybe it will make somebody be a doctor. Maybe some kid will go, 'I'm gonna do cancer research and I'm gonna beat leukaemia'. That's what I hope Sandy and I did with 'Nightbird'."

The cover of *The Wild Heart* itself would also pay tribute to Robin in its threefold depiction of Stevie. Shot by Herbie Worthington, who had become part of the Nicks extended family and one of many people on her payroll, the concept was to portray different dimensions of Stevie, dressed in a floor-length, hooded black cape against a warm, dark background. The crouching Stevie shows her private and often lonesome side, and to the right there is the star, upright and regal. But the spectral, faded figure in the centre looking down at the more contemplative Stevie represents Robin's spirit.

The Wild Heart would see a return of Tom Petty, whose song 'I Will Run To You' featured on the record as a duet. Tom and Stevie's collaborations were always stellar, their cracked, slightly wasted- sounding rock'n'roll timbres mingling together perfectly and, as Tom's then wife Jane put it, if only they would work together more, she could be "sleeping in mink". "Jane is on my side," confirmed Stevie. "Tom and I are a duo extraordinaire, and I don't have much interest in going around looking for some other guy to sing with." Bye for now, Don.

'I Will Run To You' merged that classic Heartbreakers sound with subtle synths, a blend of present and future. Lyrically, the line "I will follow you down . . .' echoes Bob Dylan's 'Baby, Let Me Follow You Down'; Dylan was a hero to both Nicks and Petty. Tom and Stevie spent a lot of time together and because Stevie respected him so much, the "swampy Floridian" felt confident enough to tell Nicks the truth, rather than regard her with awe. He loved her and was amused by her idiosyncrasies. "It's like when you've got a sister in the family nobody wants to talk about much," he said dryly. "Someone you love but who's a little bit . . . er . . . different."

"He'll say I'm like a plane that doesn't have any radar," said Stevie. "He says to me, 'You're not living in the real world', and I'm saying, 'Do you live in the real world?' and he's going, 'Well, I live in more of a real world than you do, for sure.'" But there was a logic to not living in the real world, in creating a softer existence that shuts out that which can only bring further anxiety to a sensitive soul like Nicks. The problem was that, in this case, the plane wasn't only lacking a radar, it was spiralling towards an emotional Bermuda Triangle.

Prince was another artist who noted Stevie's lifestyle with concern – she was, after all, a "drug addict", as she put it, while he was as "straight as an arrow". They would get on well, however, and share a "special" friendship – one which didn't involve going to bed, Stevie would insist, despite the inevitable rumours. Prince was "a strange and beautiful guy", there was no doubt about that.

Prince had just returned from touring his massively successful 1982 album 1999 when he received a call from Nicks. Iovine had been setting up the studio at Sunset Sound, Los Angeles, to record 'Stand Back', the song inspired by Prince's own 'Little Red Corvette', and Stevie wanted to see if the man himself would join the session. Stevie hummed the melody down the phone to him and within an hour he was in the studio with her. Stevie told Timothy White for his book *Rock Lives* that: "He listened again, and I said, 'Do you hate it?' He said, 'No,' and walked over to the synthesisers, was absolutely brilliant for about 25 minutes, and then left. He was so uncanny, so wild, he spoiled me for every band I've ever had because nobody can exactly re-create – not even with two piano players – what Prince did all by his little self."

Electronic drums were used, Toto guitarist Steve Lukather was brought in to add a guitar part and that Prince magic would ensure 'Stand Back' would be the most successful single from the album, later being nominated for a Grammy. The sound of that heavy bass and voluminous synth against Stevie's husky voice would soon be heard booming out of many a nightclub, an underground hit as well as a mainstream smash.

Prince had just one piece of advice for Stevie: sex up your lyrics. Prince's own lyrical content was always notorious for its explicit sexuality, while Stevie's words were often obscure, never literal. As Stevie explained, a sudden injection of overt raunchiness into her lyrics would make no sense because "that's not the way I am in real life. I am not a person who walks naked through the house. I will always have something beautiful on, and it will enhance me. I believe there is a certain amount of mysticism that all women should have. Even in my journals, I don't ever write about sex," she told Courtney Love for *Spin* in 1997.

And before Prince could protest any further, Stevie concluded the argument by stating: "You have to write about sex, so you must not be intrinsically sexy. I don't have to write about sex because I am intrinsically sexy. That shut his mouth right up." In your face, Prince. Stevie was a sex symbol by default, but she hadn't forgotten the one time she had bowed to pressure and gone topless on the cover of *Buckingham Nicks* – it left her embarrassed and the record barely sold any copies anyway. Stevie just had to be herself.

To Prince's credit, he cared deeply for Stevie and ran around for her when she suffered one of her many bouts of the flu, plumping her pillows and tidying up around her. "He would bring me cough medicine," Stevie recalled to *The Telegraph*'s Craig McLean, "and then I'd ask for another spoon of it, and he'd go, 'I didn't come here to start you on a new drug!' So I realised that was not gonna work out: we're two really famous rock'n'roll stars, and I'm a drug addict and he's not,*so these paths are not gonna meet well. But if I needed Prince I'm sure he would come and help me."

Stevie disliked making music videos, but in the age of MTV, if she wanted to continue to be seen as a happening young star, she had to comply. Still, the whole process wasn't "impulsive" enough. "It's being told to do it over and over again . . . It focuses in on your performance and also every little line on your face. I don't sing because of the way I look. I sing because I love the music. I don't like my body being put under a microscope. Unfortunately, if you're doing film, you have to do it. That's why I'll never be an actress."

* While this was famously true at the time, to today's reader this conclusion may seem sadly at odds with what would happen later - tragically Prince would die in 2016 after an accidental overdose of fentanyl, an opioid 50 times stronger than heroin, with evidence suggesting the star had become addicted to pain medications after trying to treat a hip injury. Nicks' close friend and comrade Tom Petty would also die the following year after an accidental fentanyl overdose.

There are actually two 'Stand Back' videos in existence – one of which was a no-expense-spared *Gone With The Wind*-inspired promo directed by Brian Grant, a colleague of Russell Mulcahy and a favourite director of the band Queen. This video showed Stevie riding on a white mare towards the manor before throwing off her hat and cape and stomping through the drawing room.

There are scenes of a ball, with a handsome man approaching her to dance (later echoed in the video for Stevie's hit 'Rooms On Fire'), more galloping and some depictions of Civil War violence, extras galore. The video would never be aired because Stevie felt she looked fat. No longer in her twenties and having imbibed enough champagne to sink the *Queen Mary*, Stevie was still uncommonly beautiful but had started to feel more conscious of how she looked, particularly after insensitive photographers had observed she had "put a little weight on around the chin". (It is unlikely Mick Fleetwood or Lindsey Buckingham would ever be addressed in this way.) Still, the 'Scarlett' version, as is it known, would eventually turn up on the DVD supplement of Stevie's 2007 collection *Crystal Visions – The Very Best Of Stevie Nicks.*

"I re-did 'Stand Back' with Jeffrey Hornaday, who choreographed *Flashdance*," explained Stevie. "This sent me into waves of panic because I am not a dancer and I am certainly not like what's-her-name in *Flashdance*." She had nothing to fear. Stevie not only had her ballet chops to back her up, but to help her she brought in the dancer Brad Jeffries, of whom she became so fond that he would star in many of Stevie's other videos, such as 'If Anyone Falls' and later 'Rooms On Fire' as the love interest.

Brad was just the latest addition to the Stevie entourage, also appearing with Stevie and the band when they performed 'Stand Back' that year on *Saturday Night Live*, hurling himself onstage mid-song and engaging in a wild dance routine with Stevie. The official video for the hit 'Stand Back', reflecting *Flashdance* and even *West Side Story* with its gang of strutting dancers, was filled with mirrors and developed into a veritable pea-souper of whirling dry ice. "It's wonderful," enthused Stevie to Molly Meldrum. "And Brad, who choreographs all my videos to this day, puts up with a lot from me because he knows that I'm sweet and he doesn't want to hurt my feelings, you know? It's difficult because I'm a rock'n'roll singer . . ."

As "wonderful" as it thankfully turned out, the making of the 'Stand Back' video did not run smoothly; Jeffrey Hornaday and Jimmy Iovine clashed significantly, according to Danny Goldberg's book *Bumping Into Geniuses.* After seeing an edit of the 'Stand Back' video, Jimmy put together a list of changes on Stevie's behalf and presented them to Hornaday, who didn't take kindly to the criticism. However, when Stevie entered the studio and watched the edit, she listed exactly the concerns that Jimmy had brought up, which caused the director to start arguing with Stevie "about the merits of his 'vision'". Goldberg remembers, "Jimmy jumped up . . . and insisted, 'There is no argument. This is Stevie's record. This is Stevie's video. You do what Stevie wants." Taken aback by Iovine's hostile tone, Hornaday answered, 'Fuck you, man.'" The contretemps concluded with Jimmy punching Jeffrey Hornaday in the face. Behind the leg-warmers and the dry ice, the world of the pop video is a volatile place. Approach with care.

*

> "*One day when I walked into Matthew's room, the cradle was not rocking. It was always rocking whenever I'd walk in, and I knew Robin was there. One day it wasn't rocking and it was very dark and the baby was very quiet. And I said, 'Robin wants this to end – now.'"*
>
> Stevie Nicks to *The Guardian*'s Craig McLean, March 2011.

The *Wild Heart* tour was soon to begin at the end of May, and there were still scenes to complete for the 'Stand Back' video. During a Friday night at home, Stevie went through her closets selecting extra outfits for the video and some of the costumes she wanted to use on tour, as her wardrobe mistress was coming by to pick them up. It was perfectly routine, but Kim, who had been gradually unravelling over the past few months, refused to let the wardrobe mistress in altogether.

"I saw this man turning into an absolute madman," said Stevie. "It was like he was building a fort around me. So on Saturday I went to finish the filming of 'Stand Back' – we were leaving on Monday – and I came back on Saturday night and he screamed and yelled at me and I screamed and yelled at him . . . and I said 'I want a divorce. I'm not Robin, I can't replace her, I wish I could but I can't'." The marriage, borne of altruism and grief, had turned into a full-blown nightmare; it wasn't healthy for anyone concerned and the time had come to face reality. Stevie admits it was about "ten days after" the wedding that she realised she'd made a mistake. Her friends and family had seen that long before they'd exchanged vows, but had been powerless to change her mind.

For some years, Stevie would not hear from Kim at all. "I suppose that Matthew will find me when he's ready, I mean I am, next to Robin, his mommy," Stevie mused to *US Magazine* in 1990. "But Kim and I can't deal with each other at all. So when [Matthew's] old enough, I have all of his mother's things and I have her life on film for 14, 15 years, I have us on tape singing, I have a beautiful book that I wrote the year she died, a roomful of stuff for him. I have his mother to give back to him when he's ready."

Chapter 20

The Wild Heart tour would certainly live up to its name. An extensive North American road trip of four legs, starting in Vegas in May, and ending in November at the Carolina Coliseum, it would whisk Stevie away from the turmoil of her divorce and throw her straight into the arms of a new man whom she would later describe as the love of her life. As Stevie remembers, "Everyone around me was in love. On the tour everyone was either getting divorced or falling in love, they'd get on the plane and see someone and fall in love instantly . . ." Stevie was no different and besides, her relationship with Jimmy Iovine had morphed into a strictly professional one – their lifestyles were just too disparate and Nicks was sorely in need of some TLC.

Mick Fleetwood, occupied with his musical side project The Zoo and the subsequent 1983 release *I'm Not Me,* decided against being in Stevie's touring band for *The Wild Heart*, giving the opportunity to drummer Liberty DeVitto, who promptly fell in love with (and later married) Stevie's friend Mary Torrey. Stevie herself, for all of her romantic tendencies, didn't believe in "love at first sight". Or at least, she didn't until this tour.

Don Henley's fellow Eagle, Joe Walsh, was booked as the support act on *The Wild Heart* tour. A successful solo artist in his own right since his 1973 breakthrough album *The Smoker You Drink, The Player You Get*, he had wittily captured the rock star lifestyle with sharp self-awareness in his 1978 hit 'Life's Been Good': the Maseratis, the mansions, the destroyed hotels, parties and paranoia are all there; the lyrics explaining that "I can't complain but sometimes I still do . . ." and concluding: "It's tough to handle this fortune and fame / Everybody's so different, I haven't changed." This song gives a pretty clear idea of what life was like for Joe, Stevie, Don and the whole Hollywood rock'n'roll scene of that era. That's if you weren't there to witness it firsthand, of course.

Now Walsh had a brand new album out, *You Bought It – You Name It,* tying in perfectly with Stevie's promotional tour. Joe was charismatic, funny and unconventional, and while Stevie was no stranger to larger-than-life rock stars (or just Eagles) during the tour, Stevie walked into the bar of the Mansions Hotel in Dallas after a show, and spotted him sitting alone. "I walked across the room . . . He held out his hands to me, and I walked straight into them." She "crawled into his lap, and that was that . . . I remember thinking, 'I can never be far from this person again . . . he is my soul.'" Joe himself has subsequently referred to Stevie as a "soul mate" himself, albeit a soul mate that wouldn't always get treated too well.

Joe would be a more than welcome distraction from the difficult year Stevie had had, although she worked hard at making the tour work, possibly harder than ever. Rather than the process getting easier, thanks to having already gone out on the road alone with *Bella Donna*, it was "probably getting more difficult," Stevie admitted to *Arizona Living*. "The *Bella Donna* tour was something like eleven concerts – that was fun and it went by really fast. This one is really fun, but every night I've become more aware that I'm singing every song. I'm very used to having a lot of songs off [with Fleetwood Mac] so I can fix my makeup, comb my hair, wipe my face and just touch up a little bit. And now I can't. I'm in such a hurry that sometimes I run to the side of the stage and I'm not even sure what I'm running there for. So it's a lot more work, physically."

Stevie was also exercising and losing weight, having been bothered by how she looked on recent photos, and her increased physical fitness also meant she didn't run out of energy during the show. "I have to stay in really good shape," she said. "In the long run, of course, it's going to make me a much stronger person because it's forcing me to take good care of myself. Otherwise I could never get through that two-hour set." It could only be a good thing that Stevie was now in better shape than she had been previously, but privately, Stevie was, as Mick Fleetwood observed, "on a slow downward spiral".

Fleetwood could see how exhausted Nicks was, how she was pushing herself hard and working like a woman possessed. "I think she suffered physically. She was running two gigs and two lives, separate lives that were equally as powerful and it took a hell of a lot out of her to retain that loyalty to Fleetwood Mac and not go, 'See ya'." It was a year since the last Fleetwood Mac album and no one was exactly beating a path to the studio to work on the next one – no one had time – but Mick was anxious that the band should not fizzle out. On the other hand, he knew he'd have a fight on his hands if he were to persuade Stevie's management to free her up for the Mac. She was doing very nicely on her own and Fishkin had already been quite clear "which direction [he] would push her in", if it came down to making a choice. It was a delicate situation.

Stevie's tour was already well underway by the time *The Wild Heart* hit the charts, then dominated by Michael Jackson's *Thriller* album. *The Wild Heart* couldn't compete with the King of Pop, but it would go double platinum, and while it would not be as lauded as *Bella Donna*, it was a "masterpiece", in Stevie's eyes. It didn't matter what the critics said (she refused to read reviews anyway – bad reviews, like horror movies, haunted her for weeks), Stevie was proud of it, not least because of what it represented to her. "Freedom," she declared. "It sets me free from Fleetwood Mac. It sets me free from Stevie Nicks. It sets me free from the person who drives me. You always have to please somebody. It is letting me go. This is two records now, so the first record wasn't just a fluke accident. I can go and do whatever I want now and no one is going to be saying to me: 'You still aren't a proven solo artist.'"

It is just as well Stevie didn't bother about reviews, because some of them were not kind, labelling the record "pedestrian" and "rambling", although this was nothing in comparison to some of the live reviews she received on this tour. Her fans were enchanted, however, and that was what mattered. Stevie wasn't writing or performing for the benefit of the critics, it was all for her fans; as far as they were concerned, she was delivering exactly what they wanted.

Punishing schedule aside, there were pleasurable moments on this tour for Stevie and her band, who just enjoyed hanging out together, playing music and introducing each other to the new artists who had caught their attention. This was one of the reasons Stevie brought together a band of people she loved being with: there would be no scurrying off to individual corners after the show, no silences, no awkwardness, as there always was on tour with the Mac. Sharon, Lori and fellow backing singers Marilyn Martin and Carolyn Brooks, who had joined the throng to fill out the sound, would regularly practice their parts and try new harmonies around the piano during down time, not least so they could be prepared should Stevie ever lose concentration or pull the rug from under them onstage. "Sometimes Stevie will do something creative and different," Lori said, diplomatically."Which forces [us] to either not sing or change our parts."

"I'm very impulsive," agreed Stevie. "So if I decide to take the upper third part harmony and then immediately sing the low part, I do it. That's the way I am, so these girls are put through a serious wringer every night to follow me."

One of Stevie's favourite moments on tour would be arriving at the new venue, empty, cavernous and echoey. There was always the opportunity to put on a favourite mixtape and blast it through the PA, filling the hall with sound. Roxy Music, Lionel Ritchie, Hall & Oates, The Commodores, Jackson Browne, Maniac, Prince and Michael Jackson were all artists Stevie loved to listen to. She'd practice her pointe exercises backstage to her Tom Petty tape (with 'TP' painted on the case in nail polish), allow Waddy to play her some AC/DC and listen to The Police during the moments before she hit the stage.

"That song 'Every Breath You Take', we open the show with it," she explained. "It gets me out of the dressing room as soon as I hear it. I don't want to miss any of it, he is talking to me! As long as I don't have to know him, just listen to him singing, that's fine. Thank you Sting!" The way Stevie talks about the intense, moody Sting possibly hints at another rock star crush – at least from afar. He gave her "palpitations", after all . . . "I've seen him but I never talk to him. I talk to Stewart (Copeland), to Andy (Summers) and the road manager, but I never talk to Sting and after I saw that video, I know why. You would not want Sting to ever be mad at you," Stevie giggled in a radio interview.

In the meantime, Stevie and Joe Walsh were keeping their relationship under wraps, which made it all the more thrilling. "It was a very great secret," she said in an interview with BBC Radio 1, before tenderly adding, "It was love." Although they didn't officially announce they were together – Stevie had only just gone through a divorce, after all – those who knew her could already see he was bringing out the generous and often fiercely protective side of her nature.

"I yelled at people at his sound checks. Someone would say, 'Joe destroyed the dressing room last night,' and I'd just say, 'Fix it,'" she laughed, relating the story to BBC Radio 1's Nicky Horne in 1991. "I bought him incredible silk shirts and leg warmers that he wore, I took really good care of him, and I think that's probably what scared Joe the most, I was too in tune with him, and he was out of tune with everything." But they were both drowning in their addictions, clinging to each other for support but aware that they would drag each other further into the depths of dependency. "We were busy being superstars and everyone was doing way too many drugs," Stevie said in later years. "But I was so in love with him."

On 25 September Nicks, Walsh and Kenny Loggins appeared as 'Stevie Nicks and Friends' for a fundraiser at the Compton Terrace Amphitheater, a venue in Phoenix owned by Jess Nicks, who was now running the promotion company Compton Terrace Concerts*. Having suffered from heart troubles himself, Jess Nicks had become involved with the American Heart Association and organised events to raise money for the cause. He'd already booked Fleetwood Mac for previous fund-raisers, raising

* No doubt after being dissatisfied by how things were being run on the White-Winged Dove Tour, Jess Nicks was also involved in the smooth-running of The Wild Heart Tour too.

tens of thousands of dollars, and now, post-retirement, had set up Compton Terrace, named after the late William Edward Compton, erstwhile programme director at KDKB radio who had given generous airplay to Buckingham Nicks during the early seventies. Nicks, Loggins and Walsh gave their time for free, and, as well as the show being a benefit for the American Heart Association, the City of Hope hospital would also receive a donation in Robin's honour.

It was a moving event to witness, not to mention take part in, and emotions were already running high. Just a few days previously, The Wild Heart Tour had taken in Denver, Colorado. Colorado, with its tranquil 'snow-covered hills', always seems to be a rich source of inspiration for Stevie but the song that would spring from this particular visit would have an especially emotional resonance. Stevie had always felt that Joe had 'a lot of pain' which he concealed deftly with his clowning and partying. But on this September day in 1983, Stevie would discover what the source of that pain was. In the *Timespace* liner notes, Stevie tells the story:

"I guess I had been complaining about a lot of things going on on the road, and Joe decided to make me aware of how unimportant my problems were. He rented a jeep and drove me to Boulder, which is like an hour and a half [away], and told me this story on the way of a little girl that was killed in an accident on her way to nursery school. His little girl.

"We walked across this park and there was this little silver drinking fountain, and it said, 'To Emma Kristen, for all those who can't, or aren't big enough to get a drink.'"

Joe explained that this had been his daughter's favourite park and that his tribute, nestling under a tree, was inspired by the time Emma once reached up to drink from a fountain only to find she was too tiny. A light snow was falling, and as Stevie approached the fountain, she burst into tears.

"Something about this story touched me so deeply that I went home to my house in Phoenix, I walked into the front entryway, where my Bösendorfer piano is, I sat down and wrote this song in about five minutes." The song would be titled 'Has Anyone Ever Written Anything For You?'. When Stevie told her parents the emotional story behind the song, even Jess Nicks had to excuse himself from the room in order to shed a tear. This song was Stevie's way of responding to what Joe had shared with her, because there was "nothing I could say to someone who had suffered a loss like that."

Walsh had tragically lost his eldest daughter when she was just three, in 1974, and he would write 'Song For Emma' that year. "So he wrote a song for her, and I wrote a song for him," Stevie concludes. "Thank you, Joe, for the most committed song I ever wrote . . . But more than that, thank you for inspiring me in so many ways. Nothing in my life ever seems as dark any more since we took that drive."

The line "poet, priest of nothing" in the song refers to Joe, and "all the rock stars in the world that I know; they're all poets, and they're all priests of nothing, and they're all legends," Stevie explained, adding that very few of them handle their fame very well. "'Priests of nothing' means they don't try hard enough. So whenever I get involved with any of them I tend to become their manager, their agent . . . 'why don't we get out your piano? Why don't we write a song? Let's arrange this!' I know that if I can just lure them to the piano, with like a glass of wine, they'll be home-free and so will I, because I get to watch them be brilliant, and probably write something, and they will be knocked out because they'll be doing what they do. They forget they have a job, you know?"

As for Stevie herself, she is "a priestess of way too much. My problem is the other extreme: how many rooms could you clean, meals could you cook, children to take care of, shows you should do, fittings you should go for, make-up hours . . . you know? I try to fit the impossible into 24 hours, and all of the 'priests of nothing'? They're sleeping."

Beyond anyone else Stevie had loved so far, beyond Lindsey, Don, Mick, Paul, Jimmy or any of the other men to whom she had been meaningfully connected, Joe was the one man Stevie would have considered marrying, and eventually he would be the one to break her heart. "There was nothing more important than Joe Walsh, not my music, not my songs, not anything." Not long before they met, there was nothing more important than her songs, so this statement is profoundly telling.

But despite the care Stevie took of him – perhaps even because of it – Joe never quite treated Stevie the way she wished to be treated. On her favourite holiday, Halloween, Joe blew Stevie off, choosing to work on his new computer instead. She felt "replaced. If computers are going to replace me in a man's life . . ." well, then it just wasn't going to work. Stevie received a further slap in the face when Walsh, after being probed mercilessly by shock jock Howard Stern about his relationship with Nicks, simply said, after a Pinteresque pause, that he had loved Stevie "as a sister. She's like a soulmate . . . we were seeking refuge in each other's presence. We were on the road, we had careers. We were both lonely . . ." Only Joe can know what he really felt, addled as he was by drugs, but the fragile Stevie was lovestruck, and felt as if the world had ended whenever he let her down.

"I remember days of misery waiting by the phone," Stevie recalled in conversation with Chrissy Iley for *Elle Magazine* in 2013. "Me in my house, with him saying, 'I'm going to visit you.' I would kick everyone out because I just wanted to be with him, and not a phone call, nothing. [I put up with it because] I was in love with him. I wouldn't now. But we were doing a lot of drugs and drugs make you needy. I don't know what my relationship with Joe would have been like sober."

Neediness aside, drugs also make you unreliable at best. Walsh probably meant what he said when he was saying it, at least. But for Joe, getting too close to Stevie Nicks was also potentially dangerous for both of them considering their lifestyle, and Nicks was not oblivious to that. "We were a couple on the way to hell."

Chapter 21

During The Wild Heart Tour Stevie had, as always, managed to find time to write and record demos for her next album – there was plenty to write about, after all. The third solo Nicks record would be trendy and upbeat, with synth arrangements reminiscent of the Art Of Noise at times and a very different feel from *The Wild Heart.*

The initial plan was to simply call it *Rock'n'Roll.* She was the queen of it, after all. But the record would not be "rock'n'roll" in the traditional sense, and Stevie decided on a working title of *Mirror, Mirror*, an obvious nod to her fascination with the trippy, magical children's story *Alice's Adventures In Wonderland.* It also conjured a sense of self-reflection, an activity Stevie was often engaged with, and there was also the subliminal reference to cocaine.

Eventually the record would be titled *Rock A Little*, however; a name that, at this point, had great significance. Stevie would explain when asked about the title that "'Rock A Little' means perseverance. [It] means cool out, rock a little all the time and you won't die." Once again, Stevie was telling herself what she needed to do. She just wasn't listening to her own advice.

Stevie had written the title track three years previously, and the song was originally inspired by the ocean, and its often unsettling power. Stevie's beach-side home was a dwelling that rocked, in more ways than one. "The beach was always shaking and I always thought it was an earthquake," she admitted. "Scared me to death every night. So I had to learn to know not to pack my bags and run out the back."

Stevie was, of course, also using the sea as a metaphor for herself with this album – the ocean was unpredictable; sometimes tranquil, sometimes raging, but even when it was 'calm', the house would 'rock a little', never quite still or stable. 'Rock A Little', like 'Bella Donna', was another warning to Stevie from her own heart.

Songs were pouring out of her, and with Fleetwood Mac still on hiatus, solo projects were flourishing across the board. Christine McVie was preparing to release her eponymous second solo album in January 1984, featuring guest appearances from the likes of Eric Clapton and Steve Winwood, while Lindsey Buckingham's album *Go Insane* would be released in July 1984, an intense, clenched fist of a record largely documenting his inevitable break-up with Carol Ann Harris.

There was an ominous shadow hanging over Hollywood as 1983 came to a close. In addition to drug problems, broken relationships, meltdowns and, for some, financial issues, there would be the tragic loss of another dear friend: Dennis Wilson. On 28 December, just weeks after celebrating his 39th birthday in typically sybaritic style, Dennis was hanging out at Marina Del Rey, not far from Stevie's condominium. He had been drinking heavily for hours and as the day wore on, a wasted Dennis decided to dive into the freezing water to look for some personal items – including a photograph of one of his ex-wives that had been flung overboard during a drunken evening on his old yacht Harmony three years earlier.

Dennis reappeared triumphantly with the photograph, but told concerned friends he was going down again for a box he knew was there. He never emerged. The people he was with suspected a practical joke, which wouldn't have been out of character, but his body was brought up by divers some hours later. New Year was cancelled and on 4 January 1984, Wilson was buried at sea off the California coast, as per his wish. From his prison cell, Charles Manson, with whom Dennis had become temporarily embroiled during the late sixties, claimed Dennis' death was a result of having neglected his priorities to him. "Dennis Wilson," he said, "was killed by my shadow . . ." California dreaming was not to be recommended if you weren't prepared for some serious night terrors.

Dennis had become close to Fleetwood Mac during his two-year relationship with Christine, who adored him and had written the song 'Only Over You', featured on *Mirage,* for him. Their engagement was broken off in 1981 when his spending and womanising became too much to bear, but the Beach Boy remained loved by the Mac as a friend and an artist. Lindsey in particular revered Wilson and the Beach Boys and would honour his memory with the track 'D.W. Suite' on *Go Insane.*

As the hard-living Californian rock elite mourned the death of their sweet, wild friend, many will have privately mused on the fact that it could easily have been any of them. There was fear behind the Aviators and a hollow anxiety at the bottom of the glass that wouldn't go away no matter how many times it was refilled. This news had to serve as a wake-up call, and indeed this would be the year Stevie herself would eventually make her first real steps towards beating her own habit once and for all. It would also be around this time that Stevie hinted she was tempted by the thought of "gracefully slipping out of" the music industry altogether to concentrate on painting and developing her ideas for children's storybooks. It was an attempt to stay in touch with innocence, light and clarity in a world – her world – that was rapidly turning dark.

*

Stevie was itching to get back into the studio with her band and Jimmy Iovine, and Jimmy, not convinced by the musical direction Stevie wanted to take, was back on the prowl trying to find songs for Stevie to use as singles. One anthemic number that had been pitched for Stevie's attention – by Bernie Taupin, no less – was the song 'These Dreams'. Stevie rejected it and it went on to be a number one hit for Heart that very year.*

* Heart frontwomen Ann and Nancy Wilson would become friends with Stevie, dropping in on her home in Phoenix when their tour hit Arizona. There they played dress up, took drugs and marvelled at how the star's own home was basically "a shrine to Stevie Nicks". "Her home was filled with pictures of her," they remembered in their 2013 memoir *Dreaming: A Story of Heart, Soul and Rock 'n' Roll.* "We spent most of the night digging through her closets trying on clothes with her. It was fun to be girls together. When it came to drugs, though, we couldn't keep up with Stevie. At some point, we had to leave to sleep."

Cue a phone call to Tom Petty. Unfortunately, this time he didn't have any songs to give, although he felt Iovine's pain. Stevie had embraced the synth-pop sound ubiquitous in the 1980s, but many of the old guard were not so keen. Petty felt "music [had] really turned to shit. People were *trying* to do something, but it was all these fakey keyboard sounds."

Iovine wasn't pleased when Petty told him he had no material "left over" for Stevie, but Petty had an idea up his sleeve. "[Jimmy] said, 'I'm frustrated, I'm trying to find writers. Who do you think would be a good writer?' And I said, 'You should try this guy Dave Stewart. He's in England. I don't know him, but he seems consistent as a writer.'" "Fakey keyboard sounds" notwithstanding, Petty had to concede that the Eurythmics' hit 'Sweet Dreams (Are Made Of This)' was a great song, and Dave Stewart – one half of Eurythmics, alongside Annie Lennox – clearly had some form.

"The next thing I know, the phone rings, and it's Dave Stewart," remembers Petty. "He says, 'Hey, I'm here, and Jimmy told me I got the gig from you. I've come over to write some stuff for Stevie and other people. Why don't you come down?'" The Eurythmics were also in the US to play some shows, and it was at an afterparty held at Stevie's home that Dave Stewart first encountered Ms Nicks. Dave apparently didn't realise who she was at the time, but their meeting would be unforgettable, even inspiring a song – although, ironically, Stevie would not get the benefit of it for her album. The track 'Don't Come Around Here No More' would be recorded by Dave and Tom Petty instead.

The night before Stewart and Nicks first met, Stevie had had a monumental argument with Joe Walsh over the phone, culminating in Joe hanging up on her. Believing their relationship was over, Stevie pushed thoughts of Joe aside as she regarded Stewart, with his dark glasses and insouciant Sunderland accent, with no small interest, and the feeling was mutual. Stewart asked Nicks if she was in a relationship. The answer she gave was "no". Stevie and Dave had plenty in common – for a start, both of them were hugely successful writers who had survived dramatic, romantic relationships with their musical partners; Annie in Dave's case, Lindsey in Stevie's.

After disappearing into her bathroom together to snort cocaine, nature took its inevitable course and Stevie and Dave staggered off to bed. But after waking up at 5am to find a troubled Stevie pacing about (and, surreally, trying on Victorian clothing), Dave suggested getting together again but Stevie, still in love with Joe, refused, uttering the now immortal words, "Don't come around here no more." In the cold light of day, Stevie had panicked. "I threw him out of bed and started dressing him," she told Chrissy Iley for *Elle*. "All this leather! All these chains I was threading through!" The whole fiasco was "very *Alice In Wonderland*," Dave observed.

With those now famous words of rejection still ringing in his ears, Dave promptly started writing, eventually recording 'Don't Come Around Here No More' with Petty at Sunset Sound – Stevie had booked a session with the boys but failed to show. Yet another example of the importance of turning up (the 'Silver Springs' debacle being another memorable one).

As Stevie remembers it, "Dave wrote that song for me and we took it in with Jimmy Iovine, then we called Tom and he came down. I went home because I was tired and when I came back the next day it was all written, and it was fantastic. Being a huge Tom Petty fan, I listened and said, 'So, what, I'm going to rewrite this song and write better words than Tom Petty did?' I was very pissed off, and at the same time, very much enamoured with the song. I knew this was going to be the second coming of Tom Petty."

"The girls that sing with her had turned up for the session," explained Tom. "[So] Dave said, 'Let's get them out here and see what they can do.'" So the song, inspired by a kiss-off from Stevie Nicks, would feature the voices of her close friends Sharon Celani and Marilyn Martin, while the subsequent video would be *Alice In Wonderland*-themed, even featuring cellos being played with pink flamingoes instead of bows. (Stevie had had pink flamingo statues "grazing" in her grounds.)

Joe and Stevie were soon back together, but Dave Stewart felt a strong kinship to Nicks; this may have been a one-night stand but he always remembered her, and in later years they would come together again, finally collaborating musically in earnest. Stewart's fondness for Nicks is detailed quite openly in his later song 'Stevie Baby', from his 2011 album *The Blackbird Diaries*: "It took one second, just one kiss / To realise all the things I'd miss. / I play *Rock A Little* just to reminisce/ I never thought we'd meet again like this . . .'" But this was all to come.

The next 18 months of Stevie's life would be devoted to making the new album, a journey which would take time to find its compass and would feature more collaborations than ever before, possibly pointing at Stevie's own lack of focus – she was drifting away from reality and, seemingly, no one, not even Jimmy Iovine, had been able to tether her. One collaboration that had worked well for her in the past was 'Stand Back', but Prince would not be available this year – being as it was the year his film *Purple Rain* was unveiled for the first time. Stevie, dressed in a white beaded gown, would be at the premiere on July 27, 1984, as would Lindsey Buckingham, Little Richard, Lionel Richie, 'Weird Al' Yankovic, and frankly everyone who was anyone in American pop culture at that time. The album of the soundtrack would go platinum 13 times and the semi-autobiographical film, starring Prince himself and the Revolution, broke new ground However, it was dark, often uncomfortable viewing. Warners had turned the option down because it was too "outrageous", and Stevie herself "freaked out" during the scene in which Prince's character slaps Apollonia Kotero, and had to go and recover in the bathroom, remaining there until the film was over.

Unfortunately, Prince noticed she had left her seat and approached her afterwards, putting her on the spot. When Stevie explained how the scene had made her feel, he simply looked at her as if "it killed him", and it would be some time until they would speak again. "It's a shame really," Stevie mused to *Details*'s Lance Loud in 1994. "We were alike in so many ways. For one thing, we both liked wearing black chiffon around the house . . ."

*

Andrew Means, Arizona Republic: Is there anything Fleetwood Mac can give you now that you don't have as a soloist?

Stevie Nicks: A headache.

For *Rock A Little* – at this point still known as *Mirror, Mirror* – Stevie suddenly decided to "move everyone to Dallas to record, with very little preparation." Stevie had been enchanted by Gordon Perry's converted church studio Goodnight Dallas, where she had recorded the piano demo of 'Beauty And The Beast' (and first met Gordon's then wife Lori, subsequently married to Stevie's brother Chris Nicks). Stevie wanted to recreate that special atmosphere for her third solo long-player.

"This was one of my bad planning moves," Stevie admitted. "I prepared, I mean the [songs were] written, but all the rock'n'roll stars arrived and Jimmy Iovine, you know, I put him in a very weird position. He had to go in and say, 'Well, I don't really know the songs either but we're going to play!' We were there for about a month and we ended up coming out with about six tracks that we could go back to that are really good."

Tracks "we could go back to" was a diplomatic way of saying that many would have to be recorded again. Stevie was a little disappointed with how things were turning out, and Jimmy Iovine was reaching the end of his rope. 'Musical differences' aside, cocaine was now running the show and ruling Stevie's daily life. Jimmy wasn't the only one who found it hard to stand helplessly by and watch someone he loved sink deeper into addiction. Stevie understood why Iovine elected to leave (although elsewhere she has stated that she fired Jimmy after the 'Don't Come Around Here No More' incident). "It wasn't fun for him anymore," she said. "It got a little bit too crazy." "Drugs were getting in the way," confirmed Lori Perry Nicks. "They weren't the unit they were previously." Paul Fishkin admitted too that "we all started getting nervous about [the escalating drug use]." But Stevie would not listen to reason. Not yet.

Keeping some of the tracks they had worked on together, Stevie contacted her friend Keith Olsen, who would take over as producer at his own studio Goodnight LA, next door to their old stamping ground of Sound City in Van Nuys. The release date of *Rock A Little* would be pushed back from late 1984 to November 1985, and the process of making this album was not a little tense at times.

"Stevie asked me [to produce] during the time I was working with Joe Walsh," explains Olsen. "We thought that doing something together would be like 'old times', even though we knew that 'old times' were gone forever."

Olsen was working with Walsh on his latest solo record *The Confessor*, an album that would feature the guitar-playing of Waddy Wachtel. Stevie herself would be a guiding presence on *The Confessor**, recorded at around the same time at Goodnight LA. "She rode shotgun with me," Walsh told DJ Howard Stern. "[She] gave me some direction, she's really good at the craft of songwriting." It often became incestuous on those LA studio complexes, and a little cross-pollination was rarely a bad thing when the artists were of this calibre. It was up to Olsen to make sure all sessions ran as they should, "musicians arriving on time, doing their thing and leaving . . . some of the time that didn't quite work out . . ."

Rock A Little would feature Stevie's song for Joe, 'Has Anyone Ever Written Anything For You?', a track that would become a collaboration with Keith Olsen himself. Keith takes up the story:

"Stevie had gotten sick and her doctor had told her to rest – period. So I went to her house and kind of just hung with her to make sure she rested and really did take care of herself. While I was there, I was playing her piano and her Kurzweil keyboard, and kept landing on this section of her song to give it another section that I thought it needed [basically a bridge] and a key change.

"I just kept playing this over and over and she heard it from her room, came out and hummed along a melody that just made it so special. [Stevie]

* *The Confessor* is about the twelve-step drug rehabilitation programme, a process Joe would have to undergo himself. One of the people he had to "make amends" to, as one does on the programme, would be Stevie.

agreed with me to put this bridge and key change into the song. (I always wanted to title the song 'I'd Rather Be Alone'.)"

When it came to selecting songs for *Rock A Little*, a number of the original tracks and demos Stevie had been developing would not be used, and it took time for the record to find its way. "For some reason it wasn't right . . . like, it was right but it was as if you had the wrong pair of shoes," Stevie explained.

"Stevie writes lots of sketches," adds Olsen. "Some good, some normal, some great . . . it's my job to wade through them and find the gems, then develop them."

A duet with Don Henley was one of the songs that wouldn't make the cut. Jimmy Iovine had, as always, been determined to have songs on Stevie's album written by others despite Stevie's wishes, and one of those songs would be 'Reconsider Me', written by Warren Zevon. "Of course, I love Warren because I've known Warren since before Lindsey and I joined Fleetwood Mac," Stevie told the broadcaster Jim Ladd on KLOS in 1998. (Warren was one of the musicians who got stoned at Stevie and Lindsey's back in the day.) "Jimmy thought it was a very important song for me to do. He thought it was like 'Stop Draggin' My Heart' was in a way. It was that kind of a career-changing song. And, of course, you couldn't tell me anything in 1985 and I just didn't want to do another person's song, you know?

"In the end, I did record it and then when all the songs were recorded in the end, a couple of songs had to go; I pulled it because it wasn't one of my songs." Stevie also had to admit she wasn't a "'reconsider me' kinda gal" anyway. Still, the track would surface again in later years when Modern/Atlantic Records were working with Stevie on collating the box-set *Enchanted*.

Tennessean guitarist Billy Burnette, son of rockabilly singer Dorsey Burnette, would also be brought on board temporarily to work with Stevie but again, because the song they worked on was not an original, the song would be shelved. Stevie and Billy first met at UCLA, where Mick Fleetwood's The Zoo were playing one night; Stevie and Billy liked each other instantly. Billy was already friends with Mick and John, and he would later join Fleetwood Mac himself when Lindsey left the band. He was clearly simpatico and Stevie invited Billy to the studio to try something out. Stevie wanted to sing the first song her beloved grandfather had taught her, the jaunty call-and-response Red Sovine number 'Are You Mine?', a song Sovine himself made famous as a duet with Goldie Hill in the fifties. It meant the world to Stevie to get it just right and pay tribute to AJ Nicks, who had started her on her journey three decades earlier with this song.

"I don't remember exactly why I asked Billy to do that," mused Stevie. "I guess because of his country roots. We did a really beautiful duet on it, but since I didn't write it and Billy didn't write it, it didn't go on the record, because it would have taken the place of another song that I did write." Their work together on this would not go to waste, however, and they would perform 'Are You Mine?' on tour.

Some covers would make it through, as would a selection of co-writes. 'If I Were You', 'Sister Honey', 'I Can't Wait', 'The Nightmare' and 'Imperial Hotel' were all collaborations, while 'Some Become Strangers' was written by David Williams, Amy Latelevision and Peter Rafelson and 'Talk To Me' by Chas Sandford. While Stevie felt conflicted about using songs written by others, if they reverberated with her, it "doesn't matter one bit. It simply saved me from having to sit down and write it," she concluded to Jim Ladd. *Rock A Little* would be the first Stevie Nicks album to feature such a high percentage of other people's work, but the opportunity to sing material written by others gave Stevie the chance to tap into her theatrical side and take on a different character. "If I can relate to you, then I can become you and see through your eyes. When I sing Tom's songs, I *become* Tom; I become more Floridian and gator-like and have more of a drawl."

'Talk To Me', a power-pop contemplation on how emotional wounds fester if communication breaks down, was sourced by Jimmy Iovine and, while Stevie wasn't instantly sold on it, it "made itself my song," Stevie said. "It sort of sang to me, it said to me something that I was going to write anyway that night, it was exactly my thoughts." Stevie took a little time to settle in with the vocals on this track, although the A-list session drummer Jim Keltner, who had been recording overdubs next door, popped in and gave her some encouragement, being her 'audience' while she worked. Whatever he said clearly had a good effect – Stevie nailed it in two takes.

The track would be released as the first single from the album, going gold no less. Writer Chas Sandford certainly knew how to craft a winning single, being the creator of John Waite's smash hit 'Missing You', and there are definitely echoes of that song in 'Talk To Me'.

'The Nightmare' was a song co-written with Stevie's brother Chris and lyrically, the song proved to be, as Stevie put it, "the final statement on how I felt about real unconditional love. As a woman, if you give out the vibe, then people will flirt with you, but boy, when you are in love with somebody, you don't flaunt or offer yourself. So in the nightmare, the fact is it didn't work, but I wouldn't trade a second of it. I'll never again settle for anything that is any less than that feeling." Keith Olsen once insisted that Joe Walsh and Stevie didn't write about each other but it's hard to imagine that there isn't a little bit of Joe in here, a window into Stevie's strong feelings for him, and an unwitting glimpse of the real nightmare that was to come. Either way, some of Nicks' sweetest poetry is contained within this song: "Thrown down through the arms of sleep / She fell through the ivory morning / Deep into the waters / Of the one she called love . . . You cannot know the dream / Till you've known the nightmare." There are whispers of the past in this song too, including some favourite themes and lyrical references to previous songs, including 'Sisters Of The Moon' ("the moon and her sisters . . .') and 'Storms' ("I'd like to leave you with something warm . . .")

Stevie found it especially difficult to pick the singles from *Rock A Little*, but 'I Can't Wait', co-written with Rick Nowels and Eric Pressly, would be the second. Rick Nowels and Stevie had known each other "since he was 13 and I was 18, there's no one I've known longer than that except Robin." But there was no nepotism behind Stevie's decision to record this track; Rick was already an established writer and when Stevie took the tape he had given her home, ran a bath, put the tape into her bathroom stereo and turned up the volume, she "went crazy. [I] played 'I Can't Wait' all night long, made up the words, danced around to it, saw the video in my head and went in the next night [to the Village Recorder, LA] without anybody else's permission and did the vocal that's on the record right now. That's the only time I ever sang this song."

One of the tracks produced by Jimmy Iovine before his departure, 'I Can't Wait' would be released in 1986, with 'Rock A Little (Go Ahead Lily)' on the B-side. 'I Can't Wait' is surely another song that, lyrically, reflects Stevie's frustration with Joe Walsh. As the title suggests, the song is about being kept waiting by a lover, and the lyrics perfectly depict how Stevie was feeling at that time: "She wonders how many more hours her heart will feel broken . . . Blame it on something at first sight . . ." The song begins with Stevie howling "I love you", more like a strident, almost desperate rallying cry than a sentimental confession.

When Stevie first listened to the backing track, it was "about the most exciting song that I had ever heard." She loved the punchy percussive rhythms and "electric" sense of vitality. While she "pretended not to be that knocked out" at first, the track, not to mention the final result, would be something Stevie remains proud of to this day. "Some vocals are magic and simply not able to beat," she wrote in her *Timespace* liner notes. "Now when I hear it on the radio, this incredible feeling comes over me, like something really incredible is about to happen."

Another co-write would be 'Sister Honey' (also the name of one of Stevie's paintings), written with the guitarist Les Dudek, who had played with the Steve Miller Band, Boz Scaggs and the Allman Brothers, all contemporaries of Fleetwood Mac who had been working the same rock'n'roll circuit for years.

Les was in Stevie's living room one evening, guitar at the ready, when he cranked up the volume and started to play the chords we now know to be the foundation of 'Sister Honey'. Stevie was hooked immediately. "I just went, 'All right, baby!' The entire canyon is ringing with 'Sister Honey'."

"You get that sparkle in the room with someone who's playing great, and they're not paying a hell of a lot of attention to you because they're playing their thing, and you just draw back and go, 'OK, I'm going to blow your mind now.' And the guitar player or the piano player or your mom or your dog look up and go, 'All right!'"

Sensing things were going well, Les suggested Stevie use some of his own lyrics in the song. He handed her some lines, starting with the words "strange fascination, some kind of temptation . . ." "I went, 'You're not serious? I don't have to sing these, right?' [But] just because I love Les, I thought, 'All right, I'll do it for you . . .'" So 'Sister Honey''s lyrics are pure Stevie with the exception of the second verse. From Stevie's point of view, there is a sense of a return to her fading connection to Lindsey Buckingham. "Come back, solemn stranger, it's your last chance . . . she's almost gone now . . ." The lines – "even if you don't need her, tell her you need her / She needs you, brother . . ." hint poignantly at Stevie's insecurity at this point, particularly around Walsh, who would soon be out of her love life for good.

The self-penned tracks that made the cut would be typically autobiographical. 'I Sing For The Things', for example, would be a sentimental portrait of the "things" that money can't buy her, the dreams and chains: a reference to the 'The Chain', and the often troubled love and permanence of Fleetwood Mac – she is "chained" to the band but her dreams struggle against that. 'I Sing For The Things' also praises the sense of romance that has the power to render all of the material luxuries in her life worthless.

"We already have so many things," Stevie said, "When I start to have several things that are similar, I can't choose. That makes me want to run away." In terms of "things" Stevie herself would rather treasure the few items that she loved, that brought her comfort and made her feel rooted, such as her favourite skirt, her boots; signature items that each had a story. (You wouldn't find Stevie Nicks wandering around an antique store murmuring to her assistant, "Do I have one of those?" a la Michael Jackson.)

The title track, 'Rock A Little', would be "shared with my father", Stevie said. It was as much inspired by the thunderous ocean as it was by her own dad, who spurred her on when she faltered. "It came from my dad saying to me, 'We don't care how you feel, you have to go up there and do a show now,'" Stevie explained. The lyric "hit it, Lily", refers to the fact that Stevie's loved ones used "Lily" as a pet name for her. "My dad would say, 'Go ahead, Lily, hit it, rock a little, get up, if you don't feel good, go home.' So this whole thing came about as a statement, it doesn't really matter what your problems are, what really matters is you have to go up and go out there onstage."

The video for 'I Can't Wait', directed by Marty Callner, would be a dramatic affair, featuring wind machines, lots of marching up and down a giant white staircase, black skirt-swishing and tambourine-bashing a la 'Rhiannon' and a strange prison cell that contains a wild Stevie, dancing and pacing within the oppressive four walls like a caged lioness. The energy is compelling but Stevie looks back on this video with genuine regret: she is clearly high, as she was for all of the videos she shot in this era, but perhaps most obviously so here.

"I look at that video, I look at my eyes, and I say to myself, 'Could you have laid off the pot, the coke, and the tequila for three days, so you could have looked a little better?'" she admitted in *I Want My MTV: The Uncensored Story of the Music Video Revolution* by Craig Marks and Rob Tannenbaum. "It just makes me want to go back into that video and stab myself." For some years now, Stevie had been relying on drugs to give her energy, drugs to bring her down, pills to help her sleep and powders to help her wake up and work the next day. The spiral had started long ago and Stevie had already started to lose people she loved because of it. She also missed her family, whom she felt she had to avoid more than she'd have liked to, again, because of her cocaine dependency. Her sense of isolation was palpable and her need for reassurance more acute than ever.

"My family is so important to me," Stevie told ABC Australia's Molly Meldrum, a note of disconnection and panic in her voice. "Last night, in the middle of the night I started to cry because I miss my brother and I needed to call him, and I didn't have any phone numbers because I don't have a book. I just needed for somebody to tell me that it's all OK. My family is very, very important to me, and you are important to me, and all the people that come to see me are important to me . . ."

Chapter 22

No amount of adulation and support could soften Stevie's latest crisis. Joe Walsh had left her, having accepted an offer to tour Australia with The Party Boys, a predominantly Australian supergroup with a rolling lineup of musicians that at various times also featured UK and US stars, including Alan Lancaster of Status Quo, Eric Burdon of The Animals and metal vocalist Graham Bonnet. Joe would stay in Australia for some time after the tour was through in 1985, forming a touring band with Waddy Wachtel called The Creatures From America. Interestingly, the live Party Boys album Walsh appeared on, released that year, would be titled *You Need Professional Help*. This he most certainly did, as did Stevie.

This was purportedly one of the main reasons Walsh chose to leave LA for Australia – to get away from Nicks and the party scene that he was afraid would kill him. Joe also admitted he couldn't give Stevie what she wanted, and that ultimately "[neither] of us could have committed to a lasting relationship in the state we were in". Stevie believed he simply "got scared". They were "complete, perfect" as a couple; a crazy, dysfunctional couple anyway. But Stevie also knew what she was prepared to give up for him: her beloved career, her lifestyle. He was unlikely to do the same for her.

Stevie was in the studio one night, getting ready to cut some new songs with Waddy. Joe had been away for weeks and, while he knew that Stevie didn't have much time in the studio that evening, he came down to hang out at about midnight and "completely screwed up the session", said Stevie.

"It would have been fine any other night," she told BBC Radio 1's Nicky Horne, "but I was angry that Joe had done that. He had everybody dying laughing because he tells 100 jokes and people were rolling on the floor, everybody was drinking and I'm going, 'This is not fair, he is not being sensitive at all to this situation. You know I would give up anything for you, I might even give up my damned career for you' – maybe, if I thought he was serious enough . . .

"I had a limousine that night because I didn't know what time it would finish and I didn't want to hold anybody up, so I said, 'Do you want to go home? What do you want to do?' and he looked at me and said, 'Actually, I didn't tell you this but I'm leaving for Australia tonight and I have to pack. So I'm just going to get a ride home with Waddy.'" Stevie's heart sank, and as she finally walked towards the door, she said, "I don't like where this relationship is going, because it's not going anywhere and I don't want to do it any more." Walsh retorted. "He said, 'If you walk out that door, you basically cease to exist.' I just didn't stop walking."

It was a harsh, bitter end to a romance that had been so important to Stevie, and it was of small comfort to her when she later received a message from Walsh via a mutual friend: "He told my friend he'd gone to Australia because he's a coward. He said, 'Tell Stevie I'm going because both of us are doing so much coke that one of us is going to die.'" Many relationships are borne of being "drug buddies" and the boundaries can become confused, but whether Stevie's love was truly requited or not, the bond would have been all the stronger because of cocaine, and to break an addiction often means breaking off a friendship for the greater good.

Stevie admittedly was convinced she was not long for this world herself and, had she continued the way she was going, there's a good chance she would have fulfilled that prophecy, whether Joe was there or not. She had spent approximately $1 million on cocaine, the drug that had famously burned a hole in her nose so large she professed she could loop a belt through it, or at least a ring . . . "a gold ring . . . with diamonds!" she added, jokingly, ever stylish and decadent even when it came to something as gruesome as this. It was harder to find humour in the day-to-day reality of what that meant. Stevie was suffering frequently from nosebleeds and blackouts. It had to be said, Walsh had a point. But to make that point, he had to break her heart, maybe even being deliberately cruel to make it easier for Stevie to turn her back on him. But it would be a break that would sadly never quite mend. 'How will we feel 20 years from now?' Stevie asked in 'I Can't Wait'. For her part, she wouldn't feel all that different. The blaze of passion might have diminished to glowing embers, but the love was still there.

"It took me a long, long time to get over it – if I ever got over it," Stevie said in an interview with *The Telegraph* in 2007. "There was no other man in the world for me. And it's the same today, even though Joe is married and has two sons. He met somebody in rehab and got married. And I think he's happy."

Rock A Little was finally finished by the summer of 1985, and would be released in November. It had cost over $1 million to record, so it's just as well that Stevie was happy with it and was already chomping at the bit to head out on tour before starting on record number four. *Rock A Little*, in Stevie's words, was "a whole tapestry of energy from a lot of different brilliant people, whom I very much respect, woven into this pattern that I hope people will understand." In reality, not everyone did understand and while the record went platinum, reviews were mixed. *Rolling Stone* expressed a concern that Stevie was "slipping out of touch . . . the real shame is that Nicks could make a good record again, if she'll only take her advice and rock a *little*."

As usual, Stevie ignored the critics and was proud of her record. She even contacted Joe Walsh, for whom she still hankered, to play it to him. It may have just been an excuse to see him and attempt to rekindle their relationship, but after tentatively suggesting she could come over, Stevie was thrilled when Joe agreed. After a final tweak of her outfit, a spritz of perfume and a primp of her super-sprayed hair, Stevie jumped into a limousine and was driven to Joe's house, which was several hours away. Crushingly, he opened the door only to flatly tell her he didn't have time after all. It was yet another rejection, and a furious Stevie promptly wrote a song about it, 'Long Way To Go', stating that it was a "long way to go to say goodbye / I thought we already did that . . ." This angry song, which would be included on the album *The Other Side Of The Mirror*, was also something of a confessional: "You were high in my life / Obsessive was my love / Worth it was my time / Oh no, you are fading out." But Stevie's memories of Joe Walsh would never quite fade to silence.

*

In January 1986, four years after *Mirage*, Fleetwood Mac finally reassembled to make a new album, *Tango In The Night*. Interestingly, it was noted that Stevie's management company Frontline "agreed" on Stevie's behalf that their artist would indeed be recording with them. Once Stevie would have dropped everything for the band, but now her cooperation was subject to her own increasingly busy schedule; she had an epic tour lined up for 1986, taking the States and Australia. Also, now that Mick was no longer managing Fleetwood Mac, everyone had their own managers, for better or worse. The members of the band had become disconnected, but in one sense this was no bad thing. Having had the chance to grow and develop away from the Mac hothouse, not just as artists but as individuals, everyone felt as ready as they ever would be to work together again, although some were more enthusiastic than others.

The process of making *Tango* started well, with Lindsey stating that it "made us feel like a band again, for the first time in a long time." Buckingham and Richard Dashut took on production duties and recording started at Rumbo Recorders in LA. However, by the time Lindsey's own home studio, 'The Slope', was built, the bulk of the work would be produced there, with Lindsey very much at the helm of the operation. There would be no more meandering jams into the small hours, no more late starts . . .

"We would start about 1 p.m. [and] shut down about 11," Lindsey said. "If people looked like they were having too good a time, I would walk in in my bathrobe . . ."

"It wasn't like he'd laid down any rules," added Stevie. "He just had very good intentions to take as little time as possible to do wonderful work and not be staying up all night playing [the] Rolling Stones, which we've been known to do . . . for days . . . The fact that it was in his own home, maybe it wasn't as much fun but we got an awful lot more done, and quicker." Stevie had to be honest, she was reluctant to go into the studio with Lindsey again, but she was tentatively pleased with how restrained his behaviour was so far.

Behind the smiles, however, there was turmoil. Of course there was. This is Fleetwood Mac. Mick Fleetwood had gone bankrupt, Lindsey was quietly fed up that, yet again, the songs he would have used on his own solo album would now be absorbed into *Tango In The Night,* John would just rather have been at sea and Stevie was otherwise engaged, joining sessions for *Tango* in earnest as late as January 1987. More worryingly, she was also now constantly high and risking permanent mental and physical damage as a result, her body already sending her signals loud and clear, with ever more frequent nosebleeds, falls and blackouts. Stevie visited a doctor to receive the alarming, but perhaps unsurprising news that she was veering ever closer to a brain haemorrhage, or even an early grave. "[He said], 'It could be the next time you do cocaine. It won't be pretty.' It absolutely scared me to death."

It was imperative that Stevie stopped doing coke immediately, but the reality was that she was almost in love with the drug, describing it in her typically fanciful way as "being swept up on a white horse by a prince. There was no way to get off the white horse and I didn't want to." And so, despite the knowledge that her addiction was life-threatening, Stevie elected not to dismount from her deadly steed straight away. Stevie was with Fleetwood Mac for three weeks in the studio, leaving them with the raw lament 'When I See You Again', before her own tour took her away from them. As Lindsey Buckingham recalled, "They weren't a great three weeks. I didn't recognise her at all. She wasn't the person I had known and moved to LA with." It had been some time since Lindsey had seen Stevie and he had never seen her so dead-eyed and disconnected.

"Cocaine is not a creative drug," Nicks conceded in 1989 to *Record*

Mirror's Robin Smith (who admiringly dubbed her "the Joan Collins of rock and a born survivor"). "It will not help you to create a masterpiece. What it will do is help you put the tiredness at the back of your mind." There was no point in being alert but mentally absent, however, let alone artistically restricted. Still, the drug gave Stevie fake courage, not only onstage but as a writer. In some cases, the songs that would appear while Stevie was on coke would be lyrically all too blatant and literal, but, fooled by the chemicals coursing through her system, she would forge ahead unstoppably. "You were likely to say more, to write down more, to give away more of the secret or to maybe say too much . . . You think it's making you better and in the long run it's not. It's taking away the actual essence of what you started out to do."

Coke also allowed Stevie to cram more activity into her life than was strictly healthy. Just weeks before her *Rock A Little* tour was due to commence, instead of resting or working on with Fleetwood Mac, she jetted off to Australia to spend time with Tom Petty and Bob Dylan on their True Confessions tour when Tom's wife Jane didn't want to go. After suggesting Tom buy Jane diamonds or even "a fucking Porsche", because, unbelievably, an invitation to go on tour with Petty and Dylan was a hard sell, Stevie shrugged and went instead. There she hung out, joined in with afterparty singalongs around Benmont Tench's piano and even appeared onstage herself – an onstage cameo playing the tambourine soon turned into something much more.

"When they finished their set, nobody really noticed that I was there, and then they went off and I didn't know what to do, so I went off too," Stevie remembered in an interview with Jim Ladd. "When they turned around and went back on, they said, 'Come back.' Tom knew it was going to be wonderful, they both motioned over to me to sing on 'Knockin' On Heaven's Door', so I did. In the next chorus [Bob] turned to me and let me sing the choruses by myself.

"It was incredible, there's no way to explain what it would be like to someone like me, who went to Woodstock and decided that was what I wanted to do . . . to stand on a stage with Bob Dylan and Tom Petty, it makes everything else that goes on that I don't love that much worth it . . ."

The crowd loved seeing Stevie onstage with their heroes, although Australian government officials weren't so impressed when they discovered she was technically performing without a work permit. Stevie revealed to *New York Magazine*'s Jada Yuan that she was told: "'If you even walk on that stage and go ping!, you can never come back to Australia. Not on a vacation, not with Fleetwood Mac, not with friends.'" As if this wasn't enough Petty-related drama, Stevie had recently managed to "accidentally pilfer" a tape of melodies that had been written for Petty, later adding lyrics to one and then innocently playing it for the man himself at a later date during a phone conversation. "All I can hear is Tom screaming." Oops.

Stevie was looking forward to kicking off what would be her longest and most colourful solo tour yet. She shrugged off concerns from loved ones and perceptive journalists, describing herself as a "road warrior", and embarked on the *Rock A Little* tour with her band, starting at The Summit in Houston, Texas on 11 April 1986. They would tour Australia too, the first time Stevie had performed in a solo capacity outside of the US. But the *Rock A Little* roadtrip was problematic. Stevie defied her doctor's warnings and continued to take cocaine and drink heavily, and the effects took their toll on her body and mind as well as decimating her performances.

Once word got out about the hole in Stevie's nose that was currently "the size of a dime", rumours spread that Stevie was having to get her fix via other, rather undignified means. Stevie has dismissed the famous speculation that she had to have the drug blown up her derriere by an assistant as "an absurd statement. It's not true," she told *Q Magazine* in 2001, although the damage to Stevie's septum "didn't stop me doing cocaine one bit." Stevie decided not to have her nose fixed in case it changed her voice. "It's so painful. I curse the day I ever did cocaine. Nothing really works right in my head now. That hole goes against God's plan . . . I'm stuck with it forever, and it slowly deteriorates . . . If it's doing that to your nose imagine what it's doing to your head, brain, and the workings of your entire body."

The use of cocaine up to that point however, and no doubt the hole itself, meant that Nicks' voice had noticeably changed on her studio recordings, becoming huskier and more nasal and her range was increasingly limited. Live, these changes were all the more noticeable, as was her persona, now morphing into something even wilder and less controlled.

Vocal discrepancies could be hidden to a certain extent by Stevie's trusty backing singers, who covered the high notes for her, but while the ever-loyal fan base layered up the lace and trooped out to her concerts in force, cheering as loud as ever, the critics weren't convinced. Watching through their fingers, they observed her unsteady dancing, frequent skips off stage for costume changes (and the rest) and strange mumblings between songs. Elements of the Stevie they knew and loved were still there, but something had cracked. There would also be cruel jibes about Stevie's fuller figure in the press, who often take issue when beautiful female stars change or age. More frighteningly, there were times when Stevie stumbled and fell onstage, "near overdoses" and incidents when "we had to just scrape her off the floor", as Paul Fishkin remembers. Stevie had become like one of her own marionettes, relying on expert puppeteers to pull and push her into position. Without them, she sank.

The Chicago Tribune's Daniel Brogan was concerned that Nicks was "riding an expressway to creative oblivion and self-destruction", while the show "provided a graphic picture of what bad shape she is in. Years of hard living have reduced her voice to a wretched rasp . . . she spent much of her 90-minute set spinning and whirling on and off the stage, often leaving her bewildered-looking band to pick up the pieces."

It was after this very show in Chicago that, as Mick Fleetwood recalls, there was "an intervention". Stevie often insists she "decided to go to Betty Ford . . . Nobody came and threw me in a van and took me, it was my decision," but Stevie's management Frontline also felt urgently that she should clean up, while Fleetwood, who played percussion on the tour, had watched Stevie "running herself into the ground, drinking, doing a lot of cocaine . . ." and was seriously concerned she would hurt herself badly. Stevie's father Jess Nicks concurs, remembering that it was "after repeated attempts to help her" that they finally flew out to convince his daughter in person to go to rehab.

"She resisted when we confronted her with it," Jess Nicks told Cox News Service's Linda Romine. "She was concerned it would be publicised and be detrimental to her career. We spent most of the night with her and convinced her it was for her help . . . It's tough, [but] Christ, the career means nothing to the parents when it comes to the health of your children." Stevie herself remembers Jess asking her, "How could you possibly even consider putting me through not having you for the rest of my life?" If anything was going to get the message through, it was that.

Stevie agreed to check in to the Betty Ford Clinic in Palm Springs after her tour, apparently using cocaine for the last time in August at the magnificent Red Rocks Amphitheater, Colorado. This show symbolically ended with the release of 25 white doves, one of which refused to leave Stevie's hand. The crowd went insane as Stevie giggled in disbelief at what could only be an omen, and she gently placed the bird in Mick Fleetwood's hat, later to be kept by Stevie as a pet (the dove, not the hat).

Stevie is especially fond of her Red Rocks concert; it was a vast venue and a powerful show and, should anyone be unfamiliar with Stevie Nicks, the lady herself has recommended that the concert film *Live At Red Rocks* is the perfect place to start. It has to be said, however, that this film, and in particular Stevie's encore of 'Edge Of Seventeen' on *Live At Red Rocks*, displays the singer at her most extreme, her performance frenzied to the point of being alarming.

Nicks has always reflected on her addiction with courage and honesty, and is philosophical about how bad it became, even stating that she "wouldn't change it", if offered the chance to go back and do things differently. "I think it all happened for a reason," she said. "But I got through it, I was so lucky. I would never lecture anybody, because I don't think that's the way to get to people . . . The ones who did make it pretty much cherish the fact we are alive, but it is difficult to accept this whole life in a different way, because for so long it was lived under that dream-cloud, dream-child world of different kinds of drugs."

Stevie used the name 'Sara Anderson' when she checked into the clinic that October; Sara being, as we know, a special name for Stevie in so many ways, and Anderson being Robin's surname – and her own married surname, of course. It's not difficult to see why Nicks chose the name Sara. Like Rhiannon, the name itself had a presence and a meaning to her that had manifested into an unseen guiding force, and Stevie needed all of the psychic protection she could muster to see her through the doors of the centre and through a tough but ultimately successful 28-day programme of rehabilitation.

There were 6 a.m. wake-up calls, daily chores and Stevie shared her room with an elderly female alcoholic. Also undergoing treatment alongside her would be the country singer Tammy Wynette, and "one of James Taylor's backing singers". Stevie herself was, she admits, a "chain-smoking, coffee-swilling mess" when she arrived there, and she also over- ate to compensate for what she was missing. Hours would be spent in therapy, scraping away at the layers of hurt that had built up, getting to the heart of why the problem had even started in the first place.

"You don't have treatment as such," Stevie explained in an interview with Lesley-Ann Jones for *You Magazine* in 1989, "but meetings with your counsellor and with everyone together. You cry and you tell all your secret stories. In three days you are out of pain and crying for a purpose. You are hopeful, but never really happy." The life of a rock star often doesn't allow much space for really paying much mind to others – one becomes so used to being the centre of attention, the draw, that many stars don't feel the need to listen to other people. This was another reason being in rehab really was enlightening for someone like Stevie. In group therapy she had to listen, and found the stories of her new comrades, many of whom were even richer than herself, very moving. These were people who'd had it all and betrayed themselves by going too far. Their confessions touched her and, crucially, motivated her to be more careful. "When you have to sit down and write on a piece of paper, 'I am not special, I am dying', that's a real serious thing to swallow," she said.

It would be during this period that Stevie really learned why she took coke – it was to give her the energy to do more than any human being could, or should, handle. More than was necessary, in many cases. She was an overachiever and it was killing her. The irony was that because she had split her focus and was doing too much, the extra work Stevie was managing to complete was sometimes of dubious quality.

"The important things I had to do got done anyway," she continued. "And all that extra time allowed me to do a bunch of stuff not that well. You know, you get crazy and say, 'Well, I'm gonna write three songs tonight. I'm gonna sit at my typewriter and I'm gonna write ten pages of my future book . . .' You don't have to do that. What I learned at Betty Ford is that it isn't necessary to go non-stop, seven days a week."

One assignment she had to accomplish at the clinic was to write an essay on the difference between being a rock star and a human being. This she found especially difficult, tellingly; she had allowed her rock star life to define her. This *was* reality to her.

Stevie's time at Betty Ford was an often tortuous month of necessary soul-searching – something Stevie was already quite adept at, one might presume – though this time she was coming through the other side with the help of professionals, rather than indulging herself. Naturally, this experience would give rise to a surge of fresh creative inspiration. 'Welcome To The Room . . . Sara', a song that would appear on *Tango*, is like a journal-entry from this time, the title a direct quote from the therapists who greeted 'Sara' as she walked into her first session. "This is a dream, right?" she asks in the lyrics, still incredulous that she is there at all. The line "You can take all the credit . . ." is apparently a sarcastic swipe at Frontline Management, who had insisted on her attending rehab.

"Frontline baby . . ." she wrote. "Well, you held her prisoner . . ."

The issues Stevie worked through in the safety and privacy of the clinic would soon appear on the page and ultimately, the record. And, lest we forget, one of those issues would be Joe Walsh's chilly treatment of her . . . "In the never forgotten words of another one of your friends, baby / When you hang up that phone / Well, you cease to exist . . ." As always, Stevie's lyrics are a patchwork quilt of vignettes, thoughts jotted down, little moments surfacing from memory as if murmured during a troubled sleep. By the end of the month, Stevie would be awake, more awake than she'd been for a very long time, if only for a moment. Something far more damaging than cocaine was about to crash into her life that would lead her by the hand into a sleep-walking half-life for eight long years.

Chapter 23

For Stevie, ditching cocaine was liberating. Once a gleaming white emblem of Stevie's freewheeling rock'n'roll lifestyle, the drug had long had Stevie in its grip, locking her into an expensive routine that now resembled an obsessive compulsive disorder. "It [became] like, 'I can't get out of bed without doing some coke. I can't go shopping without doing some coke. I can't go to a movie without doing some coke . . .'" It was a relief to be unshackled from this faceless dictator. Stevie generally hated being told what to do, so it struck a nerve when a close friend noted that cocaine was in fact telling her what to do every few minutes – go to the bathroom for another hit.

Stevie wasn't supposed to talk about the Betty Ford Clinic, but she acknowledged it was an "amazing place" that had made it easy for her to turn her life around. She felt excited about the future rather than over extended and frazzled. No longer did she hanker for the fragile, mythical image of seventies Stevie, the one that was close to fading out altogether. Stevie had lost too many heroes, although there had always been a conflict about how she felt about this. "A part of me said 'I want to go down with them also.' [But] another part of me said, 'Isn't it too bad that Jimi Hendrix isn't still here? What would he be doing now? Isn't it sad that Janis Joplin is not still here?' I wish Oscar Wilde had lived another 20 years, but he was a notorious drug addict. There would be no more work from Oscar Wilde, no more work from Jimi Hendrix, Janis Joplin . . . That's what made me say, 'I don't want to be one of the ones that people are sad about because they're no longer with us.'"

It was a monumental effort, finally prying the monkey from her back, but what was to follow would render this fresh start obsolete. Concerned friends and management still didn't believe Stevie was out of the woods, and were especially worried about how much she drank. Stevie felt better than ever after leaving Betty Ford but "the powers that be were terrified I was going to start doing [cocaine] again. And everybody thought I should go to AA," she told *The Telegraph*'s Mike Brown, even though, she insists, she was not an alcoholic. "In order to get out of that, the next best thing in everybody else's eyes was for me to go see a shrink. I really didn't want to go. But I finally said, 'all right, to get all of you off my back . . .'"

The doctor Stevie visited did not inspire confidence; he exhibited groupie-like tendencies and was eager to have Stevie in his office so he could hear some pop-star gossip and be cool by association, which Stevie saw through immediately. More seriously, he wrote out a prescription for the tranquilliser Klonopin, also known as Clonazepam, to ease any anxiety Stevie might be suffering from. "I didn't want to do it," Stevie says. "He said, 'You're nervous.' And I was nervous; I'm a nervous person. So I finally just said, 'all right.'" And so, Stevie, who was not actually depressed, was put on strong anti-depressants for the next eight years of her life . . . and one of the long-term side-effects of taking this drug would be, ironically, depression. Agreeing to this would be one of the worst decisions Stevie Nicks had ever made – far worse than taking cocaine – but the effects would take time to show.

Post-rehab, Stevie went straight into recording with Fleetwood Mac. It was about time, as far as the rest of the band were concerned. Over the past year, while the Mac had been working on *Tango In The Night*, they had been sending tapes of what they'd recorded to her home in Phoenix and Stevie, in turn, had been sending them demos to develop in her absence. However, even when she did have breaks in the *Rock A Little* tour, Stevie was nervous about turning up. She was, as Mick Fleetwood remembers, "dreading that Lindsey, in his producing capacity, would be sarcastic toward her, but he made an effort not to be as much of a martinet as he was with the rest of us." At first.

"It is wonderful that this experience of Fleetwood Mac has turned into such a wonderful thing," Stevie gushed at the time. "Something changed, because everyone is going out of their way to be sensitive to everybody else. Nobody yells at me for leaving town for over a month, and of course, being as hyper-over-sensitive as I am, I was ready for them to yell at me, and they didn't." Stevie would relay a rather different version of how things played out in the studio in later years, however.

Moments of good behaviour aside, there was undeniable friction, a friction that had been present even when the band first decided to get back together to record two years earlier. The members of the Mac had turned up to visit Stevie at a charity concert she was performing at alongside Don Henley in September 1985 at the Universal Amphitheater in LA. The benefit was for Mulholland Tomorrow, an environmental group protesting against proposed housing developments in the Santa Monica Mountains. Backstage, the Macs circled each other awkwardly – it was the first time they had all been in the same space together since the end of the *Mirage* tour. As one observer noted, "The tension was so thick you could choke on it." It was hardly better in the studio. Stevie put her hands up: "It was me that was causing [the problems], because Lindsey was the head guy and I was making him erratic. When I was not there, they all got on fine. But when I walked in it was like, 'Thanks for stopping by. We heard you were busy with your solo tour. Thanks for bailing on us.' That's the first thing I got. I don't have time for that abuse. I felt like, 'If you don't get off my back, I'm going to injure you badly.'" Happy days.

Lindsey Buckingham revealed his frustrations to writer Rob Trucks: "By the time we got to *Tango In The Night*, everyone was just a mess. I was probably the least, maybe Christine and myself, but you know, victims of the excesses that fame has to offer, victims of buying into all of our own press, shall we say . . . but mainly victims of choices we made in terms of lifestyle. Stevie in particular was not very focused. She was out there doing solo work. She wasn't there."

Be that as it may, Stevie would still feel stung when Christine, normally her greatest ally, coolly said in an interview that Stevie "phones her part in. She asks what songs we plan on doing and what songs we want her to do. The rest is decided between Mick, Lindsey and me." Stevie then noticed a quote from Lindsey Buckingham enthusing about the rapport he had with Christine, a connection which had existed "before we had even met", no less. Lindsey knew how insecure Stevie was on this subject; Stevie had felt put out when she saw Lindsey and Christine intimately working together on songs in the studio during the *Tusk* era. Lindsey was expert at pushing Stevie's buttons.

One reason, surely, for Stevie's reluctance to spend time in the studio was that she associated recording studios with hoovering up truckloads of cocaine. Now she was clean, this would be the first time in nearly a decade that Stevie Nicks would go into the studio with Fleetwood Mac and not indulge.

When Stevie did turn up, there were often huffs and atmospheres. Sometimes her input was not required, sometimes it was, but she often felt rejected, as if she were a child being waved away after trying to bother the busy grown-ups. "There've been many times when Stevie might come out in the studio and try and sing along, and we'd tend to say, 'Don't do that right now, let us work this out first.'" said Christine. "Now she'll just go, 'There's no need for me to be here.' She does feel left out."

Stevie admitted it was "lonely on the other side of the mirror", or at least on the other side of the glass in the studio. "Five hours go by and they don't even remember I'm there," she grumbled. But whatever irked her could, as always, be channelled into her own material somehow, and this detachment would be a theme on Stevie's *Alice In Wonderland*- esque record *The Other Side Of The Mirror,* her next solo album. While she sat moodily watching the others work, Stevie was determined to make her next release better than anything she'd done before.

During these moments of isolation, sometimes Stevie would close her eyes and think of Robin, the kindred spirit who had been by her side so often in the studio. Stevie still felt her presence and believed herself to be guided by her, particularly when it came to vocal takes. "She'll go,

'That's a really good song,' or 'That vocal was perfect!' She was a speech therapist so sometimes I feel her like the teacher up there shaking her finger at me saying, 'You need a few more hours sleep every night . . .'" Ultimately *Tango* would be a creative tour de force despite the inherent ill feeling – the album included strong material such as Lindsey's phenomenal 'Big Love' and Christine McVie's 'Everywhere' and 'Little Lies', her best work in years. The entire album would be a far greater success than *Mirage* and a personal triumph for Lindsey, who had worked hard on the production in his home studio with Richard Dashut. Stevie brought the hypnotic 'Welcome To The Room . . . Sara' to the table, as well as 'When I See You Again' and the radiant 'Seven Wonders', another co-write with her *Wild Heart* collaborator, synth-queen Sandy Stewart.

'Seven Wonders' was born of one of Sandy's demos, played to Stevie at her home in Phoenix. When Stevie heard the song, she wanted it instantly, and had to ask whether Sandy intended to use it for herself. "She said, 'When I wrote it I thought about you . . .'" remembers Stevie in an interview with Timothy White for *Rock Lives*. "So I said, 'Well, what do you think about Fleetwood Mac?' She said, as any wise songwriter would say, 'Absolutely. Go ahead.'"

Sandy also contributed lyrics to the song, although they wouldn't be used. Stevie explains, "The only reason for that was because we thought we'd written down exactly as I sing them, the exact words to 'Seven Wonders'. The spontaneity of that early take made it truly special.

"Sandy unfortunately didn't get me the real words before that, so I sang those words . . . and then I saw the real words and I tried to sing the real words, which are in fact very different. I couldn't do a vocal again like that first time I walked up to the mic and sang 'Seven Wonders'. There is something in that vocal that is real special, and it's because I hadn't really thought about the song much. It was my first time singing 'Seven Wonders', so when you hear it, you know that it was really the first time I was hearing it too."

After hearing Stewart sing the song first, Stevie misunderstood some of the words, hence the line "All the way down to Emmeline", which has mystified fans for years. The original line was "All the way down you held the line", but the use of a name like Emmeline is typical for Stevie, so accustomed are we to hearing her throw in women's names – Sara, Lily – and thus we look for the clues she scatters in her songs. In this case, it seems to have simply been a phonetic red herring, but it does also sound as if Stevie is murmuring the name Sara during the breaks between the chorus and verses. Another belief is that Stevie is singing "Aaron", which would also make sense: it is a family name close to her heart, as we know. Sandy Stewart's working title for the song is rumoured to have been 'Aaron' too, which may have had a hand in catching Stevie's attention.

Stevie preferred to record her vocals alone and away from the band, increasing the gulf between them. For all of *Tango*'s luminous charms, Stevie felt it didn't sound like Fleetwood Mac, not least because she "couldn't really be heard" on the record, and just three of her songs were included, while the other writers were all over it. Songs such as 'Everywhere' lacked Stevie's trademark harmonies; Christine argued that she had *wanted* her to sing on them, but the bald fact was that she had barely been there. The matter was resolved with overdubs*, layering Stevie's vocals into the mix of the album. Her voice is not especially perceptible on 'Everywhere', although her mellifluous tones contrast perfectly against Lindsey's sharp tenor in the backing vocals for 'Little Lies', sweet and sour. But the damage was done. Stevie Nicks felt "mistreated".

"We put as many things of hers on there as we could," Lindsey told writer Rob Trucks. "But if you say it took ten months to a year, I'm not exaggerating, we saw her all of two weeks. And so we had to try to cheat things, we had to try to create things out of thin air for her."

Stevie, naturally, didn't see it like that; she decided to wield her power and make a point. "It got so bad I said, 'I'm going to do a solo record,'

* The press were desperate to know who was providing the female-sounding grunts on 'Big Love', speculating that it was surely Stevie, or a new girlfriend of Lindsey's. Wrong on both counts – it was Lindsey providing all of his own sex noises, sampled through a variable-speed oscillator to change the pitch.

A mid-Eighties Stevie in all her voluminous, if glassy-eyed, glory. MIRRORPIX

The post-Lindsey Buckingham line-up of Fleetwood Mac. Rick Vito is on the far left, while Billy Burnette stands between Stevie and John McVie. Vito and Burnette joined the band in 1987, their tenure lasting until 1991. THE LIFE PICTURE COLLECTION/GETTY IMAGES

Stevie and Don Henley perform at the Concert for Artists' Rights at the Forum in Inglewood, California, February 26, 2002. KMAZUR/WIREIMAGE

Stevie Nicks steps out with British producer Rupert Hine. The pair worked together on Stevie's 1989 solo album *The Other Side Of The Mirror*. TOM WARGACKI/WIREIMAGE

. straight-haired Stevie poses in one of her favourite top hats – an enduring part of her 'Rhiannon' costume. MR PHOTO/CORBIS OUTLINE

US President Bill Clinton shakes hands with Michael Jackson as Fleetwood Mac perform 'Don't Stop' for the inauguration festivities in Maryland in 1993. AFP/AFP/GETTY IMAGES

Fleetwood Mac after being inducted into the Rock and Roll Hall of Fame in 1998. The thirteenth annual Rock and Roll Hall of Fame induction dinner also honoured Santana, The Eagles, The Mamas and Papas, Lloyd Price and Gene Vincent. JON LEVY/AFP/GETTY IMAGES

One of many emotional moments on stage between Stevie Nicks and Lindsey Buckingham during Fleetwood Mac's televised reunion concert, *The Dance*, at Warner Brothers Studios, May 23, 1997, Burbank, California. NEAL PRESTON/CORBIS

Rod Stewart and Stevie perform at Philips Arena in Atlanta, Georgia on March 24, 2012. The show was part of their co-headline *Heart And Soul* tour. RICK DIAMOND/GETTY IMAGES

Stevie and musical soul mate Sheryl Crow perform at the 10th anniversary celebration of the National Breast Cancer Coalition in New York City, March 6, 2002. LAWRENCE LUCIER/GETTY IMAGES

Stevie performs during the Epicurean Charitable Foundation's fifth annual benefit concert in her beloved Las Vegas, Nevada, December 8, 2006. ETHAN MILLER/GETTY IMAGES

Stevie, second from right, and from left, Charles Kelley, Hillary Scott and Dave Haywood, of the musical group Lady Antebellum, perform on stage at the 49th annual Academy of Country Music Awards at the MGM Grand Garden Arena, Las Vegas on Sunday, April 6, 2014. CHRIS PIZZELLO/INVISION/AP

Stevie with Tom Petty & The Heartbreakers. Stevie has always been proud of her longstanding association with The Heartbreakers, and was thrilled when Petty presented her with a platinum brooch proclaiming her 'the only girl' in their band. TIM MOSENFELDER/CORBIS

Dave Grohl and Stevie perform at the premiere of Grohl's documentary *Sound City* at the Hollywood Palladium on January 31, 2013 in Los Angeles. The film celebrates the history of the Sound City studio, where Buckingham Nicks cut their first record with producer Keith Olsen. KEVIN WINTER/GETTY IMAGES

Glamorous and poised as ever, Stevie Nicks is the proud and deserving recipient of the BMI Icon Award at the Beverly Wilshire Four Seasons Hotel in Beverly Hills, California on May 13, 2014. LESTER COHEN/WIREIMAGE

much to Mick and Lindsey's horror," she said in an interview with *The Island Ear* in 1994. "From that moment on, I got treated much worse. However, they couldn't be too awful to me, because they knew they couldn't go out on the road without me. I had platinum records and sold-out tours, why did I need to be treated like this?"

The singles were selected – 'Big Love' being the first release in March 1987 – and videos were shot, a process Stevie in particular couldn't bear, especially since being criticised for putting on a few pounds. But she appeared, swishing her ra-ra skirts and walking arm-in-arm with Christine in the video for 'Little Lies', snapping her fingers and gazing into camera, her glamorous, steampunk outfits and voluminous blow-dry incongruous with the bucolic farmland setting. Lindsey, meanwhile, wore a suit and managed to pout and lip-synch simultaneously. This was no easy feat, especially when the words being mimed were 'tell me, tell me lies', words that require the lips to be pulled back rather than pushed forward. Still, this was the eighties and pouting, quite frankly, came first.

The video for 'Everywhere', another Christine song that would become a number-one hit, was very Stevie in essence: a silvery full moon, a Tudor romance, highwaymen riding through the night . . . but other than Christine herself, the video featured lavishly costumed actors instead of the band. The potent 'Big Love' promo, on the other hand, was radically modern in approach, a multi-faceted affair costing $250,000 (or twice that, according to Mick Fleetwood); it variously featured the whole band but was really all about Lindsey, thrusting back and forth as he played guitar and made bedroom eyes at the camera.

The promo for 'Seven Wonders' would be a more traditional video in the sense that it focused on the band "playing" onstage, as it were. We find ourselves on a rosy, theatrical set to find Fleetwood Mac performing in an empty theatre, surrounded by Grecian ruins. Stevie struts among her bandmates and clicks her fingers as she sings, equal parts gypsy queen, flamboyant conductor and circus ringleader. There are moments of awkward humour here, as Lindsey goons and Mick grins. The director also plays on the Stevie / Lindsey romance element, even though said romance had long died. The pair dutifully lock eyes and touch hands, but there is sarcasm in Lindsey's kohl-rimmed eyes and nervousness in Stevie's.

Interestingly, there would be no image of the band on the album cover, just a lush homage to Rousseau by the Australian artist Brett-Livingstone Strong, a painting that was already on display in Buckingham's house. The lack of any Mac members at all on the front of the record perhaps points to the fact that there was little unity in the ranks and the image chosen will certainly have been decided upon by Buckingham. But the resulting release in April 1987 would be deemed a return to form and it would become the band's biggest seller since *Rumours*. *Tango* would spend more than ten months in the US top 40, selling a staggering three million copies and being certified triple platinum, but it was an even bigger hit in the UK, hitting the top of the album charts three times during 1987 and 1988 (and the competition was strong – Michael Jackson's *Bad* was also jostling for pole position). In the UK, *Tango* would be certified 8x platinum, but it would also be the last studio album to feature the definitive Fleetwood Mac lineup. Lindsey Buckingham had had enough.

Plans were underway for the first Fleetwood Mac tour in five years to promote *Tango* (although the tour itself would be called *Shake The Cage*). There was just one person disinclined to get back out on the road. Lindsey. He hadn't missed touring, hated the pressures that went with it and, to his mind, he had been distracted from his own work enough. In fact, he went so far as to state this publicly in an interview with the rock magazine *Creem*, to the rest of the band's outrage. "It was like he was giving his notice in the press," said Mick Fleetwood.

An emergency band meeting was called, taking place at Stevie's house that July. The plan was to persuade Lindsey to support the album they – he especially – had worked so hard on. He could even honour the tour and then leave the band if that was his wish. Everyone was dreading the meeting, and as they settled down in the paradoxically calm atmosphere of Stevie's living room, Lindsey protested he was too "fried", and didn't want to expend all of his energy on the road with the Mac when he had an album of his own to make. He'd given more than enough of himself to the band already, but Mick was determined – he needed to make money – and a confrontation ensued. Lindsey dug his heels in. "[He] wasn't prepared to do me any favours," admitted Fleetwood. But Lindsey was feeling pressured, and with good reason.

As the heat started to rise, Stevie defused the situation with a little coquettish teasing. "We can have a great time out there," she soothed. "Let's do it for old times' sake, just once more." She paused, her cheeks turning pink (surely she had only just stopped short of saying "For me?") and Lindsey smiled for the first time that evening. A breakthrough had seemingly occurred, and after Stevie assured him that things would be different this time and that "it won't be a nightmare", Lindsey agreed to mull it over.

Stevie's soft-soaping had apparently worked. The message came through to the rest of the band, via Warner Brothers boss Mo Ostin, that Lindsey would tour with Fleetwood Mac for 10 weeks. Immediately arrangements were put in place for rehearsal time, tour dates were booked and anticipation was building, although Christine McVie, who had joked that she would "break Lindsey's arms" if he refused to tour (which would render him somewhat useless if he did change his mind), couldn't quite relax, having "sensed" that this was still the last thing Lindsey wanted to do. And she was right. Suddenly Lindsey pulled out with little explanation beyond that he simply couldn't cope.

It wasn't difficult to see why. In an interview with *Montreal Gazette*'s Bernard Perusse in later years, Lindsey had to admit that "everybody's level of craziness was at the max at that point . . . and if things are crazy in a studio, it's usually times five on the road. I hit the wall. It was a survival move, pure and simple. I never regretted it for a minute." Manager Dennis Dunstan called Stevie's house with the news, preceding it with the words one never wants to hear: "Are you sitting down?"

Publicly, Buckingham released the following statement: "In 1985, I was working on my third solo album when the band came to me and asked me to produce the next Fleetwood Mac project. At that point, I put aside my solo work, which was half-finished, and committed myself for the next 17 months to produce *Tango In The Night*. It was always our understanding that upon completion of the album I would return to my solo work. Of course, I wish them all the success on the road."

The band was furious and demanded another meeting, this time at Christine's house on 7 August 1987. What would unfold was, as Mick described, "a real showdown", and he'd seen a few in his time. The gloves were off. There would be no blushes or cajoling, nudges and persuasion this time.

Strangely, it would also only be at this point that, according to an interview in 1993, Stevie really felt she and Lindsey had broken up for good, which Lindsey Buckingham found "interesting", especially considering she had been "through quite a number of men. I'm surprised to hear that," Lindsey would tell *The Dallas Morning News* in later years.

Lindsey protested, saying he'd "given 12 years of his life" to the band and couldn't "do it all anymore". The word "all" was an inflammatory one. He was referring to the rest of the band as if they were mere passengers while he was the nucleus, but this aside, Christine and Stevie's songs would generally receive more radio play than Lindsey's. The situation was turning ugly and Stevie cracked, reminding Lindsey that "there are other people in the room besides yourself."

It wasn't as if Stevie hadn't considered leaving the Mac herself, indeed she had, many times, but she was always conscious that such a move meant potentially putting a lot of people out of work – not just the band but the crew and entourage. Lindsey just wanted to move on, but his former partner was shell-shocked, bursting into tears and hissing, "You've broken my fucking heart on this." She tried to bar his path but Lindsey, a coiled spring at the best of times, coldly pushed her aside, snarling "get this bitch out of my way, and fuck the lot of you."* He was unwilling to listen to any more, but Stevie was not letting him go without a fight. Literally. The scene to follow would be a "physically ugly" one, according to John McVie.

* From Adrian Deevoy's 2013 'You Make Fighting Fun' feature in *The Daily Mail*.

"That was in the courtyard of my house," Christine McVie remembers. "There was a bit of a physical fight, and she wasn't beating him up. It wasn't nice."

Stevie ran outside as Lindsey marched towards his car, but as she grabbed onto him, he hit out, allegedly slapping her in the face and pushing her against the hood of his car, causing Dennis Dunstan and Stevie's manager Tony Dimitriades to have to restrain him as he screamed "get that woman out of my life, the schizophrenic bitch!" This was, hands down, the worst fight Stevie and Lindsey had ever had. Lindsey has often said he "doesn't remember" quite what happened on that afternoon at Christine's house, which is fair enough – it doesn't sound like an especially memorable day, after all. However, he has conceded that "it was an unpleasant situation . . . But you have to ask yourself, if someone is beating on your chest because they don't want you to leave, isn't that kind of flattering?" Way to make lemonade out of that lemon, Mr Buckingham.

Lindsey later claimed that his intention initially was to eschew the tour, not leave the band; but he had now slapped, screamed and intimidated his way straight out of the group that had made him a star. Stevie admitted that, while part of her hoped he would change his mind at first, she was ultimately happier now he had gone. Both of them now had a chance to heal and the band played on, just as it always did in the face of adversity and lineup changes. It was interesting that, after so many years of wondering if or when Stevie would leave the group, Lindsey would be the first to go. However, as Buckingham said, "Later Stevie would say, 'You know, I should have left when you left.'"

Chapter 24

Within days of Lindsey's explosive departure, there was an unusual celestial alignment which took place on August 17 and 18, 1987. This alignment was known as the Harmonic Convergence and, according to Mayan cosmology, the date marked the end of the cycles of hell, supposedly corresponding with a shift in the earth's energy – "from warlike to peaceful". Interesting timing indeed. Thousands gathered at sacred points across the world to meditate, such as Sedona in Arizona, just two hours from Stevie's birthplace and, significantly for Stevie herself, surrounded by ancient red rocks that seemed to glow in the sunlight. The rocks had formed from sandstone and limestone left by a receding sea aeons ago. Iron oxide subsequently covered the sandstone forming a rust and creating the glorious red rocks that people flocked to be near during the convergence.

Stevie herself took the cosmic relevance of these two days seriously, inviting the band to her opulent home in Paradise Valley, Arizona, and ceremoniously making a wish. She meditated on her desire that Fleetwood Mac "would be able to come back and go out in the fashion that we came in," she said. "We would not go out a dying band or slip gracefully away if we decided to quit."

The possibility of the band calling it a day was, according to Stevie, not out of the question. But in the meantime, dates had been booked and the show had to go on. Fleetwood Mac and their management pondered over the possibilities for Lindsey's replacement and the music industry speculated over who might get that plum gig, with names such as Waddy Wachtel, Don Henley and Peter Frampton being thrown around. Ultimately it would take two guitarists to replace Lindsey, the knowledge of which no doubt will have brought Buckingham some pleasure. The two musicians to be hastily brought into the fold would be LA session star Rick Vito and the Mac's old pal Billy Burnette.

The decision would be made quickly and the "audition" brought back memories of how Stevie and Lindsey first joined the band. "We went to dinner," remembers Stevie in a 1989 interview with Timothy White for *Musician*. "I walked into the restaurant and Billy Burnette was sitting there, and Rick Vito was sitting there and Mick Fleetwood and his manager Dennis Dunstan. I sat down and they introduced me to Rick – I'd known Billy for a long time – [and] everybody just started to smile . . ."

The following day Rick and Billy joined the band for a rehearsal in a small space in Venice, LA. After playing through a handful of songs, Mick was heard to shout, "Yeah, you're in!" The eleventh lineup of the band was sealed. This entire debacle had sent shockwaves through the music press, and while people were still dealing with the fact that Lindsey had left, the concept that the band would be carrying on was even harder to compute for some. But Fleetwood Mac was defiant in the face of what had happened, and the questions being levelled at them. Stevie haughtily stated that there was no reason for everyone else to quit just because Lindsey had. And as for the new lineup, the proof would be in the performances. If rehearsals were anything to go by, Stevie was convinced they were going to be just fine.

"I knew instantly that as soon as we stepped onto the big stage this was going to be wonderful," she continued. "It sounds like Fleetwood Mac. If you walk outside and listen from the parking lot, the first thing you would say would not be 'Ah, I don't hear Lindsey . . .'" And this was crucial, especially to Stevie. Mick, John and Christine were used to musicians coming and going, but for Stevie, her entire experience of Fleetwood Mac was interwoven with Lindsey's. Mick remembers her feeling privately unsure as to whether the tour would work, whether there could even be a Mac without Lindsey, but soon she was convinced, not least because

Rick and Billy were significantly "more compassionate" to her than her former beau ever had been.

To be fair, they were the new boys and they were keen to fit in to the megastar rock band they now found themselves in. Stevie was thrilled that, in direct contrast to the past, Vito and Burnette were "very interested in what I do, they're interested in my songs, they come up to my house and work with me . . . That's something Lindsey and I never did because he never wanted to be that close to me anymore," she said in an interview with the BBC. "We would always get back on the subject of why we broke up 12 years ago. After 12 years it's hard for me to remember why we broke up, or for that matter why we even went together." When inevitably asked by journalists about Lindsey around this time, Stevie simply stated that she "gave [him] up. He's a thing of my past. I hope he finds what he's searching for, and I hope he's happy, and I wish him well. And there's nothing left to say." Wishful thinking, perhaps. As Stevie fans know, their heroine has never stopped talking, or indeed writing, about Lindsey.

The first four-month leg of the tour was scheduled to commence on 30 September 1987 at the Kemper Arena, Kansas City, and the band chartered a 727 to whisk them there in the decadent style to which they had become accustomed. Burnette and Vito fitted in well and, as Stevie insisted at a press conference, "They are not just fill-in guys. They are in the group," before adding pointedly, "And everybody is playing as one unit now. Neither Billy nor Rick are freaking out on stage trying to get all their licks in."

Stevie put her all into the Shake The Cage dates, even asking for rehearsals during the tour to work on harmonies for 'Little Lies' and, while her costumes had a little of the "wedding cake" about them, according to one reviewer, she looked beautiful, swirling her talismanic shawls as the audience expected. Most importantly, Stevie's voice was generally on good form, even though her throat still caused her problems, to the extent that 'Rhiannon' often had to be left off the setlist. 'Big Love' and 'Tango In The Night', the title track to the very album the band were on tour promoting, would also unfortunately have to be jettisoned, being Lindsey's songs.

Fans had little idea quite how heroic Stevie's performances were – not only were they seeing her sing coke-free for the first time in years, she was suffering from a chronic fatigue syndrome called Epstein-Barr. This, combined with her use of Klonopin, was causing increasing problems, which is all the more lamentable as Stevie was finally starting to really enjoy being in Fleetwood Mac without Lindsey breathing down her neck. In fact, everyone was more relaxed, John McVie had recovered from his drinking problem and for Stevie, Fleetwood Mac had now become "a pleasure thing. It makes everything else all right."

Nicks was diagnosed with Epstein-Barr shortly after having breast implants removed; many hadn't realised she'd had cosmetic surgery in December 1976, but a year into her tenure with Fleetwood Mac, the sudden attention was making her more conscious than ever of her looks. Stevie believed her body to be out of proportion – "I thought my hips were too big and I had no chest . . ." – and in a bid to look better on stage, she went under the knife. "I'd advise against having [implants]," she told the *Daily Mirror* in 2003. "You will have to take them out and that leaves you scarred."

"I was in and out of hospital, at the doctor's three times a week, taking acupuncture, having IVs to clean the toxic silicone out of my body, it was awful. Once you have [Epstein-Barr], you have it always. I don't have the symptoms right now. If you get all depressed and worn out, it comes back. It has a lot to do with your state of mind."

The illness was making Stevie crave rest and she was sleeping as much as she possibly could, much to the bemusement of many of the people around her. The protective and avuncular Mick – still the band's "Daddy", as Christine called him – spotted what was happening and promptly cancelled their final shows and the Australian dates scheduled the following March, allowing Stevie to go home and rest until the European leg of the tour drew Shake The Cage to a close with a magnificent finale at Wembley Arena in June 1988.

Other than emerging to appear with Fleetwood's Zoo on New Year's Eve in Aspen (where they rang in 1988 with Eddie Van Halen), Stevie obeyed doctors' orders and hibernated, warmed by the blazing fires in her hearths, the candlelight that surrounded her and the devoted friends who rallied round. But while Stevie recuperated, she also had time to contemplate her next move as a solo artist, a move that would get underway once the European tour had been completed. Fleetwood Mac had agreed to have a break once Shake The Cage had rumbled to a close, providing the perfect opportunity for Stevie to take her time with her new album *The Other Side Of The Mirror.*

Stevie's manager Tony Dimitriades already had a producer in mind: the English songwriter and producer Rupert Hine. He was a gentle, instinctive soul with humour and vision, just like Stevie, and his success rate was impressive; he'd already written and produced for Kevin Ayers, Tina Turner, The Thompson Twins, The Waterboys, Howard Jones, Chris De Burgh and many other hugely popular artists of the day, and Tony had a feeling Hine could be the one to take Stevie forward. After speaking to Nicks herself, Dimitriades contacted Hine and arranged an introductory lunch for the pair, so they could get a sense of whether a potential collaboration would work. Tony warned Rupert that Stevie did have a bit of a habit of falling in love with her producers. Hine, bemused, thought to himself, "Well, I'm not sure that's going to happen."

*

After settling in at Le Dome on Sunset Boulevard, Stevie and Rupert started talking in earnest, Stevie's warmth and charm putting Rupert immediately at ease. "I remember liking her very much simply because when she spoke, it was only about the things that matter," Rupert remembers. "It wasn't about the things I'd done."

Dimitriades and Stevie's colleagues at Atlantic Records had engineered the meeting with the knowledge that Hine had "written big commercial hits", he said, "Although I don't think like that. Having commercial success is always second only to doing the best thing you can do in terms of writing a song that is completely communicative and successful unto itself. If you get that right, you have automatically increased the chances of success tenfold." It was clear Rupert and Stevie were on the same wavelength already, but what he was about to say next would be the clincher.

With regard to the production of the record, Rupert asked where Stevie would like to record. She had already mentioned several studios she had liked, but before she could repeat herself, Hine clarified the question. "I said, 'No, where would you like to record on Planet Earth?' She looked at me, almost incredulous," said Hine. "I said, 'Leave studios out of it. Where can you imagine recording?' Knowing Stevie a little, I thought it might be somewhere in Wales, the 'Rhiannon' factor, or perhaps somewhere exotic. She said, 'Can we do it at my house?' I said, 'I don't even have to see your house to say 'yes'.'" Rupert was known for doing whatever it took to get the results that were required, and there would be no boundaries. Anything could happen.

As far as Stevie was concerned, he was hired "before we even started talking about music. The night I met Rupert Hine was a dangerous one," Stevie would write in her liner notes for *Timespace: The Best of Stevie Nicks*. "He was different from anyone else I had ever known . . . He was older, and he was smarter, and we both knew it. It seemed that we had made a spiritual agreement to do a magic album." Evidently Tony's warning was already proving correct: Stevie was already attracted to Rupert and they hadn't even looked at the menu yet.

Soon after their auspicious first meeting, Tony contacted Rupert to confirm it was all systems go, as far as Stevie was concerned, and sessions for her fourth solo album were duly arranged at her California home. "Home" was a large mock Dutch castle way up in the Hollywood Hills, a building that radiated a sense of dark fantasy and spooky glamour. The rent was an equally glamorous $25,000 per month. For Stevie it was the ideal setting, and the sense that anything was possible with this new, innovative producer, thrilled her. She really was on the other side of the mirror here – now she even had a moat between herself and the so-called "real world".

The Dutch castle, now used largely for movie and video shoots*, was pure Hollywood let's-pretend: despite the suits of armour and antique paintings, it was built in 1974. Still, between the fusty faux medieval decor and Stevie's wild imagination, it might as well have dated back to the Dark Ages. Rupert, having been given the grand tour by the palace queen herself, was especially taken by the ballroom, and suggested making the record in there. (Stevie remembers it as the "formal dining room"; either way, it was a great big room.) Ms Nicks agreed, of course, and the console was set up right underneath a spectacular chandelier which hung from the middle of the ceiling.

"It was great until one day something went wrong with the plumbing in the bathroom above," says Hine. "All of this water was dripping, equally majestically, down the chandelier and onto the console. I would love to have had a film of that. It was so surreal." Fortunately there was no lasting damage as members of Stevie's entourage leaped in to cover the console with plastic. It was simply "funny", Rupert remembers. "One of the many surreal things that happened during those 18 months."

As they settled into working together, Stevie realised instantly that she had made the right decision in hiring Rupert Hine. Early on, Stevie had expressed how she wanted her songs to communicate as directly as possible, to resemble her demos, in a way. She had been told too many times by friends that they preferred the demo versions of her songs to those that took half a million dollars to produce, so this time Stevie decided to do things a little differently.

"It's important that what I'm saying comes through," Stevie explained in an interview for *Tyne Tees*. "In this record, [Rupert] did what I asked, he let me put my demo feeling through. In other words, if I was to sit down and play the piano not very well and sing one of my songs not that well, it might [just] hit you because you understand what I'm trying

* It is now unfortunately known as "the house that porn built", as it is a popular location for adult movie shoots, with its grottos, waterfalls and ostentatious bedrooms. However on a more savoury note, Stevie would shoot her video to 'Rooms On Fire' here, and the house would feature in Tom Petty's promo for 'Into The Great Wide Open'.

to say. As soon as they put harps and violins and incredible guitar on it, you lose that." Stevie's songs were extensions of herself, precious and personal – it was that quality that people connected with; the fewer bells and whistles, the better.

That's not to say this album would be under-produced – this was the eighties, let's not forget – but there was a freshness to it, and little standing between the listener and the song. That directness was what Stevie wanted and, judging by the response of so many of her fans, that's exactly what was achieved. Rather than hunt down another writer to provide "hits", as was Jimmy Iovine's obsession, making Stevie feel a little put out in the process, Rupert enabled Stevie to complete some of the many songs already in her canon.

This album would take considerable time to complete – it would finally hit the shelves in May 1989 – but one theory for this would be that Stevie simply wanted to take her time with it. Although, on a darker note, her worsening reaction to the daily dose of Klonopin she was prescribed likely contributed. She was effectively sedating herself while still trying to work and be creative. Nevertheless, she was enjoying working in a new way in the comfort of her own space. Rupert sat up late with Stevie as she wrote down her thoughts or tinkered on the piano before finally going to bed and it would soon transpire that the pair of them could write together very naturally. Rupert was fascinated by how Stevie developed songs and never wanted to get in the way of it by insisting her tracks be morphed into something with more obvious commercial potential.

"Stevie's audience wants the most authentic Stevie they can get," Rupert explains. "And that doesn't mean someone coming in and saying, 'I've got an idea for a much more dazzling chorus . . .' That would be horrible for her, and I'm not the kind of person that would do that. So writing together unfolded when we were together. I would play the piano and she would start singing from a [note] pad. Very organic." Co-writes with Rupert would include 'Alice', 'Fire Burning' and 'Two Kinds Of Love', a song that would develop into a duet with the singer Bruce Hornsby, whose haunting hit song 'The Way It Is' had caught Stevie's attention in 1986.

Stevie would also work with songs sent over from Heartbreaker Mike Campbell, who wrote with Tom Petty and, occasionally, would have a song that wouldn't be quite right for Tom – in the case of this album, 'Whole Lotta Trouble' and 'Fire Burning'. "He'll send them over to Stevie," says Rupert, "and with the ones she likes, she reaches for her pad and just starts singing this beautiful writing, never thinking ahead like, 'maybe these two lines will suit the chorus', she just keeps going from the top of the page until the tape runs out. This, I've seen other people be completely confused by. I love it because it's what I call 'fishing'. At any moment, the music and words [can] combine to be greater than the sum of their parts. Something rings a bell inside you and you go, 'Oh, I like that.' I think she appreciated having someone sitting by her side going, 'I get it.'" This compassionate understanding was like a balm to Stevie's spirit.

Having a British producer must also have resonated nicely with her fascination with Albion and, of course, the album's very English inspiration, *Alice In Wonderland.* But Lewis Carroll's character was not the only Alice entwined with this record; *The Other Side Of The Mirror* would be dedicated to Stevie's characterful grandmother Alice, or 'Crazy Alice', as Stevie liked to call her. Alice sadly died before the album would be released; on the "other side of the mirror" for real, as Stevie observed.

Working intimately with Rupert and having moved everyone into her home* would create a strange but inviting greenhouse atmosphere; there was plenty of room to roam, but it was a matter of time (and not much time at that) before Stevie and Rupert's relationship moved beyond the professional. Stevie was already captivated by Rupert and, as he puts it, "she was very quick to make a declaration of how she felt."

"It always seemed to me that whenever Rupert walked into one of these old, dark castle rooms, that the rooms were on fire," Stevie remi-

* Stevie's favourite photographer Herbert Worthington III, always on hand to capture a pose when his employer was in the mood, was on the payroll and also living in the Coach House at Stevie's expense. Stevie liked to keep a tight quasi-family around her at all times, a circle that included real family: brother Chris Nicks was in charge of Stevie's merchandising.

nisced dreamily in her sleeve notes for *Timespace,* and her feelings would not go unrequited.

Rupert: "Stevie's so open it's almost impossible not to fall for her. She's never provocative, just completely herself. You fall for that honesty. That magical quality, which is the phrase everybody uses, is simply because she is true to who she is. If she cared about how she came across, visually or ideologically, she wouldn't have it. It's all real." The connection between them was sensed by those around them and as Stevie remembers, everyone "respected [our] space".

It was only when Stevie had presented 'Rooms On Fire' to Rupert, and he was focusing on the arrangement of the track, that she casually revealed the inspiration behind it. "She said, 'You know this is about you, right?' I could only think of the words to 'You're So Vain': 'you probably think this song is about you . . .' I thought, 'Wow, it's kind of the reverse of that.' It made it quite difficult to finish. I haven't thought about that for a while . . ."

The sparkling 'Rooms On Fire', which would significantly be the first single from the album and Stevie's first ever UK Top 20 hit, would be a co-write with her childhood friend Rick Nowells, and detailed the potent attraction she felt for Rupert with a raw honesty; the lyric "she laughed, and she cried and she tried to taunt him . . ." denoting a certain amount of seductive teasing to draw him in, not that she would have needed to try very hard.

The song unveils a heartfelt, slightly child-like fantasy: that of a superstar who has made the choice not to get married or have children until one night everything changes. Stevie attends a party, one of those "everlasting, horrifying" celebrity shindigs that Nicks, certainly since kicking cocaine, now tried to honour with only a brief appearance. She tells the story*:

"A man comes into the room. I don't see very well so I have a sixth sense, [so] even though I can't see him very well I feel something. I close my eyes for a second and he walks over to me. I look up and he's there.

* From a 1989 interview with the BBC, via InHerOwnWords.com.

"He asks me to dance," Stevie continues, "and we end up getting married and I end up having a little baby girl and we live together for 20, 25 years. The sad thing is that I waited for him all my life and then he dies before me. I wait for him for the rest of my life and he comes back after I am very, very old and gets me. And takes me with him back to wherever he comes from."

In the wildly kitsch video for 'Rooms On Fire', filmed at the castle, a serious Stevie floats slowly down the red staircase in a long scarlet gown to attend what appears to be her own ball; she is the Red Queen with a touch of Cinderella, mingled with shades of Norma Desmond. One can imagine this is the sort of thing Stevie does regularly anyway, descending the staircase to greet her devoted entourage, dressed to the nines, wondering what the day will bring.

She meets the man of her dreams, he takes her by the hand and they slow-dance by the pool. She is then seen dancing in a dazzling haze with the baby she had always hoped in her heart for (played by her goddaughter), and there are cutaways of Stevie as we all imagine her to be: a mystical high priestess, chiffon flying in the wind as she stands on her balcony; a writer, working at the white grand piano, or poring over her diary with a fire in the hearth and a picture of herself nearby.

She cuts a contemplative figure in the video, sad-eyed as she sings, but despite her health problems Stevie Nicks still knew how to party, and it was time to celebrate her favourite time of the year: Halloween. Stevie invited all of her friends to the castle and dressed up as Scarlett O'Hara from *Gone With The Wind*, having found the perfect red dress in her temperature-controlled costume chamber. Her "belle of the ball" status was naturally assured. And did Rupert go as Rhett Butler? Not exactly. "I went as Biggles, the first world war flying pilot – pretty silly but good fun. Mick Fleetwood came as Jesus Christ on a donkey. A real donkey. They don't do things by halves."

Just days later, the rock band U2 rolled into town to premiere their *Rattle And Hum* film at the Chinese Theater on 4 November 1988. ("That was my only time in *People* magazine," said Rupert, who turned up on

Stevie's arm.) There would be an afterparty at the Paramount soundstage but Stevie wanted to throw her own celebration for the band at the castle of which she was so proud, with an A-list Hollywood set. Rupert watched in amazement as the castle was swiftly decorated and further beautified for the event. He had only been in a relationship with Stevie for a few weeks, and had no idea what to expect.

"There was all this buzzing around, and I said, 'What can I do?' And she said, 'You can just welcome the guests in your lovely English way.' So I thought, 'Well, that doesn't sound like very hard work.'" Rupert stood poised by the door, although he was convinced he would be wasting his time for at least another two hours. Stevie had told her invitees to come at 7 p.m. but, in the UK at least, party-goers tend to roll up a little later. Not in Tinseltown, baby. Let's face it, it's a party at Stevie Nicks' castle. Why would anyone want to miss a minute of it?

"On the dot of 7 p.m., the bell rang," remembers Rupert. "I opened the front door and I saw what I thought was one of those Hollywood lookalike entertainers. 'Jack Nicholson' was in the doorway. So I said, 'Jack!' and he shook hands and said, 'Yeah, how are you?' He went off to get a drink and I was looking at him thinking, 'This is too weird.'

"Lori, Stevie's sister-in-law, said 'Wow, Jack was on time, wasn't he?' It was really Jack; 7 p.m., first to arrive at a party for U2 at Stevie Nicks' house – I didn't think for a minute anyone outside of the music world would be turning up. I'd just let Jack Nicholson in . . . holy shit, this is a whole different level to what I'm used to. And there was a whole succession, John McEnroe came in with Tatum O'Neal, Cher . . . I'd just spent ten years making records in Buckinghamshire and now I'm in Hollywood with these ludicrously heavyweight A-list people turning up at Stevie's party."

Rupert's favourite memories of working with Stevie aren't those of glittering soirees, red-carpet events or even working on an album in an enchanted castle with someone he just happened to have fallen in love with. It was simply the way she talked to him, perfectly naturally, in song.

"We'd go out to dinner and she'd suddenly just start singing to me straight into my ear, things that she was either thinking or just little ideas. That was one of the strongest memories – hearing Stevie's voice away from the studio and away from the stage, only able to really tell me what she was thinking by singing."

PART IV

Never Break The Chain

Chapter 25

As ever, if one wishes to read Stevie Nicks' autobiography – and naturally thousands do – in the meantime, one need only to listen to her songs. All of them are based on her life and there is no fiction, although there may be a touch of poetic licence here and there. But Nicks has often insisted she is not a storyteller: the tales she tells in her songs are based on truth. The material on *The Other Side Of The Mirror* is no different, taking us from innocence past and the thrill of fear surrounding life's turning points ('Ghosts'*) to a bitter recrimination of a lover ('Long Way To Go'), the still-flickering flame of a past love in 'I Still Miss Someone (Blue Eyes)', and, of course, the electric charge between Stevie and Rupert in 'Rooms On Fire'.

Stevie also included a cover – 'Cry Wolf', originally released in 1987 by Laura Branigan. As we know, she also released a duet with Bruce Hornsby: 'Two Kinds Of Love', a song Stevie wrote while on tour with Tom Petty and Bob Dylan the previous year, containing revealing lyrics that describe the subject of the song, her "famous friend" as a "great temptation". So many handsome princes, so little time.

Stevie was keen to work with Hornsby but when it transpired that the two artists' schedules didn't quite click, there was only one thing for it. "We got on a Concorde to New York," says Rupert. "We recorded it and

* The arrangement of the chorus on 'Ghosts', a song Stevie described as a "hymn", is reminiscent of Tom Petty's 'Free Fallin'', released four months after *The Other Side Of The Mirror* in October 1989. Stevie would later cover 'Free Fallin'' herself for the soundtrack of *Party Of Five* in 1996.

Concorded it straight back again. It's very typically Stevie. We had one night in New York but I think Stevie still brought about six suitcases . . ."

This was when Rupert picked up a nifty time-saving device from the seasoned traveller that was Nicks. "On her luggage she has a big 'X' on the side in gaffer tape," he said. "So whenever you arrive at any airport, because she'd always have about a dozen suitcases, she would just say to the porters, 'Anything with an X on it is mine,' so she or her assistants wouldn't have to stand around working out where the luggage was. You could see it from 50 feet away." Top superstar travelling tip there.

The session with Bruce was a little tense, but the result was stellar. It was hard to put a finger on the reason behind the strange mood in the studio; one theory is that it simply wasn't the kind of song Hornsby would write himself, so it took a little while to find its centre. But there is also a school of thought that Hornsby wasn't too pleased to be on the same track as the saxophonist Kenny G, whose playing is considered by some to be the height of eighties *fromage*. But Stevie loved Kenny's playing, likening it to a fluttering human voice, and she also adored him as a friend. Frankly, Stevie didn't care what anyone else thought. It was her album, and she wasn't interested in being trendy. This is one of the reasons Stevie Nicks has endured as an icon over the decades. She has always stayed true to her own heart; a strength necessary in the music industry where one often finds oneself very much alone in various ways.

One of the more serious moments on the album that would shed a light on Stevie's inner toughness would be 'Doing The Best I Can (Escape From Berlin)'. "That's the story of my life, especially the last three years," said Stevie. "I get tired of people telling me their opinions of what I do. I want to say: 'You have no idea the responsibility I feel toward people and the guilt that I carry around, how much I want to please everybody. It's difficult, it's ageing. 'Doing The Best I Can' says, 'get off my back', basically."

Rupert: "It was quite dark for Stevie. I wanted to make that track very strong and sinewy. I enjoyed arranging that song and enjoyed that she enjoyed it, too. She always sings along when you're listening back to things

– even if her voice is already on it, she always sings, which I find very charming."

One of Stevie's favourite tracks on the album would be 'Alice', a reflection of the mind-bending children's story that inspired the record and a nod to her 'crazy' grandmother, but "there is much of Alice in Stevie Nicks", insisted Stevie, referring to herself in the third person, as very famous people are occasionally prone to do. There is also plenty of Fleetwood Mac in 'Alice', and the song describes the protagonist running back and forth between the looking glass and reality.

In December 1988, shortly after Fleetwood Mac released their *Greatest Hits* compilation (featuring 'Rhiannon', 'Gypsy', 'Dreams' and 'Sara' from the Nicks back-catalogue), Rupert Hine flew to the UK to get his own studio ready for Stevie, who would be arriving the following month. Farmyard Studios, where Rupert had recorded all of the albums he had worked on throughout the eighties so far, was situated in Little Chalfont, Buckinghamshire and this would be where the mixing and overdubs for *Mirror* took place.

Stevie instantly loved the studio's charm; this definitely had the "Rhiannon factor". "It was like being in a cottage in Wales," remembered Stevie. "It was a little spooky . . . the atmosphere was like nothing I had ever experienced." Romance aside, the result would also be Stevie's only hit album in the UK. "All those great albums with Tom Petty and Don Henley . . . they were big in America but never really translated to Europe," concedes Hine.

Sadly it would be at this point that Rupert and Stevie's whirlwind relationship came to an end, but ultimately friendship and mutual respect would endure and Stevie's time with this eccentric super-producer would leave her "a changed woman. And now, long nets of white cloud my memory," she says in her *Timespace* liner notes, quoting 'Rooms On Fire' to infer that time has made her forget some of the finer details of what happened. The main thing is that, "now I remember the rooms, the music, and how truly magic the whole thing was."

*

The Other Side Of The Mirror was released in May 1989 shortly after first single 'Rooms On Fire' hit the shops, with the album reaching number 10 in the *Billboard* charts and number three in the UK. Stevie had flown back to Los Angeles after leaving Rupert in England, but while plans for a three-month US and European tour were put in motion, Stevie was not feeling particularly inclined to do anything other than snuggle into her comfiest chair, draw the blinds and watch TV. Thanks to Klonopin, Stevie was starting to lose interest in her work during the very year she should have been riding at her highest. She couldn't even be bothered to write. This was a sign that things really were serious.

"[The doctor] kept upping my dose," Stevie told *The Telegraph*'s Mick Brown in 2007. "1988 into '89, I'm now not even writing songs any more. I was living in a beautiful rented house in the Valley, and just pretty much staying home. Ordering take-in and watching TV. And I've gained 30lb and I'm 5ft 1in tall, and I'm so miserable."

Because of the emotional gloom caused by the drug, Stevie would then supplement the Klonopin with barbiturates to try to lift her mood. Unfortunately, the doctor's decision to increase her dose of Klonopin may well have been a result of the fact that Stevie was suffering from increased anxiety this year; in June, her mother Barbara Nicks would undergo open-heart surgery. Stevie rushed to her hospital bedside in Phoenix, Arizona – "my beautiful desert"– and the five weeks that followed were "the most emotionally trying of my life". Stevie would dedicate the programme for the upcoming tour to her mother, for her courage and "her wild, wild heart". The dedication would be signed by both Stevie and Christopher Nicks.

Dosed-up and depressed, Stevie barely remembers her tour for *The Other Side Of The Mirror*, which took place between August and November 1989, and in a promotional interview she admitted blankly that "a lot of the time I'm not happy". This would be the first time Stevie Nicks toured Europe as a solo artist, but in the main, the shows were not to her usual high standard and reviews were unkind; after a show in Stockholm, Sweden, one critic went so far as to say the performance was an "insult to her fans". In the case of many of the concerts on this tour, the support acts – including Richard Marx and Philadelphia band The Hooters – received more love from the crowd than the headliner, many of whose fans walked out during her set.

It was difficult for Stevie to muster the energy to reach a healthy weight when she was feeling so under par, but eventually she would reassess her lifestyle and start exercising, buying a treadmill and pounding away as she watched *Miami Vice* and *Star Trek* to pass the time.

Fleetwood Mac would soon set to work on their next album, *Behind The Mask*, their first since Lindsey's departure. Not only were they now lacking a major songwriting presence as well as a strong singer and guitarist, they were without their usual producer in Buckingham. Enter Greg Ladanyi, a record producer and songwriter who had worked with friends of the Mac – including Warren Zevon, Toto and Don Henley – and he came highly recommended. Sessions were booked at the Village Recorder, but recording would also take place in Phoenix for the convenience of the increasingly ailing Stevie, who had now started to shake noticeably and was spending as much time as possible trying to start writing again. These were, as Stevie calls them, "lost years". "For eight years, I didn't do anything worth remembering."

Stevie also started to make bad decisions, hiring and indeed firing the wrong people, subsidising the many people in her entourage upon whom she felt so dependent on day to day, and disengaging from the life that had once been so exciting. "Did you ever see that movie *The Never-Ending Story*? There is a character in that film, a blob called The Nothing," she told *The Courier Mail* in 2003. "Well, I turned into The Nothing. If I didn't spend those years on medication, I would have done two or three great albums . . . But I have nothing from those eight years. It ruined my life. It took my soul."

Fortunately for Stevie, she had so many reams of poetry and ideas banking up that she could still provide four songs for *Behind The Mask*, three of which were co-writes: 'Love Is Dangerous' and 'The Second Time' were both collaborations with Rick Vito, and 'Freedom' was co- written with Mike Campbell. 'Affairs Of The Heart' is the only song on the record credited solely to Nicks.

Behind The Mask would take little time to record compared to the Mac's previous albums and, as usual, Stevie was not always required to be present, but the style of the album would be unremitting AOR and lacked the dark tension and mystery that had always been so appealing about their previous output. The cover of the album, created by photographer Dave Gorton, was an odd depiction of a scene by a house under a thunderous sky, a band of five musicians play together *al fresco* while a young woman, with tumbling brown-blonde locks and a white tulle dress, stands in the foreground, her arms folded and her face serious, almost disappointed. Mick Fleetwood said that no one in the band wanted to be on the cover, but it's not surprising that many fans would assume this to be a portrayal of the Mac, with the sulky 'Stevie' character standing significantly apart.

The record, released in April 1990, topped the UK album chart and was hailed by *Rolling Stone*, who loved the new lineup, proclaiming Vito and Burnette to be the "best thing to have happened to Fleetwood Mac", and compared *Behind The Mask* to *Rumours* in the sense that the songs so deftly communicated the writers' respective emotional pain. But it would not be universally loved; *AllMusic* damned it as the "least inspired" of the Mac's output, and while making it had been "fun", Stevie, fatigued and unsure of whether this was still the band she wanted to be in, was teetering ever closer to the brink of leaving the group altogether. "I've been close to leaving ever since I joined," she said, before adding, "but so has everybody else." This would be the final Fleetwood Mac album for Stevie until *The Dance* in 1997.

Publicly, Stevie presented a positive front: "In comparison to all of our other albums, this was extremely easy to record. It's not that we didn't take as much time, it's more that the time that we did take was quality time. Being in the studio with two brand-new personalities made it a lot more like being in a new band." Making the record was nowhere near as "gruelling" as it had been in the past, and Stevie's songs were strong, particularly the country blues-tinged tracks she had written with Vito.

Still, many thought *Behind The Mask* suffered from Lindsey's absence*. Despite the refreshing lack of drama with the new lineup, this loss would also be felt, privately, by Stevie Nicks. It wouldn't be long before Stevie decided she just "couldn't continue to be in a Fleetwood Mac that didn't have Lindsey in it."

*

The world tour for *Behind The Mask* – titled simply 'The Mask' – would be the longest yet for Fleetwood Mac, taking the band on the road from March until December 1990. Rather than concentrate on material from the new album, the shows provided more of a greatest hits package "high on concert pomp and circumstance," wrote *Billboard*. "The camaraderie of old friends and familiar music from the past."

But this would also be a tour tinged with sadness; after the recording of *Behind The Mask*, both Christine McVie and Stevie Nicks decided this would be their last Fleetwood Mac tour, although they still were happy to record with the band. The ladies were losing their mojo with the Mac, as were some fans and critics. What was described as an "amicable split" had transpired after a "series of heartfelt conversations", according to the Mac's publicist. Stevie Nicks was advised by her own management not to go on the road with the band at all, but she refused to let them down. "The people who surround me felt that the loss of Lindsey was devastating to the band, and that the band could never be what it was, and I had this solo career that could be a lot more successful if I had a little more time and a little more rest," Stevie told Nicky Horne in a BBC Radio 1 interview.

"For my health and state of mind, they thought it would be better for me to have just one career, like most people. Since they didn't manage Fleetwood Mac they didn't really care about [them]. That angered me, because I did care about Fleetwood Mac. I would never walk away unless I had no choice."

* His appearance on the title track notwithstanding.

The announcement would be made public shortly before the final date on 7 December 1990 at the Forum, Los Angeles, where the band would be joined, poignantly, by Lindsey Buckingham for 'Landslide', 'Go Your Own Way' and 'Tear It Up'. The timing of the news raised eyebrows in the media – Mick Fleetwood's tell-all autobiography *Fleetwood: My Life And Adventures In Fleetwood Mac* written with Stephen Davis had just been published, detailing, amongst other things, his doomed tryst with Stevie Nicks.

Had the book's revelations pushed Stevie and Christine out of the band? This was the question on everyone's lips, but the fact of the matter was a) Stevie and Christine hadn't actually read the book when they decided they wanted out and b) when Stevie *did* read it, she insisted she had no issue with how Mick had written about their affair. Indeed, his reminiscences came over as misty-eyed and sentimental rather than sordid or shocking.

"As far as what I wrote about me and Stevie," Mick told reporters, "I don't think she had a problem. We were very much in love. I think she wished that I had written more." Stevie herself later confirmed that she "wasn't displeased by anything Mick said. It was a great love affair; something I would never trade in a million years." She would even go so far as to say that, not only does she still regard Mick Fleetwood as one of her three "great loves", she wasn't ruling out the possibility that they might end up together again. "Maybe when we're real old," she mused to journalist Peter Castro. "It's possible. I'll always love Mick. It's a wild thing to say, but no one could ever take that away from me."

The reason Stevie was leaving the band was because she needed to devote her energies to her solo career, although she found it hard to take in that she was really moving on – she would conduct interviews, purportedly her last as a member of Fleetwood Mac, through sobs. In her heart she really didn't believe it was "the end".

Even so, the plans Stevie had for the future would, if fulfilled, leave little time for the Mac. While she had often talked of having come to terms with the fact that family life was not on the cards, a part of her still yearned for a child. And so during The Mask Tour, Stevie revealed not only that she was collating her first box-set titled *Timespace*, but come January, she wanted to adopt a baby girl, despite her punishing schedule and the debilitating effects of Klonopin. "I don't regret the rest of it at all, but I do regret the fact I didn't stop to have a baby," she told *Chatter*'s Peter Castro when reflecting on her life of "rock'n'roll adventures".

"I'm ready for it, and I'm good with children. And then I just may have one myself after that, if the right man walks into my life. I'll probably call her Lillian Rebecca.*She'll be loved, and she'll be the most important thing in my life – more than music, Fleetwood Mac, solo albums or anything else."

Christine's reasons for moving on from the band were quite simple – she'd come to the end of the line, had bought a farmhouse back home in the UK and wanted to spend time there, painting, writing and relaxing. She had also suffered the loss of her father and needed time away from the Mac, and the road, to reassess her future. The past few years with the new lineup, Christine admitted, had been a lot of fun, but "when the time comes for a change, you feel it."

"I would have to say this is our biggest challenge, in no uncertain terms," Mick Fleetwood told Stephen Hochman for the *LA Times* once the news went public. "But without sounding blasé, it's a decision that's come in a pleasant way, and it's understandable. Each, for their own reasons, basically wants more time to herself. And God knows both of them have given so much to Fleetwood Mac through the years."

They had indeed, and soon the group would be taking even more from Stevie, this time very much against her will.

* Lillian was a nod to Lillian Hellman, a writer with whom Stevie had always identified. It would also remind her of Robin – when the 1977 film *Julia* was released, based on the writing of Hellman, Stevie would pretend she was Lillian, played by Jane Fonda, and Robin the title character Julia, portrayed by the English actress Vanessa Redgrave. The Julia character also has a child called Lily, which is one of Stevie's pet names.

Chapter 26

The future stretched out in front of Stevie, a future free from Fleetwood Mac, free for her to tune her focus and concentrate entirely on what *she* wanted to do. Yes, Stevie had agreed to the possibility of recording again with the band, but still the separation felt like "a divorce". Once the shock wore off, Nicks had a chance to really process what was happening during the new year of 1991, the conflict and sadness transformed into tentative excitement and relief, not least because never again would she have to feel guilty about doing her own thing, with the band "waiting for [her] like anxious cats".

Feeling the way she did in terms of her health, it would be a while until Stevie could find the motivation to record another solo album; every time she tried to come off Klonopin, her hands would shake so violently that she feared she had Parkinson's, and so the daily sedation continued. However, the planning of her collection *Timespace* was a positive outlet and it was therapeutic to reflect on the past ten years as she collated some of the most meaningful moments from her solo back catalogue.

It was the right thing to do at this point in her life, it was independent of the Mac and she had more than enough songs – published and as yet unpublished – to include. Atlantic Records had suggested a "greatest hits" but, as Stevie said in the revealing and extensive self-penned liner notes, "It's really my favourite songs, my 'space in time,' the personal hits in my heart. [And] I figured if I was going to pull them out, it was time to explain why they were written." The title *Timespace* is also an invented word that Stevie loves to use, often referring to the 'timespace' of a situation she was once in, inferring that the memory is not only of its time but the place, and mental 'space', it was in as well.

The album would also include new material, including a song written for Stevie by Jon Bon Jovi and Billy Falcon, which bore the rather un-Stevie title, 'Sometimes It's A Bitch'. The inclusion of this song proved that, as powerful a star as Stevie Nicks was, she still didn't have final say over her own output, and backed down despite feeling strongly about not just the song, but the title. The word 'bitch' was not a word Stevie enjoyed singing. It was just not her style. However, Stevie's record company practically bullied her into including the song, stating unequivocally that her "career would be over" if she didn't.

"I don't have any reason to hate Jon Bon Jovi," Stevie protested in an interview with Spencer Bright for *Vox*. "He wrote me a song – that was a wonderful thing to do. I knew that just me singing it wasn't going to go over well with my fans, which it hasn't. But [my management] exerted all the pressure you could possibly exert, they scared me to death. So I did the song, and is it a big hit? No, it's not." Stevie should have been allowed more creative control and to follow her instincts. She might have been spaced-out at this stage, but this was not her first rodeo, and Stevie Nicks knew a thing or two about hits.

The lyrics of 'Sometimes It's A Bitch' were clearly inspired by Stevie, even if they might have been a little sub-Nicks and indelicate – "I've run through rainbows and castles of candy / I've cried a river of tears from the pain – but sometimes it's a bitch / sometimes it's a breeze" just didn't feel right at all. Singing a cover, unless it was a very special song that really struck a chord, or described how she was feeling anyway, was something Stevie was not always happy to do at the best of times.

Timespace would also feature Stevie's duet with Tom Petty 'Stop Draggin' My Heart Around', 'Leather And Lace', 'Edge Of Seventeen', of course, and previously unreleased songs including 'Love's A Hard Game To Play' (written by Bret Michaels and Pat Schunk) and 'Desert Angel', co-written with Mike Campbell and dedicated to those serving in the Gulf War that was raging at the time.

Stevie Nicks, like so many, was deeply disturbed by what was happening in Iraq and started writing humble, heartfelt letters of support to the troops. Stevie's earnest, imaginative missives would no doubt have brought comfort and welcome distraction to those who read them. As she wrote in her song, "I was born in the desert / So I know how it feels out there." Admittedly she wasn't being shot at, but the sentiment was keenly appreciated. She "sends the sanctuary" of her own starlit desert surroundings out to those at war, expressing "how much we love you" and also sincerely reaching out to those left behind, the mothers, daughters, wives. "Where is my father? / Where has he gone?"

In one letter, Stevie chose to share the story of Rhiannon, the goddess – and song – that had healing powers, a musical "pain pill" that had so often helped Stevie transcend the madness. "I once, a very long time ago, wrote a song about [Rhiannon]," Stevie wrote, continuing the story as if she were Wendy in *Peter Pan*, telling the lost boys a heartening fairy story before they lay down to sleep. "Rhiannon was a queen in a world far above us called The Bright World," she continued, "where all the colours were brighter, and everyone had a special sort of glow around them . . . It is said that in times of war, or strife, or pain, her song can be heard . . . It is said that the legend is true, so I send you the energy from my golden cross and the three singing birds of Rhiannon to comfort you and to keep you safe."

'Rhiannon' itself would not be featured on *Timespace*, but of Stevie's material released under the Fleetwood Mac umbrella, 'Silver Springs' was a song Stevie desperately wanted to include. It was so significant to her, especially as she had "gifted" it to her mother, who otherwise would not accept presents from her wealthy daughter. The song belonged to Barbara Nicks, who also opened an antiques emporium under the name 'Silver Springs'.

The problem was that Mick Fleetwood also wanted 'Silver Springs'. It was his intention to include it on *25 Years – The Chain**, the four-CD

* On the collection would be the previously unheard 'Paper Doll', a reggae-tinged track written by Stevie Nicks and Rick Vito during the *Behind The Mask* sessions.

Fleetwood Mac box-set he and John McVie were currently collating for a December 1992 release. Stevie knew she had to consult Mick, something she was dreading, particularly after they had wrangled over this very song back in 1976, when Mick had told Stevie it was being excluded from *Rumours*. But she duly called him, leaving an ominous message on his answering machine.

"I said, 'Mick, I need you to call me. If you don't, it's going to be disastrous.' He didn't call," Stevie said, in a frank interview with BBC Radio 1's Nicky Horne. "I finally tracked down his manager. I said, 'I want 'Silver Springs'. You tell Mick that if I don't have those tapes by Monday, I am no longer a member of Fleetwood Mac.' He said, 'OK, give me until 10.30, I'll find Mick, don't do anything yet.' At about 10.15, Dennis [Dunstan] called back and said he had tracked Mick down." Mick's response? "Over my dead body."

Stevie Nicks was always well aware she had little power in Fleetwood Mac, but the one thing she could do was remove herself from the band altogether. She made it clear that any hopes of her collaborating on a Mac album in the future were now dashed, and that Mick had "ruined Fleetwood Mac's future. I don't know [why]. I don't think that, unless he sits down and tells me, I will ever know. Knowing Mick as well as I know him, he will never tell me." Stevie officially left the group in the summer of 1991, just two months before the release of *Timespace*. Rick Vito was soon to follow, citing "personal reasons", swiftly bagging a record deal with Modern Records, Stevie's own label.

Nicks was furious that, after "15 years of fighting like a dog to keep this band together", enduring more than any self-respecting artist rightly should, in her opinion, it should end like this. "I could have dropped out when Lindsey went, but I chose to juggle two careers. When they went to Hawaii after a tour, I went straight into the studio and I toured. When I finished my album I went straight into the studio with Fleetwood Mac and they were angry because I was late. So I was constantly under the gun of them being angry because I was doing something else and not completely Fleetwood Mac."

Nicks still "adored" Christine and John, although she flatly stated she never wanted to perform with Mick Fleetwood again despite their previous intimacy, not just as lovers but as friends and performers. As for Stevie's feelings about Lindsey, not much had changed. They were still "about as compatible as a boa constrictor and a rat." She couldn't imagine them speaking again, let alone working together. And yet, at the same time, as Stevie would presciently admit to the *Boston Globe* in 1991, "Fleetwood Mac goes on like a miniseries. It's one of those *Gone With The Wind* things that goes on and on. I never really know what's going to happen . . . I never burn bridges but right now I don't think I'll work with them."

Once compiled and sequenced, *Timespace: The Best Of Stevie Nicks*, her first retrospective, was released on 3 September 1991, ultimately going platinum in the US, gold in the UK and spending an impressive four weeks at number one in New Zealand. She supported the album with a tour, titled tellingly, Whole Lotta Trouble, after the track she wrote with Mike Campbell. Joining her on tour would be her old friend Les Dudek on guitar, with whom she had so enjoyed working on *Rock A Little*.

And so, in a show of defiance after leaving the Mac and no doubt under continued pressure from her label, Stevie Nicks packed her costumes, her make-up and her medication and embarked on an extensive US tour, taking her from 9 July at the Woodlands Pavilion in Houston, Texas, to 14 November at the legendary Whiskey A-Go-Go in LA. Stevie loved being on tour, no matter how tired she was. She couldn't stay still for very long and the energy she received from her super-tight band and the adulation from her most devoted fans would keep her going. As the ribbons trailed from her mic stand and Stevie hollered and purred, swathed in some of her most spectacular outfits yet – all plunging sweetheart necklines, glitter and giant puff sleeves – she mesmerised the crowds with her undiminished presence and glamour, even if her backing singers still had to cover some of the high notes at times.

Stevie returned home with her entourage (which once again included Sara Recor, who had separated from Mick Fleetwood – no doubt she and Nicks would have plenty to talk about) to enjoy a quiet Christmas in

Phoenix, Arizona, and make plans for the coming year. In the meantime, Lindsey Buckingham was still working on his solo album – the one he'd been working on since he left Fleetwood Mac in 1987 – and readying it for its eventual release in the summer of 1992. *Out Of The Cradle* was recorded with Richard Dashut and featured many co-writes with the producer, as well as a Rodgers & Hammerstein cover ('This Nearly Was Mine'), a version of 'All My Sorrows' by the Kingston Trio, the group Lindsey had so loved as a youth, and a fiery song that echoed a sentiment on *The Other Side Of The Mirror*, practically sharing a title: the 'Big Love'-esque 'Doing What I Can'. This epic 16-track album would also connect Lindsey with his old Fritz bandmate Bob Aguirre, with the closing track a twinkling co-write between the two, 'Say We'll Meet Again'. Be careful what you wish for.

*

In 1992, it transpired that the Fleetwood Mac song 'Don't Stop' was being used by US presidential candidate Bill Clinton as the rousing theme tune for his campaign. So when he won the election, succeeding George H. W. Bush, Clinton could think of nothing better than having Fleetwood Mac themselves perform the song at his inaugural ball on 19 January 1993. The fact the group had technically disbanded didn't stand in his way. He was the President. He could do what he wanted.

Stevie was in the full throes of Klonopin addiction by now and had become self-conscious about how her weight had been affected. Despite her reluctance to take the spotlight, she couldn't say no to Clinton and the rest of the definitive Mac lineup felt similar, although Lindsey took a little convincing. It had been five years since he'd been in the same room as the group, more than a decade since they'd performed together live, and Buckingham was wary of throwing himself straight back into the toxic situation he'd worked so hard to get out of, especially as the final parting hardly a peaceful one. Even after all of this time, it would take the President of the United States to get Lindsey to appear on stage with them again, much to Stevie's incredulity. Nicks herself had only recently stated she never wanted to perform with Mick Fleetwood again and yet here she was. Some opportunities are just too good to miss – it was just one song, after all. "I called [Lindsey] and said, 'If you cheat me out of this honouring moment, I'll never speak to you again,' so he did it." They didn't particularly speak at the time anyway, to be fair.

On that cold January night, the band made their way to the Capital Center in Landover, Maryland, to perform for the man who was about to become America's 42nd President. It was, as *Ultimate Classic Rock*'s Stephen Lewis wryly noted, a "summit" and testament to the politician's "tactful ability to finesse broken relationships." It would take more than Clinton's smooth charm to permanently fix the Mac, but that night Mick Fleetwood recalled looking at his bandmates before they went onstage, to be watched live on TV by millions. "John and Chris were holding hands. Lindsey was holding Stevie's hand. That really got to me."

The crowd were howling with excitement and Fleetwood Mac rocked, giving a flawless performance as they played in the round to thousands of people, and millions more in their homes. It was a special moment, not least because it was fascinating to see them play together again and looking so excited to be doing so. They certainly didn't look as if they were playing under duress.

Stevie chose to wear her classic black chiffon and top hat, Lindsey was in a baggy suit, smiling at Stevie as he sang, looking like a man who couldn't quite believe what he was doing. The audience, including the whole Clinton clan, looked on, smiling, dancing and clapping along with this progressive anthem that had meant so much to them for quite different reasons. Stevie glanced over at Lindsey for the line, "I never meant any harm to you." She still looked a little blank from the sedatives, as she would, but the Mac magic was weaving around the audience and everyone on stage, unifying everyone, if only temporarily. It was a night filled with hope.

The performance took an even more memorable turn when they were accompanied onstage by the entire Clinton family – "Bill, will you join us, please?" requested Christine, cool as a cucumber and as if she did that sort of thing every day. Michael Jackson sang along next to Stevie as the song played out and a full-scale (but quite civilised and very smartly dressed) stage invasion occurred, including Aretha Franklin in a full white gown Stevie would have very much approved of, and actress Sally Field, who appeared to be making eyes at the dashing Lindsey Buckingham. Earlier in the evening, there had also been performances from Elton John, Aretha herself, Barbra Streisand, Michael Jackson, Bill Cosby, Jack Lemmon and Chevy Chase to name but a few. Clinton had star power himself now, but, just like John F. Kennedy, he always had the ability to attract the showbiz element and Stevie herself would become a regular presence at Clinton administration events. (Although a little later down the line Nicks herself admitted in an interview with David Letterman that, perhaps, "Clinton isn't old enough, I think he needs to be more experienced. He's my age, and I have trouble figuring out who's going to go on which bus, he's got to decide on, you know, Russia . . .")

"[The inaugural gala] was something I don't think any of us will ever forget," Stevie told Howard Cohen of *The Miami Herald* afterwards. "Walking out [on stage] . . . and knowing that we were walking out because Bill Clinton wanted us. You couldn't feel more special than we did that night." For Stevie, one of the stand-out memories of that night would be when Clinton walked onstage to join the Mac. "I started to move towards him and he got this terrified look on his face. I just handed him my tambourine and said, 'Go to it, Mr President.' And he did – he rocked out." What was amusing was that the tambourine Stevie had handed Clinton was dampened, as it always was, with gaffer tape. It looked beautiful, with its long flowing ribbons, but its only function was to give Stevie something to do with her hands while she wasn't singing. Nicks was a little embarrassed when she realised Clinton was trying to get a sound out of the instrument to no avail. Still, at least he had something to do with his hands.

Despite the undeniable exhilaration Fleetwood Mac clearly felt onstage together, in the cold light of day little had changed. Lindsey, according to Stevie, was still "not able to have any kind of relationship with me. I just bug him to death. Everything I do is abrasive to him. He's scary when he gets mad." They would return to their cold war, but what was especially sad was that because of her addiction, she now felt largely indifferent.

Her sister-in-law Lori Perry Nicks, who, with husband Chris and daughter Jessica, was living with Stevie at her Paradise Valley home, was heartbroken to see her friend like this. "There was nothing anybody could really do. She was very sad for a long time. There was nothing that she could find in life that really mattered very much to her." It was a cruel contrast after the thrill of that enchanted night in Maryland, a glimpse of how things had been, and how they might just be again.

Little could happen of any value or substance until Stevie finally wrenched herself free from prescription drugs, however. Inertia aside, the physical effects were becoming increasingly worrying, but while this destructive habit had been developing insidiously for eight years, it would take something major, something dreadful, to shock Stevie into going into rehab and kicking Klonopin out of her life for good.

*

Stevie had been collating work for her sixth solo album, *Street Angel* – her first since leaving Fleetwood Mac – as best she could since 1992. It was a slow process, but at least she felt as if she was moving forward. "I think it is a good time in my life," Nicks said at the time, unconvincingly. "I was very excited to begin this record. I started in my house with [former Eagle] Bernie Leadon and [guitarist] Andy Fairweather Low, and we just started playing songs. By the time we went into the studio, we had become like a little band, and it was very happy because it was more fun for me."

British super-producer Glynn Johns was hired to work with Stevie on the album, a man who had famously worked with The Beatles, Bob Dylan, The Band, The Rolling Stones, The Who and many other iconic artists. This wouldn't mean he and Stevie were the best fit, however, with Glynn appreciating a rather more cut-and-dried approach which was at odds with Stevie's generally more fluid, heart-led way of working.

Many of the songs on this album were outtakes from previous records, thanks to the writer's block Stevie had been suffering from, but the pressure was on to release at least something – the main reason for leaving Fleetwood Mac was to concentrate on developing her own career, after all. Now here she was, free from the Mac and, as she described it, she was "vegetating". It was a relief that there was plenty of material to work with, but whether it would add up to a make a hit album was another matter entirely.

The tracks 'Love Is Like A River' and 'Listen To The Rain' were *Rock A Little* off-cuts, 'Rose Garden' was a song Stevie had written as a teenager while the pre-Mac 'Destiny' was recorded but rejected from *The Wild Heart.* The record would also include a bevy of Nicks/ Campbell co-writes, including 'Blue Denim' (another paean to Lindsey Buckingham's eyes), 'Kick It' and 'Greta'. There would also be a cover of Bob Dylan's 'Just Like A Woman', featuring the man himself on harmonica, a Sandy Stewart song, written with Dave Mundy, titled 'Unconditional Love' and the Trevor Horn/Betsy Cook track 'Docklands'.

In short, it would be something of a patchwork quilt and it didn't bode well that it consisted mainly of songs that, under different circumstances, would have previously been far from Stevie's first choice. The self-penned title track, a duet featuring David Crosby, was pretty and intriguing, telling the story of an unreachable homeless young woman, a "Charles Dickens character with your top hat and scarf", reflecting Stevie's own favourite style that she'd persuaded Margi Kent to recreate ("like an urchin on the wharves of London"). But as much of a departure as this record was in terms of theme, mood and writing, it was rather prosaic and not a patch on Stevie's previous work. "Fun" aside, even Stevie herself wasn't a fan of it, and she blames the result on her addiction to the "soul-sucking" Klonopin. "That's what everybody heard when they listened to that record," Stevie said. "They heard that I really didn't care."

The drug might have dulled Stevie's edges, but an incident was around the corner that would force her to wake up, setting off the chain reaction needed to close the door on her dependency, no matter what it took. While hosting a baby shower at her home, Stevie opened a bottle of Lafitte Rothschild, took a sip and blacked out, cracking her head on the fireplace.

"The girls said they found me lying on the carpet," Stevie told *Us Magazine*. "They got me up to bed. Later I looked at myself in the bathroom mirror and saw I had some blood on the side of my head. I'm one of those people who doesn't injure themselves. I was horrified to see that blood. I hadn't had enough wine. I knew it was the Klonopin." Stevie is sure "some little spirit" must have tapped her on the shoulder and made her see what was happening before her problem went even further. "Having a little bit of the spiritual is ultimately better than having none," Stevie said in *Interview Magazine* in 1998. "I believe there have been angels with me constantly through these last 20 years, or I wouldn't be alive."

Once she had recovered from her fall, now convinced the prescribed drug she took every day was "killing" her, she decided to conduct an experiment on the willing Glenn, her trusty personal assistant. She sat him down and asked him to take the same dosage of Klonopin she'd been taking, just to see the effect it had. "I said, 'It won't kill you, because it hasn't killed me, but I just want to see what you think'," Stevie told *The Telegraph*'s Mike Brown. "Because Glenn was terribly worried about me – everybody was. I was taking two in the morning, two in the afternoon and two more at night. At that point if I could find a Percoset, because I'm so miserable, I'd take that, or I'd take a Fiorocet [barbiturates] – anything."

So Glenn agreed to take exactly the same medications that Stevie had been taking up to this point, his employer keeping a close eye on him. At one point he was given the task of setting up a stereo in Stevie's living room. After half an hour, Stevie popped in and found him "just sitting there", unable to fix the stereo or even move from the spot. "He was almost hallucinating," Stevie remembers. "It was bad. I called up my psychiatrist and said, 'I gave Glenn everything you've prescribed for me.' And the first words out of his mouth were, 'Are you trying to kill him?' And the next words out of my mouth were, 'Are you trying to kill me?'"*

Stevie called her management to announce that she wanted to go to

* For those of you concerned about Glenn the human guinea-pig, please be reassured that he was fine, and the experiment was only "for one day".

rehab and get every trace of Klonopin out of her system, the drug that had stolen away her "precious forties", the drug her "powers that be" had led her towards so she could keep working. The irony was not lost on her. Work had become almost impossible. "It's very Shakespearean," Stevie said. "It's very much a tragedy." "She was in dreadful pain," adds Paul Fishkin. "But she just willed herself to do it."

"I spent 45 days in [hospital]," Stevie said. "When you go on those tranquillisers, you'd better start saving your money so you can afford to go into rehab and stay for two months." Better still, if your doctor suggests Klonopin, just "run screaming from the room."

And so, Nicks admitted herself to the Daniel Freeman Memorial Hospital in Venice Beach and "nearly died". Her hair went grey and fell out, her skin flaked off and she had a headache from the withdrawal symptoms from the day she arrived to the day she left. The agony of this lengthy detox was almost unbearable, far harder than kicking a cocaine addiction. Stevie had brought in as many favourite items as she could to comfort her during two long months of torture. One was a picture of her niece Jessica. "I kept saying, 'I'm so sorry I'm not going to be there for you. I'm so sorry I'm not going to be able to teach you.'"

The temptation was always there to "call a limo, go to another hospital and ask for Demerol because I was in so much pain," but instead Stevie stoically persevered, choosing life – and quality of life – over complacency and substance addiction. Stevie watched others come and go; the heroin addicts would be there for "12 days, three days of psychotherapy and they're gone, and I'm still there". The entire ordeal was like someone opening a door "and pushing me into hell . . . But I did it."

Chapter 27

After checking out of rehab, Stevie returned home to Phoenix. She had let her LA rental go after an earthquake had struck the previous year, but Los Angeles was also full of associations she needed to distance herself from. "It was] not a good time," Stevie said, in an interview with *The Guardian*'s Craig McLean." I was freaked out. In rehab, when you're leaving, the last thing they say to you is, 'Don't get married, don't sign contracts, don't buy a house, don't sell a house. Nothing heavy.' Because your judgment is impaired. And you need to go out there and find out who you are, not on tranquillisers."

So, retreating to the desert she loved, Stevie licked her wounds before returning her attention to *Street Angel,* a record Stevie would dedicate to her niece, Jessica James Nicks, the little girl whose sweet face Nicks had gazed upon every day in the clinic. Stevie was still "very much grieving" her lost years and creativity. And soon she would be mourning *Street Angel.* She loved the songs – regarding them, as many songwriters do, as her "children" – but the new album failed to match the quality of its predecessors by rather a long way.

After the inevitable departure of Glynn Johns, much of the production had taken place under the watchful eye of producer Thom Panunzio, a comrade of Tom Petty's, while Stevie had been away. When Stevie emerged, *Street Angel* was not only far from how she'd have liked it to be, it was also "unfixable. [It was] a terrible record," she admitted. Nicks tried to improve the recording by adding overdubs, even re-recording some of the material, but the fact was she had bigger things on her mind. The ordeal she had just gone through, if nothing else, had given her a new perspective. "You're lucky you're still alive," she mused. "Lucky to live in this incredible house, lucky you didn't lose your fortune or scare all of your friends away . . ." She was also four years away from celebrating her half century. Makes a girl think . . .

Street Angel, released in May 1994, would be certified Gold, her only solo album so far not to go Platinum in the US. As she embarked on a three-month promotional tour, Stevie became increasingly downcast by the reaction of the media, who were apparently nearly as disappointed as she was. The nineties was a harder, more cynical decade than the eighties; grunge and alternative rock singer-songwriters like Kurt Cobain and Alanis Morisette were making visceral, angry music that expressed their pain and simultaneously gave their fans a vehicle onto which they could project their own rage and torment. Times had changed, a spell had broken and there was, in some circles, a sense of slight impatience with Stevie's persona – a persona she had arguably long since outgrown.

As *Rolling Stone*'s Kara Manning observed, Stevie's "child-woman personality has served her 20 years, [and] it's overdue for the doe-eyed innocent to get tough. Refusing to spit and kick like Bonnie Raitt or Kim Gordon, she trembles instead, a little girl made helpless by uncaring men and her own isolation."

To be fair to Stevie, this, of all times, was when she really did need her friends to rally round and one friend in particular stepped up to the plate. Heartbreaker Mike Campbell had always been a close ally of Stevie's; "very generous" and supportive, not just in terms of giving her melodies but as an understanding presence in her life. Realising how hard it would be for Stevie after coming out of rehab, facing the same people, throwing herself back on the road and suddenly encountering thousands upon thousands of fans, Campbell, who had written with Stevie on *Street Angel*, stayed close to the fragile Nicks. Stevie hints in the film *In Your Dreams* that he, indeed, was the mystery man she "made out across America" with on the tour bus, according to Stevie, a "forbidden romance" that she insists saved her life.*

The Street Angel Tour would be Stevie's first to use a bus, rather than a private jet. It was time to cut costs. "[It's] a difference between $700 a day or $5,000 a day," she admitted. Stevie made sure she was comfortable, however, decking the coach out with veils to sleep under, the plumpest of feather pillows and a king-size quilt she retreated to once she finally was ready to sleep at "five or six in the morning". There would also need to be a special place on the bus for all of the thousands of gifts she received from fans: teddies, jewellery, flowers, all of them thrown at her feet and all of them accepted with sincere grace. The toys would be taken to Phoenix and given to hospitals or children's charities and the flowers Stevie would keep, drying them to make potpourri, putting a handful into small velvet bags and handing them to the crew at the end of the tour.

Stevie looked radiant on the tour, her long blonde hair a voluminous mass of crimped waves (she braided her locks into hundreds of tiny plaits before she slept to create the effect) that gave her fuller shape greater proportion. Fans were as supportive and adoring as ever, praising her performances and enjoying the appearance of guitarist Rick Vito, who accompanied her on a rendition of 'The Chain'. However, it irritated Stevie that the critics seemed more inclined to concentrate on her weight, saying with understandable bitterness, "I guess talent no longer matters."

Seeing pictures of herself at her heaviest had broken her heart, as did some of the comments made in the press about how she looked. Unfair as it was, being judged on her weight rather than her songs, she made a decision. "I just wouldn't go on stage and perform any more if I didn't lose the weight. It was just too hard to have everybody expect me to be a different way and not be able to get back to that. I was very

* Nicks would write a song about this tryst, titled 'For What It's Worth', which would emerge later on the 2011 album *In Your Dreams*. As Stevie matured, her lyrics seemed to become far less cryptic – perhaps time really did make her bolder as she noted in 'Landslide' – either way, the lines in 'For What It's Worth' are unambiguous: "You said even if I left my girlfriend . . .", "only a few around us knew . . ."

depressed about it." Worse than the reviews were the shocked and disappointed faces she encountered wherever she seemed to go – she wasn't the version of Stevie Nicks wanted to see. She almost felt as if she had to apologise.

By the end of the tour, Stevie resolved to "make [*Street Angel*] go away completely. I have never listened to it since", and her fuller figure depressed her to the extent she even considered getting a regular job in which she was no longer scrutinised for her looks. It was hard – having been regarded as so sylphlike in her youth, this contrast was all the press could talk about. Had she not been a "sex symbol", whether she wanted to be or not, perhaps people would have only focused on her work. But the two elements – her fairy-queen looks and her music – were forever intertwined. It was time to make some changes and Stevie promised herself that she would "never forget this feeling".

One member of her management had already been sacked by Stevie after he warned she would ruin her career if she didn't lose weight. A further portent, her contract with Atlantic was nearing its end, but she was obliged to provide one more album for them – and there was nothing on the horizon so far. With that in mind, Stevie did what any self-respecting rock star would do: she became a recluse; drawing, writing and exercising, dancing in her ballet room (complete with "fabulous ballet barre" carved for her by a fan) and spending hours on the treadmill with the TV on, her high-heeled boots replaced with platform Reeboks.

As Stevie worked hard to pull herself up and out of her funk, Mick Fleetwood was pushing on, some say ill-advisedly, with yet another version of Fleetwood Mac. This time they had Bekka Bramlett taking the 'Stevie Nicks' role, and Mick accepted an offer to open for REO Speedwagon on the Can't Stop Rockin' Tour, a development that left the estranged members of the definitive Mac understandably dismayed. "It was really disturbing when they wound up on a nostalgia tour triple-bill package as the middle act between Pat Benatar and REO Speedwagon," Lindsey Buckingham told *Salon Magazine* in 1997. "Mick could rationalise it, because continuing the band was the same thing he had done after Peter Green had left." But this new phase was in danger of devaluing the band's legacy, and many critics and fans agreed. The sight of the undoubtedly talented Bekka Bramlett strutting onstage instead of Stevie prompted many audience members to, as one witness put it, "go their own way – out to the parking lot."

Slowly Stevie started to build herself up again, recording new demos with her backing singers and emerging into the outside world. On one occasion, when Tom Petty was playing at the Ritz-Carlton nearby, Stevie went to meet him for dinner. What followed was "one of the quintessential lectures of my life". During their meal together, Stevie agonised over her regrets during her time on Klonopin – "I had done many things in those eight years that I was not proud of, that were not me, things that I would never do . . ." – and begged Tom to write her some material, because, despite repeated attempts, it appeared that the well had all but dried up. Petty was having none of it.

"He said, 'You know what? Everybody makes mistakes. You can't blame yourself for the Klonopin – you didn't go out on the streets looking for that. That's just a nasty thing that happened to you, so now get over it. You're upset 'cause you're 20 pounds overweight – lose it, you can do it. That's not your problem.

"Your problem is knowing and remembering that you're a great songwriter. I'm not going to help you write songs, I don't have to help you. You need to go home to your piano and sit down and do what you love to do. You never married, you never had children because your love is songwriting, and what in the world is up with you telling me that you need me to help you write songs?'"*

Stevie had to admit that had anyone else attempted to address her so directly, she would have stormed out. But Stevie loved and respected Tom, and the feeling was mutual. It was the "kick in the butt" she needed, and she promptly went home, set up her surroundings to be suitably atmospheric and sat down at her piano. One of the songs to emerge

* From a Stevie Nicks interview with Barnes & Noble website, 2001.

from this time would be 'That Made Me Stronger' – a tribute to Tom's strong but friendly advice. This, and much of the material Stevie produced from this point, would appear on Stevie's 2001 album *Trouble In Shangri-La*, a title that succinctly illustrated Stevie's life; a surreal kind of paradise that was spiked with anxiety.

One seam of trouble that had run through Stevie's life was about to reappear in a rather more palatable form, proving that time heals, history repeats and hell does sometimes freeze over. The following year would see Stevie Nicks and Lindsey Buckingham (yes, the pair who were never going to speak again) duetting on Nicks' stand-alone song 'Twisted' for the soundtrack to the Helen Hunt movie *Twister*. The track would also feature Mick Fleetwood on drums – they were just three fifths away from a full-scale reunion – and this would be one of the sessions that would push the band towards reconvening in earnest. This time they didn't even need to be urged by the President of the United States. Things were different now and everyone had had a chance to grow as individuals, beat their demons – or at least go some way towards doing so – and find the love for one another again.

"I was always available to give this another try," Stevie added. "In an eerie sort of way it felt as if we had only been apart for a year. Some things you just never forget. [Lindsey's and my] voice are just good together and we know it. I love my solo career, don't get me wrong. But it will never be quite as exciting as Fleetwood Mac."

*

In March 1997, a slim, healthy Stevie Nicks turned up to rehearse with Fleetwood Mac for two shows for MTV that would be filmed at the Warner Brothers soundstage in California. There were plans afoot for a live video and album titled *The Dance*, and the entire lavish affair would be filmed before a huge and justifiably excited audience. A short tour would follow. Stevie's mother Barbara was excited for the band, not least because they now had a second chance at seeing the world together. (They were "so screwed up" before that they simply slept all day.)

Once the offer had come through from MTV Stevie, already on a roll with her weight loss thanks to that treadmill and the Atkins diet (she'll only touch a carb if it's "killer"), also decided to quit smoking for good. At her most addicted, she smoked three packs of Kools a day, but she needed to make sure her voice was as strong as it could be for *The Dance*. The night before Stevie gave up, on New Year's Eve 1996, she decided to binge on booze and cigarettes – "about 500" – to make her feel so wretched she would never want to smoke again. Nicotine patches would get her through in the meantime.

Stevie would also knuckle down and work on her voice with 40 minutes' worth of exercises every day under the initial supervision of a vocal coach, and as for indulgences, a cup of Paradise Tea (and maybe a shot of tequila before hitting the stage) would have to suffice. The former party queen of the LA rock scene was now 49 and she knew she had to stay healthy if she wanted to continue doing what she loved long into the future. "That's my first priority now," she said. "To be in shape so I can walk on the stage and be great." The Mac would, as it always had, take precedence over any romantic involvements for Stevie; she had started seeing someone at the time, but he would ring her up during rehearsals, pull her focus and question her as to when he could expect her home. "All of a sudden it's defensive," Stevie told *Salon Magazine*'s Michael Ryder. "And I'm thinking 'you're endangering what I do'. That's just the way I am." He had to go.

Another priority for Stevie was to stay on the right side of Lindsey Buckingham, but it appeared he had softened since their previous encounters. He was more fulfilled, having been able to use his own ideas for his own output without being under the Mac cosh, was "reoriented" and, most importantly, had "finally got some closure on Stevie after having to be around her all those years".

Everyone had been "at their worst" during their final sessions together for *Tango In The Night* ten years earlier, but as the rehearsals happened, Lindsey observed Stevie's behaviour and realised he wasn't the only one who had evolved. Stevie was also making an effort to be more open to

Lindsey, and Lindsey in turn was 'kinder' in his dealings with her. "This was the girl I used to live with," he said rather touchingly, "and it was no longer bittersweet, it was sweet." Yes, it would still be "an emotional minefield", he would add, remnants of past grudges and hurts still close to the surface and, as Mick Fleetwood observed as the days went on, "there are places you don't go and buttons you don't push, but the most important thing was that the circle had been completed and they all knew they were exactly where they were supposed to be.

"We decided to do this a long, long time ago," said Stevie, specifically of herself and Buckingham. "We decided to search for the pot of gold together and we never gave up until we got it. So now, that's a pretty great thing. Now the two of us can link arms and walk out on stage and say we worked very hard for this."

And so, on 23 May after six weeks of rehearsal, Fleetwood Mac hit the stage at the Burbank Studios in California. They had all come a very long way as artists and as people, and, at seemingly the perfect time, they had reunited. The stars had aligned; if ever there was a harmonic convergence, this was it. As the opening beats to 'The Chain' kicked in and Stevie raised her arms in silhouette to the sky, the spell was cast once again. Some genuine magic was happening and while the band might not have realised it at the time, *The Dance* would come to be remembered as one of the most memorable, spine-tingling moments in modern rock history.

Performing their greatest hits (and a few new songs) onstage in front of an ecstatic audience was, Stevie admitted, "trippy. We really didn't think that we would ever do that again," but the result was "as magic as it gets." For the first time in 15 years, they were back onstage together playing a full Mac set, but it was the first time in at least 20 years that they'd all been quite this happy to perform with each other. There were plenty of smiles, meaningful glances and flirtatious exchanges. Everyone looked healthy and sharp, the familiar gleam was still in Mick Fleetwood's eyes, John had, happily, eschewed his trademark shorts and was looking rather dapper, Christine was stylish and coiffured, Lindsey looked sharp as always and Stevie's California-girl looks had matured beautifully, her eyes reflecting greater warmth now she was clean. Stevie nervously "flubbed" the start to 'Dreams', but didn't seem to care, in fact she liked the fact that the audience could see that just because you were a star didn't mean you didn't make mistakes or act like an "airhead" from time to time. Moments such as these tend to break the ice and connect the audience to the person on stage all the more – everyone in the house was rooting for her.

Naturally, one of the most engaging elements of the Fleetwood Mac story is the relationship between Stevie and Lindsey and this concert would deliver to fans exactly what they wanted to see, although that was not the motive at the time. The pair appeared to be singing to one another, but in contrast to previous shows on previous tours, they were not exchanging angry curses and furious looks. Quite the opposite. After Stevie and Lindsey's touching acoustic duet of 'Landslide', a song that took both of them back to old, if not happier, times, there was an embrace and a coy: "Thank you, Lindsey . . ." "Thank you, Stevie." But during the performance of 'Silver Springs' . . . well, no one could quite believe what they were seeing, and what unfolded onstage was not planned. "In six weeks of rehearsal, it was never like that . . . Only on Friday night did we let it go into something deeper."

As the song progressed, Stevie turned to Lindsey and just sang with all of her might as he watched her and took it, as if she was casting a hex upon him, her finger pointing at him as she sang, "You'll never get away from the sound of the woman who loves you . . ." Since that night, some might say Stevie and Lindsey played up the emotional warfare of their relationship on stage – a relationship that developed its own persona and arguably became a member of the band in its own right – but what happened on the MTV Special was real and unexpected, even for Stevie herself.

Nicks would subsequently sing 'Silver Springs' to Lindsey "almost every day" on the tour that would follow which was, she had to confess, somewhat cathartic. "Lindsey and I get to say things we wouldn't get to say to each other in real life," she said in an interview with *Miami Herald* during the tour. "It's like a release. Even now we don't talk much, so when those songs come around and are directly involved with our relationship it's very therapeutic to work that stuff out."

The Dance Tour, lasting from September to November, coincided with the 20th anniversary of the release of *Rumours* and was a gratifyingly successful venture, as was the live *The Dance* album. It featured that incendiary performance of 'Silver Springs' and earned the group several Grammy nominations. Stevie believed that the band now "plays way better than we did in the beginning" and also agrees the material chosen for *The Dance* album displayed new arrangements that surpassed the originals in many cases; 'Rhiannon' being just one example – opening with an extended introduction of just voice, keys and percussion as Stevie takes on the role of the troubadour, telling the tale of the man who "still cried out" for the enigmatic protagonist.

New tracks on the record, such as Lindsey's soft-hearted 'Bleed To Love Her', boast lyrics that seem all too clearly to point to Stevie at her most mystical and capricious. "Once again she calls to me, then she vanishes in thin air . . ." There's a sense of affectionate ribbing in this song, as well as genuine, enduring love, and even longing. It certainly appeared that at least a part of Lindsey was still crying out for her, and vice versa. After all of these years, they were still writing about each other, and would continue to do so. Stevie would be writing songs about Lindsey even as they toured together for *The Dance*.

Thanks to the nature of simply being on the road together, i.e. trapped in confined spaces with little else to do, Stevie and Lindsey would finally start to talk properly, chipping away at the thick ice that had formed over their shared past.

They had, according to Lindsey, "some really good talks", even going some way to sorting out their differences, or at least accepting them. It wasn't easy. "We've known each other all our lives and yet we're still trying to figure out what's going on," lamented Lindsey. "Obviously [there's] a lot of love as a sub-text. But where is that love? How do we get in touch with that? For all of us, the decisions we make now are going to determine how we are as people until we die. Stevie and I are trying to look at it . . . with care."

Meanwhile, there was someone else in the group who was feeling uneasy. *The Dance* tour would only take in key US cities, never making it to Europe or Canada as hoped, because Christine just didn't want to be on the road. She missed England and wanted to retire and this news, broken during the US dates to the rest of her bandmates, would hit Stevie the hardest. Nicks was emotional enough as it was and it wasn't unusual for her to burst into tears onstage after Christine's announcement. "It happened at a certain part in 'Sweet Girl'," she explained, the song that celebrated "dancing across the stages of the world", as Stevie has spent her life doing. The lyrics also asked, "What do you want to do?" For Christine, she just wanted to go home, and Stevie was devastated. "I was just thinking about how Christine didn't want to go back out on the road and it upset me, I was thinking of her as 'Sweet Girl'. I have to be careful because I'm real emotional and I could go that way every night if I let myself."

As the tour came to a close shortly before Thanksgiving 1997, everyone said goodbye to each other again, all of them somewhat transformed by the experience of being together again. But there was dissatisfaction. The tour had gone so well, the album was a hit, it felt as if they were starting something again . . . only to suddenly stop. "It's like, 'Well, now what?'" said Stevie. "I feel bad for Mick, because I would have liked it to have gone its karmic wheel; when you do a record, there's a certain kind of life that it has, and I feel that we should have gone to Europe. We should have finished the tour. But I don't think that we should've risked Christine's sanity. It wasn't worth that."

The question was often raised as to whether the band could simply continue without Christine McVie. As far as Stevie was concerned, "without her, it won't ever go back together". This assertion would be proved wrong just five years down the line. In the meantime, both public and press were in raptures over *The Dance* triptych of album, TV special and tour, and there was no doubt about it, Stevie had stolen the show. "Let's face it," said *Rolling Stone*. "That Fleetwood Mac tour was all about Stevie Nicks . . ."

Wheels were already in motion for Nicks' new album and a solo collection, the planning of which had been postponed because of the Fleetwood Mac tour. Stevie was a little wary of dropping her own work for the sake of a Mac venture that could suddenly fall apart or suffer another dramatic Lindsey Buckingham exodus but as it happened, the timing was serendipitous: thanks to *The Dance*, interest had never been higher and the new, "improved" Stevie Nicks had won everyone over with her performances.

After the disappointment that was *Street Angel*, she was keen to present something to the world that reflected her more positively. Nicks' contract with Atlantic Records was coming to an end, and Warners' Reprise label had been in touch to suggest she release a box-set to see out her old contract before moving on and working on a new solo album.

"Atlantic decided that they would like to box up all of the songs that I loved," Stevie explained in a radio interview with DJ Chuck Nowlan. "It was better to do it this way because, it wouldn't have been so good to have to muscle together solo records from different record companies. So this way, you know, my whole solo life is on Atlantic and now it's all in a perfect little box where everybody can have what they want out of it."

Stevie holed up at home with her closest friends, including her assistant Karen Johnston and old friend Sara Recor, to devise the track list for what would be a three-disc collection spanning her whole career as a solo artist. Stevie remembers: "We said, 'Okay, everybody make your own list: what would you like to see on the boxed set off each record?' And there were some things that weren't on anybody's list, and there were other things that we kind of fought back and forth about. It took a good 10 days to work it around to exactly what songs would go. "These songs played a big experience in our lives. Sara's been my friend since 1978; they're my really close friends who were there at the end of the seventies when all this started, when the idea came to go and do a solo career. That was a big deal when I decided to do that, because it did upset Fleetwood Mac. These ladies watched it all go by . . . So when we went through all these songs, it was like we were going through home movies. They bring up all the experiences that were happening."

Like *Timespace*, Stevie wanted the box-set to include liner-notes written by herself, unseen photographs and even some pages from her famous journals. The release would be titled *Enchanted,* a suggestion of Chris Nicks' that Stevie fell for instantly. After the success of the recent Fleetwood Mac tour – particularly her part within it – the album could only soar.

Chapter 28

Enchanted would be like a treasured photo album, a highly personal scrapbook filled with "tumultuous songs"; hits, rarities, B-sides and gems that had long languished in Atlantic's vaults up until now. "There is a memory and an experience that goes with each song," Stevie said, adding that the process of preparing for the box-set and going way back into her repertoire to select the right songs was like "seeing all of my experiences spread out over the floor."

Putting together this extensive retrospective would find Stevie occasionally having to accept, with humour, the quixotic naiveté and defiance of her youth. "I wish at certain places that I had put a little more time and effort in, or that I had listened to people who said, 'This is not that good of a vocal. Either do it over or let's see what else we have in all these tracks,' and I would stand up: 'No, it has to be the first vocal! It's the true thing.' Which we all say in the beginning; you say stuff like, 'It has to be the virgin part!' You find out all these years later it totally sucked and they were totally right."

Stevie was always prepared to be open with herself and her fans and in the album's liner-notes, she was ready to reveal more secrets and opportunities to read between the lines in search for clues. Sometimes Stevie was opaque, sometimes she was blatantly honest, but everything from her love for Lindsey to the relationship with Prince that never was, would be touched upon.

"There isn't a song in here that isn't about something intense," said Stevie. "To hear all [of them] in a group, I didn't even realise that my life was that intense. When I proofread all the words for the songs, I went, 'Wow, even I'm amazed that you're still alive.'"

"'Thousand Days' was written about my non-relationship with Prince," she told *Billboard*'s Timothy White (adding that he still hadn't actually "set up his payment on 50 per cent" of their co-write on 'Stand Back'.) The song recalls an all-night recording session with Prince at his home in Minneapolis during which Nicks smoked a joint or two, an old habit of hers of which Prince staunchly disapproved, before falling asleep on his kitchen floor.

"Prince and I were just friends," Stevie would confirm in a *Mojo* interview in 2013, quashing widespread speculation to the contrary during the eighties. "I think he would have been happy to have a relationship. But I wanted a musical relationship and I had smartened up, even then. You'll break up and never speak again. But he wasn't interested in just that . . . I like him, but we were so different there was no possible meeting ground." So that clears that one up then. Who's next? Ah yes, Don Henley . . .

Enchanted would feature Stevie and Don's duet 'Leather And Lace' from *Bella Donna* as well as the previously rejected Warren Zevon-penned track 'Reconsider Me', featuring Don and Stevie once more. This track would be selected as *Enchanted*'s first single. According to Stevie in later years, not only did Stevie not wish to include this song on *Rock A Little,* the record Jimmy Iovine had originally sourced the melodious track for, but her reluctance to sing it actually sparked the final argument between the pair before Iovine threw his hands up and stormed out on Stevie, and the album, for good. Stevie was at her most obstreperous and coke-addicted during this period, and not only was the idea of singing someone else's song on her album unappealing, she didn't like the sappy sentiment of the track one bit. Stevie Nicks beseeching someone to "reconsider" her? Please. In Stevie's opinion, every song on the record had to represent her, whether the writing was her own or not.

"[Jimmy] thought it was going to be a key song in my career," Stevie told *Tampa Bay Times's* Steve Morse in 1998. "But I really don't like to do other people's songs that often. That's why I write my own songs. I was pretty crazy at that point in my life, and you couldn't tell me anything. And I said to him, 'I would never ask somebody to reconsider loving me.' Well, he thought that was the biggest bunch of crap he'd ever heard, so we had a big fight about it and that's just about the last time Jimmy and I ever worked together."

All the same, the track had been recorded and duly put out to pasture for over a decade. It was time to bring it out of mothballs and, as Iovine had predicted, 'Reconsider Me' was a winner. Those who knew the Stevie story were intrigued to hear her crooning with ex-lover Don. Those who didn't just loved the sound of their voices together, a Mac and an Eagle, two figures who were always destined to appeal to each other creatively as well as carnally; with songs such as 'Witchy Woman' and 'Journey Of The Sorcerer' in their canon, the Eagles radiated mystic Wild West vibes just as much as Stevie.

Another Henley/Nicks collaboration to feature on *Enchanted* would be 'The Highwayman'. This, and 'Leather And Lace', had been developed from demos recorded in 1977 while they were seeing each other, so these were two duets that had not been engineered by Jimmy Iovine, despite both of the tracks having been included on *Bella Donna*. 'The Highwayman' was inspired by the Alfred Noyes poem of the same name, which tells the gripping tale of a star-crossed secret affair between a highwayman and an innkeeper's daughter. Stevie's lyrics reflect the galloping meter of the Noyes original. "And she . . . out in the distance / Sees him against the sky / A pale and violent rider /A dream begun in wine."

For Nicks, the "highwaymen" her life were figures such as Don and the Eagles; they were dashing rock'n'roll marauders, and she had to be a highwaywoman to keep up with them. You didn't really think Stevie was going to cast herself as an innkeeper's daughter, did you? (Even if her father had once run a bar in LA.) Yes, Outlaw Stevie was an equal and could match any Eagle desperado that she came across. And, as we know, she certainly came across a few.

Speaking of which, the male lead in the B-side 'One More Big Time Rock'n'Roll Star' ("just what I need . . ." she grumbles) sounds familiar.

With regard to the lyrics, as Nicks said in an interview with *The Boston Globe* at the time, "It's such a rock-star thing to send flowers. It's sick to send a $150 arrangement of flowers and think that that's going to make it OK." Hello again, Don. That hot/cold "Love 'em and Lear 'em" attitude strikes again.

Another duet to turn up on *Enchanted* would be 'Whenever I Call You "Friend"' with Kenny Loggins from way back in 1978. The track, a true-blue seventies soft-rock love song, was included on Loggins' album *Nightwatch*, but evidently Nicks was given permission to feature it here, too. Musically, it was a departure from Nicks' usual style but, as Loggins puts it, "It seemed like she could sing just about anything and make it a hit. Hers was a rambling, free-form lyrical style that she would then arrange into a musical form."

Stevie's duets remain some of her most classic moments as far as Loggins is concerned. She had spent years harmonising and blending her voice with Lindsey's, and it showed. "My favourite stuff of hers was when she teamed up with Tom Petty," adds Kenny. "I thought their voices were great together. Her duet with Don Henley ['Leather And Lace'] was pretty great too."

Naturally, the Nicks/Petty track 'Stop Draggin' My Heart Around' would feature on *Enchanted*, and there would also be a glimpse of Lindsey Buckingham, thanks to the inclusion of Stevie's Buckingham Nicks-era song 'Long Distance Winner'. Naturally, Buckingham would be present in all sorts of other ways too, not least because so much of Stevie's writing has always centred around him. The track 'Gold And Braid', a live favourite developed with Tom Moncrieff and shelved during the *Bella Donna* sessions, is "about Lindsey wanting more from me in our relationship," Stevie said in a 1998 interview with Timothy White for *Billboard*. "But wanting to know everything about someone, which goes hand in hand with being in love, was never something I've ever wanted to share with anybody. Professionally, everybody always wanted me to be their idea of what I should be. I'd flat-out look at people and say, 'You know, I'm not gonna do what you want, so why do you bother?'"

'Gold And Braid' takes us back to a time when one of Lindsey's main problems was how Stevie was onstage, in comparison to how he would have liked her to be. Back when Buckingham Nicks first joined Fleetwood Mac and started touring, Stevie, as Lindsey's partner, was "acting too sexy on stage, with my dancing and all that. But I like doing that. [I] told him: 'I can't be your Stevie up there.' I'm not telling *him* how to act. It bothered him when the audience would go crazy about me.

"I always took the line a performer should decide for him/herself what he/she wants to do on stage," Stevie continued. "Other people shouldn't interfere in that. Lindsey didn't agree. He's the kind of man that likes timid women, very introverted, serious. I like talking to people. Sometimes I'd go to the edge of the stage to say 'hi' to the people who, after all, did come for me." Perhaps Stevie's blithe (if realistic) assumption that the audience had largely "come for her" irritated Lindsey too. Still, the lyrics to 'Gold And Braid', a song written when the couple were very much at war, resolve her feelings and reach out to him. "I never did not love you, I never did run from you . . ."

Another favourite on the box-set would be 'Ooh My Love', a very Stevie-story about a "trapped princess" who is terrified of the outside world, and, of her earlier songs, the paranoid 'Kind Of Woman' would appear, detailing Stevie's fears of Lindsey straying. Fellow *Bella Donna* track 'After The Glitter Fades' was also selected, a song written before the glitter even glittered, indeed, in 1972, shining a light on Lindsey and Stevie's early days in LA and their love of singing together. (Stevie had originally wanted Dolly Parton to sing this track but was, at the time, unable to reach her.)

The box-set takes us from pre-Buckingham Nicks, with 'It's Late', a favourite of Stevie's grandfather AJ, to 'Rose Garden' and more contemporary releases, including a pensive cover of a Sheryl Crow song, the blues-inspired 'Somebody Stand By Me', part of the soundtrack for the 1995 Drew Barrymore vehicle *Boys On The Side*. Disc three of *Enchanted* was very much a cornucopia of Stevie's movie songs, while the first two discs were selections from her solo albums. *Enchanted* would hit the shelves, amid much anticipation post-Mac reunion tour, on April 28, 1998*, exceeding initial sales projections for the first week (shifting 56,000 units) and remaining a fan favourite to this day. The final track, a minimal piano version of 'Rhiannon', draws the curtain on the collection.

A 37-date US tour kicked off a month later on 27 May in Hartford, Connecticut, one day after Stevie's 50th birthday. Nicks celebrated her half-century in style and was, naturally, lavished with "fabulous presents". "I got a diamond pendant and a diamond ring," she boasted mischievously, as well as 50 silver roses from Don Henley, no less.

The pair had recently worked together for Henley's Walden Woods conservation benefit at LA's Wiltern Theatre. The Walden Woods organisation was formed in 1990 to preserve the land around Walden Pond in Concord, Massachusetts, where the transcendentalist *Walden* author and naturalist Henry David Thoreau lived and worked. For the benefit, titled 'Stormy Weather', a bevy of major league female artists including Joni Mitchell, Björk, Natalie Cole, Gwen Stefani and Sheryl Crow appeared, as did, of course, Stevie Nicks. Stevie strode on in a sensational red ball gown and performed Etta James' 'At Last' to a jubilant crowd. Backstage, the stars mingled and Stevie and Sheryl Crow made a beeline for one another. They had previously met at the Grammy Awards after-show party for *Boys On The Side*, but, as Stevie said to *The Independent*'s James McNair in 2002,"It wasn't until we both did [the] charity benefit for Don Henley that we sat down and talked properly about recording together. I thought, 'If it doesn't work out at least we'll each have a new friend.'" Stevie knew she wanted to write with Sheryl on her next solo album, *Trouble In Shangri-La*, the record she had put on hold when Fleetwood Mac reunited the year before. All in good time.

After the benefit, Stevie and her band threw themselves into rehearsals for the Enchanted tour, with Nicks telling everyone, "Well, this is our big chance to be 'enchanted'. When I do my next record it's definitely on a

* This would also be the year that Fleetwood Mac were inducted into the Rock'n'Roll Hall of Fame, and in addition to this honour they were given the Outstanding Contribution accolade at the BRIT Awards, presented to them by the producer Sir George Martin.

much more serious vein . . .*" This tour would indeed be rather more fun than usual, not least because Stevie was promoting a box-set rather than a conventional solo album, freeing her up to sing what she wanted onstage.

On this tour, Stevie would also address her audiences far more than she normally would, sharing nuggets of information hitherto unknown – providing a live version of her revealing liner-notes, perhaps – such as the background to her early track 'Garbo'. The song was actually inspired by the "infamous *Buckingham Nicks* album cover . . ." After having been snapped at by Lindsey – "don't be paranoid, don't be a child . . ." – Stevie had wondered to herself whether the Hollywood stars before her had ever felt similarly upset at having to do things against their will, "for art, for music . . ." said Stevie with a sardonic smile. She wrote 'Garbo' straight after the photo session that had caused her so much anxiety.

Clean, energetic and with a full schedule ahead of her, not to mention some rather splendid new diamonds, this was the perfect "enchanted" start to a new phase in Stevie's life, and she was feeling better and stronger than ever, having evolved from waif-like gypsy urchin to wise woman of rock. Ms Nicks was no longer a rock'n'roll princess; she was now a queen. In some people's eyes, she was also still a witch; not even a white witch, but a Satanic, black magic-conjuring occultist. Stevie had lost count of the number of times she tried to explain that her interest in the metaphysical was strictly positive and that her witchy costume onstage was exactly that – a costume – but the ignorant few saw the image and ran with it.

May 28 was a travelling day on the Enchanted Tour, but as the band and crew made their way from Connecticut to Detroit, a news story was breaking about a ludicrous incident way down South, in Huntsville, Alabama. The previous Sunday, a group of students had been chastised just moments before their baccalaureate service. The reason? They wanted to sing Stevie's song 'Landslide', deeming it an appropriate song with its

* As told to Chuck Nowlan on Boston station WZLX in 1998.

lyrics about growing older. The music minister at Huntsville High School disagreed, banning the students from performing the song altogether on grounds of Satanism.

"The music minister said the leader of Fleetwood Mac is a witch and a Satan worshipper," said Emily McDowell, who had intended to sing 'Landslide', to *Deseret News*. "I was in shock. So I pointed out the fact that I was a Christian and I wasn't singing the song to go against God."

All anyone had to do was listen to Stevie's lyrics and look at the work she was doing to see that she was clearly not a Satanist. In fact, her principles fitted the "Christian" ideal rather more than those belonging to many in the church. There was always a strong sense of "service" in her attitude towards her music and her performances – she wanted to "bring magic" to people's lives; she wanted her lyrics to show them they weren't alone. In addition, Nicks generously gave time and funds to numerous charities, was sincerely moved (and not just to tears, to action) by those in need and in the light of both of her parents' heart problems, Stevie donated 25 cents from every ticket sold on her *Enchanted* tour to the Arizona Heart Institute Foundation, raising funds and awareness in one swoop. The donations went towards research, the Heart Healthy Lessons For Children programme and the building of a research and education centre on the Arizona Heart Hospital campus in Phoenix.

Stevie was the ideal poster girl for the charity. As her father Jess Nicks, then the chairman for the Heart Institute's International Council, explained: "I've had open-heart surgery twice, her uncle had open-heart surgery twice, her mother had open-heart surgery once, and her grand-mother died of heart disease. [Stevie is] a prime candidate for heart disease." Stevie Nicks has a prolapsed heart valve herself and considering her previous lifestyle, it is amazing the cocaine abuse alone didn't put her coronary health in serious jeopardy.

As Stevie toured *Enchanted* she would be protected by her usual coterie of friends and colleagues, which was just as well – rock stars are vulner-able at the best of times but in July 1998, it transpired that a certain fan had become dangerously infatuated with Stevie. A recently discharged patient from the West Pines mental institution in Denver, Colorado, was planning to kidnap Nicks, believing she was a witch who could "heal him" and help him to "get along with others and find a woman to marry". His intention was not to hurt her, only to "abduct and impregnate her". If he neglected to take his medication, he had the potential to become very aggressive.

Ronald Anacelteo, a "self-proclaimed homosexual", he had been diagnosed with schizophrenia and noting that Nicks was on her *Enchanted* tour, had turned up to see her play only to be banned from entering. Having talked obsessively about Nicks while he was in hospital, clinic staff had alerted the police when they learned he had bought tickets to two Stevie shows, with the hope of getting as close to her as he could in order to receive the healing he needed. He readily admitted that if he had the opportunity, he would kidnap her in order to "make babies", having been taken in by a vile homophobic church campaign that proclaimed gay people required "healing" to make them straight. Stevie, naturally, took legal advice and had a restraining order brought out against him, barring him from all of her concerts, studios she was likely to be working in and, of course, her home.

It was a frightening time and the Nicks entourage was on red alert, not least because Stevie's deranged admirer had also worked out where she lived. Trouble in Shangri-La indeed. The entire ordeal was symptomatic of the very theme Stevie had chosen for her next solo album – the unique extremes and fears, the darkness under the glitter, the issues that arise from fame and fulfilled dreams that can be too hard to handle.

Fortunately, Stevie would be safe; it wasn't such a bad thing that she was rarely alone. She would also appreciate the support of her inner circle in light of the news she had recently received about Lindsey Buckingham. On 8 July Stevie's former lover had welcomed his first child with partner Kristin Messner, a boy called William Gregory. The news was bittersweet; he still occupied a huge place in her heart and her mind and perhaps their earnest talks, renewed closeness and fiery onstage passion during *The Dance* had given Stevie hope that they might end up together after all.

She would later admit, with a chuckle, that when she saw him behaving with such uncharacteristic gentleness with his new family, she would say to herself, "Oh Stevie, you made a mistake . . ." During an interview with MTV.com's Kim Stoltz, Stevie bravely confessed that despite previous incidents that came close, the day she truly knew her romance with Lindsey was over was "the day his first child was born. I knew that was it . . . that was the definitive thing." Stevie was still clearly nursing the embers of a life-long love.

The *Enchanted* tour concluded on 14 August 1998 at A Day In The Garden, Woodstock, with Stevie flying in on a helicopter over the hordes of people to whom she would soon be singing. "It was so incredible!" she enthused to the audience as the rain clouds rolled in over Bethel, New York. Despite the dramas that had punctuated the dates, a youthful, bright-eyed Stevie hit the stage with a wide-open smile and a pitch-perfect voice. However, during that final show at Woodstock in the open air, Stevie broke down as she performed her encore number 'Has Anyone Ever Written Anything For You?' The crowd wept with her as she struggled through, the meaning of the song, written for Joe Walsh and the loss of his daughter, still so close to the surface. But it was also clear that Stevie, her euphoria mingled with sadness, was still fragile. This was her first sober solo tour. She was finally seeing and engaging with just how much love there really was out there for her.

"Can we do this again?" Stevie asked the audience, as she tearfully closed the final Enchanted show, before adding tellingly: "It would be so good for me." The crowd howled their approval as she bit her lip, her eyelashes wet. This was as good as therapy – night after night Stevie had been immersed in the unquestioning love of her fans, unimpeded by the usual hazy wall of drugs and alcohol. In her lonely moments, when she remembered she had no cocaine as a crutch, no future with Lindsey, no children of her own, that helped.

Chapter 29

Nineteen ninety-nine beckoned and work on *Trouble In Shangri-La* had been postponed long enough. Nicks had started writing and recording demos for the album back in 1994; 'Love Is' and 'Trouble In Shangri-La' were early contenders and provided "the beginning and the end" of the album, according to Stevie and 'That Made Me Stronger' – that nod to Petty's pep-talk – was another song from this period just bursting to be heard. Meanwhile, the "trouble" to which Stevie refers in the album title would not only symbolise her (ultimately successful) fight against her own demons, in contrast with her 'fairytale' life, but the many stars struggling away on their apparently diamond-studded path.

"If you're in show business, there is a price," she told *Scottsdale Life* in 2000. "You get to have Shangri-La, but people just go crazy. It's not [as] wonderful as everybody thinks sometimes. [The title track was written] in the last few months of the O.J. Simpson trial*; it wasn't really about them, it was just about how people make it to the top of their field and can't seem to handle it. I've seen so many people screw up paradise, including myself."

All in all, it would take several years for *TISL* to finally emerge, having lain dormant due to the Fleetwood Mac reunion and *Enchanted*. However,

* Ex pro footballer and actor O.J. Simpson was tried on two counts of murder after the deaths of his ex-wife, Nicole Brown Simpson, and a waiter, Ronald Lyle Goldman, in June 1994.The case has been described as the most publicised criminal trial in US history. Simpson was acquitted after eight months. At the time of writing, Simpson is incarcerated in a Nevada prison after being jailed in 2008 for armed robbery and kidnapping.

anticipation for the release was high: it would be the first Nicks solo album to feature new work since *Street Angel*, therefore it would also be her first solo album recorded drug-free, and that clarity would make a considerable difference to the quality of the finished product.

As soon as Stevie had recovered from the Enchanted tour, she resumed project Shangri-La, lining up a crack team of producers and musicians that would include her friend Sheryl Crow, who contributed the song 'It's Only Love'. Most of the Heartbreakers would feature, of course, and the producer and songwriter John Shanks, who had previously worked with Melissa Etheridge, Bonnie Raitt and Joe Cocker. The 13-track album would eventually be released one year into the new millennium – Stevie never did like to be rushed.

The flamboyant John Shanks was, as one friend observed, "a bit of an LA professional, perhaps not the best fit". To be fair, Stevie had actually earmarked Sheryl Crow to produce the whole record, but clashing commitments meant she "produced as much of it as she could and then had to go and do her own thing," Nicks explained to chat show host Rosie O'Donnell. "Then she came back and helped with a little more of it, and really has been my saving grace. She's like my angel." Small world that the music business is, 1999 would see Sheryl in the studio with Prince to sing on his album *Rave Un2 The Joy Fantastic*, as well as making her acting debut in *The Minus Man* alongside then-boyfriend Owen Wilson. Meanwhile back in Shangri-La, Mike Campbell stepped in on production, as would Rick Nowels, Shanks, of course, and Stevie herself.

To Sheryl, Stevie has always been "one of the few people who takes care of me. If I'm sick, Stevie will come over with a cashmere blanket; that's how she is. She's a big rock star and she doesn't need to drop everything, but she cares about people," she told *The Independent's* James McNair in 2002, going on to quash any assumptions that Nicks could possibly be competitive, egotistical or anything other than sweet. "When I was first Grammy-nominated she was very supportive. Other female artists seemed to ignore me but Stevie didn't have any of that.

"Stevie can never know how much of an inspiration she's been to me," Sheryl continued. "Her singing style . . . she came out of blues and country, and when I first heard it, it validated what I liked. To me she was the greatest female songwriter of her generation, and I don't know of anybody today who gets so lost in the mystery and power of their music." That's not to say Crow and Nicks shared the same traits or tastes – Stevie loved shawls and frills while cowgirl Sheryl had more androgynous tastes, and, in the studio, Stevie found Sheryl to be rather more organised than her, while Sheryl observed that Stevie didn't always look after herself, preferring coffee to water, even if her voice started to dry out. Sheryl's main observation during sessions, however, was that Stevie had previously been in the studio with male producers, who, in many cases, "want to make her into something that is maybe not as intimate as what she sees her music as being".

Whether Crow noticed this from the point of view of a fellow female artist contending with the same issues in her own career, or simply as a sensitive person on the same wavelength, Stevie loved that Sheryl "gets it, she understands the life of a woman in rock'n'roll. There's no room for playing games with her or saying, 'You don't understand what I'm going through.' She understands and that's brought us closer than I can explain." Normally there were few people Stevie could really relate to, but both women had walked a similar path: finding solo fame at 29 years old, taking care of everyone on the road and acting the "matriarch" . . . Now Stevie had a female friend with whom she had plenty of experiences in common and was on the same level – another star in her own right rather than an employee, or someone who would inevitably defer to her. Nicks whisked Sheryl to Hawaii for a holiday in a luxurious rented abode, just as she had done with Sara Recor, Sharon and Lori and all of those she felt close to. "She knows how to live," laughed Sheryl. The friends took a catamaran and "sailed to Molokai for 10 days", remembers Stevie. "It was great, because nobody was going to mess with Sheryl and me together. We were like Thelma and Louise."

The pair would record Nicks' early song 'Sorcerer' as a duet and the track would be released as the album's second single (the Shanks-penned

'Every Day' being the first). Sheryl challenged Stevie to "explore different parts of my voice", and for Nicks, the process was reminiscent of singing with Lindsey. The resulting version of 'Sorcerer', with its sensual, confident country-rock arrangement, shone, stomped and rang out just as Stevie had hoped it would. After thirty years of being knocked from pillar to post – performed live by Buckingham Nicks, considered then rejected for *Tusk*, recorded with Marilyn Martin on backing vocals for the 1984 movie *Streets Of Fire* – 'Sorcerer' had found a home, and this song would be one of the highlights of the album.

Stevie also wanted to include two more vintage songs, one the mysterious, mandolin-led 'Candlebright', a track born in 1970 that reflected the nomadic streak of this curious "lady from the mountains", before she even was a nomad. "I'd never lived away from my parents when I wrote that song. I had no idea what was coming. But I think that song is a pretty amazing premonition, because it really is about how I would always travel and basically keep the light in the window so I could find my way back." And Stevie expresses that gypsy-like tendency even when she isn't on tour. When she needs fresh surroundings, she simply throws her favourite things in a bag and moves on, "for no special reason".

'Candlebright' is another strong moment on *Trouble In Shangri-La*, although, as far as many die-hard fans were concerned, you could rarely go wrong with any of Stevie's output. There was always a sense of familiarity thanks to the fact that she generally used the same chords and phrasing, always fond of the notes that took her rasping voice from "fah" to "mi" to "do" on the "do-re-mi" scale. (Sing it and you'll see what I mean.)

While perhaps the effect on fans was subliminal, this was something that had inevitably been noted by the musicians around her, particularly Stevie's musical director Waddy Wachtel. He found it frustrating at first, but soon realised the repeated use of the same chord progression was actually Stevie's secret weapon when it came to introducing unfamiliar work live – something artists are rarely wont to do if they want to hold their audience's attention.

Waddy: "I said one night on tour, 'Once again you amaze me . . . normally if one plays new songs for people, they go, 'We don't want to hear that.' But *your* songs, because they embrace those same chords, you're in. It's so funny because it's always been like a criticism between her and I: 'Stevie, you gotta get off those fucking chords!' But afterwards, I had to say: 'Well, I'm wrong again!' It's a comfort factor for her fans. It's a security blanket."

Like 'Candlebright', 'Planets Of The Universe' would be another song to be brought into the light after twenty years waiting its turn, a *Rumours* reject dating back to when Nicks and Lindsey Buckingham's relationship was imploding. This was no 'Dreams', however and, lyrically, "Planets" presented something of an issue; while Stevie normally managed to remain admirably magnanimous in her dedications to Lindsey, this song contained a verse written in the heat of the moment that addressed her ex-lover a little "too spitefully", Nicks confessed. Therefore, the version on *Trouble In Shangri-La* does not include the bitter lines that command Lindsey to "take your leave" . . . "don't condescend to me . . ." before stating: "I wish you gone / And I don't care / I don't care / I don't care . . ." Protesting too much, naturally, but either way, Stevie wanted to neutralise the poison on this, the third single from *Trouble*, even if it was obvious that the story behind the song was now ancient history anyway. (The full, unedited version would be included on the 2004 reissue of *Rumours*.)

However, the more recent track 'Fall From Grace' would show that, while much of the ire had dissolved, confusion and dissatisfaction raged on between Nicks and Buckingham. 'Fall From Grace', written on *The Dance* tour the previous year, asked quite openly, as the protagonist sits alone in her hotel room: "Was I so wrong? Why am I always so intense?", trying to pluck answers from the air. She was experiencing a melancholy sense of *deja vu*, "in this same place I sit / The same place as before . . ."

The dramatic, revealing 'Thrown Down' was also written during this time, chronicling how the estranged lovers had again become confidants on the tour. (This song would not, ultimately, be included on *Shangri- La*, turning up later on the 2003 Fleetwood Mac album *Say You Will*.) The lyrics to 'Thrown Down' describe how "he fell for her again, she watched it happen . . ." – as did everyone else – and goes on to note "how difficult it had been to be without her." The barricade had been "thrown down" after many years and changes had passed between them, and "maybe now he could prove to her", Stevie sings in the chorus, "That he could be good for her / And they should be together." Stevie might have been known for her often obtuse poetry but there was nothing cryptic about that. These words were like the jottings in a love-struck teenager's diary. Was it fantasy? Reality? A little of both, maybe . . . and it's uncertain as to where Lindsey's wife Kristin fits in to all of this. Admittedly, she must have accepted that, in a strange way, "Lindsey and Stevie are always going to be an item of sorts," as Mick Fleetwood put it. "They have an unsquashable alliance whether they like it or not." And at the moment, it appeared they quite liked it.

"Lindsey and I have come through this whole thing," Stevie said breezily. "He lives ten minutes from me. I can jump in the car and go over there." Would that be wise? Or appreciated? Who can say? But their cautiously salvaged friendship meant the world to them, they had been through so much together and nothing, no one, could take that away from them. For *Trouble In Shangri-La,* Ms Nicks also invited Lindsey himself to play on the unambiguously titled 'I Miss You' (the first time Buckingham had played on a Stevie record). "Time and distance never matter," Stevie crooned.

'Fall From Grace', meanwhile, would meet with some opposition from John Shanks, who felt it had too many verses. Many Nicks songs do have an abundance of stanzas, having started out as poems, but Shanks wanted Stevie to get ruthless, just as she'd had to be with her beloved 'Silver Springs' three decades ago. Chopping down her creations was always painful.

One day, however, some avenging angels came to the rescue. Sheryl Crow had invited her actress friends Laura Dern and Rosanna Arquette into the studio as Nicks was agonising over 'Fall From Grace'. The women saw the original draft of the lyrics and loved the words so much, they rounded on Shanks, forcing him to change his mind.

With Stevie it was, as the more empathetic producer Rupert Hine has observed, never about the rules, the technical side, or indeed about "musical masturbation, [rather] she wants the song to communicate. Sometimes the mechanics of verses and choruses and bridges and middle-eighths can be a bit wearing for her. I think she's had less successful relationships with producers when they've been more bothered by that side of it." 'Fall From Grace', to Stevie, is the perfect leveller to 'Edge of Seventeen' in terms of energy and it's interesting that, on this most feminine of albums in terms of who collaborated on it, it should be a strong band of ladies to protect one of Stevie's cherished songs.

As always, collaborations and duets would loom large on Stevie's album, but this time, most of the team-ups would be with other women. Perhaps inspired by her sisterly new friendship with Sheryl Crow, Stevie invited singer-songwriter Sarah McLachlan to provide piano, guitar parts and backing vocals on the track 'Love Is'. (McLachlan also drew the dragon that makes up the 'S' in Stevie's name on the album cover.) Stevie likes to have the radio on as she drifts off to sleep and she first discovered McLachlan's music when she was drifting off one night only to be "pulled out of sleep" by the sound of Sarah's haunting voice and dark, passionate lyrics. Now wide awake, Stevie listened for the DJ to announce who the track was by. All he said was "That was a new thing from Sarah that's called 'Possession'." Stevie expands on this in conversation with McLachlan herself for *Interview Magazine* (1995):

"I wrote down: 'Sarah. Possession.' The next morning I said to my assistant, 'You have to go get this record that's called 'Possession'. I don't know if that's the name of the album or the song. All I know is that this lady's name is Sarah . . .' which, of course, is my favourite name."

It was meant to be. As Stevie concluded, Sarah has been "a total part of my life ever since". There was no doubt that Sarah McLachlan was talented, but she had something else, something that Stevie had seen back in the late sixties at the Fillmore in San Francisco. "[Your] music reminded me of how I had felt about Janis [Joplin]," Stevie told Sarah. "I thought, 'Somehow this woman reminds me of the incredible music that came out of San Francisco when all of us were so knocked out to be alive.' I thought, 'Wow. She's ticked into an incredible thing here. Somehow she's new, yet she must be a very wise, old soul, because she's put it all together now, but she's still a little antique.'"

Stevie would also invite The Chicks [formerly known as Dixie Chicks] singer Natalie Maines to lend her vocals to the song 'Too Far From Texas', a Sandy Stewart track. Stevie contacted Natalie through Sheryl because, "of course, Sheryl Crow knows everybody in the world," joked Stevie. "If you need anybody, call Sheryl – she'll have a number."

After listening to Sandy's song with Sheryl by her side at home in Phoenix, Stevie turned to her friend and said, "What do you think? Do you think Natalie and I could sing this?" Sheryl suggested sending the song to Natalie. "Within two days, me, Natalie, Sheryl Crow on bass, Waddy Wachtel, Mike Campbell, Benmont Tench and Steve Ferrone went into Michael's home studio, and basically it's like Natalie and Stevie and Sheryl and the Heartbreakers, without Tom," chuckled Stevie. "We replaced Tom with us."

A break in the proceedings would be called for in January 2001. President Bill Clinton was leaving office, handing America over to the Republican George W. Bush, the eldest son of George H. W. Bush, who had preceded Clinton back in 1993. Hillary Clinton had organised a farewell party and to "complete the cycle" as Lindsey Buckingham said, invited Fleetwood Mac to play – as a surprise – at the ball. Just after Christmas 2000, during that post-turkey lull when nothing much happens, the band received the call from the White House.

Fleetwood Mac had just two weeks to get their heads together and prepare for the performance, which would take place on 6 January 2001. They hadn't played together for three years. Lindsey picked up the phone and called Stevie. "I said, 'Jeez, do you think we can pull this off? We need to rehearse, right?' They wanted an hour," Buckingham explained to *Rolling Stone*'s Andrew Dansby, "so we figured we could rehearse for three days and put together just the workhorses for the set, which we did. Christine's lack of presence wasn't really felt too much. We have some singers who filled in those parts and it went very smoothly. We were involved in a small way in ushering in his administration, so it was nice to kind of complete that cycle."

Stevie knew it would be a high-security event, but was still amazed by just how hard it was to get into the White House (although little did Stevie know she would soon have her very own flag on Capitol Hill in honour of her charity work). The Mac played eleven songs, sticking to the hits, and Stevie was touched when she glanced over to see Bill Clinton dabbing his eyes during 'Landslide', its lyrics no doubt especially poignant to him at this stage in his life. It was a more reflective song than the strident 'Don't Stop' of the Clinton campaign of yore, he *was* getting older . . . and, come to think of it, maybe the word "landslide" wasn't exactly what he wanted to hear in the light of the current situation. His own victory over Bush senior had indeed been a landslide but as the song describes, changes were afoot, anxiety abounded and a new season was underway, making America feel distinctly chilly.

*

Back to work, and the pop singer Macy Gray would be the latest voice to appear on *Trouble In Shangri-La*, although Stevie admitted she wasn't her first choice. Stevie was looking for an unusual, high but husky vocal for her song 'Bombay Sapphires' (*not* inspired by gin, she has insisted, having included the "s" on the end in an attempt to clear up any confusion) and originally wanted to feature her old crush Sting, but "chickened out".

"The only reason Macy is on the record is because we're managed by the same people," said Stevie a little bluntly. Nicks was clearly in a better mood when she was called upon to provide quotes for the album press release in 2001, however, gushing about Gray's "wild, intense vibe. She walks into the room and it's like everything starts to move. She's like a walking tornado. She's a total blast. We had a great time working on the song. Our voices blended so well together."

Away from the party line, Stevie Nicks admitted in an interview with

NPR's Ann Powers that "some people cannot sing harmony . . ." Macy Gray was, apparently, one of those people. "I wanted her to sing the harmony and she said, 'Stevie, I can't do it.' So I had to go out and sing the harmony without the melody, and then she went out and sang in unison with me, in order to get her to sing the higher harmony. She was like so irritated with herself. I'm like, 'It's fine, it's fine.' It's amazing and she sounded great, but we had to work really hard on it, because that's not what comes to her. She wants to sing straight melody." Macy Gray ain't no backing singer.

The 'Bombay Sapphires' we hear on the final cut was the third version that had been recorded, and this one was produced by Stevie Nicks. "It was easy," shrugged Stevie in an interview with VH1.com, "because it was exactly what I wanted to do. It was done in one night. I really did have a vision for that song, and [on earlier attempts to record it] nobody else saw my vision. The first time it was too R&B, the second time it was too Wagner, dirge-like. The third time it was back to its little funky reggae self." As for the title, well, 'Bombay Sapphires' was inspired by actual sapphires from Bombay. (Again, *not* liquor – and Stevie would never write about gin anyway, because "it makes you *mean*.") "It's a blue-grey kind of star sapphire," Stevie explained. "It's the colour of the ocean." Or the colour of, say, the glass bottle used to contain a certain brand of gin, the name of which escapes me at this moment.

Despite the wrangles, 'Bombay Sapphires' would be Stevie's favourite track on the album; it conveyed a message she wanted to share with the world: "You don't have to stay in a bad situation – you can see past the problem and to the 'white sand and ocean . . .'" This line would be inspired by a trip to Hawaii two years earlier, where Stevie retreated to take stock of the changes in her life. She found that "if you take yourself to a great environment, you can just about get over anything." True, not everyone can whisk themselves off to a luxury resort when they're feeling glum, but we can always use our imaginations (in the meantime). "I was looking outside one day and it was like I was almost seeing my past as something I really wanted to leave behind for a while," Stevie said. "I was looking *past* the past, out to the ocean and how beautiful it was and how white and inviting the sand was . . . For me, it was very important that that song be on the record."

Moving on was very much a core theme for Stevie at this time, especially after having been so involved in retrospective work over the preceding three years. "The box-set really was all about the past, and the Fleetwood Mac reunion was all about the *Rumours* songs . . ." Stevie said. "I felt a necessity to go into the future. Because when you're in a great old band that still exists, you can always live on that. Or you can go ahead and do your own thing [alongside] that."

Much of the album would be recorded in intimate studios such as Mike Campbell's, but Stevie always loved to use her home as much as possible, and the album cover itself would display the glorious sunset view from Stevie's "back yard", as she refers to it. (The words "back yard" conjure up images of the terraced houses in the British soap opera *Coronation Street.* Stevie Nicks' ocean-facing "back yard" is not *quite* the same.)

The image, taken by the renowned photographer Neal Preston, is of Stevie with her back to the camera, looking out over the view, the colours heightened as the 'magic hour' just before twilight descends. In actual fact, the picture of Stevie to grace the cover was meant to have been taken from the front, but Preston took a quick Polaroid for lighting as Stevie walked through the archway and onto the platform that jutted nerve-rackingly over the sea below from a considerable height.

"After the whole session was over and everyone had gone home, [the Polaroid] was lying on a desk and I picked it up and went, 'Oh, this is it! We don't even need to go through the rest of the film.' And there was not a picture in the rest of the film that would have worked."

"I said, 'Every little girl at three is going to want to be her, and every 90-year-old woman is going to want to be her too, because that really is a fairytale princess image.'" And it was; with her long hair and peach chiffon flowing in the breeze, her platformed feet in motion, there is a hint of Rapunzel gazing at the horizon from her tower – although *this*

Rapunzel looks as if she is about to take flight and glide into the sunset – no rescuer required, thanks.

Back on Earth, the album itself would soar; released on May Day 2001, an auspicious date*, the record would enter the *Billboard Top 200* at number five, something that had evaded Stevie's releases since *The Wild Heart* in 1983. Stevie would have been immensely proud of *Trouble* anyway, but it didn't hurt that it would be certified gold within six weeks of its release, and even prompted the usually critical Lindsey Buckingham to break tradition; not only did he praise the album, he proclaimed it the best solo album Stevie had ever made. Well, he was on it himself, after all.

* The ancient festival of Beltane or Bealtaine is celebrated on or around May Day. This holiday marks the halfway point between the spring and summer solstices and would be a day of feasts, fires and rituals to encourage growth, abundance and fertility, hence the dancing around the phallic maypole.

Chapter 30

Also released on May Day 2001 alongside *Trouble In Shangri-La* was Destiny's Child's *Survivor.* Here was another record bursting with female energy in a way that was, whether consciously or not, wholly appropriate to the sexy, eldritch energies of the first of May – Beltane – that turn of the ancient wheel of the year that celebrates goddess energies as they come into full bloom. *Survivor* also featured the hit single "Bootylicious', a song very much made by the fact that it samples the one-note riff from Stevie's 'Edge Of Seventeen'.

The story behind how Destiny's Child came to use the sample is subject to some dispute; Beyonce claims to have heard 'Edge Of Seventeen' while on an aeroplane, the riff putting her in mind of a "voluptuous woman" with attitude. She started humming along, eventually writing a song around it that celebrated the curvaceous female form, the lyrics a reaction to the constant media scrutiny over her weight. That's one version of the story.

The other version is that producer Rob Fusari had the idea of using the riff from 'Eye Of The Tiger', but after not being able to secure it, used the 'Edge Of Seventeen' riff instead. He wasn't happy when he heard Beyonce claiming credit, and rang Destiny's Child's manager (and Beyonce's father) Mathew Knowles to complain. The upshot was that Knowles "explained to me, in a nice way, [that] 'People don't want to hear about Rob Fusari, producer from Livingston, N.J. No offence, but that's not what sells records. What sells records is people believing that the artist is everything.' And I'm like, 'I understand the game. But come on, I'm trying too. I'm a squirrel trying to get a nut, too,'" Fusari told *Billboard*'s Craig Marks in 2010.

Stevie only realised her song had been sampled when, during an interview with Barnes & Noble, the journalist asked whether she had heard it. Stevie was thrilled – she kept up with MTV and VH1, so Beyonce Knowles and co. were no strangers to her. "I love Destiny's Child," she enthused. "I'm totally honoured! I think these girls can really sing, so they're OK in my book." On learning that, during the chorus, the words "I don't think you're ready for this jelly/My body too bootylicious for you, babe," are sung, Stevie was mock-shocked. "Oh my goodness," she squealed. "I'll try not to turn into my mother, Barbara, and give them a quick call."

She wouldn't have to. During the week of *Survivor* and *Trouble In Shangri-La*'s release, Stevie was promoting her album on *The Rosie O'Donnell Show*, while Destiny's Child were up the hall rehearsing for *Saturday Night Live*. During a break, Stevie and Destiny's Child got talking and the result would be a cameo performance from Stevie Nicks herself in the 'Bootylicious' video, being filmed in LA later that week. Stevie, looking at least 15 years younger than her actual age, is seen strutting on the spot with a guitar around her neck, playing the riff normally taken care of by Waddy Wachtel, greeting the camera with a mean glare and a pout.

Nicks, visible for just a few fabulous seconds, had great fun on the shoot and would maintain an enduring admiration of Beyonce, later proclaiming her "great. She's got her alter ego [Sasha Fierce], but Beyonce the girl, the woman, is very sweet and nice and polite. She's a good role model. I'm glad we have her." Stevie doesn't dish out compliments like that to everyone, as those who recall her reaction to Britney and Madonna's publicity stunt smooch, or Nicki Minaj's attitude problem on *American Idol*, will testify.

May 2001 was a particularly special month for Stevie; not only would she celebrate her birthday and release a solo album she was proud of, but a circle was being completed. The remastered, expanded version of *Rumours* would be released on 29 May and the track list would include 'Silver Springs'. Better late than never. No doubt a result of the public response to Stevie's astonishing live rendition of the song on *The Dance* didn't hurt.

"It's incredible," said Stevie. "Because they're putting the old 'Silver Springs' back where it should have been all the time." Stevie and the rest of Fleetwood Mac had been summoned to the Valley to hear the record and, "I really didn't want to go," said Stevie. "I've heard *Rumours*, I do [the songs] every time I'm onstage but they said, 'No, you have to OK it.' So I sat in the studio, and I swear I cried three different times because I heard things that I [haven't] heard since the day we were in the studio doing them, because in stereophonic sound you can only put so much, so a whole lot of that great stuff is like mush, and you can't hear it. On this you can hear all of the incredible instrumentation that went onto that record."

It was a triumphant moment for Stevie and the new *Rumours* would be a hit, especially in the light of *The Dance* – yes, the MTV Special had taken place three years previously but the effect of it cannot be overstated. The world wanted more classic Fleetwood Mac magic, and it would have been rude to refuse. This explosion of Mac love would clear the way for a new Fleetwood Mac album to boot. The *Trouble In Shangri-La* tour commenced on July 6 in Burgettstown, Pennsylvania, after high profile appearances on the *Late Show With David Letterman* and *The Tonight Show With Jay Leno,* on which Stevie was joined by Sheryl Crow, as she would be on tour. Sheryl subtly slunk onstage to provide backing vocals on 'Gold Dust Woman', joining Stevie on six songs from the album and performing a solo spot with her own song 'Every Day Is A Winding Road' as Stevie refreshed her make-up and brushed her hair as it did battle with the humidity.

Sheryl was "part of the band", as Stevie put it and the tour, augmented with this star guest, was a hit, grossing more than $13.3 million. "It was fun musically to have Sheryl there," said Waddy Wachtel. "She's a total pro. I like her a lot." It helped Stevie to have Sheryl around, and Sheryl in turn would draw a lot of support from her new mentor, although she found Stevie to be "way too tough on herself," particularly in terms of how she looked in a climate that was somewhat cruel to women who dared to get older. "Stevie should tell herself the wonderful things that she tells me," Sheryl insisted. "It's hard to be in the public eye, and getting older isn't easier for any of us gals. Stevie's still gorgeous, though, and I get frustrated with her because she doesn't realise it."

The set-list for the tour, initially a balance between *Trouble* tracks and old favourites, changed as the tour progressed from July to October, and the alterations were not always to Stevie's liking. "I started out with five or six songs [from the new album] in the set, but by the last concert, not one was in the set. That was heartbreaking." It was Waddy Wachtel's job to make sure the songs for the live show had sufficient impact to keep the energy up – not only for the fans' sake, but the band. Three months worth of playing the same songs every night risked becoming a little routine, and nobody becomes an artist because they like a routine.

"Getting the Petty tune ['Stop Draggin' My Heart Around'] to open – that was my insistence," said Waddy. "It gave us a great way to go. When she walks out on that stage, I want her to be comfortable. She's got to feel like singing, feel like entertaining, feel like smiling – or no one is going to be smiling," he added ominously.

Waddy was also pushing to mix the set up a little with the inclusion of a loved but lesser-used song from Stevie's bursting canon of hits; "something unique, something you don't do often," he beseeched Nicks. "Like 'Bella Donna' . . . then we listened to it and went 'Too much work! Too hard. Did we actually used to perform this?'" Back to Plan A.

If you believe in self-fulfilling prophecies or simply the magnetic power of the words we choose, which Stevie of all people surely must, perhaps the appealingly descriptive 'Trouble In Shangri-La' was not the best name to use. This tour, as successful as it was, would indeed be beset by trouble, ranging from sound problems to ill-health. By mid-August, Nicks had already cancelled eleven shows on account of acute bronchitis.

"Stevie was sick a lot in the beginning," remembers Waddy in an interview with *Black Cat.* "It was very tough. [And] the monitors sucked for her. Every night it was: 'I don't feel good,' or 'The monitors stink,' and she wasn't having fun." Morale was sinking. When the front person is unhappy, everyone is unhappy. Thankfully Lori Perry Nicks knew what to do. "[Lori] saved our asses, basically, on that tour," continues Waddy. "She said, 'Turn Stevie's vocal down!' As soon as it was turned down, everything started to focus."

Stevie and her assistant Karen Johnston would fly with Waddy Wachtel and a chosen few by private plane from show to show while the rest of the band would be on a tour bus. But if Stevie thought she'd had some drama on this tour, it was nothing in comparison to the genuine disaster that was about to strike. As Waddy gravely recalls: "We were out there when the world blew up." On 11 September 2001, Stevie Nicks was travelling from Toronto, Canada, to Rochester, NY. On September 11, Stevie "became a New Yorker."

"Part of my heart went down with those towers . . ." A line from Stevie Nicks' journal on the tenth anniversary of 9/11.

After the show in Toronto on 10 September, Waddy started to feel unwell. In order to protect Stevie's health in case he was infectious, it was decided that Waddy would not be flying with Nicks to New York. In fact, he decided to stay the night in Toronto to rest, promising to meet the band and crew in Rochester on the 12th, the day of the show.

But as the night wore on, Waddy started to feel inexplicably uneasy. "I went to bed kind of uncomfortable. And woke up much more uncomfortable, like we all did." As morning broke in Toronto, Waddy received a phone call telling him to turn on the television. And so, the catastrophic events that had struck Wachtel's birthplace that day were replayed before his very eyes, the destruction, the devastation . . . and the shockwaves of that tragedy would reverberate across the planet to this day. Suddenly Waddy remembered that Stevie was in New York herself, having touched down at 2.30 a.m. Despite repeated attempts to reach her, "you couldn't get hold of anybody in New York."

When Stevie landed in the small hours of 11 September, the sky was clear after a heavy electric storm. As she stepped into the limousine at the airport, she couldn't have anticipated what the day would bring, but she was fairly sure it would incorporate sight-seeing, luxury shopping and generally enjoying her day off. "It's always a romantic drive for me . . . like something wonderful could happen." As the limo finally purred up to the entrance of the historic Waldorf Astoria Hotel at around 4am, Stevie was excitedly visualising her show that was scheduled to take place at the Radio City Music Hall that week, "one of my favourite places to play."

The Waldorf itself was a source of fascination for this dyed-in-the-wood West Coast girl and as she took in the "great arched windows" and the stunning decor, she wished those walls could reveal the secrets of the many guests who had passed through that foyer, the movie stars, the dignitaries, the royalty . . . As Stevie and her coterie settled into their suite, gossiped, drank coffee and unpacked, the sun rose and filled the room with dazzling pink light. Stevie gazed out of the window onto the streets below, now already full of cars and people on their way to work. She was tempted to go out for breakfast and start getting busy with the platinum card, but decided to get a little sleep instead. Wise decision. "I went to bed, dreaming of going out later, maybe finding a little diamond something . . ."

Stevie drifted into a much-needed slumber only to be woken urgently several hours later by her assistant Karen. It was shortly after 9 a.m., moments after a hijacked jet had hit the south tower of the World Trade Center just six miles from the Waldorf. Eighteen minutes earlier, at 8.45 a.m. New York local time, a hijacked 767 commercial jet had flown into the north tower. In shock, Stevie Nicks jumped from her bed and ran to the window. "Suddenly I felt like I was in the middle of history. Looking down at that same street – no cars, no cabs, and no people," she reminisced in her journal. "Just empty. Not beautiful – just frighteningly silent. No way out – just fear." And there really would be no way out. The hotel "went into lockdown," Stevie wrote, adding that "it is the President's hotel, so lockdown is something they do well." At one stage, hotel guests realised there was a "military escort on our wing. That whole period nearly drove me into a mental home," Stevie admitted.

All anyone could do was watch, weep and wait as office workers jumped to their death to escape the blazing towers less than 30 minutes away, smoke and dust billowed through the city streets and panicking citizens ran for their lives. It's testament to the images we are so frequently exposed to in popular culture that the scenes looked sickeningly familiar; it was as if we'd seen it all before in a disaster movie. Stevie and her entourage flicked through every international news channel, watching the horrifying footage and wondering what was going to happen next. Naturally, the shows in Rochester and at Radio City Music Hall would be cancelled, and during those three days, all Stevie could do was remain in her suite, watch the news, put wet towels up at the windows to keep out the stench of burning metal, write and peer out as the sun set on New York each day through the unnatural haze.

"The sunsets were extra beautiful," adds Stevie wistfully in her journal. "Like smoke on stage makes the lights more beautiful. After that, soon after that actually, I developed an allergy to dust and smoke. I don't use smoke on my stage anymore." As soon as she was able to emerge from her hotel room, she reached out to New Yorkers in person, delivering lunch to a group of firefighters at Ground Zero. Stevie's big-hearted decision to share her perceptions and feelings at this dreadful time by publishing pages of her journal would also bring comfort to many, as would the fact she continued her tour once she'd left New York for Atlanta. It wasn't as if she hadn't considered abandoning the rest of the dates altogether, but, "my parents and friends like Tom Petty and Don Henley kept saying, 'People paid to see your show, and if they're willing to go out in this frightening world, don't you dare come home.' It was hard to walk on stage and not burst into tears. All my songs suddenly seemed to be about 9/11."

One of the most significant songs Stevie wrote shortly after this time was 'Illume', which would be included on Fleetwood Mac's next album *Say You Will* in 2003. "It's just about making it, you know," Stevie would explain. "I was sitting there, thinking about those horrible tragedies, and the candle was lit, and my heart was still so heavy, and I didn't know quite what would happen, and we were all like that, confused.

"I didn't set out to write a September 11 song, it just happened. I also wrote one called 'Get Back On The Plane,' and a song called 'The Towers Touched The Sky,' but it was just too depressing." Mick Fleetwood would describe 'Illume' as Stevie's "modern-day 'Gold Dust Woman'" after listening to her rudimentary demo. Nicks wasn't sure whether the groove was too simple, but Fleetwood reassured her. "It has that Edith Piaf element coming through, where the singer's relationship with the lyric is incredibly personal and powerful," he said.

The remaining shows on the *Trouble In Shangri-La* tour would take on a sombre tone, and it was during this dark period that Sheryl Crow really witnessed the intense restorative properties of Stevie's music up close, as fans shed tears and looked to Nicks for solace. That healing extended to Stevie herself too – the power of her heartfelt songcraft, or her "heart songs" as she refers to them, helped to bring her through the trauma. Once she and the band finally arrived back in Los Angeles to play to a home crowd, Stevie was so relieved to be back she could have cried.

"When we played in LA, it was like a church revival," Crow told *The Independent* the following year. "You could feel it in the air. It was right after September 11 and Stevie had people in the palm of her hand. She gave [them] a lot of strength that night. Stevie says that her songs go out and work on her behalf. And they do, because they are very healing for people. I've yet to make that peace with my work because it doesn't have that depth. But if I ever wrote something as good as 'Landslide', say, I'd just get in my car, drive to Tennessee and have kids. I'd feel completely sated."

Chapter 31

As 2001 drew to a close, Mick Fleetwood was keeping a close eye on Stevie Nicks and Lindsey Buckingham, hoping they would soon put their solo careers aside for a while in order to return to Fleetwood Mac and start recording their first studio album together in 15 years. Stevie was enthusiastic, John preferred not to be in the studio and persuading Lindsey to do anything "Mac" was always a little tricky. Christine, meanwhile, would remain in England, working on her own solo projects. "Christine deserves, like everyone else does, to do whatever the hell she wants," said Fleetwood, while Nicks made it publicly clear that "if we thought there was any chance she would come back we would have waited to do this record."

"You can't make people do stuff," Stevie said to *Wall of Sound*'s Gary Braff (2001). "[But] Mick and I are going to make this happen. We're the strong ones and we're going to push this through if it kills us." Fortunately it would be a little easier than that. Before long, Mick and Lindsey were already back in the studio, preparing for *Say You Will*.

Work was already surreptitiously underway when on 6 December, Mick and Lindsey joined Stevie for a Stevie Nicks and Friends benefit show for the Arizona Heart Association, alongside Don Henley and some of the many pals who had appeared on *Trouble In Shangri-La* – including Sheryl Crow and Natalie Maines. Sheryl impressed Stevie once again, being the first star to say an unequivocal "yes" to playing on the bill. As soon as she agreed, others followed. "Sheryl did a benefit for my father and the Heart Association, so my family loves her as much as I do. We raised enough to build a hospital. Now that's girl power," said Stevie.

Mac power would be deployed too, of course, when Stevie invited Lindsey onstage, introducing him as "someone who is very special" to her for 'Landslide'. The crowd witnessed a loving moment between the pair when Stevie held his hand and Lindsey kissed her head. Mick Fleetwood then joined the pair and the audience would be delighted further when Lindsey announced that, "Mick and I have been spending a lot of time together because Fleetwood Mac are working on a studio album right now." Once the crowd – now going nuts – eventually calms down, Buckingham adds solemnly that one must "learn to be responsible for yourself, and then you can take care of others . . . We're learning how to do that again." The idea would be that the chemistry would thus remain, while the baggage would largely be left behind (or at least squashed).

Yes, that was the *idea*. The reality was as it always had been with Fleetwood Mac when they hit the studio: highly creative, sometimes enjoyable but often excruciatingly uneasy and resulting in a mix of material that would, in many cases, polarise the band members. Now they were missing a key writer, and, while the most radio-friendly tracks on the album would be those written by Stevie, *Say You Will* was, like *Tusk*, very much Lindsey's record, appearing at times as simply a vehicle for indulging his wish to make experimental, angry music that wouldn't always be easy to listen to.

Mick clearly wanted everything to work between all of the personalities, organising sessions in a comfortable rented house in Bel Air instead of a conventional studio, running around after Stevie as if pandering to a confident child when she strides in late with a large "spirit-catcher", brought from her home in Phoenix to bring luck to the proceedings. John McVie simply wanted to be on his boat. "Back in the studio, *love* to be there," he says sardonically in *Destiny Rules*, the Candlewood Films documentary of the making of *Say You Will* for VH1. "150 replays of the same track . . ."

Stevie had been working hard for *Say You Will* in her own time, having written 17 potential tracks before she had even completed her Trouble In Shangri-La Tour, but the 9/11 attacks on New York had left her "world forever changed", as she told her bandmates, and as a result she wanted more time to write new material. She was given four weeks and knuckled down at home with her typewriter and her piano, honing four songs at first, recording them as demos and bringing them to the studio once her month was up. 'Illume' was one track. Another would be the upbeat title track 'Say You Will', (which would, when recorded, feature the dulcet tones of Stevie's niece, Jessica and John McVie's daughter, Molly). 'Silver Girl', dedicated to Sheryl Crow and "all the rock'n'roll women", and 'Thrown Down' – "I'm talking to you," said Stevie as Lindsey listened – completed the initial four. Stevie turned to look at Buckingham to gauge his reaction, only to realise he was in tears. Then that set her off. "I cried, we all cried, and then we set to work," said Stevie somewhat matter-of-factly.

"If you write a few more songs like that, we'll make this a double album yet," says Lindsey, and the room soon breaks into applause. Stevie bows theatrically . . . rather a different atmosphere to the scenes she described having to endure during the seventies, which saw her staying out of the way, compromising her songs, feeling unwanted or tolerated. But as she leaves at the end of the day, Stevie says to Mick, and not for the first time, "I had no rest . . . but I wrote four songs," as she reaches up to embrace him, like a little girl in need of approval. To this day it still matters to Stevie what the others in the group think, whereas Lindsey appears to remain more self-assured, sometimes to the point of bullishness. Nicks was getting better at sticking up for herself and her songs, especially thanks to that hugely successful solo career, but little had changed when it came to people criticising Buckingham's work. Nobody dared.

Emotions ran high, not least because, as Lindsey laid down backing vocals to Stevie's songs, he found it strange "singing about myself" again. "He continues to be a well of inspiration, which is terrific," said Nicks dryly, although not all of the songs she provided for *Say You Will* were drawn from that abundant source. 'Illume' as we know, was inspired by 9/11 but the idea for the track 'Say You Will' was also partly borne of a film Stevie had seen about the legendary Cuban jazz trumpeter Arturo Sandoval, which resonated with her on various levels. "I just loved the way that through all the pain, they managed to [make] music and stay happy and keep love alive," observed Stevie. "Dancing and rhythm and music . . . how healing it was. That was really my inspiration for that song." 'Say You Will' is about second chances, softening the pain of the past and seeking peace through music.

Stevie's song 'Running Through The Garden', on the other hand, was inspired by a combination of *The Twilight Zone*, Nathaniel Hawthorne story *Rapaccini's Daughter* and a strange, beautiful picture of a girl that Christine had drawn for her. "It's her, it's the girl in the song," Nicks insists. Written in 1985 with Benmont Tench, Gary Nicholson and Ray Kennedy, 'Running Through The Garden' is "the story of a girl who's raised in this beautiful Italian villa," Stevie explained to *Performing Songwriter*'s Bill DeMain. "Her dad is this gardener and he's raised all these poisonous plants, and she became poisonous. If anybody were to kiss her, they would die. She could never leave because she's addicted to the poison." This deadly garden and its doomed prisoner takes the concept of 'Bella Donna' even further; 'Running Through The Garden' presents us with a toxic plant and a beautiful woman combined. (Originally the track was to be titled 'Rapaccini's Daughter' but, because of publishing rights, Stevie chose the alternative title.)

The symbol of the garden, "running towards what you know is wrong", and the plaintive apology for the inevitable entrapment of the man who comes near, clearly paints a picture of Stevie at the time she wrote those lyrics in the mid-eighties. The "poison" may well represent the cocaine that ruled her life at that time, and it is little wonder that Hawthorne's story spoke to Stevie. When the gardener and his daughter attempt to leave the garden and breathe the pure air away from their dangerous grounds, they start to fade. The garden could well represent Fleetwood Mac; a dark, toxic, co-dependent situation that was often damaging, but almost impossible to leave. A poignant, intimate track of Stevie's, 'Goodbye Baby', would close the album, many fans speculating that the protagonist is expressing her heartbreak over a terminated pregnancy. "Don't take me to the tower and take my child away," she sings. " . . .I who went to sleep as two / woke up as one."

One Stevie track on *Say You Will* that we know to be about Lindsey is, of course, the powerful 'Smile At You', written in the seventies with Tom Moncrieff, the title belying the song's furious lyrics. 'Smile At You' had been rejected from *Mirage* on account of the fact that they "weren't in that place any more". Does that mean they were back in "that place" again now? Possibly. It's more likely that it was just a great song that needed to be heard after nearly four decades in the dark. Its rancour was as potent as ever, however, and Stevie's biting vocal take would be like pure fire, as Lindsey's silvery backing vocals weave around a malevolent, percussive groove, culminating in one of the strongest moments on *Say You Will.*

Lindsey's material here seems to swing between compellingly strange and experimental and very reminiscent of past Mac glories; the opening guitar riff for 'Miranda' is almost the same as that of 'Big Love', while the chord progression on 'Steal Your Heart Away' puts one in mind of a slower (and friendlier) 'Go Your Own Way' at times, and even the guitar part on Stevie's 'Destiny Rules' is appealingly similar to his finger-picking on 'The Chain'.

'Bleed To Love Her', debuted on *The Dance*, is uncharacteristically warm and sweet for Lindsey, despite the extreme passion denoted in the title, as if the idea of "bleeding" to love someone was quite normal. If this is too affectionate for you, the spiteful 'Come' will certainly redress the balance. Allegedly written about Buckingham's former girlfriend Anne Heche, who would later go on to have a civil partnership with TV host Ellen DeGeneres, 'Come' sneers nastily, "Think of me, sweet darlin' / Every time you don't come." Stevie wasn't happy about the inclusion of this song at all, feeling it was far too controversial. They had never addressed sex so blatantly on their records and this was, perhaps, an unpalatable way to do it. Still, such is the artist's dilemma. Are you creating for the sake of your audience, or yourself?

There would be moments of fun during sessions for *Say You Will*, and occasionally work would be pushed aside in favour of reminiscing but largely, or at least once the veneer of good behaviour had worn off, old tensions started to raise their heads. Lindsey, as ever, made the point that his songs were complete, having intended them for inclusion on a solo album – now, yet again, they were being absorbed by Fleetwood Mac so maybe that gave him leeway to be, at times, very un-Mac indeed. Stevie, on the other hand, insisted that *her* songs were written very much with the band in mind, as if they were "in the room" with her. Changes and cuts suggested by Buckingham would be sullenly rebuffed – "would you say that to Bob Dylan?"

Lindsey also made a point about the fact they had to work on Stevie's songs "for six months" before they could add his tracks and overdub her vocals, insinuating that Nicks' material needed a lot of attention. Therefore it sounded all too familiar when, after the album was complete in 2003, Buckingham publicly complained that "she's yet to say: 'Good work on my songs, Lindsey . . .'" It was a sulky snipe that harked back to his issues from 30 years earlier, after they'd first broken up, and yet he still had to arrange and produce her work. Stevie was shocked, to say the least. "Did he say that? My God. All I can say is he worked his butt off. I give him all the credit."*

In a bid to lighten the mood, as Lindsey worked and Mick and John sat, slumped and awkward, on the sofa, Stevie frivolously invited the cameras into the kitchen to show them the treasures that lay within. It was a veritable land of temptation – red liquorice laces, Fritos, Doritos . . . "It's a boys' kitchen, full of great stuff," Nicks told *Rolling Stone*'s Jancee Dunn. "I just say to myself, 'You can never eat this, or you will weigh 170 pounds at the end of this project.'"

Another attempt to "inject some humour into this recording", something she evidently felt was desperately needed, saw Stevie bringing in a 'Big Mouth Billy Bass' singing fish wall mount – ubiquitous at the time

* As told to Gavin Martin, *Daily Mirror,* 21 November 2003.

– which waggled its tail and sang 'Take Me To The River'. Stevie gives a demonstration and dissolves into giggles, something we don't see too often in this documentary. For a moment we get a glimpse of the younger, girlish, fun-loving Stevie rather than the older, tougher Ms Nicks. But she was tougher because she had to be.

The fact was that making *Say You Will* was as difficult as everyone had feared, and Stevie openly admitted to Dunn that "[Lindsey and I] have a lot of the same problems that we've always had, which is our egos. And we're filming a documentary at the studio, so there's a crew with us at all times. There were a couple of times where I've gotten just furious and walked out of the room yelling, and I've nearly run over the sound guy. It's like the TV show *Big Brother*. If we could vote each other out, we'd be fine! My vote would come up 'Lindsey'. Lindsey's would say 'Stevie' [laughs]." This observation was close to the mark, and the cutaway conversations between individual members of the band, confiding to camera – and therefore, the world – were reminiscent of the *Big Brother* Diary Room.

One of the many things Stevie and Lindsey were arguing about was the fact that Lindsey wanted to make *Say You Will* a double album. Stevie warned that this would be an unreasonable move during a recession, expecting people to spend their hard-earned cash on a double album made by a group of people who, in a few years, would be eligible to draw a pension. Put simply, Stevie just didn't think anybody would buy it, and where would that leave them? Well, hardly scanning the ads in the back of the newspaper for work, admittedly, but they all had lifestyles they were quite keen to maintain. Warners had taken a risk on them. It needed to pay off. After much wrangling, Lindsey addressed the camera himself, stating that it was "his call" to make it a single album, adding, "I have a new house to pay for, a family . . ."

Stevie gritted her teeth, exhausted by the now constant aggravation but determined to see the project through. All that mattered right now was that the album would soon be finished and released to the world on 15 April 2003, another addition to Fleetwood Mac's golden legacy. In the meantime, "if we have that final fight that means we can't walk back into this house and Lindsey and I blow up into a mass of exploding timbers, the fact is the record will be done, and even if we're dead, people will at least have the record to enjoy and the music will live on . . ."

Not everyone *would* enjoy *Say You Will,* however, and one of those who found the album difficult to listen to was Stevie Nicks herself. "I'd be lying if I said that record is what I wanted because it isn't," she said frankly in an interview with *The Age.* "I argued with Lindsey all the way through it and he argued with me. It wasn't very much fun and I wasn't that pleased with the music. I felt my demos were better." However, Stevie assured readers, and herself, that as soon as the band hit the stage on the obligatory tour, "we get lost on the fun parts of the show. We're always going to rise above and concentrate on the good things." "The good things" wouldn't just come to mind on their own – Stevie and Lindsey would have to work at this, and after having suffered the mother of all fall-outs during the making of *Say You Will,* it took Stevie to make the first move and ensure the 136-date five-leg *Say You Will* tour wasn't going to be a complete nightmare for all concerned.

Fleetwood Mac would set off on 7 May 2003 in Columbus, Ohio, touring the US until October before heading out for the European leg in the second week of November. The band would then take in Australia from February 2004 before the fourth and final leg of the tour in North America, the last show taking place on 14 September 2004 in Michigan. Knowing they would be on the road together for well over a year, Nicks steeled herself and invited Lindsey over for a heart-to-heart. It was better to thrash out whatever needed to be thrashed – metaphorically speaking, of course – in advance than endure a living hell. Judging by some of the scenes during the making of the album, this was a talk that needed to be had.

Stevie sat Lindsey down and told him: "I believe you and I need to remember who we were when we were 16 and 17 years old. We need to remember we were really good friends before we ever had a date. We need to remember how much we respected each other, how much fun we had – and how much fun we can have when we're both in good spirits. And we need to take that power couple on to the stage. Or we need to not go on tour."*

The tête-á-tête was successful, much to the relief of Mick Fleetwood, but one of Lindsey's gripes that would surface was Stevie's stage wear. We all know that Lindsey, according to Stevie, had a problem with her being "sexy" onstage in the past, grabbing the attention with her sparkling, low-cut costumes that flowed and moved as she whirled around the stage. This time, Stevie agreed to compromise. She knew she was going to look spectacular whatever she wore anyway.

"Mr Buckingham is never crazy about my flamboyant clothes," said Stevie. "His comment to me is, 'Can't you just be a little more casual?' So I said, 'OK,' and went into a little black sweater with little pearl buttons and I did exactly what he wanted. It was a little more sedate but still fabulous." Naturellement. A liberal spritz of her favourite fragrance (a floral number called 'Fracas' by Robert Piguet), a last minute zhuzh of her wavy locks and "Mama", as those in the Mac entourage called her, was ready to rock.

Contrary to the experience in the studio, there was much merriment to be had on the *Say You Will* tour. Lindsey's niece Cory Buckingham was in the entourage, working for the band as something of an ambience director and an assistant to the tour manager, fixing the ribbons to Stevie's mic stand, making sure those last minute tweaks that make all the difference have been made and, much to the delight of fans, publishing an online tour diary which gave Mac fanatics an inside scoop into life on the road with their favourite band. She wrote humorously about Stevie's manager's Maltese dog, who had become friends with Nicks' two beloved Yorkies (oh yes, the dogs were on the tour too). Cory was in pieces when she spotted the Maltese performing his favourite trick. "Stevie's manager holds a treat in the air and says, 'Stand back!' and moves her hand in a circle, and he stands up on his hind legs and twirled just like Stevie. [She]

* As told to *The Telegraph*'s Craig McLean in 2013.

got a huge kick out of that one." Cory also reported back on how Stevie just couldn't stop singing. She sang as she walked off stage, sang while she had her make-up refreshed . . . Nicks even serenaded Cory down the radio after a show, filling the loading dock with the sound of that inimitable voice.

Something else that amused Cory was how much Stevie loved taking pictures, although "The best part, I say this with love, is that she doesn't really know how to use [the camera]," writes Buckingham's niece. "Every time she takes a picture, she has to take it three times, while saying, 'This damn camera . . .'" Stevie was determined to capture every moment for posterity. In the meantime, Lindsey would read, John McVie would be "happy with a cup of coffee and a computer" and Mick, as always, took care of everybody and kept them laughing. Stevie in particular missed Christine McVie, but everyone was putting extra effort into keeping the vibe up. On one occasion, knowing that Stevie turned up every day at the venue with her long hair in rollers, one "very creative crew member" who enjoyed teasing Ms Nicks about her maiden aunt look ordered in a "truckload of velcro curlers and distributed them to the whole crew and staff", writes Cory. "When Stevie showed up and saw every single member of the crew with a curler in their hair, she died. To top it all off, John wanted to play too, so we put some double stick tape on a curler and put it next to him so he could stick it to his hat before she turned and looked at him during 'Gold Dust Woman'. We like practical jokes around here . . ."

One of the highlights of the Say You Will Tour for everyone involved would be the Australian leg – even if Stevie did have to leave her precious pooches at home ("It was terrible!"). The weather was stunning, the general mood was happy and the shopping opportunities were out of this world. One slightly unusual little store Stevie went into was 'Just White', a doll shop in Perth owned by a certain 74-year-old lady called Margaret Michaels. That lady would earn herself a nightly dedication from Stevie on stage, much to the fans' bemusement. "You just made my life so much better," she purred, before dedicating 'Beautiful Child' to the shop owner. Before the tour left for Australia, Stevie had visited a close friend of hers who was in hospital with cancer. On the day Fleetwood Mac hit Perth, on 27 February 2004, Stevie received the awful news that she had passed away.

Needing a little retail therapy, Stevie wandered the streets until she happened upon 'Just White'. As any self-respecting Stevie devotee knows, Ms Nicks is extremely fond of dolls. Once inside, one doll stood out to Stevie. "I looked at [it] and [my friend's] spirit was just there. I just felt it so strongly. I've had the doll with me since then and I sit her up near me and it has really helped me get through this very difficult period." And Ms Michaels? Well, she's "not really into that sort of thing," she admitted, but "she was so warm and so sincere, lovely."

Stevie would celebrate her 55th birthday during the North American leg of the tour on a beautiful early summer's day and she would be presented by band and crew with a rather unusual cake: made with dark chocolate, it was covered in little gravestones – each represented a song that she'd had to retire from the set due to vocal issues she'd suffered from during the tour. Fortunately she saw the humour in it, as macabre as it was.

The Say You Will Tour was a triumph, grossing $27,711,129 and the band parted as friends. It was time for a break, a long one, although a break for Stevie isn't really a break at all. It's just a break from Fleetwood Mac.

Chapter 32

Hawaii was, as always, the go-to place to relax after a tour, and Nicks whisked some of her closest girlfriends off with her to soak up some rays. Stevie being Stevie, however, as soon as her mind had cleared, was ready to start brainstorming on her next creative project – in this case, a musical adaptation of Evangeline Walton's *Mabinogion Tetralogy*, the stories that inspired Nicks' song 'Rhiannon'. Stevie and her friends knuckled down to some serious study of Welsh mythology in the incongruous surroundings of glorious Maui.

"It could be a movie. It could be a record. It could be a couple of records. It could be a mini-series. It could be an animated cartoon . . ." Stevie said, listing off the possibilities to *The Telegraph*'s Craig McLean. It had been some years since Stevie had last considered the idea in earnest – of course, she had wanted to work on a *Mabinogion* reimagining for the big screen before she'd even made *Bella Donna*. Maybe this idea's time had finally come. Or . . . maybe not. A call came through from Stevie's management, summoning Ms Nicks to the very un-Rhiannon-like surroundings of Las Vegas. Celine Dion and Elton John were playing shows back-to-back at Caesar's Palace and, presumably wanting to have a break, suggested Stevie Nicks perform there for one week for a handsome fee.

"I'm, like, 'Howard, I am on a spiritual quest here; I really cannot come to Vegas.' And he's, like, 'Stevie, you have to, please, just come tomorrow . . .' We went to Vegas." The *Mabinogion Tetralogy* would just have to wait. Stevie's residency began on 10 May 2005.

Nicks was excited by the idea of performing at kitsch Vegas, and she loved that she could sashay straight from the stage to her hotel every night rather than pack up and leave for the next city. Admittedly, when she and Waddy headed over there to check out Celine and Elton's show at Caesar's before starting their own stint there, they were dumbstruck by the sheer size of the stage. Waddy and Stevie nicknamed it the "flea circus", concerned they'd look miniscule onstage, and Stevie was pretty small to begin with. The sound on the other hand would be huge and Stevie and her band would enjoy their time at Caesar's so much that, in Nicks' opinion, Vegas would certainly be an option for her golden years. She could see herself performing there as "a little old lady".

Even after this week was complete, however, Stevie would still not be able to return to her *Mabinogion* venture quite yet. Don Henley had been in touch, suggesting the pair of them embark on a co-headline tour in June, and, "when Don Henley asks you to rock with him, you don't say no," Stevie said mock-solemnly. "Plus, I thought, 'I have this amazing show left over [from Vegas] . . . what the hell, let's do it.'" And so the work began, commencing with the swapping of set-lists and the inevitable "arguing", joked Henley. There were also certain logistics Stevie required for performing that weren't necessary for Henley: in order to look her best, Stevie needed "special lighting, proper performing temperature, time for costume changes . . ."

Henley was a little lower maintenance. "I'm just a guy . . . Guys don't mind sweating. I'm just going to go first and that will make my life a lot simpler." The tour would be titled simply 'Two Voices', and while the pair performed separate sets, Don would join Stevie on their duet 'Leather And Lace' amongst others, and even slow-dance with his co-headliner during 'Gold Dust Woman'. Fans were beside themselves with excitement to see another little slice of this long-gone rock'n'roll romance seemingly springing back to life before their very eyes.

After ten dates together, Don unfortunately had to return to LA to reconvene with the Eagles who would be touring for three months, but Stevie continued to play shows for the rest of the summer, booking 23 more dates and adding the singer-songwriter Vanessa Carlton as a support artist. Carlton was "a special one" in Stevie's eyes, and an artist Nicks often found difficult to watch without crying in the wings, so much did Carlton remind her of herself as a younger artist.*

The dates were titled The Gold Dust Tour, and the final show would be at the Coliseum at Caesar's, Las Vegas; Stevie's new favourite place to play. With a long, black "cold-shoulder" gown and her hair tied up for the encore, Stevie looked more like an operatic diva than a rock singer, although her voice naturally proved that nothing had changed. After this exhilarating closing show at Sin City, Stevie headed back to the tranquillity of Paradise Valley. Four days later on 10 August 2005, her father Jess Nicks passed away. Jess was 80 when he died, and had suffered from heart disease since 1974. He had joined his daughter on her most recent tour, zooming around the venues on a mobility scooter, but he was elderly, his health was failing and just before Stevie's tour concluded, he suffered a fall in his hotel room. He died the following week.

Stevie was philosophical. She knew he was no longer physically robust, especially having had three operations on his heart, but he'd had a happy, successful life and loved touring with Stevie and watching her star rise over the years. "I took [his passing] with the grace he would have wanted," Stevie wrote in her journal. "I'm just glad he's not in pain anymore." Stevie noted that her "force of nature" of a father had also timed his departure perfectly. "He waited until the Fleetwood Mac tour was over – I asked him for that. He waited until this summer tour was over – I asked him for that. He couldn't leave us during a tour. The last show was Saturday in Vegas. I got here to Phoenix Sunday night. It is Wednesday night. He waited for me."

* Stevie and Vanessa would become so close that Stevie would even be invited to officiate Carlton's marriage in December 2013 to Deer Tick frontman John McCauley. A year earlier, Stevie had written out her "rules of engagement" on a stack of hotel stationary for Vanessa, titled: "How to get what you want out of life and men . . ." one of them being:"He must have a good job. He must be happy and satisfied with his own life. You are there to enhance his life, not take away from it, and he is there to enhance your life, not fuck it up.""That's my favourite one," laughed Vanessa. "Thank you, Stevie!"The world awaits the Stevie Nicks Guide To Life.

Stevie Nicks would, as so many of us do when faced with such a loss, throw herself into work once the initial grief had become more manageable. From February 2006, Stevie resumed the Gold Dust Tour, taking it to Australia and New Zealand, countries she always enjoyed visiting. Supporting Nicks on this leg of the tour would be none other than old friend Dave Stewart, and they loved staying up late together, reminiscing and listening to music.

"We decided to stay one time in this resort, and it was pouring with rain, so there was no point in being there," remembers Dave. "So we went for this strange meal and then went up to her room and she said, 'I always watch this channel', and she put on the TV and it was a music channel called Rage. This is about 2 a.m. now, and she put it on and shouts over the top of every song, 'This is my favourite one!' She loves music, rocking out . . ." Little did they know they would be working together in the studio in the relatively near future. Better late than never. This year would also see Stevie touring with Tom Petty & the Heartbreakers, the "best summer I've ever had. And you can interpret that any way you want," she said, not a little slyly. After 27 shows on the road together, Tom presented Stevie with a diamond-studded platinum sheriff's badge, engraved with the words 'To Our Honorary Heartbreaker, Stevie Nicks' and on the back, much to Stevie's delight, she noted the inscription: 'To The Only Girl In Our Band.' "I keep it on my black velvet top hat," she says proudly. "It goes with me everywhere. It's probably the most beautiful piece of jewellery a man has ever given me, ever."

But during breaks from touring, Stevie would continue with a mission she had first embarked on a year earlier. Stevie's manager, who also handles Chris Isaak's career, had visited the Walter Reed Army Medical Center with Isaak in Washington. When the *Gold Dust* tour hit DC, the suggestion was made that maybe Stevie herself could visit the troops. "And there changed my life," declared Nicks, who was sincerely touched by what she saw and learned that day.

She would go on to spend a great deal of time with hospitalised soldiers in the coming years, as well sending baby supplies to war widows, writing to injured GIs, bringing them T-shirts and even loading up hundreds of iPods, programmed with music from her and her niece Jessica's collection to give to the soldiers to pass the time and use the power of music to lift their spirits. The time she spent with the patients was worth more than any amount of money she could donate, and the "rock'n'roll fairy princess", as she described herself, couldn't help "falling in love with every one of them". And in turn, her genuine concern and kindness would change their lives, too.

Nicks would spend increasing amounts of time on the road over the following few years, which can't have been easy during this time, struggling, as she was, with the menopause. "I fight it every day," she admitted, explaining that it made her feel down and affected her sleep. Still, she worked and wrote on, motivating herself with a sense of guilt: Stevie always feels that, unless she has achieved something, or done something special, she cannot relax at the end of the day. "Sometimes I'll get out of bed in the middle of the night and go into my office and put the paper in the typewriter and get out my books that are inspirational to me – Oscar Wilde, Keats, Canadian poets, European poets – and I'll just open a page and read something and say, 'OK, this is my information for today, this is what is supposed to come through to me today.'" Duly inspired, Stevie would start to write "for one or two hours", and only then would she be able to go to sleep.

Yet another Best Of Stevie Nicks album was on the horizon, this one being titled *Crystal Visions*, her ninth album over all. Again, it presented all of the old favourites, 'Edge Of Seventeen', 'Rhiannon', 'Stand Back', but also a dance remix of 'Dreams', courtesy of the Iranian-American DJ duo, Deep Dish. In addition, fans purchasing *Crystal Visions* would also be treated to a live version of Stevie singing Led Zeppelin's 'Rock And Roll', a version of 'Landslide' performed with the Melbourne Symphony Orchestra and, if you went for the deluxe DVD package, exclusive audio commentary from Nicks and some rare footage from the *Bella Donna* sessions. The album, released on 27 March 2007, hit number 21 in the *Billboard* chart and would be certified gold in Australia, perhaps unsurprisingly given the presence of the Melbourne Symphony Orchestra.

Stevie would spend the summer of 2007 on a US tour to promote the record, adding one-off dates during the rest of the year before continuing to tour the States in 2008. Stevie was nothing if not a grafter, but the fact was that *Crystal Visions* had not been a smash hit. Nicks needed a fresh approach. On discussing her plight with Dave Grohl (as one does), the Foo Fighter and former Nirvana drummer suggested she make a documentary film, and he had an idea of who would be the perfect director – someone she knew rather well, indeed. Dave Grohl commanded Stevie to "Go home and call Dave Stewart right now."

As well as being a sought-after producer, Dave Stewart was an avid filmmaker. In this visual age, having a DVD to accompany her next album could be the perfect way to freshen up Stevie's career, but the idea of being filmed wasn't immediately appealing. It would require hours in hair and make-up, for one thing, but Stevie did at least have a little time to think about it. Fleetwood Mac had scheduled their extensive Unleashed Tour – their first in five years – to take place from March 2009 after several weeks of rehearsals, so there was nothing Stevie could do until they had returned home at the end of the year. Stevie would also be releasing The Soundstage Sessions on 31 March, the first live album of her solo career, featuring Vanessa Carlton. The Soundstage Sessions had been recorded two years previously in front of a select audience at WTTW's Grainger Studio in Chicago, and would include a cover of Dave Matthews' 'Crash Into Me'. Intimate, slickly produced and atmospheric, Stevie was "as proud of this" as any of her previous work.

Stevie and Fleetwood Mac knew all too well that hitting the road was the best way to make money in the now somewhat broken music industry – a world of downloads and stolen music – as was reissuing work from their already well-wrung back catalogue. The Unleashed Tour would not only bear the irresistible subtitle 'Fleetwood Mac's Greatest Hits' (i.e. no unknown quantities for the audience's ears to contend with) but it would mark another *Rumours* package, with previously unreleased tracks and "never seen before" DVD footage. Music was no longer enough these days, especially if you were essentially repackaging work that fans would already have in their possession; you had to add visuals and "extras" if you wanted to survive the digital age. And most importantly, you had to get back out there and play some shows. The tour was titled Unleashed because, according to the band's press statement on the announcement of the dates, that was how they all felt once they hit the stage together. For Stevie, it was still strange without Christine, although Lindsey Buckingham admitted he preferred the band as a foursome. Either way, all of them would have been thrilled to have McVie back in the fold, not that anybody thought that could possibly be on the cards. And so, as each show was about to start, Lindsey and Stevie linked little fingers as they ascended in the backstage lift together, Nicks as ever eager to squeeze her former paramour for that little bit more. She'd appeal to him, telling him she was nervous, her puppy-dog eyes wide open and a worried look on her face. "What do you want me to say?" was the unsatisfactory response. Worth a try.

Lindsey would insist to interviewer Rob Trucks that the one thing he has never done is "cheat on my wife", but Stevie revealed during press for Unleashed that they were still attracted to each other and the audience sees that connection onstage – not least because they want to see it too. And so the fantasy is retained in a kind of parallel universe; after the show, they go back to normal and leave the theatre in separate limousines that drive them to separate hotels, which is interesting in itself.

"When you had a love affair like we did, it never really goes away," Stevie would explain to *Rolling Stone*. "Obviously I didn't go out with him because he was a jerk, I went out with him because he was a beautiful guy with a gorgeous smile and a wonderful laugh and he was a lot of fun in the beginning . . ." Say no more.

It was on the Unleashed tour that Stevie would write 'Moonlight – A Vampire's Dream'. Nicks had watched *New Moon*, the latest movie adaptation of Stephanie Meyer's *Twilight Saga* books and she was hooked, as one might expect. She wept as she watched the rejection of the female protagonist, thinking of all of the times she'd felt the same. A demo swiftly followed. "I finished it in Australia and my assistant recorded it on a camera," explained Stevie. "She went and hid it down the hall like she wasn't listening but she was, and I was by myself and I played the song. [Then I] said, 'OK, you can come out now, Karen. I'm ready to make a record.'"

*

Stevie already had plenty of material for her next solo album, but she was also excited by the idea that her new record would be accompanied by a unique DVD. It would be enjoyable to work on, especially if Dave Stewart was involved; one mutual friend affectionately described him as "as batty as she is" and no doubt new visual content would boost sales, too. The concept Stevie had in her head was that of a compilation of archive footage at this stage, although Stewart had other ideas. But in the meantime, the call was made, and Dave Stewart was more than happy to work with Nicks on her next opus, *In Your Dreams*.

There were a few dates in Stevie's diary to honour before work could commence in earnest, among them the 2010 Grammy Awards in January. Stevie had been invited to appear alongside the singer Taylor Swift. "I didn't want to do it," said Stevie flatly. "I didn't want to stand next to her, at five foot 11 and 100 pounds, and be broadcast to 50 million people. But she wouldn't hear it. She had a plan." Swift, who just an hour earlier had graciously accepted a Grammy for Best Country Album (for *Fearless*), hit the stage in a white blouse and jeans to sing 'Today Was A Fairytale' before being joined by the now perennially black-clad Nicks with whom Swift attempted to harmonise on 'Rhiannon'. The results were mixed, but Nicks was pitch-perfect.

Taylor Swift was fortunate to have Stevie onstage with her, particularly as Nicks had very strong feelings about younger female singing stars and she was vocal about it because she wanted them to learn from her advice – and her mistakes.

The publicity stunt kiss between Britney Spears and Madonna at the

MTV Video Music Awards in 2003, for example, was, "the most obnoxious moment in television history. Madonna will be fine, but will Britney get over it? [She] should be smarter than that," Stevie said, adding that both Spears and Christina Aguilera should "wear more clothes and try writing decent songs. I have never been to a strip club, but I turn on MTV and see in every single video what it must be like."

Katy Perry, on the other hand, was tops with Nicks. Perry, alongside John Mayer, would have the honour of having 'Landslide' dedicated to her by Stevie onstage during the Fleetwood Mac Live Tour in 2013. They'd spent time together and got on, but Perry was already a favourite of Nicks because her music was on her "treadmill list", i.e., tunes to walk on the treadmill to.

Miley Cyrus also gets Stevie's vote of approval. Despite the bizarre tongue-out "twerking" performance with Robin Thicke in 2013 – again, at the MTV VMAs and again garnering priceless publicity thanks to the world's apparent outrage – according to Digital Spy, Stevie would insist that "unlike some of the other singers / actresses that we are always worried about [no doubt referring to Lindsey Lohan here*], Miley has an ability to become a great actress and a great singer and probably a great songwriter and go on until she's my age.

"When you're young, you don't think about even five years from now. I actually didn't either, but I was really focused on who I wanted to be and what I wanted to be and I knew I was going to be in this business for a long time." And she was right. The year 2010, more than 40 years after Stevie had first picked up a guitar and started to play, would see her approaching her 62nd birthday and preparing to make a new studio album that would coincide with the 30-year anniversary of *Bella Donna* – her first foray as a solo artist.

* When asked by the *New York Times* what she thought of the rumour that the actress Lindsey Lohan was slated to play Ms Nicks on the big screen, Stevie blurted: "Over my dead body. She needs to stop doing drugs and get a grip. Then maybe we'll talk."

Chapter 33

After initial discussions with Dave Stewart, who would be producing *In Your Dreams*, Stevie decided sessions should be held at "Tara"*. Tara is her white 1930s mansion which is empty and free for her to use for special occasions such as this, where they could save money (rather than spend $2,500 every day at a studio), work as long as she liked, dress everyone up in her costumes (and oh, she did, engineers and all) and allow people to stay if they wished.There was also a complete top-of-the-range studio built into the house: pro-tools rig, microphone hanging over the coffee table to capture any spontaneous moments of musical genius, the lot. Work began right after the Grammy Awards ceremony on 1 February 2010 and when Dave Stewart first suggested filming themselves as they made the record, Stevie's "life passed before [her] eyes". In fact, the words she uttered were actually "in your dreams", hence the title. Archive footage she was happy to work with. This, on the other hand . . . "I've known him since 1984 and I was thinking I can be pretty grubby for this experience, and he said, 'Well, darling, what if brilliant things happen and we don't film it, and then we are really sorry?'"

What really swung it for Stevie was watching the 2007 Tom Petty documentary *Runnin' Down A Dream*, particularly the section that touched on the Travelling Wilburys, Petty's supergroup with Bob Dylan, Roy Orbison, George Harrison, Jeff Lynne and Jim Keltner. "We got to see them really be who they were, just looking so handsome and playing this

* "Tara" being a reference to the fictional plantation in *Gone With The Wind*, a favourite movie of Stevie's.

amazing music . . . and then within minutes it seemed two of them had died. If they hadn't have done that, what a shame that would have been. That was what came into my head: what a shame that would be if you, Miss Vanity, said no to this because you don't want to spend half an hour in make-up or pick a uniform."

Stevie herself would generally stay at her condominium overlooking the sea, developing some of her songs there in private and bringing them into "work", having nurtured them protectively in the dark first. But when Dave Stewart suggested they write some songs together, Stevie smilingly agreed while thinking "Not a chance . . ." However, Nicks would give him a chance, and the results would be beyond what she had hoped for. For one thing, Dave and Stevie's friendship didn't have the "baggage", as Stevie puts it, that she'd had to consider with Lindsey. It was an obstacle that had stopped them from even trying to write together; it was all just too personal. So, tentatively, Stevie decided to give Stewart one of her treasured books of poetry to see what he made of it, and what chords and melodies her words inspired in him. Dave already had the vague structure of a song in mind, a track reminiscent of 'Don't Come Around Here No More'.

"I did not expect him to read all of that poetry," Stevie said in an interview at Hamptons International Film Festival. "If I'd have given it to Lindsey, he'd have been like, 'Yeah sure, I'm gonna read all this . . .' And it's all the fairies and the lost love affairs . . . so I didn't expect Dave to read this book, but he did." Sitting with Stevie one afternoon by the fire, blazing away as always, Dave picked out a poem and, peering at Nicks through his ubiquitous dark glasses, suggested they work it up into a song.

Impressed that Dave had actually sat down and pored over her writings, Stevie decided to go with it. Dave picked up his guitar, Stevie leant in to the microphone, someone pressed "record" and "within five minutes [we] had a song that was really good. That was the first song we wrote, the first time I have ever written a song with someone else. I have written with Mike Campbell but he sends me a CD in the mail or in a car – he doesn't come with it." Ordinarily Stevie would receive a disc of a dozen songs and play them through, listening to them with Lori and Sharon and thinking about what would be a good fit. But this time she simply "recited my words in a singsongy way" as Stewart played. "It was like an epiphany for me. I thought, 'Now I understand why Paul McCartney and John Lennon wrote songs together.' Together, they're more than the sum of their parts."

The rapport between Nicks and Stewart was partly because they'd had parallel pasts – both had been one half of a famous duo, both had been in love with their intense former musical partners, and both had had to cope with everything that this brought with it. In turn, they became a duo themselves. "I've become somebody who collaborates a lot," mused Stewart. "There's a great thing about collaboration: you learn how to become calm and patient and not really take yourself too seriously all the time, but on the other hand you've got your eye on the vision. I allow people to feel like they can do anything. Whoever is in the room, they realise, 'Fuck, I can do anything I want.'"

That first song they wrote together was the moody 'You May Be The One' ("wonder who that one's about . . ." crooned Stevie in jest, when describing the song). And so began the "most fun year of my life", an 11-month, five-day-a-week "magical mystery tour", as Nicks described it, very much in her element. Her beautiful home was filled with people, music, creativity and laughter and quite frankly she didn't want it to end (and to be fair, the engineers alone must have been wondering whether it actually was ever going to end. Eleven months might be an average timescale for Fleetwood Mac, but . . .).

Dave had "created a magical sandbox in my house – which is a very *Alice In Wonderland* house – and allowed us to play. "We had dinners every night and it was like the old wild crazy days," Stevie said. "I'd bring down clothes and make everybody dress up, and we filmed it. It turned into more than a documentary, it's really a film. We made serious movie videos as we went along in the back yard of my house. All these amazing fairy-tale animals . . ." That was one thing Stevie learned about Dave – if she suggested something, no matter how outlandish, her trusty producer would make it happen. "Like, don't say, 'Dave, I think there should be a white horse out in the backyard tomorrow.' And then you wake up and you look out your window and there's a beautiful white horse in the trees in your backyard." He'd also laid on a fog machine for extra atmosphere. That's Dave Stewart for you. (Said white horse would accompany Stevie on the cover image of the album.)

The documentary presents us with the album's trajectory, the often surreal and theatrical video concepts and something of an inside track of how Stevie likes to work, and indeed play. Naturally she is presenting herself in a certain way; she knows young girls revere her and thus requests that the editors exclude any film of her swearing like a sailor, ("Take that fucking track off," she barks at one point. She later admits: "I tried very hard not to swear in this film, because that's not the role model that I want to be"). We see how much she loves to kick back at the end of the day and have a "disco" in her own home, how her beloved dogs are always present when a cuddle with something small and hairy is required, so to speak, and how, with Dave Stewart's help, she is able to inject that sense of fantastical whimsy she loves so much directly into her sessions like never before. Acclaimed as it undoubtedly would be, this might not necessarily be her greatest solo work in many people's eyes, but Stevie would enjoy making *In Your Dreams* so much that it would be her favourite record, her "own little *Rumours*". It was being made in an utterly different way and it was certainly the first time pictures of the recording sessions would be posted on Twitter in real time (again, thanks to Dave).

In addition to the songs written with Stewart, *In Your Dreams* would include songs from way back, one of which was written when Stevie was just 17. 'Annabel Lee' was inspired by the Edgar Allen Poe poem of the same name, although arguably this track dates back even further if Stevie's suggestion that she actually wrote this "with" Poe in a former life is true. 'For What It's Worth', the song written for the man who "saved her life" after rehab, would also find a home here (and be later released as a single), as would 'Moonlight (A Vampire's Dream)', written on the last Fleetwood Mac tour (Stevie would have a picture of *Twilight Saga* romantic leads "Bella", portrayed by Kristen Stewart and "Edward', played by Robert Pattinson, on her piano as they recorded this song) and the twinkling 'Italian Summer', a song inspired by a trip to Ravello, Italy. One magical night Stevie and the girls had gazed out from their window in the Palazzo Sasso hotel, high up in the hills above the Amalfi coast, watching the drama of an electric storm followed by a wild fireworks display in the town – it was as if nature was joining in with the celebrations. Stevie was moved to write a poem, which would become the lyrics to 'Italian Summer' and she gave the original to the hotel's owner as a gift.

Two other particularly special songs would be 'New Orleans', a heartfelt gesture of solidarity dedicated to the Louisiana city that was still picking up the pieces after Hurricane Katrina, and 'Soldier's Angel', naturally borne of Nicks' time spent with hospitalised troops*. This track would kickstart a healing process, not just for those who heard it, but because accompanying her on the song would be Lindsey Buckingham, and joining Stevie and Dave for sessions at Tara would be "like a big cashmere hug, and he's not used to that", said Stevie. "Everybody was lovely to him and everybody was thrilled with what he was doing, Dave was filming him from every angle, and Lindsey felt a part [of it]. He could not deny how beautiful our situation was or how much fun we were having, and this was a very serious song we were doing." Stevie had called on Lindsey because she knew he was the only person who would be able to do her original piano demo of the song justice. "It's very old school Stevie and Lindsey," she observed, and working on the song gave them "a moment of clarity" together in a new context. Lindsey was not in control of the sessions, he was out of his comfort zone and, strangely, that meant he could actually relax more.

Naturally there would be a duet with Dave on *In Your Dreams*, a sweet if rather weak moment for the pair. 'Cheaper Than Free', a repetitive ballad, would feature lyrics that bordered on the banal ("what's deeper

* Stevie has set up her own charitable foundation, Stevie Nicks' Band Of Soldiers. She says, "I refuse to be pulled into the politics of war. But once these soldiers sign up, go to war and come back to a hospital, I will do whatever it takes to make them better."

than a deep well? The love into which I fell . . .. / More exciting than high fashion? High passion . . ." You get the idea). The title, 'Cheaper Than Free', was inadvertently given to Dave and Stevie by the movie star Reese Witherspoon, who was hanging out with Stevie and co. during an early session at the Village Recorder nearby. When Stevie started talking about how much money would be saved if they used her house instead of a studio, Reese chuckled that it would be "cheaper than free" . . . and immediately the Stewart/Nicks songwriting cogs started whirring.

By December 2010, the album was complete one year after its inception and Stevie had a moment to breathe, give Tara a bit of an airing and build up her strength for her next move. Stevie had agreed to tour with Rod Stewart in the spring of 2011, two months before the release of *In Your Dreams* in May. It would be another co-headline show, just 18 dates, and the pair were sure to have some laughs on the road, singing all the old favourites in a three-hour show. The initial idea to team them up had actually come from Rod's daughters Kimberly and Ruby – "They love Stevie," Rod said. "She's just ultra-cool – she has a cult." (Hopefully he means a cult following.)

Stevie and Rod hadn't worked with each other in the past, although they'd partied together during the seventies. Nicks remembers attending a New Year's party at Stewart's home in Los Angeles where her eye had inevitably been caught by Rod's collection of Tiffany lamps. As she made her way towards them, glass of wine in hand, the host himself swooped in and took her drink away, fearing she was drunk and was about to cause some expensive damage. Stevie was horrified, although Stewart smoothed it over. "Oh, the bitch I am sometimes, I probably wanted more wine for myself," he laughed in interview to *Rolling Stone*. Rehearsals would show the fundamental differences between Rod and Stevie: Nicks was "a professional, nervous, doesn't want any mistakes". Rod admitted he was "just the opposite. I like the element of risk. Just not when it comes to Tiffany lamps."

Stevie was also wearily amused by the fact that, whenever they stayed together on the tour, "at six o'clock every morning he would put on 'Do You Think I'm Sexy?' as loud as it would go to get us out of bed." Some alarm clock. All the same, despite what Rod calls a "shaky start" he had to admit she was "wonderful to work with. By the end of the tour, she'd bought all my children a piece of jewellery, the three girl singers in the band jewellery, she bought me a piece of jewellery and what did I buy her? A Jo Malone candle. I felt so cheap," he said in an interview with Hitfix's Melinda Newman. They would tour again together the following year which at least presented Rod with the opportunity to buy her something even more glamorous. (Candles are, to be fair, très Stevie.) *

During rehearsals with Rod, it had transpired that the smash-hit teen TV show *Glee* had released an album featuring a version of 'Landslide' sung by Gwyneth Paltrow, who had made a guest appearance on the show. And, as it turned out, the record was doing rather well. "The *Glee* album with Gwyneth's 'Landslide' just hit number one," Stevie grinned the night before her tour with Rod began. "Ka-ching, ka-ching . . . I don't care who sings it, as long as they keep singing it."†

In Your Dreams would enter the *Billboard* chart on 3 May 2011 at number six (and at 14 on the UK album chart), and so, warmed up by the short tour with Rod, Stevie, with her band in tow, "stomped around the world like a door-to-door salesman" to promote the record and entertain her fans.

"Stevie is married to that microphone," said Waddy. "She can't do without it. She loves it, she needs it, and it's her. It's an incredible reality. Stevie is married to that tour, she is married to her fans, and married to the responsibility of being that girl for all those people. People think that artists are selfish, but Stevie Nicks is selfless. Hey, her only vice is wanting a fine hotel

* Rod would join Stevie onstage for a duet of 'Leather And Lace', although he wouldn't take it entirely seriously, gooning about with a pair of frilly knickers for Stevie's line "Take from me my lace." Ahem.

† Stevie visited the set of *Glee*, thrilling the cast and crew, and she was devastated when she heard that Cory Monteith, one of the show's stars, had died at the age of 31 on 13 July 2013. The cause of death was a toxic combination of heroin and alcohol. Stevie wrote to the cast of *Glee* expressing her sadness, also calling Monteith's fiancée and co-star Lea Michele to offer her support."She sent me the most beautiful letter, as well a necklace that was hers and a beautiful book of pictures," Lea told MTV.com.

room, since she spends so much time on the road." But she also knew she had to sell that record; "the state of the music business" left her no choice. Fortunately for her, and all of Fleetwood Mac, the interest in the group as a whole and as individuals was, in Lindsey's opinion, higher than ever, as generation after generation of younger listeners discovered the band for themselves.

But Mick Fleetwood was getting a little edgy. Stevie wanted to spend another year on the road for *In Your Dreams*, which clashed somewhat with what Fleetwood had in mind for the Mac – a world tour that would take them into the New Year of 2014. "I was fed up with waiting," he admitted in an interview with *The Sunday Express*' Charlotte Heathcote. "I was being a brat. I said, 'I don't think Fleetwood Mac is going to work again. We may not ever do this.' It all worked out for the best, Stevie was made aware of this and it all happened." She wouldn't budge until she was ready, however.

Mick was not the only member of Fleetwood Mac keen to get Stevie's attention. Still basking in the afterglow of that "cashmere hug", Lindsey Buckingham revealed to the writer and broadcaster Pete Paphides, during an interview for BBC Radio 4's *Follow Up Albums* series, that he wanted to record with Stevie again as Buckingham Nicks.

"I would love to record with Stevie again," he admitted, adding coyly, "if you talk to her, put in a good word for me. I have written a bunch of songs and I do want her to hear them, and I hope that we do [work together again]." It also appeared that, perhaps, Lindsey was sending a message to Stevie by pulling his Buckingham Nicks-era instrumental 'Stephanie', a favourite of Stevie's, and adding it to his own setlist on his solo tour. Even if the Buckingham Nicks reunion was a no-go subject for Stevie, Lindsey had evidently softened more than ever, indicating that touring with the Mac would be an ever more appealing prospect.

Even so, from Stevie's point of view, as well as feeling *In Your Dreams* "deserved" another year on the road, she also believed Fleetwood Mac "should stay off the grid for three years," she said to The Herald in 2013. "It's just smart to keep us out of the spotlight for three years." Three was also a 'magic' number, of course; and it would be, as Stevie put it, a "perfect harmonic convergence" when they did reconvene in January 2013 for rehearsals. "Everyone went along with it. And now they all know it was really a great idea – because we were gone long enough that it was us coming back. I told the press last year that 2013 was going to be the year of Fleetwood Mac. And I was just hoping with all my heart that this big statement was gonna come true!" And it would. 2012, in the meantime, was all hers to do with what she wished. But Stevie would have another, more personal reason for wanting more time before Fleetwood Mac went back out on the road; four days before New Year 2012, the Nicks family was hit by personal tragedy. Barbara Nicks, Stevie's beloved mother, died after a battle with pneumonia. She was 84.

Stevie was about to resume editing her *In Your Dreams* documentary when Barbara passed, and in response Nicks retreated altogether, even going down with a two-month case of pneumonia herself, almost in sympathy. Stevie had long suffered from respiratory weakness, and the grief struck her immune system hard. Fleetwood Mac were recording an EP simply titled *Extended Play*, to be released on iTunes, but "I didn't go [to the studio]. I didn't want to go. I didn't want to go anywhere. I didn't leave the house for almost five months," Nicks confessed in an interview with Herald Scotland. All she wanted to do was pack up her favourite things and retreat to Tara, where she stayed in bed and watched the HBO series *Game Of Thrones*, which at least distracted her, the archaic supernatural themes, mythical beasts and dark saga-like storylines making for perfect Stevie viewing material. (The show even inspired Stevie to write a series of poems into the bargain, one for each of the characters.) Nicks did manage to drop in on the very final sessions for *Extended Play*, which is when the previously impatient Lindsey, the man she used to dread seeing at the studio, presented her with the song 'Sad Angel'. "I wrote that song for Stevie," he told *Rolling Stone*. "She always had to fight for everything. She was coming off a solo album and was in the process of reintegrating herself mentally in the band, and we're all warriors with a sword in one sort or another. I just wrote, 'Sad Angel have you come to fight the war / We fall to earth together, the crowd calling out for more.'"

The death of Barbara Nicks, the woman who had encouraged Stevie's dreams and guided her when she was lost, left Stevie by her own admission "a little crazy," to the extent that, after an "exhausting day of interviews", she spoke out about the behaviour of the 'outspoken' Nicki Minaj on the TV show *American Idol* a little too openly, and her words swiftly flew around the internet in a miasma of scandal and outrage. Singer Minaj, a judge on the show alongside Stevie's friend Mariah Carey, had lashed out at Carey, allegedly referring to her as "her fucking highness" before. Again, allegedly, saying, "If I had a gun, I would shoot the bitch."

Asked for her response to the story by The Daily.com, Stevie let fly. "How dare this little girl! If I had been Mariah I would have walked over to Nicki and strangled her to death right there . . . I would have killed her in front of all those people and had to go to jail for it." Mariah Carey had reportedly hired security to protect her from Nicki Minaj on the show. It sounds like all she really had to do was call Stevie Nicks. In all seriousness, Stevie herself was stunned by what she'd allowed herself to blurt out, fatigued, unhappy and riled to hear of her friend being insulted. "That was the first time that something really awful happened that I couldn't call my mum and say, 'What do I do?'" she said. What Stevie could do, however, was imagine what her mother would have said to her in a situation such as this.

"I spent a whole night not sleeping, that first night when it was all over the internet, and I could just hear my mother saying to me, 'Rushing in to save your friend was not wrong. But the words that you used were unacceptable, so apologise to this girl and she'll move on. But you should never move on, you should always remember to step back and take a breath before you say anything in a super emotional experience like that, because words are treacherous.'"

It was almost a "visitation" as Stevie describes it, and the following day Nicks issued a statement, apologising to Minaj. Stevie explained how protective she felt towards Carey and how exhausted she was that day. "I spoke without thinking," she wrote. "I think all artists should be respectful toward one another and that includes me. I am truly sorry." Stevie would appear on *American Idol** herself (fortunately Nicki Minaj was not present) alongside her sometime producer and former lover Jimmy Iovine some months later, just before Fleetwood Mac began their tour, and while she had previously joked that she would be a sharp-shooting Simon Cowell-type on the show if she had the chance. Stevie was of course a warm and sympathetic mentor and the contestants adored her. She was kind and encouraging, harmonising with the hopefuls as they sang and urging them sincerely to put their hearts into it. She bantered with Jimmy, whom she insisted she still found "gorgeous", cheekily complimenting his "little Greek body", and as he referred to one contestant's song choice – 'Sweet Dreams' – as "the way you think of me", Stevie added, quick as a flash, "or a beautiful nightmare". Possibly the best back-handed compliment one could receive. But Stevie's loss was still close to the surface, and she was close to tears throughout the show. "My mom died, so now I don't have any problems. That's my problem, my mom isn't here anymore." No matter how close she still felt to Barbara spiritually, her mother's rings "dancing on my fingers" to remind her of their closeness even after death, nothing would ever feel quite the same again.

✝

Another lesson Stevie took from the memories she had of her mother was that it was "really easy to say you're sorry. Just walk up to someone and say 'I am really sorry' . . ." Stevie said, quoting Barbara. These words came back to her on the threshold of the Fleetwood Mac Live Tour in the spring of 2013. She realised it was time for another pre-tour heart to

* Stevie Nicks would appear on the small and indeed silver screen increasingly during this period. As well as *American Idol* and her own film *In Your Dreams,* Stevie also starred in Dave Grohl's *Sound City* documentary, focusing on the studio of the same name that had kick-started her career. She was also given a cameo role in an episode of *American Horror Story: Coven*, playing herself as the "white witch" and singing 'Seven Wonders', 'Rhiannon' and 'Has Anyone Ever Written Anything For You?'. For someone who always shied away from acting, Stevie was a natural.

heart with Lindsey, but this one would finally "change everything", according to Nicks.

"Sorry" was "something we didn't say very much [to each other]", at least until now. Having thought long and hard about what she wanted to say and inviting Lindsey over, Stevie poured her heart out, the past unfurling before them once again. She set the record straight and delivered a few home truths and he at last seemed prepared to accept them.

"[His] response was good. It was more or less, 'I wish you'd told me all this a long time ago.' I didn't take the time to explain that I wasn't happy because I thought [he] knew." A weight lifted from both of them, although Stevie admitted feeling some frustration that they hadn't had this chat three decades ago. Imagine the angst they could have saved themselves, although it is hard to say whether or not Buckingham would have just stormed off. Everything has its proper time and this, it would seem, was it. The result would make Fleetwood Mac a happier place to be than, perhaps, it had ever been. There was just one missing piece of the jigsaw now: Christine McVie. Stevie had thought about her every day since her "big sister" had left the band in 1998, declaring in an interview with *The Observer* in 2009 that she would "beg, borrow and scrape together $5 million and give it to her in cash if she would come back. That's how much I miss her." Well, that wouldn't be necessary. Rumours were flying almost as soon as the world tour had been announced that Christine might be coming back to the Fleetwood Mac fold, but Stevie batted away the barrage of questions, telling the press that "as much as we'd all like to think that she'll just change her mind one day, I don't think it'll happen."

However as the months rolled on, Christine McVie stated publicly that she might "pop back to do a little duet or something when they're in London". Lo and behold, on 25 September 2013, during Fleetwood Mac's three-night residency at London's O2 Arena, just before the band played 'Don't Stop', Stevie Nicks would introduce to the stage her "mentor, big sister, best friend . . ." and the writer of that very song. On came Christine McVie to thunderous applause, although Stevie would reveal in the cold light of day that Christine could have performed more songs with the band if Lindsey had allowed it. "I think his words were, 'She can't just come and go . . .' That's important to him," she told *Mojo*. "but it's not so important to me."

Lindsey needn't have worried. Four months later, the worst kept secret in rock'n'roll would be officially revealed when Mick Fleetwood announced that Christine McVie would be rejoining Fleetwood Mac for their 2014 On With The Show Tour of the US. So what had changed? Well, Christine initially started to shy away from touring when she developed a fear of flying. Then she convinced herself that she wanted to stay at home and be a "country lady", renovate a house in Kent, walk dogs, drive a Range Rover and "bake cookies. I don't know what I was thinking," she admitted, calling it a "deluded idea". Clearly it was what she needed at the time, but the road was calling her – and the fact that she was now 70 years old, the age at which most people would be quite happy to start baking cookies and communing with canines, didn't make a blind bit of difference. After a course of therapy to help her with her phobia of flying, she was ready to join her friends once again. One reason for her change of heart might have been seeing how John had suffered with his health in recent months. In October, John McVie had been diagnosed with cancer of the liver.

The Australia and New Zealand legs of the tour were cancelled so he could undergo treatment and Christine felt "renewed love" for how her stoic former husband was handling – and beating – the illness. Shortly after the On With The Show announcement, Stevie reassured the press that John was going to be just fine. "I'm not the least bit worried about John," she told *Us Weekly*. "He's very, very strong and a man of very few words. He's not a person to mess with." John admittedly looked suddenly older in publicity shots, but McVie was in remission and the dates were going ahead. Well, when you're faced with a command like "On with the show", what choice did a pro like McVie have but to rise to it? The tour began in September 2014 and the love for Fleetwood Mac just keeps on growing, as it does for Stevie herself. LA band Haim are among a new generation of Stevie fans, and influential style blogger Tavi Gevinson announced in her TED talk that year that "the lesson is to just be Stevie Nicks". No doubt many of you reading this now have long been aware of that.

In true unstoppable Nicks style, amid the chaos of hitting the road again with the most dysfunctional rock'n'roll family in history, she released *24 Karat Gold – Songs From The Vault*, her eighth solo studio album. The record featured new versions of old Stevie songs and demos dating back to 1969, and sold 33,000 copies in the first week. To accompany the release, Stevie curated an exhibition of previously unseen Polaroid self-portraits, also titled '24 Karat Gold', at the Morrison Hotel Gallery in West Hollywood, offering stunning, intimate glimpses of the rock queen herself in snatched quiet moments on tour during the Mac glory years.

Stevie would also make a return to *Rolling Stone Magazine* as their cover girl in 2015 during the On With The Show Tour. Waddy Wachtel told his friend he was "so proud" of her before adding, "Boy, they're going to be pissed off!" And it seems they were. *Rolling Stone* writer Brian Hiatt reports that after a brief greeting, Mick Fleetwood "pointedly ignores" him while Lindsey, installed in the neighbouring dressing room during the interview, crossly bangs on the wall before requesting – via Stevie's assistant Karen Johnston – that Stevie "turn the music down". On with the show, on with the rivalry, on with the unique, frictional magic that can only be the Mac.

*

And so, to the future. Stevie Nicks has always talked about the long term, discussing how she would still be performing as "a little old lady", taking better care of her health so she could do just that. Stevie still wants to release the children's stories she'd written in the eighties: 'A Goldfish And A Ladybug' and 'The Golden Fox Of The Last Fox Hunt', and would love to make a record for children. "You can teach children an incredible amount through music," Stevie says. "I'd also like to record an album of songs by my grandfather, AJ Nicks." In her heart, her career is at least partly dedicated to him, the man who set her on the path to showbusiness at such a young age, with greater success than he could ever have imagined. "He wanted to be a famous country and western star. I have to believe that he is enjoying this with me," says Stevie."He would be really happy for me, because for the first time in a long time, this is fun."

In addition to all of these plans, there is still the *Mabinogion* movie concept, and a "ten-song ballet opus of 'Rhiannon'." As for a book, Stevie has warned her fans there will not be a "tell-all" book, unless everyone else in her life is so old by the time she writes it that they just won't care anymore about what goes in. "If I ever write a book, it will be vignettes, you know, 'the day I met Lindsey', 'the day I joined Fleetwood Mac', 'the day I decided to do a record with Dave Stewart'," Stevie told the audience at the Hamptons International Film Festival after a screening of *In Your Dreams*. "It'll be the magical moments. I am never going to write a book to drag people through the dredges of my life. I've done enough interviews, everybody knows that there were some very bad times in my life, but I survived." Rather, it would be about the "beautiful, romantic things. That's the stuff I'd like to tell you about."And as for a title, as Stevie revealed to *Rolling Stone*'s Rob Sheffield*, 'maybe [it should be] *There's Enough Shawls to Go Around*."

Stevie is admittedly at that age where, for most people, their memories are in bolder relief than their dreams. However, Stevie is still dreaming, still creating and still sharing the magic and escapism the world so sorely needs. She has no teenage children to worry about, no "failed marriage" to lament having lost, or having given her "best years" to. And as for death? "I'm not afraid of it at all. I try to get as much done as I can, because you don't know how long you're going to be here," she told *Playboy*, way back in 1982. An old soul. "That's why it's important that I type a page or two every night – even if that's at 11 a.m. See, I think you live on earth a certain number of times until you finish what it is that you were meant to do here. And then you go on. I don't think I'll be back. I think I'm done."

* In this 2019 *Rolling Stone* interview, Nicks would also discuss her treasured temperature-controlled 'shawl vault', a revelation that sent the press into a frenzy. As *Vanity Fair*'s Kenzie Bryant put it: "like a trademark Nicks shawl, this news is huge."

In the meantime, "they'll probably be wheeling me out onstage in a wheelchair with rhinestones and raven feathers hot-glued to it. You know me," she continued, with a twinkle in her eye. "It has to be fabulous." The future may take her back to her past, in that Stevie still hankers for San Francisco, just as she did in her song 'Gypsy'. Little has changed in her heart. San Francisco was the place where it all began for her and Lindsey back in 1967 and where all of the rock'n'roll ghosts – those of Jimi, Janis, Jim Morrison – can still be sensed hanging around at the Fillmore.

"So," added Stevie. "If you're in the Haight 10 years from now and a blur of feathers and rhinestones whizzes past you on a rocket-powered wheelchair and someone goes, 'What was that?' you can say, 'Oh . . . that's Stevie.'"

Afterword

When I learned that my unauthorised biography of Stevie Nicks would be re-released as part of Omnibus Press's Remastered series, I was thrilled: *Visions, Dreams & Rumours* was always unashamedly a celebration of a truly special human being, written with affection for those who, like me, love her work and what she stands for, rather than an academic appraisal*. It was a lovely surprise to know this book would be up there alongside some of Omnibus's most classic titles. I was also keen to include an afterword to reflect on the past ten years since the book was first published and to update and revise the text.

The intention behind the project is, more than ever, to acknowledge Nicks's lifelong commitment to creativity, self-empowerment and the forging of a more magical kind of life, inspiring in us the possibilities afforded to us by our imagination and how powerful that can be, both personally and politically. In my opinion, to continue to look for and create beauty, magic and kindness when life seems determined to show us the opposite, whatever our circumstances, is a radical act of resistance and rebellion. As we've seen in the example of Stevie Nicks, this doesn't mean checking out or escaping reality – it means engaging with the world on our own terms, understanding what's real and standing up for what we know in our hearts to be right.

* I recall the first edition being described by one critic as a "hagiography" – elevating the subject to a saint-like level – and to this I'd simply say, why yes, it's a book about Stevie Nicks. If you *aren't* worshipping at the Church of Stevie, what are you even doing with your life? Get yourself some "Saint" Stevie Nicks prayer candles and give in to it.

From being the inspiration for the hit series *Daisy Jones and the Six* to being celebrated in the form of a Barbie doll, Nicks is as relevant and inspiring as ever: a vibrant symbol of self-empowerment, individuality, self-acceptance and strength at a time when heroes can be hard to find and things are not always as they appear to be. And while, as we know, Nicks has remained circumspect on whether she is indeed a witch, she has become a totem of inspiration amid the witchcraft revival and surge of interest in goddess culture. (Who could be a clearer embodiment of the Divine Feminine in popular culture than Stevie Nicks?) All of this circles back to creativity, female empowerment, an open-mindedness, a tolerance and a way of thinking and living that takes the power back. It makes sense that people of all genders have looked to Stevie, who has candidly reflected on the challenges in her life and how she has handled them, and shared the lessons along the way. Her lessons regard substance abuse, health and the changes that come with the privilege of getting older as a woman, as well as renewed perspectives on shifting relationships, with a priority on self-care.

The last decade has been one of reflection, resilience and new milestones for Nicks. One doesn't have to be a fan of Fleetwood Mac to be aware that in 2018, the turbulence caused by her volatile relationship with Lindsey Buckingham did, sadly, cause what appears to be an irrevocable split between not just the pair professionally and personally, but Buckingham and Fleetwood Mac. Buckingham would be replaced by Mike Campbell (The Heartbreakers) and Neil Finn (Crowded House). Manager Irving Azoff reportedly told Buckingham that Nicks could no longer go on stage with him, with Stevie later clarifying (after Buckingham had been giving what she referred to as a "revisionist" version of events, claiming that Stevie was trying to "shape the band in her own image"*) that she had "dealt with him for as long as she could", releasing the following statement in 2021:

"Following an exceedingly difficult time with Lindsey at MusiCares in

* 'Lindsey Buckingham Won't Stop', *Rolling Stone Magazine*, Stephen Rodrick, 9 September 2021.

New York in 2018, I decided for myself that I was no longer willing to work with him. I could publicly reflect on the many reasons why, and perhaps I will do that someday in a memoir, but suffice it to say we could start in 1968 and work up to 2018 with a litany of very precise reasons why I will not work with him. To be exceedingly clear, I did not have him fired, I did not ask for him to be fired, I did not demand he be fired. Frankly, I fired myself. I proactively removed myself from the band and a situation I considered to be toxic to my wellbeing. I was done. If the band went on without me, so be it. I have championed independence my whole life and I believe every human being should have the absolute freedom to set their boundaries of what they can and cannot work with. And after many lengthy group discussions, Fleetwood Mac, a band whose legacy is rooted in evolution and change, found a new path forward with two hugely talented new members."

Buckingham's attitude at the MusiCares benefit concert might not have been incendiary in relation to previous blow-ups, but it was the straw that broke the camel's back. In 2024, Stevie would tell *Rolling Stone's* Angie Martococcio that while she still respected him as an icon and wished him well, his behaviour that night prompted her to re-evaluate how she wanted to move forward. He "wasn't very nice to anybody; he wasn't very nice to Harry Styles." This was no small thing, indeed it was tantamount to insulting Nicks's own child: Nicks has mentored many young artists but she loves Styles like a son, and has duetted with the former One Direction star numerous times*. While more dramatic incidents had gone down over the years, seeing Styles disrespected proved a tipping point for Nicks, and she could sense the voices of her parents advising her once and for all to cut ties with Buckingham. "I could hear my mom saying, 'Are you really going to spend the next 15 years of your life with this man?' I could hear my very pragmatic father – and by the way, my mom and dad liked Lindsey a lot – saying, 'It's time for you guys to get a divorce.' Between those two, I said, 'I'm done.'"

* Memorably the pair would perform 'Landslide' together at London's Hyde Park in honour of what would have been the late Christine McVie's birthday in July 2024.

The band played on, as did Nicks in her solo capacity and she would be honoured at the Rock & Roll Hall of Fame the following year (2019) as a solo artist, making her the first female artist to be inducted twice (Fleetwood Mac had been inducted in 1998). "I feel I definitely broke a big rock'n'roll glass ceiling," she said in an interview with CBS. During the ceremony, Nicks delivered a poignant speech, acknowledging the late Tom Petty, who had died just two years earlier, and performing their famous duet 'Stop Dragging My Heart Around' with Harry Styles in tribute during the ceremony.

Life would change suddenly and swiftly, and for two years the live music industry (and many other industries) ground to a halt due to the global Covid 19 pandemic. But an incident would rock the Mac on a more personal level, stopping the band in its tracks once and for all. On 30 November 2022, the news broke that Christine McVie had died after a short illness at the age of 79. She was, as Stevie Nicks put it to *Rolling Stone*, her "music soulmate, my best girlfriend. We kept that band afloat by keeping the peace. We were the keepers of Fleetwood Mac, and that is why we cannot replace her. We did replace Lindsey two times, and it was OK. No fighting, super fun. But Christine was different. There's no more Fleetwood Mac now." As for Lindsey, Stevie would only speak to him again briefly at Christine's LA funeral in January 2023. While Mick Fleetwood has expressed hopes that there might be a reconciliation between the pair, only time will tell. But, as Nicks herself has said, it's not like she hadn't given him "more than 300 million chances" in the past. And while Fleetwood Mac could often seem like the ultimate drama, there were further dramas unfolding on the world stage that Stevie had something to say about. Her energy was needed elsewhere.

"I never voted until I was 70, but now I regret that," she said on MSNBC's *Morning Joe*. "And I've told everybody that on stage for the last two years. I regret that, and I don't have very many regrets." In 2024, as another Trump presidency loomed, Nicks, who publicly endorsed the Democratic nominee Kamala Harris, urged Americans to take the time to vote and encouraged her fellow artists to step up and write a protest song in support. Nicks herself had released a single, 'The Lighthouse', to support the fight for women's reproductive rights.

"In the end of the Fifties and Sixties and going into the Seventies, everyone was writing protest songs," she continued. "Bob Dylan, Joan Baez, Joni Mitchell, Stephen Stills, it was lots and lots and lots. I would say to all my musical poets that write songs to write some songs about what's happening, like I did. Whoever wins [the election], the lighthouse needs to keep shining its light and also keep those ships from crashing into the rocks." To Nicks, Kamala Harris was "the lighthouse". "She is our great hope to save the world," she told *Rolling Stone.*

'The Lighthouse' was acknowledged as a rare protest song for our times, a call to action that was praised by the activist filmmaker Michael Moore, who wrote on his Facebook page that this "powerhouse anthem" was "fierce. Inspiring! A beacon of light guiding the rest of us to the polls en masse as we build, vote by vote, our blue wall that will end this Gender Apartheid once and for all . . ." Nicks responded, thanking Moore for "so eloquently saying what I've been trying to express. Your words remind us of the urgency to act . . . Let's be the lighthouse guiding each other toward real change." Trump would, as we know, defeat Harris at the polls. But that lighthouse is still there, unextinguished and defiant.

More turmoil would come as Stevie's beloved LA would be hit by devastating wildfires in the early days of 2025, which would see Nicks moving to a hotel for 92 days to stay safe until the fires were eventually brought under control. But out of that 92 day stint, under what must have felt like another lockdown of sorts, would be the emergence of a new solo album. Being in the hotel made Nicks feel as if she was on the road, "but there's no shows . . ." she said, speaking at the Pollstar Awards in April 2025, and she added that this prompted her to "get back to work."

"I have seven songs," she revealed, "and they are autobiographical, real stories where I'm not pulling any punches, for probably the first time in my life. They are not airy fairy songs that you are wondering who they're about, but you don't really get it. They're real stories of memories of mine of fantastic men." Speaking from the podium, she then eyed Jimmy Iovine in the audience and warned, "you're next".

The initial inspiration for the new record came from an incident with her late friend Prince: as we know, she walked out of the premiere of *Purple Rain*, upset by the scene when Prince's character slaps Apollonia. She admitted to Prince afterwards that she only saw the first half and gave him a 24 karat gold necklace with gold hearts on it. But Prince rejected it, saying, "You always bring me a gift, you never bring me you." The resurfacing of this memory was what prompted Nicks to start writing the material for her new solo album, her first LP release since *24 Karat Gold: Songs From The Vault* in 2014 and first new material since 2011 (*In Your Dreams*). With, at the time of writing, promises of new songs that bring the magic and spill the tea on her tumultuous romances on what she refers to as her "ghost album", plus unveiling plans to tour with Billy Joel, Stevie Nicks is approaching her eighth decade with characteristic style, energy and a twinkle in her eye. As she told *Billboard*'s Gary Braff in 2013, "I plan to be out there singing when I am a seriously older woman. I think my voice will still be good, because I'm not going to let it go. And you just can't make a comeback. Comebacks are no good. You have to just keep singing."

High Priestess, rock goddess, wise woman, dreamer. Survivor, sorcerer, queen. All of these things and more besides, and always with a foot in both worlds. Shine on, Stevie Nicks.

Pick 'n' Nicks – A Stevie Nicks Fact File

Because, whether she's your specialist subject on *Mastermind,* you've a pop quiz coming up, or you just want to impress people with your knowledge, who doesn't want a handful of Stevie fun facts up their voluminous sleeve?

Five key facts about Stevie Nicks' early years:

1) Stephanie Lynn Nicks was born to parents Jess and Barbara on 26 May 1948 at the Good Samaritan Hospital in Phoenix, Arizona.

2) Barbara Nicks gave birth to Stephanie Lynn when she was just 20 years old, one year after marrying Jess Nicks. Jess would later become the chairman of meatpacking company Armour and Co., and executive vice-president at Greyhound Corp. The family would move around a lot – to Utah, California, Texas, New Mexico, Los Angeles . . . Despite this, Jess Nicks insisted his famous daughter always felt "like an Arizonan".

3) Jess loved the name Stephanie, but his first-born became known as Stevie because, as a small child, she just couldn't pronounce her name properly. It initially came out as "Teede" (her mother would still call her "Teedee" and "TC Bird" long into adulthood).

4) Stevie's favourite childhood memories stem from staying with her maternal grandmother in Ajo, Arizona. (Ajo means "garlic" in Spanish, in case you were wondering.)

5) But it would be Stevie's paternal grandfather who would steer her firmly onto her life's path. Aaron Jess Nicks was a nomadic country and western singer who took the four-year-old Stevie with him when he went to perform in bars, teaching her to harmonise and sing the "answers" when he sang call-and-response classics. The first song they sang together was 'Are You Mine?' by Red Sovine.

Animal magic:

A great dog-lover, Stevie is especially fond of Yorkshire terriers. Sara Belladonna, Sulamith India Grace, Lily and Mana are the names of just some of her beloved Yorkies from over the years.

In addition to her own extensive wardrobe (and temperature-controlled shawl vault), Stevie has another wardrobe filled with tiny shawls, Ralph Lauren cashmere and Rhiannon outfits which were made especially for her Chinese-crested Yorkie, Sulamith.

Music

Stevie Nicks' favourite record for inspiration: Joni Mitchell's 1974 album *Court And Spark*.

Style

Three influences on Stevie Nicks' style:

1) Eye make-up: silent movie goddesses

2) Clothes: California sunshine, fairy queens, children's books.

3) Hair:Victorian society beauty meets Lillian Gish in San Francisco.

Stevie always looked to old school Hollywood for make-up inspiration, but especially the European actresses, such as Marlene Dietrich and Greta

Garbo, highlighting the eyelids and brushing darker colour in the sockets. "I'd always done my eyes like that.To me, Marlene and Greta are just totally glamorous without people saying they were sex symbols," Stevie said in an interview in 1977.

Stevie doesn't like to throw any clothes away, especially if they were gifts. Even if they don't fit her. "It's like a piece of love. I could outfit everybody in Los Angeles in these things."

Stevie Nicks first really fell in love with lace when she visited the Antiquarius antiques emporium in London.

Nicks has personalised stationery with an image of a top hat and tambourine in the top right corner, and a gypsy-like woman with flowing locks in the bottom left corner. She's been known to write notes to her fans on this pretty paper and have them scanned onto the site The Nicks Fix.

"When I stop singing I'm gonna have a garage sale like you're not gonna believe," Stevie said while on the Wild Heart tour in 1983. "We're talking chiffon, chiffon, and more chiffon."

Beauty

Don't do Botox. Stevie tried it once. Never again. In 2020, she would tell *The Guardian*'s Jenny Stevens: "Botox only makes you look like you're in a satanic cult. I only had it once and it destroyed my face for four months. I would look in the mirror and try and lift my eyebrow and go: 'Oh, there you are, Satan's angry daughter.' Never again. I watch a lot of news and I see all the lady newscasters looking like Satan's angry daughters, too."

Take off your make-up when you go to bed. "I have always taken very good care of my skin," Stevie insisted to Oprah Winfrey. "Even on the days you are just very, very drunk and everybody else goes to bed with their make-up on, not me." Stevie would also advise steering clear of sun exposure and cigarettes.

Steam. During the *Rumours* tour, Stevie's voice took a pounding and she was susceptible to colds. On the advice of fellow rocker Boz Scaggs, she invested in a facial sauna into which she plunged her face before each show in a bid to clear her sinuses. The byproduct of this would be that her pores would be purified and her complexion left dewy. "It may not help my voice but I'll have terrific skin," she joked.

Wellbeing

Ballet exercises. Every day, Stevie would stretch to keep her limbs lean and prevent injuries during the show. She would also do ballet exercises to Lindsey's demo tapes, although as soon as he added lyrics (usually negative) the feel changed and she'd have to abandon them. But the main thing is that ballet takes focus and discipline, and the results are worth it. Before one concert in Japan, she challenged Richard Dashut to get his leg up on the barre, which he managed with some pain (he was wearing tight jeans) before staggering away, muttering: "That's all right, I didn't want to have kids anyway . . ." The other advantage of ballet is, as Stevie says, it's a meditation, a mindful act. "It's so physically difficult, that if you're worried about anything, and you do this for 15 or 20 minutes even, you can't think about anything else."

Drop the internet addiction. "[It's] ruining our society and making everybody rude. I think it's the reason why people just don't care and the reason why nothing lasts and people don't meet anybody . . ."

Keeping a journal is a must when it comes to Stevie-style solutions. It gets all of your concerns out on the page – privately, as opposed to on Facebook – and is cheaper than therapy. Stevie journals constantly, also creating tour diaries that she binds together like a scrapbook and gives to everyone at the end of each tour. "I tell people all the time that they should keep a journal, even if it's just, 'I had a terrible day today and I don't want to talk about it, love Stevie,' or 'I dreamt last night . . .' Even if it's just three sentences, because at the end of five or six days, you would have created a habit and you will find over a month that you have a whole story growing." You might even get a song out of it too.

Keep reading

Stevie is a voracious reader, enjoying everything from fiction (Taylor Caldwell is a favourite) to poetry collections. "I just read anything that comes in my way that's interesting," she told *High Times*. "I pick up bunches of little old poetry books. I love serenity since I don't have much of it in my life."

Candid camera

When Stevie was being made-up for the famous *Rolling Stone* cover shoot with Annie Leibovitz in 1981, she popped a tape of her then new song 'Wild Heart' into the stereo and sang along with it, Lori harmonising by her side as Stevie's make-up artist Liza attempted to beautify her employer even further. Somebody filmed it, Nicks herself is not aware of whom, and put it on YouTube. It has become, she admits,"quite a little phenomenon".Watch it. It's adorable and at the time of writing, has had over 1 million views.

Precious things and talismans

Stevie's favourite item: her precious Tiffany blue lamp. She even wrote a song about it – 'Blue Lamp' (which turned up on *Enchanted,* left over from the *Bella Donna* sessions). A gift from Stevie's mother, it dates back to the time Buckingham Nicks first joined Fleetwood Mac and "symbolises the light that shines throughout the night", Stevie told Storytellers in 1998, "Because Fleetwood Mac was a definite light at the end of the tunnel." Stevie has kept that lamp switched on for decades. "It was the first really beautiful thing that I got. I ended up carrying it back from Phoenix to Los Angeles on the plane and they didn't want to let me on with [it], and I said, 'Well, you're gonna have to run over me, 'cause we're not going without the lamp.'"

Nicks's house contains a crystal ball, a moon-and-stars light given to her by her goddaughters (Mick Fleetwood's daughters Amy-Rose and Lucy), a doll in a birdcage, a painting of a gypsy who "rules the room" and is possibly getting younger, in reverse Dorian Gray-style and, most importantly, a "fainting couch".

Nicks has a fabulous grand piano . . . with bullet-holes in it. The instrument was caught in a drive-by shooting while being transported from LA to Phoenix.

What would Stevie take with her in a fire drill? Tapes, notebooks, guitar, "two or three dolls . . ."

House and home

Nicks would sell her gated home on Chautauqua Boulevard in Pacific Palisades ostensibly because she didn't want to have to worry about the state of the pool or the gardens while on tour. But, according to the Hollywood rumour mill, she wanted out because she believed the property to be haunted.

Mornings are not to be rushed in the world of the rock goddess. Stevie's morning routine often involves waking at 9 a.m., drinking coffee (Folgers) and enjoying some me-time until 12 noon, then taking a bath and doing some vocal exercises. You could expect Stevie to be dressed and drifting down the stairs by 2 p.m. On days off however, Stevie's "top priority" would be to get up by 11 a.m. "to watch my soaps: *All My Children, One Life To Live* and *General Hospital*."

Stevie home essentials: candles, cashmere, good speakers, good friends.

Stevie's favourite dish to make at home: an omelette.

Favourite movie

Stevie's favourite horror movie: *The Haunting* (An adaptation of the Shirley Jackson book *The Haunting Of Hill House*).

Hey Barbie!

In November 2023, Mattel released a Stevie Nicks doll as part of their Barbie Music series. It was designed with a flowing black dress (reminiscent of the outfit worn on the cover of the 1977 *Rumours* album) and platform boots. Nicks announced the initial Barbie release during a concert at New York's Madison Square Garden.

Manifesting magic

Not only did Stevie write a song called 'Rose Garden' as a teenager, describing an imagined golden future that would soon become real for her, the concept for the 'Rhiannon' costume was born long before you might think."In fourth grade, I wore a black top hat, a black vest and skirt, a white blouse, black tights and black tap shoes with little heels. I did a tap dance to Buddy Holly's 'Everyday' with my friend Colleen," she told *Music Spotlight*. "I had a definite knowledge of how I wanted to look even then." And, to paraphrase the song, every day it was indeed getting stronger.

Famous fans

Celeb Stevie-worshippers include Smashing Pumpkins frontman Billy Corgan, Florence Welch from Florence + The Machine, Courtney Love – who was empowered by listening to *Bella Donna* during her days as an erotic dancer in Japan – and designer Anna Sui, who created a line heavily inspired by Stevie's style. "She's the iconic California woman," says Sui. "Everyone has their version of her."

Date for your diary

Every May in Manhattan there is a drag parade called 'Night Of A Thousand Stevies', organised by Chi Chi Valenti. Everyone dresses up according to the given Nicks-related theme and, one day, "The Goddess herself" has promised to turn up in disguise. "Not one of you will know it's me until I walk onstage and sing 'Edge of Seventeen'," she has said enigmatically.

"*I'd like to be remembered as a notoriously eclectic person: a collector and a dancer and a singer and a songwriter and a fairy-dust spreader.*" Stevie Nicks to *Us Magazine*, 1990

Acknowledgments

Thanks, love and white-winged doves must go to the following gold dust men and women:

The brilliant, wise and supportive Dylan Howe, to whom this and all of my work is dedicated whether he likes it or not. Thank you. To Keith Olsen and Rupert Hine – RIP; to Fay Armstrong, Kenny Loggins, Mandi Davis, Shannon Trotta, Ian Sanders, Rudy Noriega, Dave Stewart and Waddy Wachtel (for warm vibes on initial approach, I appreciated it), the NBT massive, David Fricke, Gavin Martin, Daryl Easlea, Paul Silveira, Gareth Thomas at UCA, and all of those who assisted me, or at least tried to, in my quest. Your support, contributions, interviews and generosity are very much appreciated. (Oddly enough, it appears I am long-lost cousins with longtime Nicks collaborator Benmont Tench from the Heartbreakers. Did that help me get an interview with him? No, it did not.)

Thanks to my editor Chris Charlesworth, who also made contributions to the original text on the subject of Peter Green's Fleetwood Mac; to Neal Price, Claire Browne and Millen Brown-Evans – I've really appreciated being able to revisit the text; to Matt Bourne; to the always inspirational and definitely magical Vivien Goldman; Jenny Boyce; David Barraclough; the cats: Marzipan, my forever familiar, Pipistrelle and Moonbeam (aka The Lovely Brothers); Jacqui Black, Charlie Harris at Midas PR, my lovely family and friends, you for picking up this book, to the readers who gave me feedback, and, of course, Stevie Nicks for being the most fascinating, magical and inspiring subject to write about. This book was, by happy accident, originally completed on the full moon before Stevie Nicks' 66th birthday and was revised, with perfect cosmic timing, during Mercury and Venus Retrograde one month before her 77th.

Bibliography

BOOKS

Everything You Want to Know About Stevie Nicks, by Ethlie Ann Vare and Ed Ochs, Ballantine, 1984;

Fleetwood - My Life And Adventures In Fleetwood Mac, Mick Fleetwood and Stephen Davis, William Morrow, 1990;

Musicians in Tune by Jenny Boyd, Holly George Warren, Simon and Schuster, 1992;

Songs in the Rough by Stephen Bishop, St Martin's Press, 1996;

To The Limit: The Untold Story of the Eagles by Marc Eliot, Da Capo, 2004;

Conversations With Tom Petty, Paul Zollo and Tom Petty, Omnibus Press, 2005;

Read Between My Lines - The Musical & Life Journey Of Stevie Nicks, Sandra Halliburton, SK Halliburton Enterprises, 2006;

Storms - My Life With Lindsey Buckingham and Fleetwood Mac, Carol Ann Harris, Chicago Press Review, 2009;

Bumping Into Geniuses - My Life Inside The Rock and Roll Business, Danny Goldberg, Penguin, 2010;

Fleetwood Mac's Tusk (33 1/3) - Rob Trucks, Continuum, 2011;

Making Rumours - The Inside Story Of The Classic Fleetwood Mac Album, Ken Caillat and Steve Stiefel, published by John Wiley & Sons, 2013;

It's Not Only Rock 'n' Roll, by Dr Jenny Boyd and Holly George-Warren; John Blake Publishing Ltd, 2013;

Kicking and Dreaming - a story of Heart, Soul, Rock and Roll, Ann and Nancy Wilson with Charles R Cross, It Books, 2013.

ARTICLES

Billboard review, 3 March 1974

Buckingham Nicks feature, *Rock Magazine,* Dan Hedges, December 11, 1974;

"Innerview" with Fleetwood Mac, Jim Ladd, 1976;

'Fleetwood Mac: John and Christine and Stevie and Lindsey and Mick . . .' Vivien Goldman, *Sounds*, 30 October 1976;

Big Mac: Two All Gold Albums . . . *Crawdaddy Magazine,* John Grissim, November 1976;

Stevie Nicks interview, H P de Tijd, Peter Van Bruggen, April 30, 1977;

'The True Life Confessions Of Fleetwood Mac' , *Rolling Stone,* Cameron Crowe, March 24th 1977;

Emotion Runs Deep Between Stevie Nicks and her Dad, Cox News Service, Linda Romine.

Christine McVie interview, *Creem,* Patrick Goldstein, 1980;

BBC news report, death of John Lennon, December 8th 1980;

Fleetwood Mac's Siren Soars With Her First Solo Album . . . *Bam Magazine*, Blair Jackson, September 11th 1981;

Stevie Nicks interview, Special RKO Radio, December 21, 1981;

Stevie Nicks solo live show review (Bella Donna), Steve Pond, *LA Times,* 1981;

Stevie Nicks interview, *Glamour,* December 1981;

Stevie Nicks: Poetry In Motion, *Hit Parader,* Blair Jackson, January 1982;

Stevie Nicks, Macrame Goddess: Confronting the Gates of Elmo, *Creem,* Sylvie Simmons, 1982;

Stevie Nicks: Back To Mac, *The Record,* Michael Goldberg, February 1982;

Stevie Nicks interview, ABC News;

Molly Meldrum, ABC Australia, The Meldrum Tapes;

Interview with Liz Derringer, *High Times,* March 1982;

Lindsey Buckingham: Pop Renegade, *The Record,* David Gans, April 1982;

The Wild Heart Press Kit, 1983; (Modern Records)

20 Questions *Playboy* interview, David Rensin, July 1982;

WBNC Boston radio interview, July 5, 1983;

'Arizona's Bella Donna Comes Home', Michael Lyons, *Arizona Living,* September 1983;

'She's Smiling Now', *Rock Magazine,* Vicky Greenleaf and Stan Hyman, October 1983;

Rock A Little interview, *MTV interview* in LA, May 11th 1985;

Stevie Nicks interview, BBC One To One, 1989;

'Last Tangos, New Beginnings', *Musician,* Timothy White, February 1989;

Stevie Nicks interview with Roger Scott for Tyne Tees, ITV, 1989;

The Rebirth Of Fleetwood Mac, *The Music Paper,* Mark David Henrickson, June 1990;

The US Interview, Stevie Nicks, *Us Magazine,* Steve Pond, July 1990;

Stevie's Wonder, *People Magazine (*Chatter), Peter Castro, August 13th 1990;

Interview, *The Sun (Columbia, MD)* July 17th 1991;

A Solo Stevie Nicks, *Boston Globe,* Steve Morse, July 14th 1991;

BBC Radio 1 *Timespace* interview, Nicky Horme, 1991;

The Second Life Of Don Henley, *GQ,* Christopher Connelly, August 1991;

Timespace Liner Notes, Modern Records / Atlantic Records / EMI Records, September 1991;

Come Into My Parlour, *Vox Magazine,* Spencer Bright, February 1992;

Stevie Nicks, In the Studio with Red Beard, May 1992;

Stevie Nicks, Tommy Vance show, May 1994;

Stevie Nicks Survives Storms, *Miami Herald,* Howard Cohen, June 6th 1994;

'Would You Stay If She Promised You Heaven?' *Details,* Lance Loud, August 1994.

Stevie interview, *Details Magazine,* August 1994;

Q&A by Ryan Murphy, *US Magazine,* August 1994;

Q and A (Stevie Nicks), *Rolling Stone,* Jancee Dunn, September 22nd 1994;

Stevie Nicks and Sarah McLachlan, *Interview Magazine,* March 1995;

Stevie Nicks interview, *Allure*, April 1995;

Stevie Nicks interview, *Microsoft Music Central,* 1997;

'Rumours' Are True: Mac Is Back, *USA Today,* August 12th 1997;

Billboard Magazine report, Larry Flick and Melinda Newman, August 16, 1997;

Lindsey Buckingham interview, *Salon Magazine,* Michael Snyder, August 29th 1997;

Fleetwood Mac Takes Reunion Right To The Top, *Philadelphia Inquirer,* Steve Appleford, September 21st 1997;

Interview with Chrissy Iley, *The Scotsman,* September 30th 1997

'Stevie Turns 49, Barbara Nicks Interviewed', Randy Cordova, *The Arizona Republic,* October 21, 1997;

Airy Godmother, *Los Angeles Times,* Booth Moore, October 23rd 1997;

'Back On The Chain Gang', *Rolling Stone,* Fred Schruers, October 30 1997;

'Blonde On Blonde', Courtney Love and Stevie Nicks, *Spin Magazine,* October 1997;

Stevie Nicks interview, Total TV.com, 1997;

'Trip To Stevieland' , *Harpers Bazaar,* Wendy Goodman, November 1997;

High Priestess - Stevie Nicks, *People Magazine*, Steve Dougherty, January 19th 1998;

How We Met; Mick Fleetwood And Lindsey Buckingham, *The Independent*, Lucy O'Brien, March 8th 1998;

Stevie Nicks radio interview with DJ Chuck Nowlan, WZLX Boston, April 13th 1998;

Long Distance Winner, *Billboard* interview, Timothy White, April 18 1998;

'Songbird', *Rolling Stone Interview,* April 19, 1998;

The Rebounding Talents Of Nicks, *Entertainment Weekly Online,* Chris Willman, May 1st 1998;

Church Axes Song At Baccalaureate, *Associated Press* report from Huntsville, Alabama, May 28th 1998;

Stevie Nicks interview, *MTV Storytellers,* 1998;

Stevie Nicks Showers Fans With Music And Emotions, *San Jose Mercury News,* Brad Kava, August 3rd 1998;

Rumours BBC Radio 2 radio special, November 11th, 1998.

Waddy Wachtel interview, *Musician* magazine, David Simons, April 1999;

Rolling Stone Millennium Issue Stevie Nicks Q&A, December 30, 1999;

Stevie Nicks interview *Us Weekly,* June 11-18 200;

Interview, *Scottsdale Life,* Andrew Means, July/August 2000;

Off The Record interview with Joe Benson, September 24th 2000;

Fleetwood Mac Play Surprise Farewell Gig For Clinton, *Rolling Stone,* Andrew Dansby, January 8th 2001;

Stevie Nicks VHI Interview, April 14th 2001;

Queen Of The Stoned Age, *Q Magazine,* Paul Elliott, May 2001;

Nicks In A Hard Place, *Barnes and Noble* Interview, May 1st 2001;

Exceptional Women, 106.7 Magic, Boston, Candy O'Terry interview, 2001;

Stevie Nicks by Sheryl Crow for *Interview* Magazine, May 2001;

Stevie Nicks, Borders.com Interview, June 2001;

Waddy Wachtel interview with *Black Cat,* 2001-2003;

Stevie Nicks Keeps Rocking And Twirling, *Cincinnati Post,* Rick Bird, December 12th 2001;

Tom Moncrieff / Javier Pacheco (Fritz) Q&A, Penguin Q&A Sessions;

Sheryl Crow and Stevie Nicks, *The Independent,* Sunday July 21st 2002;

Women In Rock 2002: Stevie Nicks, at 54, is still the coolest chick in the room, *Rolling Stone,* Jancee Dunn, October 31st 2002;

'Everybody Was Pretty Weirded Out', *Uncut Magazine,* Nigel Williamson, May 2003;

How Stevie Nicks escaped the chaos of Fleetwood Mac and soared solo, Classic Rock / Louder Sound, Bill deMain, 2003/2025;

Sex, drugs and Stevie Nicks, *The Courier Mail,* Nui Te Koha, September 27th 2003;

Madonna-Britney Kiss Angers Stevie, *Herald Sun,* Nui Te Koha, September 19th 2003;

Stevie Nicks, *Queen of Rock* Interview, 2003

Cory Buckingham Q&A, FleetwoodMacUK.com, 2003;

You Magazine (Daily Mail, Sunday Edition supplement), Interview by Maureen Paton, November 16, 2003;

'Confessions of a Rock Chick', Gavin Martin, *Daily Mirror,* 21 November 2003.

Take It To The Limit, *Mojo Magazine*, Phil Sutcliffe, December 2003;

Nicks' song sung for shop owner, *Daily Telegraph* (Australia), Dora Tsavdaridis, March 9th 2004;

'Going Your Own Way Easier Said Than Done', Mark Brown, *Rocky Mountain News*, July 9, 2004;

Eagle Flies With Nightbird, *Boston Herald,* Sarah Rodman, June 8th 2005;

Gold Dust Woman, *San Francisco Chronicle,* Bill Picture, July 24th 2005;

Stevie Nicks interview, *Australian Women's Weekly,* December 2005;

Still Going His Own Way, CanWest News Service, Bernard Perusse, April 15th 2007;

Stevie Nicks: A Survivor's Story, *The Telegraph,* Mick Brown, September 8th 2007;

Stevie Nicks: The men, the music, the menopause, *The Guardian,* Craig McLean, March 25th 2011;

Stevie Nicks: Wild At Heart, *Harpers Bazaar,* Christine Lennon, April 2011;

Robert Llewellyn *Carpool* interview with Paul Fishkin, 15 December 2011;

BBC Radio 4, Follow Up Records, Pete Paphides and Lindsey Buckingham, reference from *The Quietus,* May 2012;

Styling Stevie: Margi Kent interview, *District MTV,* November 21 2012;

Hamptons International Film Festival Q&A for *In Your Dreams*, 2013;

Dave Stewart Q&A with Mike Fishkin, Mill Valley Film Festival, 2013;

The Return Of Fleetwood Mac, *The Observer,* Caspar Llewellyn Smith, January 12th 2013;

Mick Fleetwood interview, *Sunday Express,* Charlotte Heathcote, February 3rd 2013;

'When We Walk Into The Room, We Have To Float In Like Goddesses', NPR Music, Ann Powers, March 17th 2013;

Fleetwood Mac's Stevie Nicks on addiction, Botox and the burying of hatchets, *Daily Telegraph,* Craig MacLean, 2013;

Lindsey Buckingham On Surviving Fleetwood Mac, *Men's Journal,* Brian Hiatt, April 2013;

Lindsey Buckingham Talks Fleetwood Mac Tour, New EP, *Rolling Stone,* Andy Greene, May 7th 2013;

For Sale: Honky Chateau Where Elton And Bowie Recorded Classic Hits, *Observer,* Kim Willsher, August 4th 2013;

Stevie Nicks on *Loose Women,* September 12th 2013;

The Story Behind Christine's Live Return, *Mojo Magazine,* James McNair, Sept 26th 2013;

Fleetwood Mac's Stevie Nicks on music, Game Of Thrones and her ties to Prince, *Herald Scotland;* October 1st 2013;

Stevie Nicks: The Fairy Godmother Of Rock, *New York Magazine*, Jada Yuan, October 6th 2013;

Stevie Nicks: The Original Rebel, *Elle UK,* Chrissy Iley, October 2013;

Stevie Nicks: The Queen Of Rock, *Sunday Night Australia,* Alex Cullen, November 8th 2013;

Lea Michele Credits Stevie Nicks With Helping Her Through 'Worst Year Of My Life' , *MTV.com,* Jocelyn Vena, November 12th 2013;

Jimmy Iovine: What I've Learned, *Esquire,* Cal Fussman, December 11th 2013;

'Fleetwood Mac's Stevie and Christine: 'We Were Like Rock'n'Roll Nuns', *The Guardian,* Tim Jonze, December 12th 2013;

'You Make Fighting Fun', *Daily Mail,* Adrian Deevoy, December 28th 2013;

Stevie Nicks Talks Filming *American Horror Story . . . Us Weekly,* Ian Drew and Justin Ravitz, January 8th 2014;

Mick Fleetwood Goes His Own Way: Custom Fashion, *Sunday Express,* Mick Fleetwood, March 2nd 2014;

'I Believe In The Church of Stevie', *Rolling Stone*, Angie Martoccio, October 24, 2024;

Stevie Nicks is 'not pulling any punches' on her new album, Mikael Wood, *LA Times,* April 18th 2025.